OPERA TODAY

Also by Meirion and Susie Harries
The Academy of St Martin in the Fields
The War Artists (in conjunction with the Tate Gallery
and the Imperial War Museum)

OPERA TODAY

MEIRION and SUSIE HARRIES

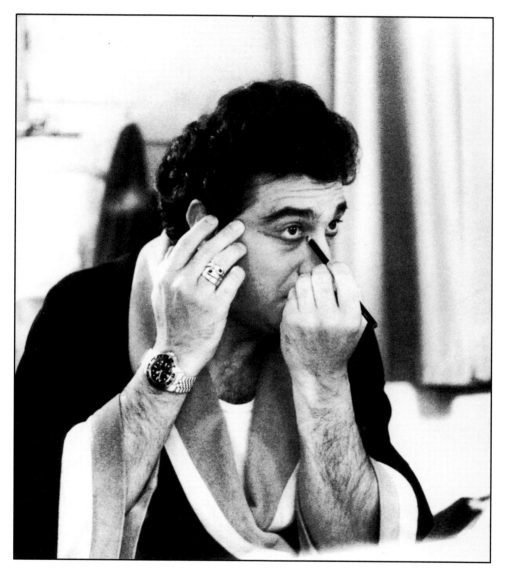

ST. MARTIN'S PRESS · NEW YORK

To Rachel Catherine Harries

Library of Congress Cataloging in Publication Data

Harries, Meirion, 1951–
    Opera Today

    Includes Index.
    1. Opera.   2. Music as a Profession.   I. Harries,
    Susie.   II. Title.
    ML 1700.H35 1986   782.1   86–15460
    ISBN 0-312-58675-2

            First published in Great Britain by Michael Joseph Ltd.
                        First U.S. Edition

            10   9   8   7   6   5   4   3   2   1

Photographs by Zoë Dominic
and Catherine Ashmore

Jessye Norman in *Ariadne auf Naxos* with Harlequin and Truffaldino (Olaf Baer and Eric Garrett) (Covent Garden, 1985).

Contents

I – OPERA ADMINISTRATION
1 The Width of the Spectrum   3
2 Funding   12
3 Planning the Season   23
4 Casting   41

II – THE SINGER
5 Building the Voice   57
6 Building the Performer   69
7 Building the Career   76

III – THE CONDUCTOR
8 Conducting Opera   99
9 Preparing the Music   116
10 The Orchestra   121
11 The Chorus   128
12 Working with the Principal Singers   135
13 Working with the Producer   148

IV – THE PRODUCER AND DESIGNER
14 The Producer's Job   159
15 Evolving the Conception   170
16 Working with the Designer   176
17 The Sets   193
18 The Lighting   208
19 The Costumes, Wigs and Armour   222
20 Working with the Performers   234

V – IN PERFORMANCE
21 In Performance   257

CONTENTS

VI – THE MODERN COMPOSER

22 Why Write Opera Today?   271
23 Choosing a Subject   274
24 What Makes a Good Libretto?   285
25 Composer and Librettist   290
26 Setting the Text   295
27 Getting New Opera into Performance   302
28 The Problem of New Opera   311
Acknowledgements   322
Index   325

I

OPERA
ADMINISTRATION

1

The Width of the Spectrum

'Opera is dead.' 'Opera is booming.' 'The new breed of acting singer is the envy of every straight theatre company.' 'If you want acting, go to Stratford-upon-Avon/Stratford, Ontario.' 'Performers now don't begin to match those of the 1950s/1940s/1920s/1890s. Well, it's the inadequate diet of post-war Europe/the dearth of dedicated singing teachers/the invention of the jet aeroplane.' 'This is the age of the producer.' 'This is the age of the designer.' 'Opera is grotesquely over-subsidised/atrophying for lack of funds/collapsing under its own weight.' 'The structure of the opera world is being undermined by creeping homosexuality.' 'People go to the opera not to see but to be seen.' 'Opera should be taken into the arena, out to the people, away from the bourgeoisie.' 'Opera libretti are ridiculous.' 'Opera has the greatest power of any of the arts to move the human heart.'

To generalise about opera is as misleading as it is tempting, and each of these statements should be subjected to the same question – 'What opera, where?' Within an art form that is itself a hybrid (of visual and aural, verbal and musical, intellectual and emotional, fundamental and trivial), it is hardly surprising that there should be an almost infinite number of variations on what is broadly the same theme, *dramma per musica* – differences in the scale and scope of operations, different tastes, different aims, different kinds and degrees of success.

Opera exists as an entertainment on the grandest scale – at the 'big four' opera houses (the Metropolitan Opera House, New York; the Royal Opera House, Covent Garden; La Scala, Milan; the Vienna State Opera), or on the most modest – *The Story of Carmen* in church halls in Wales. Opera is equally Franco Zeffirelli's production of *La Bohème* for the Met with a cast of 280, an orchestra of about 100 and a support staff of some 300 or more – or Stephen Oliver's two-hander, *A Man of Feeling*, at the King's Head pub in Islington. Production styles range from the most lavish and elaborate (the Met's *Francesca da Rimini*, with real gold leaf, moving drawbridges, flying fireballs), to the most aggressively austere – the 'poor theatre' approach of Opera Factory or of David Alden's production of *Mazeppa* for English National Opera, in which river banks were reduced to chalk lines on the floor and the scaffold and ceremonial axes for a public execution to a cubicle of screens and a power saw.

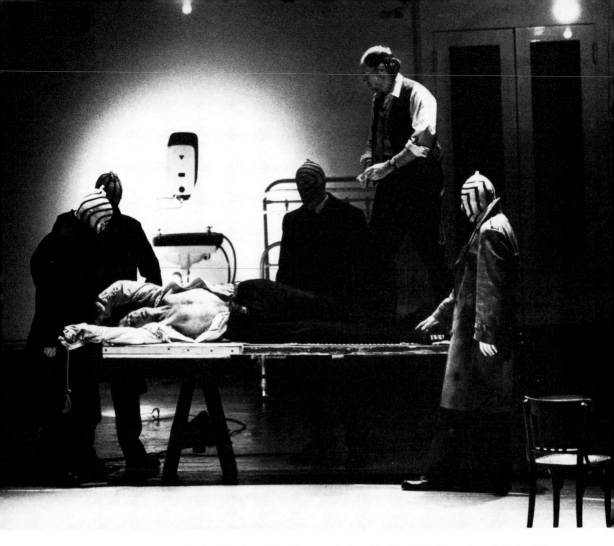

A severe stage-setting for Tchaikovsky's *Mazeppa*, designed by David Fielding. (*centre*) Richard Van Allan as Kochubey (ENO, 1984).

The opera company itself may be the most permanent of organisations, complete with general manager, music director, director of productions, orchestra, chorus, administrative hierarchy, music staff, wardrobe, wig room, armoury and production departments, all operating all the year round. The Royal Opera House at Covent Garden, for example, in a performing season of forty-eight weeks shared with the Royal Ballet Company, gives about 120–140 performances of some twenty to twenty-five different productions, Vienna 240 performances of thirty-six productions in forty-four weeks, and the Met approximately seven performances a week in a New York season of thirty weeks. Alternatively, for the greater part of the year the 'company' may consist solely of an administrator and possibly, in the interests of continuity, a conductor and a skeleton administrative staff, with everyone else – singers, designers and technical staff, producers and musicians – assembled afresh for each production, and sets and costumes makeshift or rented. The regular staff of the Virginia Opera Association in Norfolk, Virginia, for example, consists of a general manager, a principal conductor and a chorus master; singers, orchestra and chorus are hired individually for four operas performed one after the other between October and March each year. Betwixt these two extremes are the opera festivals (like Santa Fe and Glyndebourne) which in the course of a few weeks – usually in the summer – put on a larger number of operas two or three at a time; and a number of houses which have a constant and elaborate administrative structure but perform for only part of the year. The Lyric Opera of Chicago, for example, has a single season in the fall, the San Francisco Opera separate seasons in fall and summer and, until recently, New York City Opera had only one long summer-fall season – though from 1986 it will be adding a spring season to keep the house open for thirty-six weeks a year.

The character of the product on offer in an opera house will depend to a considerable extent on whether the company runs itself as an ensemble or prefers to invite guests from outside. Among the most thorough-going ensemble companies – those which cast all their productions (principals, *comprimarii*, conductors and even producers) from within the company – might be counted the Bolshoi, most of the smaller German houses, and New York City Opera which is, in fact, the only large-scale ensemble company in the USA because so few companies can afford to keep singers, orchestra and technical staff together on a permanent basis. At NYCO, all the principal roles are shared among the company singers, as its General Director Beverly Sills describes: 'The girl who's doing *Traviata* tonight [Leigh Munro] covered *La Rondine*, did the ingénue in *Sweeney Todd*, alternates as Cunégonde in *Candide* and sings in *The Student Prince* . . .' The Met, on the other hand, gives all its principal roles to guests, as do the rest of the big four and other 'international' houses like Munich and Paris. Smaller roles in these companies, however, do go to 'in-house' singers with long-term contracts, whereas organisations like Virginia, the Opera Company of Philadelphia and the summer festivals hire even their supporting players on a freelance basis.

Other companies, falling somewhere between the two systems, might best be described as 'semi-ensembles'. English National Opera, for instance, supplements a central core of company singers both with the occasional 'star' guest and with associate artists who, whilst not members of the company, work with it on a regular and organised basis. The Deutsche Oper in Berlin similarly maintains a large resident company, with some fifty singers on contract, but in any season will invite on average well over a hundred guests and the houses at Hamburg, Frankfurt and Cologne preserve the same balance. Even the smaller German houses, which operate in essence as ensemble companies, may take guests from each other for the sake of variety. Performances on offer range from the most painstakingly prepared to the almost laughably impromptu. Where many German houses will allocate six weeks of rehearsal to a new production (perhaps more for a Wagner opera – Bayreuth frequently stipulates two months or more), and both Covent Garden and the Met will try to allow for four weeks, at lower levels 'instant opera' is endemic. A cast and orchestra of sorts is assembled with three or four days to spare, sets and costumes are procured from a hire company and a 'producer' employed to direct stage traffic. In between come the houses which in preparing new productions spare neither expense nor effort – but then revive the same productions with the minimum of either. One major European house is particularly famous for the despatch with which it puts revivals on to the stage; as one observer describes it, 'People arrive the day before, they meet in a rehearsal room – "Hello, I'm Fricka/Sieglinde/Brünnhilde." "How do you do? I'm singing Wotan/Siegmund/Siegfried – this is the rock, this is the door, this is the sword, that's where the conductor is, see you tomorrow at seven o'clock."'

Some opera companies are rarely seen outside their own four walls – the Paris Opéra, for example, or Covent Garden, for whom it has now become too expensive to tour (at home, that is, for as Paul Findlay, the Royal Opera House's Assistant Director, points out, it costs neither the house nor the Arts Council any extra to tour abroad, where the fees paid by the host cities are enough to cover all expenses). At the other extreme one finds the Welsh National Opera which has no permanent theatre of its own and is in effect on tour all year round.

Many of the larger companies both have permanent homes and tour more or less widely – La Scala, for example, the Bolshoi, and the Met, which in terms of the number of performances given has been in its touring guise the fifth largest company in the USA, visiting eight cities in eight weeks, from Washington to Dallas and Minneapolis to Memphis (though in 1987 the Met is to abandon the tour – like Covent Garden, largely for financial reasons). Other houses have formed separate and subsidiary touring companies – San Francisco has the Western Opera Theater, for example, and Houston Grand Opera the Texas Opera Theater Company.

There are houses which are as exclusive as they can practicably make themselves – Anthony Besch, invited shortly before the Islamic revolution in Iran to produce *Madam Butterfly* at the Shah's own opera house in Teheran, was not sure that anybody at all was allowed to come and watch – and others which are compulsorily popular. Lilian Baylis founded English National (then Sadler's Wells) Opera with the express intention of bringing music and drama to working people at prices they could afford and in a language they could understand. New York City Opera has a similar mandate (a legacy from Mayor Fiorello La Guardia) to keep its ticket prices within the reach of any and every New Yorker. More expensive than ENO but more welcoming than the Shah, Covent Garden is anxious to rid itself, without becoming un-smart, of an 'establishment' aura – Paul Findlay comments, 'We don't want to create any one image which will be offensive to another sector of the public' – and has promised that in the unlikely event of increased subsidy, its first action would be to reduce ticket prices.

Certain features, however, almost all opera companies have in common. The most obvious, perhaps, is a more or less urgent need for money – which may yet prove the great leveller. For as long as funding for the arts is inadequate, there is nothing certain or immutable about the current structure of the opera world. Scale and splendour of operations, number of productions and performances, sizes of staff, calibre of guests and consequent position within the national or international opera hierarchy all depend on money. The big four maintain their superiority partly by virtue of tradition (less so in the case of Covent Garden, essentially a post-war foundation), largely by virtue of money, as Sir John Tooley, General Director of the Royal Opera House, recognises all too clearly: 'What of course could bring us down is our inability to finance a sensible programme. One of the debates we have at the moment is about the minimum number of opera performances that you can give and still maintain your credibility as a great opera house. Rather a negative way of looking at it, but a question you have to ask when your finance is declining' – and all major houses whose subsidy, like Covent Garden's, in real terms decreases annually, face the same prospect of planning on a downward curve.

Opera companies are also uniform, to a far greater degree than theatre companies or even symphony orchestras, in the repertoire they present. All over the world, with relatively minor regional variations, opera administrators compile their seasonal programmes from very much the same ingredients – it has been estimated that a core repertoire of some one hundred pieces (a large proportion of them nineteenth-century) accounts for at least two thirds of the world's opera performances. In international houses the common bond may be even more conspicuous in that the same pieces may be presented by the same protagonists. In putting together their casts, administrators fish from the same pool of international singers – their relative prestige and cash flow determining whether they are competing for the sturgeon or the sardines – and there are similar reservoirs of producers, designers and conductors all of whom distribute their favours impartially between the major houses of Europe and America. Even administrators move from house to house – Rolf Liebermann, for instance, from Hamburg to Paris and back again, Massimo Bogianckino from Rome to Florence to Geneva to Paris, Sir Rudolf Bing from Glyndebourne to the Met – their passage assisted by the universal predilection for the non-native. In Britain particularly where a national operatic tradition has only been securely re-established within the last forty years, the tendency has been to defer to the greater experience and charisma of the Continentals. Glyndebourne was started under the aegis of Fritz Busch and Carl Ebert and continued into the sixties under Vittorio Gui and Gunther Rennert. Covent Garden meanwhile appointed as successive Music Directors Karl Rankl, Rafael Kubelik and Sir Georg Solti: as Sir Colin Davis has pointed out, in some circles it is considered more convincing for an international house to have an 'international' (i.e. foreign) musician at its head.

Also, broadly speaking, the administrative structure of any opera house above a certain size will be articulated along similar lines, with separate departments handling music, production, technical (lighting, sets, the stage etc.), finance, and general administration, under the overall control of an administrative head and/or a board of management.

Every opera house in existence, however, has its own individual character, attractive or otherwise, bestowed on it by the people who work there, the building itself, the aims it pursues and a wide variety of other influences. The difference in atmosphere between houses which in repertoire, casting and general objectives have much in common is noted by Placido Domingo, among others: the machinations and intrigues of Vienna as compared with the friendliness, albeit in less stately surroundings, of Covent Garden; the elaborate bureaucracy and luke-warm audiences of the Met as compared with inspired chaos and near-manic passions at La Scala.

Some houses revel in tradition – the Met, for example, in the singers that have been associated with it over the years, La Scala in its status as 'Verdi's house', though the commemorative spirit is not surprisingly at its most pronounced at Bayreuth. While production styles at the Festspielhaus have for over thirty years been among the most adventurous in Europe, the prevailing attitude towards the music of Wagner remains reverential. Other companies have no tradition to speak of – since 1975 well over 250 new opera companies have been founded in the USA alone – and from this very lack of encumbrance derive their strength and their freshness.

Some opera companies are characterised in the eyes of the outside world by the personalities of those in charge. Glyndebourne Festival Opera, for example, is still essentially a family business and while it remains one, however financially successful it may be, it is unlikely ever to become a glossy and commercialised operation to compare with some of the larger European festivals. James Levine's Metropolitan Opera is very different from Sir Rudolf Bing's – more accessible, more overtly interested in marketing and public relations, arguably more American and less European-oriented. In some houses national traits seem to dominate. Peter Wood on Milan: 'I couldn't work in Italy – I couldn't take the siesta. I went to meet Lila de Nobili at La Scala, and it was like a movie: I searched right through that great building and it might have been *The Sleeping Beauty* – seamstresses asleep at their machines, prompter dozing in the prompt corner, stage hands propped up against the scenery – one of those great ideas you felt you really wanted to film. After forty-five minutes I found her painting away as usual – the only person awake in the whole building.' Other houses derive much of their individuality from their physical environment – La Fenice, for example, approachable on one side only by gondola, or the Roman Arena at Verona, packed on a fine night with over twenty thousand people, eating, talking, holding lighted candles. Or Glyndebourne again, set in a dip of the Sussex Downs with sheep and cows one side of the ha-ha, while on the other – even on a cold and miserable evening – the more determined among the audience eat and drink their *alfresco* suppers (after which, according to one singer, 'you could turn cartwheels and most people wouldn't notice').

The Arena di Verona: the audience of 25,000 at a performance of *Turandot*.

More significantly, though, opera houses are distinguished from one another by their differing priorities. For a considerable proportion of *habitués* opera is about beautiful singing, very largely for its own sake, and several major houses openly acknowledge its primacy in their scheme of things. Their first imperative is to secure the services of as many of the world's leading singers as they can, and the other elements (largely theatrical rather than purely musical) which can go to make up the ideal opera performance, though not disregarded, are subordinated to a greater or lesser extent. Covent Garden, for example, made the following formal 'Statement of Opera Policy' in 1983: 'We attach importance above all to standards of musical performance since we believe that in the performance of opera even the most imaginative stage presentation will not wholly compensate for short-comings in musical standards.' Even more single-minded in the pursuit of vocal excellence (though there are signs now of a shift of emphasis) has been the Lyric Opera of Chicago, which was described in 1984 by its General Director, Ardis Krainik, as having been for decades 'basically a conservative grand opera company, with top singers and conservative productions'. The company had a particular affinity for the Italian tradition of *bel canto*, and a large Italian audience. (In 1958 it was given a sizable grant for the specific purpose of importing Italian producers and *comprimarii*).

It is easy, though a serious over-simplification, to dismiss this approach as 'canary-fancying', and its critics are particularly vehement when the system appears to operate to the disadvantage of home-grown canaries. Some houses feel it more worthwhile to advertise the talents of national rather than international singers. New York City Opera lays great stress on the importance of nurturing the careers of native artists and its private fund-raising is deliberately geared to that end, as Beverly Sills explains: 'What's terribly appealing to people who have come to this country, perhaps as immigrants, and made their fortunes here, is to assist the young American artists. . . . Individuals have set up all kinds of scholarship programs . . . for the singer who has made the most promising début of this year, or of last year and lived up to the promise this year, or who is already doing leading roles but needs a little extra help for more coaching or more language tuition. . . These people don't want to pay the superstars' fees, it doesn't interest them, not the people who give to this company.'

A third type of opera company believes that imaginative stage presentation *can* compensate, and more than compensate, for less than the best vocal standards, and it gives strictly dramatic values a very much higher priority. The Opera Theater of St Louis, for example, as its name suggests, vigorously promotes the notion that opera is to be seen primarily as a form of theatre; it employs young and not yet established singers, but places them in the hands of experienced producers (such as Colin Graham and Jonathan Miller) and gives them rehearsal time which by American standards is very generous. At English National Opera, while the Music Director, Mark Elder, is adamant that drama is not *more* important than music, it is arguably considered *as* important, and the company's most successful productions of recent years – among them Jonathan's Miller's *Rigoletto*, David Pountney's *Rusalka* and Colin Graham's *War and Peace* – have been lavishly praised by critics from the straight theatre. A strong emphasis on theatrical values is the natural corollary of the decision taken on principle by ENO and a majority of the smaller German houses to perform opera in the language of its audience. Singing in the vernacular, however, can have one unfortunate side effect: translation seems, on occasion, to strip away the veil of enigma and the exotic, revealing situations that are now recognisable and words that refer to the audience's own experience. Thus vernacular opera may be felt to be dingy, even laughable, on principle, and some – though not all – administrators have snobbish reasons, besides those usually proffered, for shunning it. Even surtitles can be suspect, as posing another threat to the comfortable and superior glow of cultivation which an evening in a foreign language can generate. Designer John Conklin explains, 'What the surtitles do is take all the mystique out of it, so you don't have to know a language or have inside knowledge of opera. Anyone can come in and look at it – and they're terrified of that, terrified that like the Emperor's new clothes, people are going to come in and say – "This is shit, guys. This makes no sense at all and we're going to the movies."''

Glamour is an attribute that an international opera house can often ill afford to lose. It may be a significant factor in fund-raising, whether the house is looking to the government or the private patron for support. Even in a country with a socialist government, an international opera house, as Harold Rosenthal, Editor of *Opera* magazine, points out, is traditionally a national asset in terms of prestige; the gala night at the opera has long served a minor political function as a suitable environment for impressing visiting dignitaries – a custom that major houses have now institutionalised with their premium schemes by which expensive seats are made available on a regular basis to business firms and companies for the purposes of entertaining clients. And while they may not sympathise with it, few administrators of international houses are blind to the fact that a significant proportion of their best-paying clientèle comes to the opera largely or solely in order to maintain a high social profile. Vienna, Salzburg, the Met, La Scala, Covent Garden, Paris, Glyndebourne, Munich are all often accused, with varying degrees of justice, of playing host to contingents of what *Punch* unkindly describes as 'woodentops'.

At the other end of the spectrum are opera houses characterised by a stern sense of social commitment – houses which feel a duty to their communities, not merely to divert but to inform and improve them. As Götz Friedrich, the Intendant of the Deutsche Oper in West Berlin, recently observed, in his house one could still see 'how much composers, writers, philosophers needed the opera as a means of exploring ideas or issues of the present moment' and that at the Deutsche Oper 'more of the audience was intellectually involved in what it did, because the management did more than any other management I know of to communicate with the audience, and because in Berlin you felt more conscious of the fate of Europe than elsewhere'.

2

Funding

No professional opera company exists on its income from the box office. Glyndebourne, perhaps the most adept of any in balancing the eternal equation of box office, expenditure and artistic standards, covers only 65% of its operating costs from ticket sales, and is justifiably proud of the achievement. The Met's percentage – between 38–43% of costs covered – is higher than the American national average of 35–38%, which is what Covent Garden also usually recovers. The Paris Opéra averages some 21%, La Scala 17% and in the Soviet Union, although exact figures are not available, 'as long as the companies keep their value to the Soviet Union, they are accountable only in terms of artistic standards and international critical success.'

It is up to every administrator to find the most profitable relation possible between, on the one hand, the number of seats in his house and the price of tickets; and on the other, the scale of his operations – the number of performances given, the manning levels of the company, the cost of productions and the prestige of the singers involved. Some of the factors in the equation are variable (usually those involving expenditure), while others are not (those involving income). The number of seats in the house cannot be altered, for example, other than very occasionally. The administrator may make an effort to improve attendance figures, but unless attendances have been unusually low to start with, the increase in income is unlikely to be really significant. Bayreuth, Glyndebourne, Salzburg and Vienna are almost invariably sold out and at the Met, where average attendance is around ninety per cent, those seats left unsold at the end of the day tend to be the cheaper ones anyway.

The most obvious method of making more money, raising seat prices, is severely limited. Not only is there a healthy consumer resistance, but some houses are anyhow committed to 'popular' pricing – the Deutsche Oper, Berlin, for example, or New York City Opera. Beverly Sills explains: 'We call ourselves the people's opera. . . . There was a time when our yardstick was, "Whatever the Met charges, we charge half" – though that's no longer true, because the Met is up to eighty-dollar seats, and our top seat is twenty-eight dollars. . . . Our people are working people, without enormous amounts of money. I'm fond of saying that the Met has the senior partner in the law firm, and we have the junior partner who's just come in. Our patrons have babies and need baby-sitters; they find the cost of parking extremely expensive, not to mention the cost of restaurants in the neighbourhood, which has got to be quite fancy because of Lincoln Center. . . . For my "walk up to the window and buy a ticket" sale, I've got to keep it priced so that somebody who opens the newspaper in the morning and sees that *Akhnaten* is playing tonight, can find a price bracket so he can say to his wife, "Let's go see Philip Glass – for twenty-four dollars we can both go", and make a casual attempt to come. . . . Twelve dollars is a casual purchase: sixty dollars is not.'

Nor can the opera administrator often hope to amortise his costs in the manner of the Broadway impresario by extending the run of performances of a successful show and thus, as it were, getting more return on the money spent on sets, costumes and rehearsals.

The costs of an opera house, on the other hand, are by no means fixed. Materials become ever more expensive and the processes to which they are subjected more elaborate. It is now necessary, for example, for every costume, prop and piece of scenery which appears on a stage to have been chemically fireproofed, often before it reaches the theatre (a process which adds thirty per cent to the cost of plywood, for example). Singers' fees continue to rise; recently inflation has been

To economise on hire charges, a mould is taken from the decorations of an original in order to produce a series of chairs in Covent Garden's own workshop for John Schlesinger's production of *Der Rosenkavalier* (1985). This economises on hire charges.

perhaps less noticeable in the fees paid to the stars than in those requested by middle-rank singers taking advantage of the state of the market. It is not, however, the singers who make opera expensive, contrary to popular belief. Opera is the most labour-intensive form of entertainment so far devised, and a major opera house can expect to earmark up to two thirds of its expenditure for annual wages to its permanent staff.

The gap between expenditure and income from the box office is widening all the time, and the methods of bridging it vary. In Europe the difference is generally made up to a large extent by public subsidy. The Vienna State Opera, for example, is effectively 100% funded by central government; the Deutsche Oper looks to its local government authority for some 84% of its income; the Paris Opéra and La Scala both receive about 79%, the former from central government, the latter from both central and local government; Munich is given 75% of its funds by the local authority, Hamburg about 73%, and in the 1983–4 season Covent Garden received 54% of its income from the Arts Council.

However in Britain at least, there is still a shortfall. In the 1983–4 season, subsidy plus box-office revenue accounted for only 88% of Covent Garden's total expenditure. 'Other earned income' helps whittle away the deficit – income from the sale of advertising in programmes, merchandise (such as books, T-shirts, calendars and *L'Elisir d'Amore* eau de toilette), and the proceeds from television and video. Glyndebourne (which receives no public funding at all, other than for its touring operation) has been described as 'the last stronghold of private enterprise' – a bastion maintained by the Christie family and loyal supporters mobilised under various headings, principally the Glyndebourne Festival Society, and the Glyndebourne Association America. The Festival has been very successful in securing corporate sponsorship for particular projects (the Glyndebourne Chorus Scheme, for example) and for individual productions, occasionally finding the perfect sponsor – like Cointreau for Prokofiev's *The Love for Three Oranges*. Covent Garden, through the Royal Opera Trust (formed in 1974), has also increasingly attracted business sponsorship – from IBM for a season of schools' matinées, Midland Bank for the Proms, Commercial Union for *Don Giovanni* in 1981 and bullion dealers Mocatta and Goldsmid for *Der Rosenkavalier* in 1984, Barclays Bank and J. Sainsbury p.l.c. for Sadler's Wells Royal Ballet touring. ENO has for some years been enabled to record selected productions by a special grant from the Peter Moores Foundation and, until the petrol market went into a temporary decline, Welsh National Opera's London seasons were financed largely by Amoco.

Private funding in Britain, however, is on a relatively small scale, and is unlikely ever to reach a level where it would diminish the need for government subsidy – at least, without a major change in British tax laws to make donations to the arts deductible as they are in the USA. At present, the amounts that corporations give are usually forthcoming only for specific projects and not as contributions

OPPOSITE A schools' matinée performance of *La Bohème* (Covent Garden, 1984).

towards the general running expenses of a house, where they are equally if not more urgently needed. As Paul Findlay puts it, 'When you attract private money, you inevitably do it on the basis of something which has visibility. Wages and salaries don't have visibility in the same way as a new production.'

It is in comparison with the situation in the USA that private patronage in Britain dwindles into insignificance. In 1982–3, for example, when Covent Garden's private funding of some £700,000 amounted to under 4% of its income (though by 1984–5 the percentage had risen to nearer 7%), the Met's, at $25,800,000, constituted 36% of its total; and New York City Opera, because of the constraints on its pricing policy, regularly has to raise 60% of its income from private donors. Sir Claus Moser, Chairman of the Board of the Royal Opera House, has spoken of the need for 'a major change in the attitude of the British public towards giving', and it is no coincidence that in recent years American firms such as Citibank (*Manon Lescaut* 1983 and *Samson* 1985) and IBM (*Simon Boccanegra* 1980) have been among Covent Garden's most generous patrons. In Britain it has been considered somehow distasteful to associate the fine arts with commerce; Sir George Christie has referred to Glyndebourne's anxiety to 'minimise sponsorship's visual presence', (whilst at the same time recognising that Glyndebourne is beholden to such support), and Covent Garden's acknowledgement of generous and continued support from the Midland Bank, in the form of a banner in Floral Street reading 'Midland Bank Proms', caused – in Sir John Tooley's phrase – 'a paranoia to exist at 105 Piccadilly' (the home of the Arts Council). In America, money has no stigma attached and a donation that was *not* prominently acknowledged would stand little chance of being repeated.

But the problem goes deeper than a simple distaste for commerce. The Englishman's reluctance to sponsor the arts has to do with a firm conviction that they are his right, a service already paid for in taxation: the electorate is entitled to galleries, concert halls and theatres as it is entitled to schools and hospitals. This contrasts with the view held by recent American governments who have considered the arts a luxury, and individuals who prize them have accepted the need to pay for them. 'Philanthropic giving', in the words of the Met's Centennial Appeal literature, 'is a deeply personal matter, reflecting the donor's values, priorities and concern for the quality of life within our society and its future wellbeing.' And this is an attitude of which the Met has taken full advantage. As the 'General Motors of the arts' in America, it has both the largest budget (by far) and the most pressing need for contributions. Accordingly, in addition to its fifty-odd marketing personnel whose job it is to boost routine ticket sales, it employs a further fifty staff solely for extra fund-raising – on which it *spends* over three million dollars a year, more than ten per cent of Covent Garden's annual total budget.

The public contribute voluntarily to the Met's upkeep in a variety of ways. Those applying for subscription schemes (by which, before the start of the season,

OPPOSITE Façade of the Royal Opera House, Covent Garden: Midland Bank Proms season, 1982.

they book the same seat for a series of performances) are invited to add a gift to the price of the tickets and in 1982–3, for example, did so to the tune of over a million dollars. The 100,000 members of the Metropolitan Opera Guild (an organisation comparable to 'Friends' groups elsewhere) pay a minimum of $30 a year for a priority booking facility and a subscription to *Opera News*. A carefully graduated hierarchy of 'Patrons' of the Met pay considerably more for proportionately greater privileges. For $1800 per annum, the Supporting Patron is rewarded with priority booking, his or her name in the programme, access to the Patrons' Room in the opera house, a Backstage Tour and a chance to Meet the Artists. The Sponsor Patron, at $3000 p.a., receives even higher priority in booking tickets, access to dress rehearsals and an invitation to the Opening Night Dinner. The Benefactor Patron, at $6000 or more, is given the highest priority booking, the chance to attend certain working rehearsals, and an invitation to a dinner held on the stage itself. Above $10,000 a year one enters the President's Circle, whose members are specially mentioned in the programme, are admitted to briefings on artistic and institutional planning with senior management, and enjoy behind-the-scenes dinners with board and management. The Second Century Circle is subdivided into Second Century Sponsors ($25,000 plus), Second Century Benefactors ($50,000), Second Century Guarantors ($100,000) and those acknowledged to have displayed Leadership for the Second Century ($250,000 or more); all four categories are entitled to privileges so exclusive that they are not listed in the publicity material.

Of the Met's more than 200,000 contributors, all of whom are making gifts to the Met over and above what they pay for any tickets they may buy, a large proportion are individuals. Their contributions begin at a relatively modest level – about half the contributed income is composed of average gifts of $100 – and rise steeply to gifts of over $100,000 from Mr and Mrs Gordon P. Getty, for example, and Mr and Mrs Walter Annenberg. Individuals may choose to donate directly to a specific production, by way of the Fund for Productions; the last new production of *Arabella* was underwritten by Mrs Michael Falk, and the Zeffirelli *Bohème* paid for in its entirety by Mrs Donald D. Harrington of Amarillo, Texas, one of the Met's most generous individual donors.

Attracting and maintaining the interest of patrons is an art which the Met has mastered, by identifying its clients' needs and desires. What an individual contributor wants may well be the sense of personal contact with the organisation, admission behind the scenes and the feeling of being an insider. What a *corporate* contributor, of which the Met has many, will want is more severely practical. In the words of Barbara Lorber, former Director of Public Affairs at the Met (now Vice President at Hill and Knowlton, an international public relations firm where she counsels corporate clients on their charitable giving), 'What they're after is access to our audience. They want to position their product or company with that upscale audience, people with a lot of disposable income . . . They want to make what they do visible in a positive way.' As a member of the Met's fund-raising staff, Barbara Lorber's job was to match each potential corporate contributor with a particular activity in need of finance, persuade the company in question to under-write it and make sure that adequate public acknowledgement was made to enable the executive responsible to justify the expenditure to his superiors on 'a hard-nosed business basis'. If necessary, she could furnish them with evidence that exposure of this type produced results. 'People who care about an organisation really check those donor lists in the program, they know who's taking care of something they love. They really do use consumer power as a reward for the cor-porate donors. . . . Texaco has bound volumes of letters from people all over the country saying they drive miles out of their way to go to a Texaco gas station because Texaco brings them the Met on the radio every Saturday.'

The producers of luxury goods make especially suitable sponsors for the Met. Barbara Lorber recalls an occasion on which thirty-six dummy bottles of champagne were needed for use on stage in one scene of *La Traviata*, and the designer was anxious that the labels should be authentic. Discovering that the Cordon Rouge label had not been changed since the early nineteenth century, she asked the product manager at Mumm's for three cases of empty bottles. When, obligingly, he presented in addition a few full ones for the use of the company, she seized her chance and asked for free champagne for consumption by the Patrons in the intervals, explaining to him what Patron Donor level means at the Met. 'Perfect – in the first act there's the *Brindisi*, Alfredo sings, everyone drinks champagne and then in the intermission the Guild Members go to the Belmont Room and the Patrons to the Patrons' Lounge, and all over the place are Mumm Cordon Rouge bottles and little cards saying "Champagne compliments of . . ." One of the ladies, who is very prominent socially, changed her usual champagne purchases from Moët to Mumm. . . . Two years later it was a six-figure contribution from Seagram's, the parent company, to help underwrite the Centennial Ball, plus product all over the place. . . .'

Beverly Sills and the New York City Opera have also had extraordinary success in keeping themselves afloat, using very similar methods. The Met, however, enjoys several advantages as a fund raiser – in particular its undisputed status as a *national* organisation. Its carefully orchestrated claim to represent the whole nation is substantiated by four of its activities – the National Auditions, an annual nation-wide search for talent under the auspices of the National Council of the Metropolitan Opera; the tour, which for a century brought fifty-six opera perform-ances to 250,000 people in eight other cities every year; live or recorded television broadcasts, occurring with a frequency – about seven a year – that Covent Garden, for one, very much envies; and above all the live Saturday afternoon radio broad-casts, sponsored by Texaco, which have been running for over forty years. The fund raisers play up the notion of 'the Met family' to considerable effect; while its live audiences are naturally drawn for the most part from the greater New York area, two thirds of its contributors live elsewhere.

Annual contributions, individual and corporate, have played a crucial part in the survival of the Met. In the late sixties and early seventies, the move from Broadway to Lincoln Center and a very damaging strike helped to exhaust capital reserves. Frank Taplin, President of the Metropolitan Opera Association, summed up the situation: 'We had to take one of three decisions. We could close down, we could cut back and become a regional company with a season of three or four months, like Chicago or San Francisco, or we could go for it.' They went for 'it' in the shape of a broader donor base, got it, and between 1976 and 1982 it was contributions plus the income from merchandising, television, radio and video rights which enabled the Met to bridge the gap between ticket sales and expenditure – except in the 1980–1 season when there was another crippling strike.

But even during that period of financial success, the fundraisers were dubious as to whether annual contributions could in the long term be more than a partial solution. They (correctly) anticipated costs escalating faster than contributions and were anxious to create some sort of financial buffer. 1983, the Met's centenary year, seemed to offer the perfect focus for a campaign to raise an Endowment Fund as such a safeguard, and in 1980 the Metropolitan Opera Centennial Fund – its motto 'To Endow a Second Century of Greatness' – was launched with a target of a hundred million dollars. 'Since 1929', the campaign leaflet explained, 'with the exception of the last few years, the company has been living in a "survival syndrome", and has never had the financial flexibility to make artistic choices solely for artistic reasons rather than financial ones.' The purpose of the Centennial Fund was to make long-term planning both more secure and less inhibited; eighty-five per cent of the money raised was to be used to generate interest with which the income/expenses gap might be bridged in perpetuity. The remainder was to be spent in the immediate future on such pressing needs as refurbishing and eventually improving the stages, lighting and stage machinery (described by critic Martin Mayer as being 'at the state of the art in America in 1965', viz. in line with German technology of the 1950s).

Since 1980 the Centennial Fund Appeal has been run with prodigious efficiency and zeal. At one extreme, a National Telefund effort has involved personal telephone calls to every member of the Metropolitan Guild. At the other extreme is a special incentive scheme for donors prepared to contribute $100,000 or more – the 'Gift Recognition Opportunities Scheme' by which opera lovers are given the chance to have their generosity publicly recognised. In return for very large sums indeed, donors have the opportunity to name a part of the opera house or a facet of its activities or the post of one of its employees. To name the auditorium, for instance, costs $25,000,000, the stage $10,000,000, the seventy-five-foot teak and leather Serpentine Bar $2,500,000, a student score desk or a backstage elevator 'used by artists and members of the company' $250,000 each. To append his name to one new production a year in perpetuity, the donor must be prepared to pay $10,000,000; for naming a revival fund devoted specifically to reviving the works of one composer, $2,500,000; for one performance per season for ten years, $250,000 (this last designed to appeal to donors 'wishing to mark a special annual occasion in their lives or seeking an appropriate method to memorialize a loved one to whom the Metropolitan Opera was important'). Were the post of Music Director to share your name, it would cost you $5,000,000; the prompter and first clarinet come cheaper, at $1,000,000 and $500,000 respectively.

Among the other forms of contribution encouraged by the Centennial fund raisers are 'Planned Giving' – leaving money to the Met in your will, the setting up of charitable trusts or Pooled Income Funds, and direct gifts of paintings, antiques, jewellery, rare books, real estate 'or other property of value you no longer wish to own'. In 1982–3 the opera house broke even largely by virtue of the liquidation of a company that had been bequeathed to it. By the end of 1984 the Centennial Fund had all but reached its target of $100,000,000, and the fund raisers were contemplating a new goal of $150,000,000. Not a few of the Gift Recognition Opportunities had been accepted; by mid-1984 there had been fourteen gifts of more than $1,000,000.

Outside New York, the opera world is very fragmented, and fund-raising is almost entirely localised – a state of affairs that Andrew Porter, principal music critic for the *New Yorker*, regards as deplorably wasteful: 'So many companies, and so many of them part-time, each of them with its own administrative resources, its own house, its own company managers and staffs; and each production being put on so few times and not revived ... There's enough money in most large areas – the Eastern seaboard, for example – to support a year-round company of the highest possible standard, but each city wants its own company. ... There's an awful lot of local pride, and local money involved in local pride.'

The fragmentation is partly the result of the pattern of public subsidy in the USA, especially during the Carter administration when more funds were made available to the arts and particular encouragement given to the setting up of regional organisations; of the 645 opera companies existing in America in the 1983–4 season, 178 (i.e. 27%) were created between 1975 and 1980, as compared with 187 in the previous twenty years. This trend towards decentralisation was reinforced by the policy of the National Endowment for the Arts. Founded in 1965 'to encourage and assist the nation's cultural resources', the NEA makes annual grants to individual artists, companies, arts agencies or service organisations. Under its Opera-Musical Theater Program, it provides funds for opera companies all over the USA – for touring, for the development of new pieces ($5000 in 1983–4, for instance, to the Vice Versa Vision Company of Connecticut towards Conrad Susa's *The Love of Don Perlimplin*), for education, for special projects like concert performance of opera, for the employment of American artists, for their general administration and for specific projects. In 1983–4 $3750 went to the Arkansas Opera Theater in Little Rock to hire a professional set designer for three productions; the Des Moines Metro Opera received $7875 to engage American singers for the coming season; and the Chicago Opera Theater was given $20,000 towards its revival of Virgil Thomson's *The Mother of Us All*, including the hiring of an American artist to design the set.

There can be no doubt that these grants – which must not exceed 50% of the company's budget and are in practice rarely more than 10% – are invaluable for regional companies, as a lever for private funding. The Opera Theatre of St Louis, for example, was awarded $400,000 by the NEA as a Challenge Grant in 1984 – on condition that every one dollar of this money was matched by three from private sources. Indeed, the NEA concluded in 1984 that with the reduction in federal grants to the arts (a policy favoured by President Reagan, resisted by Congress so far as it is able), private support nationwide is lagging.

One can hardly overemphasise the importance of the type of funding a company receives, affecting its very character and policy. In the words of David Reuben, the Met's Press and Public Relations Director, 'If I had to think of one word to sum up the difference between the Met and other houses, it would be *risk* – the amount we can take as opposed to the risk the European companies can take, whether it's in repertory, staging, schedule, singers. We can't *afford* to lose.' Subsidised houses, though accountable to their government sponsors, have the freedom to experiment: some fully subsidised houses, especially in Germany, seem to feel a positive duty to do so. Whereas American donors very rarely succeed in dictating artistic policy, they can intimidate by simple virtue of the fact that they possess the ultimate sanction of being able to withdraw their support at any time. This is a course of action not likely to be adopted by a government: any attempt to cut off funds altogether would provoke a public outcry. The worst the larger European houses have to fear is a reduction – English National Opera, for example, was seriously affected by a one per cent reduction in its grant imposed *ex post facto* – or, inconvenient enough, a delay: La Scala is informed by the government of the amount it can expect in subsidy so late that it regularly has to borrow at twenty-five per cent interest in order to finance the first part of its season. For the larger companies at least, there is a reasonable assurance that there will *be* a subsidy next year – no mean vantage point from which to renew the annual struggle to make ends meet, as the American houses would be the first to agree.

3

Planning the Season

In the past, responsibility for the extraordinarily complex task of running an opera company has tended to rest on the shoulders of one individual – a single Intendant in overall charge of all aspects of the house's administration. At the Met, Sir Rudolf Bing was a General Manager rather in this mould, but the arrangement is more characteristically a European one and still exists in many German and Austrian houses. The intendant now is usually an artist rather than exclusively an administrator by background – for example, Michael Gielen and Wolfgang Sawallisch at Frankfurt and Munich are both conductors, Michael Hampe, intendant at Cologne, a producer – and he is expected to involve himself equally in policy and in practical matters.

The modern trend, however, is to separate administrative (particularly financial) responsibilities to a certain extent from artistic policy-making. The General Manager (General Administrator/General Director/Managing Director, whatever his particular title might be) is responsible for the day-to-day running of the house, including its fund-raising, liaison with the board, negotiations with the unions, and the task of giving the house a public profile and maintaining its discipline and morale. At his side will be a Music Director, responsible for everything you hear in a performance and, sometimes, a Director of Productions, responsible for everything you see. Occasionally both hats are worn by a single 'Artistic Director', as is now the case at the Met where the split between artistic and administrative affairs became complete at the retirement of General Manager Anthony Bliss at the end of 1985. His successor Bruce Crawford – a specialist in fund-raising and chairman of BBDO International, the sixth largest advertising company in the world – took up his position knowing that he would primarily be required to concentrate on the Met's finances, and in this respect alone would he exert any influence in artistic matters. As the editor of *Opera News*, Robert Jacobson, commented when the appointment was announced in November 1984, 'What the Met's general manager needs to be is a firm, savvy, productive businessman, since the millions of dollars needed to keep the company functioning escalate dramatically every season ... The man, too, has to serve as a counterbalance to the artistic leadership of James Levine. ... As in the US Senate and the House of Representatives, a checks-and-balances system is thereby assured.'

Elsewhere the demarcation between 'art' and 'administration' is less absolute. At La Scala, for instance, *Sovrintendente* Carlo Maria Badini works in conjunction with *Direttore Artistico* Cesare Mazzonis and *Direttore dell' orchestra* Claudio Abbado (until 1986, when he will be succeeded by Riccardo Muti). When Abbado moves to the Vienna State Opera in the 1986/7 season as its Music Director, he will be working with General Director and Producer, Claus Helmut Drese. Beverly Sills and Ardis Krainik, as General Director and General Manager of New York City Opera and the Lyric Opera of Chicago, have Music Directors to oversee the musical standards of their houses. Scottish Opera and English National Opera both have triumvirates – at Scottish Opera, a General Administrator (John Cox), Artistic Director (Sir Alexander Gibson), and Director of Productions (Graham Vick); at ENO a Managing Director (from 1972 to '85 Lord Harewood, from 1985 onwards Peter Jonas), a Music Director (Mark Elder) and a Director of Productions (David Pountney). The post of Director of Productions is one that has been considered at Covent Garden (where control is at present shared between the General Director, Sir John Tooley, and Music Director, Sir Colin Davis) but never fully implemented. Sir John now feels that in a house run as a showcase for the world's most outstanding artists – singers, producers, designers and conductors – it would be inappropriate for any one individual to take the lion's share of the new productions on offer, as a Director of Productions would certainly expect to do. Nor, with specialist staff on hand (Technical Director Tom Macarthur and lighting consultant Robert Bryan) is there any obvious need for a Director of Productions to co-ordinate and monitor the technical aspects of productions – as, say, John Dexter was required to do at the Met in the mid-1970s. Similarly, Welsh National Opera now has only a General Administrator (Brian McMaster), a Musical Director (until 1986, Richard Armstrong, thereafter Sir Charles Mackerras) and a Technical Director (John Harrison), having scrapped in 1978 the post of Artistic Director previously held by producer Michael Geliot.

In all these cases, the General Managers work closely with their artistic directors in such matters as choice of repertoire and casting. Many of them feel, however, that their first and most important duty as administrators is in itself the assembling and developing of a successful artistic team around them. One of the inducements which took John Cox from Glyndebourne (where he was Director of Productions from 1972 to '82) to Glasgow was the prospect, with the examples of Diaghilev and Max Reinhardt before him, of *building* a team rather than simply being a member of one. Once the team is formed, the art, as Lord Harewood explains, is to offer advice without interfering: 'Sometimes you have to try and persuade them to alter something. You can't usually alter a concept once it's going, but you can try to get them to tone down something that's going to be exaggerated, remove something that's going to irritate the audience. Sometimes you succeed, sometimes you don't. You most often don't, and then find you're right and the audience giggles.'

OPPOSITE Beverly Sills, General Director of New York City Opera

Brian Dickie, General Administrator of the Glyndebourne Festival Opera, similarly advocates *détente* between the administration and the artistic team: 'Obviously one goes to stage and orchestra rehearsals, as another pair of fresh, experienced eyes. But in the end it's up to the producer and conductor; you can't say, "I will not have that on my stage." You *could*, I suppose, but you'd probably only say it once.'

Brian Dickie, like Sir George Christie, exercises a considerable influence on the artistic standards of the house and the direction it is likely to take; he and Sir George are responsible between them for auditioning most of the singers who appear at the Festival and both have pronounced ideas on the type of repertoire to which Glyndebourne is best suited. But, as Brian Dickie explains, 'Every artistic institution does have to have quite clear artistic leaders, and I don't think that any general administrator can give a house a coherent artistic identity by himself. . . . Why does Glyndebourne need a Music Director or Director of Productions? Because, I think, Bernard Haitink and Peter Hall contribute inspiration on a permanent basis, unlike guests, whose influence over what happens in the house cannot extend beyond work on their own pieces . . . Both Bernard and Peter have inspirational qualities which, combined with their positions, mean that there is a sort of excitement there when they're round the house. If people actually hold an office, as well as being what they are, their ability to influence others, to lead them, is considerably enhanced . . . Glyndebourne's position was never as secure when we had no artistic directors as it was when Ebert and Busch were there – it hasn't really been that secure again until now.' And his most pressing short-term ambition is to make the most of this situation, 'to get the best out of the Haitink-Hall partnership'.

In discussing 'artistic policy' it is essential to acknowledge (as critics of those in charge of opera houses are often reluctant to do) that opera planning is rarely achieved in peaceful isolation, free from market pressures, financial necessities and other factors entirely beyond the planner's control. Sir John Tooley observes, 'People think you can just say you're going to do X, Y and Z. They're quite unwilling to accept that there are any other forces at work.' The more 'international' and prestigious a house, the more likely, paradoxically, is its artistic policy to be a compromise – not so much the administrator's vision unalloyed as the product of extended negotiations between a variety of interested parties: administrator, singers, producers, designers, conductors, agents, television and recording companies, subscribers, Boards of Trustees, even (on occasion) sponsors.

The logistics of planning a season in an opera house will obviously also vary according to the length of the season and the number of productions being mounted. Glyndebourne, for example, presenting only five productions a year under excellent and relaxed festival conditions, tends to plan over an eight- to ten-year period; year-round houses, mounting anything between fifteen and thirty productions, are less likely to plan for more than three or four years at a time. Rather than explore the complex ramifications of long-term planning, however, it will

Placido Domingo with Sir John Tooley in the auditorium during rehearsals for the televising of
Die Fledermaus, Domingo's début as a conductor at Covent Garden (1983).

be less confusing here to consider the planning of a single season as if it were
executed in isolation.

Most houses, other than those whose brief is obviously specialist, aim at a
balanced repertoire within the season – a judicious mixture of German and Italian,
for example, and within the German repertory, some sort of balance between
Mozart, Wagner and Strauss; within the Italian repertory, a mixture of the *bel
canto* works of Rossini, Bellini and Donizetti, and the romantic repertoire of Verdi
and Puccini. Some administrators like to ensure that French opera is represented,
or Eastern European pieces other than the Russian standards – Janáček, Dvořák,
Smetana, or Prokofiev, for instance. Many houses now incorporate in their standard repertoire baroque opera in one form or another – certainly Handel (in 1984
his operas were played at the Met, New York City Opera and seventeen other
American houses, and this was before the centenary in 1985) and, increasingly,
Monteverdi and Cavalli as well; in Germany, designer-directors are tempted to

resuscitate even earlier works by the scope they offer for spectacle and stage effects. It is not unusual in countries with a relatively slender operatic corpus – England, America or Scandinavia, say – for national composers to feature in programmes as a matter of policy; and most administrators, with greater or lesser degrees of enthusiasm, acknowledge an obligation to include at least one contemporary work per season. In many year-round houses, the mixture is leavened with operettas, even musicals. The specific ingredients of the mixture, however, and the proportions in which they are combined depend to some extent on the individual circumstances of each house. Wagner is made more difficult to programme at the Met by the size of the house and of the voices needed to overcome it; equally, the Met is less well-suited to Mozart than a house the size of Glyndebourne. Conversely, there is a risk at Glyndebourne of Verdi sounding overblown.

Every season must be balanced from the economic as well as the artistic point of view. Much as the artistic team may despise it, the box office has to be considered – though the degree of attention paid it may vary. At Glyndebourne, for instance, 'We decide what we want to do', according to Brian Dickie, 'and then see what it will cost. . . . We're never flush with money, but as a festival opera we have a certain flexibility, so, for example, if a season is a bit more expensive than we can afford, we can save on next year.' Glyndebourne is, however, at the fortunate end of the financial spectrum. Most houses must look first to their budgets, *then* formulate what in an ideal world they should like to do, and then compute as accurately as possible both what their plans will cost, and what can be recouped at the box office. Different houses operate different systems for estimating box office returns, and set different targets for themselves. English National Opera, for example, aims at about 70% attendance, but predicting how that average is to be achieved is not an easy game to play, as Lord Harewood complains: 'You can get it wrong – though it sounds totally mad – by as much as 20% in next-door pieces. We put *War and Peace*, out of canniness, much too low this season [1983–4], and were 15% out in our estimate – sales were substantially up on it. Then *Rosenkavalier*, which got rather good notices and is a good revival – about 15% down in the same period. What can you say? The weather?' If it is decided to include in a season operas which no one believes will manage 70% attendance, then other works which invariably sell well must be incorporated to compensate. There are traditionally reckoned to be some two dozen operas which are sure-fire successes at the box office; different countries might have different candidates for the lower end of the list (*The Magic Flute*, for example, would certainly be included in Germany but probably not in Italy, and vice versa for Ponchielli's *La Gioconda*), but most houses would agree that in the upper echelons are *Aida, Carmen, La Bohème, La Traviata, Faust, Rigoletto, Madam Butterfly, The Marriage of Figaro, Der Rosenkavalier, Tosca, Cavalleria Rusticana* and *Pagliacci, Il Trovatore, Lucia di Lammermoor, The Barber of Seville, Lohengrin, Don Giovanni, Tristan und Isolde*, with *Die Meistersinger, The Tales of Hoffmann, Otello, Così fan tutte, Manon, L'Elisir d'Amore* and *Fidelio*, all contenders. The *Ring*, when it comes to measuring box-office viability, is something of a special case because although it almost invariably sells well, its costs are usually higher than those of the rest of the repertoire.

While the central core of the repertoire, reflecting popular taste, will be much the same from house to house, each company may be characterised partly by its approach to that core repertoire, partly by the more unusual pieces (excluding new commissions) it chooses to add. Since the early 1970s English National Opera, for instance, has presented with its *Aida*s and *Figaro*s and *Barber*s such works as Ligeti's *Le Grand Macabre*, Penderecki's *Devils of Loudun*, Dvořák's *Rusalka*, Szymanowski's *King Roger*, Bartók's *Duke Bluebeard's Castle*, Monteverdi's *La Favola d'Orfeo* and Britten's *Gloriana*. Covent Garden in a comparable period put on Massenet's *Esclarmonde*, Meyerbeer's *L'Africaine*, Bellini's *I Capuleti e I Montecchi*, Ravel's *L'Enfant et les Sortilèges*, Verdi's *I Lombardi*, Donizetti's *Lucrezia Borgia*, and Berlioz' *Benvenuto Cellini*, showing if nothing else a greater fondness for French opera, including 'grand opera' in its strictest sense. (One might make a similar comparison between New York City Opera and the Met, though since the era when Julius Rudel was at the head of one house and Sir Rudolf Bing at the head of the other, the contrast has perhaps become less pronounced.)

On the whole, festivals, under the impetus of a holiday atmosphere and assisted by a strong tourist presence, can afford to be more adventurous. Glyndebourne, for all the 'establishment' tags attached to it, has made important contributions to the repertoire in Britain, introducing *Così fan tutte*, *Idomeneo*, and *Macbeth* for the first time, leading the way in the baroque revival, making *Intermezzo* part of the accepted Strauss canon and, in Sir George Christie's phrase, 'having a crack at Haydn'. It is hard to imagine a programme like the 1984 season at Santa Fe outside the context of a festival: Korngold's *Violanta*, Cimarosa's *Il Matrimonio Segreto*, *Intermezzo*, Zemlinsky's *Eine Florentinische Tragödie*, and Henze's *We Come to the River*, all receiving their US professional premières, with only *The Magic Flute* to represent what might be called the mainstream. (The 1985 season again included the US première of a Henze work – *The English Cat* – plus the world première of John Eaton's *The Tempest*). A festival with no more than four or five performances of a production to sell and no obligation to revive it can risk experiments that conceivably have little more than novelty value – Wagner's version of Gluck's *Iphigénie en Aulide*, for example, or Richard Strauss's edition of *Idomeneo*.

Every administrator must also find the right proportion of new productions to revivals. No one would deny that new productions are the lifeblood of any company. Whether they are simply replacements for old ones that have worn out their welcome or their physical fabric, or works being brought into the repertoire for the first time, a certain number of new productions in a season is crucial both if a house is to keep its audience (Paul Findlay reports that when Covent Garden *did* reduce its number to two per season, there was a serious fall in box-office returns), and if it is to maintain the morale of the company itself. Nevertheless for obvious reasons few companies, however limited their seasons, exist entirely on new productions. At Glyndebourne, for example, out of five productions per year, two are new and the remainder either 'repeats' (productions coming back after two years or less with roughly the same cast) or 'revivals' (coming back after three years or more, substantially recast). And in houses like the Met, Covent Garden, ENO, La Scala, the Vienna State Opera or any other year-round house, the great preponderance of productions will be revivals of various degrees of antiquity. When ENO's *Count Ory* was revived in 1985, for instance, it was well over twenty years old (described in the brochure as a 'vintage' production); and the Met's *Don Giovanni*, *Madam Butterfly* and *Eugene Onegin* are all thirtyish. Covent Garden's *Dialogues of the Carmelites* dates from 1958, its Zeffirelli *Tosca* likewise; in fact, twenty-five per cent of the Royal Opera House's stock is over twenty years old, and it has productions in store dating back to the 1940s.

In selecting new works, therefore, the administrator has traditionally needed to have an eye to their revivability. This season there may be an audience for *Lakmé* or *Euryanthe* or *La Wally*, but how many people are going to want to see them again within the next ten or fifteen years? For the same reason it behoves him to tread warily with unorthodox interpretations. A risk at the best of times, the losses attendant on a flop are compounded each time the production is revived. Many large houses feel that in the long term they have a responsibility to have on offer to the public fairly straightforward 'library' versions of standard works, rather than essays on those works by distinguished interpreters. Gerald Fitzgerald of *Opera News* argues, 'You can't spend two million dollars on *Tosca* and have it made out of stainless steel and fibreglass – that's for a festival, for four or five performances done in a unique way – not *Tosca*, but one director's concept of *Tosca*: it can be fascinating and throw light, but it's not durable.'

So when considering a new production, the administrator has a choice. He can play safe, select a producer and designer likely to be conventional, and spend a lot of money in the confidence that this will be recouped over a long period. Or he can allow for unorthodoxy, acknowledging the possibility that the production's life will be shorter and, preferably, spending less on it on that assumption. ENO has been tending towards a higher turnover of less expensive, less traditional productions – partly, perhaps, through an ideological opposition to the more lavish forms of 'grand' opera; partly through the feeling that an opera house should not be allowed to become clogged with the familiar. It is also partly in protest against the inhibiting effect that the concern for revivability can have on creative energy at the outset of a production, as David Pountney explains: 'It makes each production even more like a piece of porcelain in a glass case. And yet, in the theatre one must have the right to fail; the right to break the piece of porcelain and then stick it back together again. The theatre is too dangerous a place for precious objects. Our aim has been to cut the Gordian knot by severely reducing the cost of several of our new productions. We aim to do more new work, fewer revivals, and create an atmosphere in which the burden of responsibility with each new production lies where it should – on its artistic vitality – and not on its status as a crucial investment in the company's future.' David Pountney would like eventually to see no production lasting longer than four years, but the most immediate effect of the policy has been the decision to mount – under the auspices of Norwest Holst – a series of rarely-performed operas, such as Wagner's *Rienzi* and Tchaikovsky's *Mazeppa*, on the understanding that they will be done as cheaply as possible and never revived. Sets and costumes are simple, since after the production's first and only run they are scrapped or put back where they came from and considerable economies are made by not requiring the chorus to perform the music from memory.

Another way of financing 'experiments' is to share the costs and halve the risk of a new production with another company. Increasingly, the larger houses are prepared either to borrow (that is to say, rent) already-existing productions from one another, or to collaborate on equal terms in evolving new productions together. In both cases, sets, costumes and, ideally, the original production concept, are transferred from one house to the other; in the latter case, the same cast may travel with the production.

Managements have always kept an eye on what each other is doing – most commonly in order to *avoid* doing the same. While ENO and Covent Garden will inevitably have *Butterfly*s and *Traviata*s in their repertoire at the same time, they will generally try not to mount them during precisely the same period, and the same applies to the Met and New York City Opera. Beverly Sills is perfectly realistic about the need to avoid seeming to compete on the same territory with the Met: 'I cannot afford to have a *Bohème* that looks cheap compared with Mr Zeffirelli's million-dollar production – mine has to be extremely innovative and imaginative, approached from a totally different point of view.' But as costs escalate, collaboration is on the increase throughout the opera world. Taking Covent Garden as typical of the major European international houses, in its 1984/5 season four out of the seven new productions involved the participation of one or more other companies – *Samson* (a co-production with Chicago and the Met), *The Barber of Seville* (borrowed from Cologne), *La Donna del Lago* (a co-production with Houston Grand Opera) and *Ariadne auf Naxos* (borrowed from Paris). On the European scene as a whole, Jean-Pierre Ponnelle is closely associated with the idea of the 'travelling package' opera. His production of *La Cenerentola*, for instance, premièred and owned by La Scala, has been seen widely all over Europe in the past ten years, as has his Monteverdi cycle evolved in Zurich with Nikolaus Harnoncourt; he is currently working with Daniel Barenboim on a Mozart series which migrates between Paris and Washington.

The phenomenon is even more significant in the USA. New York City Opera, for example, in 1984 borrowed its *Carmen* from Philadelphia, *Lakmé* from Chicago and *The Rake's Progress* (designed by David Hockney) from San Francisco (a production which that house had in fact bought from Glyndebourne and had remade in Italy); the Ponnelle *Cenerentola*, identical in every physical detail to the European version, has been in circulation in the States for years, rented by San Francisco (who first mounted it in 1969) successively to Houston, Dallas and Chicago. This

free and easy commerce in productions is in part due to the efforts of two organisations set up in order to combat what some critics see as the parochialism of American opera, which vigorously promote the exchange of information and closer
collaboration. The Central Opera Service, run under the auspices of the
Metropolitan Opera's National Council, publishes statistics on the repertoire of
every company in North America and the major ones abroad; on performances
in the US – when, where and by whom; the availability of musical materials, transla-
tions and surtitles; new developments in scenery and costumes, and their availability (for rental, sale or exchange); companies' schedules, the size of their
auditoria, their staffing, union contracts, budgets, income, prices, subscription per-
centages and attendances; on touring, opera education and so on. Its principal
role, as described by its Executive Director, Maria Rich, is as a service organisation
which caters equally to educators and performers. Opera America, on the other
hand, is an association of performers, a forum established by the major American
companies for networking information amongst themselves.

There is no question but that the rented production is a godsend to a tight-
stretched budget, both for borrower and lender, but it can on occasion turn out
to be something of a pig in a poke, as when costumes and sets seen at a distance
appear considerably less alluring at close range or, more straightforwardly, simply
do not fit their new hosts – a problem which also affects production-sharing.
Jonathan Friend, one of the Met's three artistic administrators, points out: 'Basically, a production that is conceived, designed, built and lit for one stage will
never be actually right for another. It saves money in that we don't have to build
a new one of our own. . . . But when you see on the stage a production that doesn't
look right, you're not going to be able to revive it as many times as if you'd spent
the money and got something you liked.' It makes perhaps most sense to share
costs and ownership of a piece that neither party sees as a staple of the repertory,
and that neither would necessarily have undertaken independently. The costs of
mounting Philip Glass's *Akhnaten*, for instance (co-produced in 1984 by Houston
Grand Opera and New York City Opera), would have been prohibitive for any
one company, as Beverly Sills explains: 'It isn't so much the expense of the physical
production itself – actually the Glass is quite simple and primitive, at his request
– it's the rehearsal time that is needed. When I do a *Traviata*, my orchestra has
done three or four hundred performances of it. If there's a new conductor, we
get three healthy readings and he puts his stamp on it and marks the parts and
we're in very good shape. You can't do that with a Philip Glass work. The number
of orchestra and chorus rehearsals is quite awesome. We have a synthesiser in the
pit, and we've never used one in anything before. It's a totally different combination
of instruments. It requires a great deal of work from the chorus and orchestra. . . .
Since we're sharing the costs, we *both* pick up the tab for whatever extra rehearsals
are needed.' And as far as the composer is concerned, the arrangement has the
added benefit of exposing the work to two different audiences.

But the graver drawbacks of production-sharing become apparent when the original director is not able, or not required to travel with the production to ensure that the original conception, which sets and costumes were designed to complement, is respected. Designer John Conklin recalls, 'I did a *Werther* in Houston with David Alden, who is not your standard director. If you hire him, you know he's going to be wilful. His *Werther* was not so strange, but it was not run-of-the-mill. It was for five houses, and he directed the first two; from then on, it was chaos. . . . We're all trying to have some vision of *Werther* – and David Alden's and my version is going to be specific, the choices are going to be specific. You can't expect somebody else to come in and move people around in the same way. . . . Other directors said, "Where's the tavern, how do you do the scene without a tavern?", and "Why is the graveyard there?" . . . In another house it was supposed to go to, we had moved it up to *c.* 1812, and someone there said, "You can't do it unless Werther is wearing his blue and yellow Werther costume that he wore in the novel." I held out – and having paid their share of our production, they rented a whole other production from San Francisco so they could do it 1790 in blue and yellow.'

Among the other factors which may affect the planning of a season, the preferences and availabilities of singers are probably the most influential. While planning round singers is considered by many critics to be in some way reprehensible – in artistic terms not absolutely pure – it is a fact of operatic life, especially but not exclusively in international houses. For prestige reasons, international companies must attempt to present most, if not all of the dozen or so singers who are at the top of the profession at any given moment. It is not unusual for such companies first to secure the services of the singers and then to ask them in which operas they would like to appear. Provided the pieces fall within the framework of house policy, they will be staged, and some frameworks are loose enough to accommodate virtually anything – hence the occasional appearance of works whose sole virtue is as vehicles for exceptional voices. What may not always be appreciated is that negotiations between singer and administrator rarely relate to a single opera. More usual is a process which might politely be described as horse-trading ('If the house gives you X in 1986, in 1987 you will perform Y for it'), more accurately as blackmail ('If you *don't* give me X in 1989, I will not be singing Y or Z for you this season or next').

Prestige aside, certain pieces require performers of a particular type and calibre – *Carmen*, for example, or *Lucia di Lammermoor* – and without singers who are able and willing, it is considered rash to mount the works at all. At a press conference in 1984, Covent Garden explained the absence from their 1985 repertoire of both *Fidelio* and *The Midsummer Marriage* entirely in terms of casting.

Ensemble houses may not be in thrall either to the whims of international singers or to their schedules, but if they have exceptional performers within, or within the reach of their own companies, they may well respond. New York City Opera, for example, has in the past put on *Lucia* and *Manon* for Gianna Rolandi, Massenet's *Don Quichotte* for Samuel Ramey, *Werther* for Jerry Hadley, and Ambroise Thomas's *Hamlet* so that Erie Mills might play Ophelia; and Welsh National Opera's productions of *I Puritani* and *Norma* were largely prompted by the availability of Suzanne Murphy. Certainly if at any moment a company has a singer capable of taking a particularly difficult role (a Salome, Brünnhilde, or Medea, an Ochs, Otello, or Falstaff), it is well-advised to take advantage of the fact – always assuming, of course, that it is possible to cast the rest of the opera satisfactorily, as Lord Harewood explains: 'If you've got a good young soprano who is rather inexperienced but has a smashing voice . . . you decide that the kind of role that would be the right stretcher, in which she would be only one of four main pillars, would be something like *Trovatore* – and you then have to see whether you can cast the rest of the parts satisfactorily or whether you can't. Certain things are much easier to cast than others. If Rosalind Plowright was to say (which she has not done) that she would like to do *Medea* here, anyone knows that the other parts are relatively easy to cast. If she were to say that she wanted to do *Anna Bolena*, they're actually very difficult to cast, because you've got to get a very good bass who looks like Henry VIII or sufficiently so (and *we* really know what he looks like, unlike La Scala), and to persuade him to sing it is not easy as there isn't an aria. You've also got a massive second soprano part, Jane Seymour – and she's got to seem a winner, which is very awkward when it's Rosalind as Anna. I don't mean that Rosalind won't co-operate, but that she looks splendid, and you've got to get somebody who looks at least comparably splendid. Just to say Henry VIII liked short dumpy ladies and not very tall slim ones is an awkward thing to convey to an audience.'

In the same spirit, some companies will schedule operas to suit conductors (elusive maestri like Carlos Kleiber, for example, who is only prepared to conduct certain pieces) or to entice producers whose names will add cachet to a season. Glyndebourne, while it will virtually never mount a vehicle for a singer, quite happily admits to selecting an opera in order to forge a team of producer, designer and conductor which may be of permanent value to the company. On the whole, however, Glyndebourne's programme-planning is governed by more abstract considerations. At its heart are themes pursued over several seasons – a particular period or genre of opera, the work of a single composer, even one aspect of a composer's work. The most successful of these have come to be considered typical Glyndebourne repertoire and the fiftieth anniversary season in 1984, designed to be representative, embodied almost all of them. It opened with *The Marriage of Figaro*, followed a month later by *Così fan tutte*. These were the two operas which constituted the first ever Glyndebourne season, and Mozart operas have remained

OPPOSITE Glyndebourne Festival Opera planning meeting in Sir Peter Hall's office at the National Theatre, 1985; (*left to right*) Brian Dickie, Sir Bernard Haitink, Sir George Christie, Sir Peter Hall.

archetypal 'Glyndebourne repertoire' – what they do best, as well perhaps as any house in the world. (The Festival has mounted all the major Mozart operas except *La Clemenza di Tito*, and on principle they revive the three Da Ponte operas – *Figaro*, *Così* and *Don Giovanni* – every decade or so.) Then followed a baroque opera (Monteverdi's *L'Incoronazione di Poppea*), reflecting the part which Glyndebourne and Raymond Leppard played in the baroque revival of the 1960s; and *Arabella*, the last in a sequence of Strauss's domestic comedies produced by John Cox. The season also included Britten's *A Midsummer Night's Dream*, less the continuation of an existing theme than the initiation of a new one; temperamental incompatibility cut short the promising association between Glyndebourne and the English Opera Group in the 1940s which had begun with the world premières of *Albert Herring* and *The Rape of Lucretia*, but in 1985 Glyndebourne presented a new production of *Albert Herring*, and other Britten operas may follow.

Perhaps more typical of the Festival's repertoire would have been a Rossini opera, commemorating the series – *The Barber of Seville*, *Le Comte Ory*, *L'Italiana in Algeri*, *Il Turco in Italia*, *La pietra del paragone* – introduced in the 1950s by Vittorio Gui, but the planned revival of *La Cenerentola* was in the event postponed. A theme pursued in the 1960s, perhaps more surprisingly, was nineteenth-century Romantic opera – *Werther*, *Eugene Onegin*, *La Bohème*, *The Queen of Spades*. These, all tragedies virtually by definition, were less obviously attuned to the Glyndebourne ambience which is generally speaking lighthearted. Nevertheless, under the artistic management team of Hall and Haitink, the next Glyndebourne theme will be Verdi, starting in 1986 with *Simon Boccanegra*.

With guidelines such as these, Glyndebourne's programme-planning is relatively straightforward. 'You get themes going', according to Brian Dickie, 'you pick something from each – and you've got a balanced season.' But few year-round houses find it easy to pursue themes in any systematic way, given far more acute scheduling difficulties and a much greater volume of productions which tends to submerge all but the most obvious of the administrator's fixations. At the Paris Opéra, as Harold Rosenthal points out, Massimo Bogianckino has successfully introduced a sequence of classical operas presented in the versions specially prepared for Paris at the time when it was the capital of the opera world – Rossini's *Moïse et Pharaon* (or *Mosè in Egitto*, as it is more commonly known), *Jérusalem/I Lombardi*, *Alceste* and *Macbeth*. And ENO's fondness for Eastern European opera, sustained through the reigns of two music directors, might be called a recurring motif. Under Sir Charles Mackerras the company presented Prokofiev, Janáček, Penderecki, Szymanowski and Bartók; and in the 1984–5 season under Mark Elder, out of twenty-one productions five were Eastern European – *Osud*, *Rusalka*, *The Bartered Bride*, *Mazeppa* and *The Makropoulos Case* (with *War and Peace*, *The Gambler*, *The Queen of Spades* and *The Adventures of Mr Brouček* still warm in the repertoire). This might be compared with Covent Garden, only one of whose twenty-four productions in 1984–5 – *Boris Godunov* – was Eastern European, or the Met, which has always passed over this repertoire and in 1984–5 managed only *Eugene Onegin*.

Outside the confines of a festival, however, it is hard enough to schedule cycles of operas, let alone to pursue themes. Houses do occasionally attempt Mozart cycles, all the major works in a single season – Cologne, for example, presenting all seven operas in Ponnelle productions. And for every company with aspirations to permanence, a *Ring* cycle is sooner or later obligatory, although the logistical problems it poses are unique. To present a whole new cycle in a single season is virtually impossible for a repertory house; only the Bayreuth Festival tries to do this, and the first year of a Bayreuth *Ring* is widely regarded (though not perhaps by the paying public) as a trial run, with part of the budget held back for spending after the first season. Even where the four new productions are acquired gradually, to schedule them in the end as a cycle within, as it were, spitting distance of one another – not more than a week apart, say – is made extremely difficult by the technical resources required and the demands on the singers. It is far easier, where it is possible – and Seattle and San Francisco, for example, have both adopted this approach – to schedule the *Ring* separately, in a quasi-festival setting apart from the rest of the season, and even this can be disruptive.

Once the individual components of a year's programme have been chosen, how they are arranged within the season depends chiefly on whether the house is run on the *stagione* or the repertory system. In the *stagione* (literally 'season') system, a period of preparation is followed by a run of performances (usually about seven to ten) as closely grouped as possible, with the same cast and conductor in each. '*Stagione*' may mean the presentation of one opera at a time, but more often means that a maximum of two or three operas are being performed in any one week.

To run on the repertory system entails having operas 'in your repertoire', i.e. ready-prepared, and giving performances of them usually singly and without rehearsal at intervals throughout the season. Under this arrangement it may be possible to see the same opera once a month for a year and, equally, to see a different opera virtually every night for a month; the Vienna State Opera has in the recent past been known to stage twenty-seven different operas on consecutive nights.

Few companies now operate either *stagione* or repertory in their purest forms. The smaller non-international German companies still operate on a repertory basis, and the Bolshoi often presents thirty operas a month, while at the other end of the scale some quite large American companies (Philadelphia, for instance) rehearse and perform one opera at a time – presenting, say, five different operas, one each in September, November, December, February and May, though they rarely give enough performances of any of them to justify the title of 'season'. Most houses, however, work on watered-down versions of one system or the other. In the bigger houses, the *stagione* system is usually considered to produce the best results. At Covent Garden, new productions are prepared and performances given in blocks – with revivals, allocated rather less rehearsal time, handled in the same way. In neither case, however, will the cast necessarily remain intact. (In the 1984 London production of *Turandot*, for instance, it was originally planned that there should be two Turandots, two Timurs and three Calafs during a run of seven performances.) The Met is now moving towards a similar application of *stagione* principles: where there are particular reasons for a production to run all through the season – to satisfy subscribers, for example, or for the purposes of radio or television broadcasts which do not start until the season is well-advanced – two blocks of performances are scheduled (though the conditions under which the second block takes place are closer to those of repertory in that casts more often differ from performance to performance, and rehearsal time is more limited).

Lorin Maazel tried hard to convert the Vienna State Opera from the repertory to the block system but met with stiff resistance from an audience which prefers to feel that it may, if it wants, go to different operas every night of the week and demands the opportunity of hearing four different singers take the same role in the course of a season. The State Opera might now best be described as a modified repertory house, as might the Bavarian State Opera in Munich; here both new productions and revivals of productions which have not been seen for over two years are thoroughly rehearsed and performed (albeit with cast changes) in blocks, but these are diluted later in the season by a considerable number of single-performance revivals mounted with little preparation. (Two rehearsals are scheduled for a one-off: one for the principals to work on ensemble with the conductor, another with the producer to work on stage moves – neither with chorus or orchestra.)

The repertory system is now responsible for some of the most severely criticised features of international opera – in particular, for singers and conductor arriving at short notice and being given so little time to rehearse that 'having an opera in the repertoire' means little more than having the sets and costumes in store and the music in the library. Ironically, repertory was once considered the only way to achieve high standards. What has happened, as Thomas Hemsley points out, is that its schedule (the five to six opera week) is being applied outside the organisational framework within which it originally developed – the resident ensemble company where the same singers, conductor, often even the same producer (the resident *Oberspielleiter*), were always available. Together they could explore the repertoire and evolve joint interpretations cohesive and resilient enough to withstand gaps of weeks, even months, between performances. When different freelance singers are assembled for each of the isolated performances and given no more rehearsal than if they had been working together for years, the strengths of the system disappear while the glaring disadvantages linger on.

Aside from the grand overall design – *stagione* or repertory, and all the various permutations – there are other, lesser factors which influence the order in which operas are presented within a season, the number of performances given and their precise timing and spacing. Singers, as usual, must be consulted at an early stage. A soloist who is already booked to sing Don José in three different houses between September and November would naturally prefer a fourth administrator to schedule *Carmen*, while the role is still in his voice, for December rather than the following July. And within the run of a single opera, how the performances are distributed will be dictated by how frequently singers are prepared to perform in a week. Some insist on having three days clear between performances, and a minimum of two is usual; few are willing to do more than five performances in a fortnight, although this will depend to some extent on the piece – *in extremis* an administrator might risk scheduling a run of *La Bohème* or *Rigoletto* with only one clear day between performances, but rarely *Aida*, *Arabella* or *Tannhäuser*. The dictates of the box office must also be respected, so the works selected for a season will not necessarily be given an equal number of performances: the shrewd administrator will learn to milk his most commercial productions to the maximum without actually overexposing them, and simultaneously to avoid the possibility of poor houses for works whose popularity is less certain. In 1984–5 English National Opera, for example, gave its new production of *Madam Butterfly* twenty-one performances, its revival of Rossini's *Count Ory* five.

Composers must be spread throughout the season, and the work of the chorus distributed as evenly as possible to keep its members busy and interested without overtiring them; to be performing *Nabucco* whilst rehearsing *Die Meistersinger* or *The Midsummer Marriage* is not a good idea. Even more fundamental is the need to regulate the flow of labour for stage staff and technical departments, bearing in mind the physical limitations of the house. For many theatres, especially the older ones, some permutations are simply out of the question; it is impossible to programme two large-scale productions at the same time – either because there is insufficient space in the stage area to handle the props and scenery for both, or because the stage hands cannot exchange them in the time available. Before the Royal Opera House, whose wing space is very limited, acquired the neighbouring Floral Hall, large sets (as Clifford Starr, Deputy House Manager, recalls) came to the stage from a pantechnicon parked in Floral Street to which, after the act, each was returned and driven back to store. If productions cannot be neatly dovetailed by expedients such as these, it may become necessary to schedule a 'dark' day – one in which there is no performance and the technical staff may work undisturbed – with an inevitable loss of box office. This is less of a problem for the larger German opera houses with their superior technical resources, which include separate side stages on which whole sets can be built in advance and then trucked on to the main stage in minutes. Similarly at the Met, strictly speaking almost anything is technically *possible*, but some things are more expensive: in terms of overtime paid to the stage staff, it is far cheaper to combine the Zeffirelli *Tosca* with the company's stock production of *Madam Butterfly*, which is small, than with the Zeffirelli *Bohème*, which is not.

The planning jigsaw puzzle, with so many awkwardly shaped pieces to be manipulated, is extraordinarily complex. Jonathan Friend, as Artistic Administrator (Planning) at the Met, has a perhaps uniquely daunting task in a house that does nearly as many performances as any year-round repertory company but is also bound by the stringencies of the *stagione* system. 'Once we've chosen the new productions, we make a guess as accurately as we can as to how many performances the box office will take of those pieces and then find approximately seventeen or eighteen other operas from our repertoire that we need to revive and make a guess at the number of performances that each of those will take. Then we put them together in a season, trying to make sure that we don't have three Verdi works on at the same time, otherwise we'll just run out of baritones or tenors; that the pieces which need a lot of orchestra rehearsal (which also tend to be those from which you can get fewer performances at the box office, say *Pelléas*, which has to have a lot of orchestra time but can't be played for more than six performances without the box office dying) are suitably interspersed with the *Traviata*s which we can play for more performances with less orchestra time. . . . You may suddenly think it would make life easier to swap two operas, take one out of the early part of the season and put it in the later part and vice versa. But then you realise you've got three huge chorus operas on at once, and another in rehearsal. Then you realise three of James Levine's operas are on at the same time. Then you try rearranging it, and realise you've got four Mozart operas on at the same time. . . . You keep shuffling it round till you arrive at what everyone assumes is what you really *want* to do that season – and what is really the only way you can find to keep the curtain up seven times a week.'

4

Casting

The ability to cast well, with the right mixture of caution and inspiration, is perhaps the most valuable gift an opera administrator can have, whatever the conditions under which he is required to exercise his talents. As Brian Dickie puts it, 'Casting is an immensely important part of my job. The performances are the important thing – if they're not right, to hell with the restaurant, and the central heating, and the dressing rooms.'

In an ensemble house, casts will be chosen largely or exclusively from within the company. When ensemble companies were the norm in Germany and Austria, casting was systematised by means of a structure of '*Fach*s' – literally 'drawers' – by which all the variants of the human voice are categorised according to range, weight and character. In the smaller German repertory houses, the *Fach* system still operates. The house has its quota of each of the different types of voice, which might be categorised broadly as: soprano – *coloratura*, *soubrette*, lyric, dramatic; mezzo-soprano – lyric, dramatic; tenor – lyric, *spinto*, *Helden*; baritone – lyric, *Helden*; bass – *cantante*, *buffo*, *profondo*; and, if the budget is generous, perhaps representatives of other more specialised *Fach*s – the *Spieltenor*, or comic tenor, the *Kavalierbariton* (especially suitable for Don Giovanni), or the *Zwischenfach Sängerin*, the lowish soprano or high mezzo-soprano who literally falls 'between drawers'. In each *Fach* the singers are arranged in order of seniority – 'first lyric soprano', 'second lyric soprano', and so on.

Over the years, the standard repertoire has been similarly analysed and classified, and each of the principal roles allocated to its *Fach* – Constanze is a *coloratura* soprano role, for example, Blonde a *soubrette*, Abigaille (in *Nabucco*) and Turandot dramatic sopranos, Nemorino a lyric tenor, Andrea Chénier a *spinto* tenor, Siegfried a *Heldentenor* and so on. To cast a role the administrator has merely to ascertain its classification and take the company singer from the corresponding *Fach*. Each singer, knowing his or her precise classification and status, has both the right to be offered the appropriate part and an obligation to accept it (though modern operas offer some scope for negotiation).

The *Fach* system had, and still has, some obvious advantages. Provided every *Fach* in a company is adequately filled (and it is in fact at the initial auditions for the company that the real 'casting' takes place), forward-planning can present few problems for the administrator. For the singer, the system offers security (a certain guaranteed level of employment) and protection against unsuitable casting – a sheltered and convenient method of learning one's trade. However, because modern travel gives everyone more choice – the management the choice of bringing in from outside a second lyric soprano, say, and the second lyric soprano the choice of singing elsewhere the first soprano roles consistently denied her at home – the *Fach* system is being undermined.

Even outside the relics of the *Fach* system, in any house which has principals on contract the administrator will have to devise some kind of rationale for casting from within the company. A hierarchy of sorts, formal or informal, will exist among the resident singers, which will have at least to be acknowledged if not invariably respected; and generally the administrator must meet the needs and ambitions of his company singers. Mark Elder explains: 'To build the principals' seasons is a very important part of what we try to do, because one needs the loyalty of the people in the company.' Major international houses by definition cast few, if any, principal roles from within their own companies, looking instead to freelance guests – and to a large extent competing with each other for the same ones.

The phenomenon of the international 'superstar' is hardly a new one. There has always been an appetite, both among operagoers and to some extent the public at large, for the particular brand of glamour and success, generated by skill as publicly and perilously displayed as possible, which the *diva* or *divo* embodies; and with the help of extravagant publicity, stars have always emerged to satisfy the craving.

What may be new is the relative scarcity of top-class singers. To compare the standards of the present with those of the past is always a dangerous game – in Harold Rosenthal's words, 'The Golden Age of opera is always the era *before* that of the questioner' – but in absolute terms it is perhaps fair to say that at all the leading houses singers quite frequently appear who are either not yet ready for the roles in which they have been cast (and arguably never will be) or are too old for them, because there are simply not enough genuinely first-rate performers to go round.

Sir Colin Davis worries specifically about the shortage of top-class male voices: 'I've got into trouble for saying there's a paucity of singers. Everyone knows there is . . . but they don't want to hear it. The older generation of baritones – they're nearly as old as I am, fiftyish, and where is the next generation? . . . And when it comes to doing the pieces which require the grand voices, there are three tenors in the world.' Götz Friedrich, in his capacity as Intendant of the Deutsche Oper, claimed in 1983 that there were only twenty to thirty supreme artists in the world,

OPPOSITE Katia Ricciarelli and Luciano Pavarotti as Luisa and Rodolfo in Verdi's *Luisa Miller* (Covent Garden, 1978).

fifteen others who were worth paying for and ten more who have been catapulted into the leading rank by recording companies and are *not* worth the money they request and receive. And while supply has dwindled, demand has dramatically increased. No longer is it simply the big four houses which vie for the top singers, or even long-established competitors like Paris, Chicago, San Francisco, Munich and Geneva; increasingly American money makes its muscle felt as newer companies like Houston, Dallas, Miami and Philadelphia bid for the leading names.

There is not a great deal that is healthy about this particular form of competition; it has, in fact, various damaging side effects. Perhaps most seriously, administrators feel obliged to plan ever further in advance if they are to secure the singers they want. Few care to admit exactly how many years they will book singers before they actually need them – it has about it something of the stigma attached to hoarding – but the two to three years once considered extraordinary are no longer enough. Vienna and La Scala have recently acknowledged the necessity to look further into the future than they do; Paris and Covent Garden are slightly ahead of them, but none works consistently as far in advance as the Met which was described rather enviously by Lorin Maazel as 'having set new standards in the business of planning ahead'.

American houses, of course, have problems imposed by their geographical isolation which European companies do not share. An engagement at the Met, for example, means five or six weeks during which singers may accept no other work besides the eight to ten performances the house may offer; whereas, as Jonathan Friend explains, 'In Vienna they can go and do one performance a week, go to Munich for two performances the next week, back to Hamburg for two performances the next week, Covent Garden for three weeks, to Vienna for another one performance – appearing in many different cities in the period which they'd have to spend at the Met on just one engagement.' While regular appearances at the Met remain an essential element in an international career, an engagement there – in financial terms at least – may be considerably less attractive than some of the others on offer to a major singer. Hence the necessity for the house to get ahead of the field in staking its claims, and in the 1983–4 season it was already booking for 1988–9. (In fairness, one should add that Glyndebourne draws up its 'shopping list' for the leading roles in its major productions four or five years in advance – in 1984 a Falstaff had already been approached for 1988, for instance; and, also in 1984, Houston was rumoured to have booked a baritone for 1991.)

The risks of long-range casting are obvious. Most houses are subsidised on an annual footing, with the result that many contracts are negotiated and signed on the basis of non-existent funds. Equally, singers may be unable to deliver what they in their turn have promised. In a profession where a career in the top flight may last no longer than ten years, a singer booked when he is just approaching his prime may be well past it by the time he is actually called upon to perform. Nor should one ignore the wrecking effect of organisations with the power to operate on a short-term basis at the expense of other people's five-year plans –

the most conspicuous being the Salzburg Festival. Such is its prestige that artists with even an outside chance of an offer are reluctant to commit themselves to summer engagements anywhere else; or having done so, beg to be released when the summons arrives from Salzburg. Sir George Christie remarks, 'Salzburg does not cast much more than twelve months ahead – a thoroughly arrogant way of going about things. It is a thorn in the side of all of us, because agents tend to sit back and wait for the invitation to come in. It makes for great difficulties for other summer festivals, including Bayreuth.'

With all the major houses, and many of the lesser ones, now competing for their favours, both top- and middle-rank singers have inevitably succumbed to the temptation to boost their fees – charging, quite understandably, what they judge the market in its present straitened state will bear. The houses which feel the effects of this inflation most acutely and are least able to withstand them (houses such as Paris, Covent Garden, Florence, Stockholm, San Francisco, La Scala and the Met), have made various attempts to form cartels within which the maximum fees payable to certain singers are fixed. But their resistance has repeatedly been sabotaged either by one of the members (usually the same one) reneging on the agreement and paying a higher price, or by companies outside the cartel – and regarded by many of its members as *nouveaux riches* – simply overbidding and whisking the artists away from under their noses. As one of the big four administrators commented sadly, it is hard for a year-round house to compete with a company like Philadelphia which, with a grand total of ten performances a year, is in a position to spend 'rather a lot' on each of them.

Some singers may prefer to be remunerated in kind: in return for performing the role they have been asked to perform, they will request/demand the opportunity to play another part which it might not have occurred to the administration to offer them. Alternatively, the *quid pro quo* may be to hire the conductor of the singer's choice. The bargaining power of some artists is virtually unassailable, and it is not unknown for their agents to take advantage of it – to make it a condition of their acceptance of roles, for example, that lesser singers, also on the agency's books, accompany them.

The company which is not in the market for the world's leading singers is, therefore, in some respects at an advantage. Glyndebourne, being in the enviable position of selling out virtually every production it puts on, has no need of the pulling power of the big names; nor, for that matter, can it afford them. Nor, since it specialises in ensemble work with a tightly-knit company in a small house, does it necessarily want them, as Brian Dickie explains: 'One of the problems of the megastars is that however much you paid them, you still wouldn't get them here for four or five weeks' rehearsal, and you wouldn't get them to do twelve or fifteen performances. So there wouldn't be any particular advantage in having all the money in the world – we'd turn into something quite different. . . . If we did have £10,000 to spend per performance, what would we do with it? Invite one of the superstars? If he got paid £10,000 per performance, what would the

others get paid? Probably their normal fee, whatever that may be – say, one or two thousand pounds. It'd probably end up by destroying the whole character of Glyndebourne performances.'

Instead the Festival specialises in identifying those singers who are teetering on the brink of major careers, using the stars of tomorrow while they are still affordable and while they are still prepared to work as Glyndebourne works. Brian Dickie continues, 'We, like Bayreuth, are very dismissive of people who come for four performances. It doesn't work there and it doesn't work here – we have different priorities. Many great singers share these priorities: others don't, and are perhaps not so successful here, even if we manage to entice them.' And if the objective is to secure the quality of performance associated with the stars without the ballyhoo and the bad habits that some (though not all) bring with them, then the list of singers who have appeared at Glyndebourne early in their careers is witness to its success – including as it does Kathleen Battle, Josephine Barstow, Régine Crespin, Montserrat Caballé, Ileana Cotrubas, Lisa Della Casa, Mirella Freni, Edita Gruberova, Barbara Hendricks, Sena Jurinac, Pilar Lorengar, Birgit Nilsson, Margaret Price, Elisabeth Söderström, Dame Joan Sutherland, Dame Kiri te Kanawa, Dame Janet Baker, Teresa Berganza, Frederica von Stade, Luciano Pavarotti, Thomas Allen, Sir Geraint Evans, Ruggero Raimondi, Hans Sotin and Ingvar Wixell.

Keeping oneself informed of present and prospective talent obviously constitutes a very important part of an administrator's job, and each must evolve his own methods of staying in touch. New 'discoveries' will usually be brought to his attention by way of a flourishing operatic grapevine – made up of producers who have used promising performers, other singers who have enjoyed working with them, conductors inclined to regard them as protégés. Some houses have long served an invaluable function as 'feeders' for others – New York City Opera, for example, for the Met and several of the major European houses. Tatiana Troyanos, Shirley Verrett, Placido Domingo, José Carreras, Cornell MacNeil and Sherrill Milnes all made their first major American appearances at NYCO; and Beverly Sills takes great pride in having groomed La Scala's latest Figaro: 'This house prepared Samuel Ramey's Figaro, and he walked right into the new production at La Scala and had a triumph and then recorded it. He didn't have to do it, as in the olden days, via the Met. You don't need the Met stamp any more and that was my pioneer, I did that. I showed you could become an international star without the Met label.' And in the last few years several of the NYCO company singers have taken major roles at Glyndebourne – Jerry Hadley as Idamante, for example, Carol Vaness as Electra, Gianna Rolandi as Susanna and Zdenka, Ashley Putnam as Arabella, and Delores Ziegler as Dorabella. Glyndebourne itself might be seen as a 'feeder', as the last in a series of opera festivals which have traditionally been regarded as stepping stones leading the way to a major international career – Wexford,

OPPOSITE Birgit Nilsson as Brünnhilde in *Götterdämmerung* (Covent Garden, 1962).

Aix-en-Provence, Glyndebourne and eventually on, with luck, to the big houses.

The administrator will have an eye to the major singing competitions, to the critics – one isolated notice, good or bad, may not signify, but a unanimous press is not lightly discounted – and, with discretion, to the agents. Some houses specifically employ 'spotters'; Sir Rudolf Bing had regular scouts out in Europe, and the Met now employs Joan Ingpen in that capacity. Other administrators prefer (and have the time) to do their own travelling. Sir George Christie and Brian Dickie, for example, go twice a year on 'fishing trips' to North America which for the last decade has provided a large proportion of Glyndebourne's principal singers; in New York, San Francisco, Houston and other operatic centres they audition dozens, even hundreds of hopefuls.

The formal audition – selected arias performed to piano accompaniment – while obviously the most practical method of hearing a large number of voices in a limited time, can give an accurate impression neither of a singer's musicianship when confronted with an unfamiliar work, nor of how they will project themselves other than musically on the stage. Many casting teams therefore prefer to inspect prospective employees under performance conditions. Occasionally, though, where a house is unusually large, has individual acoustical properties, or is in any other way unique, it may be necessary to fall back on a formal audition held on the team's home ground as the only means of assessing how well a given voice might adapt to a particular stage. The National Theatre in Munich, for instance, sounds like no other house and auditions are held there twice weekly to identify voices which are suited to it; and every artist hoping to be cast for the Bayreuth Festival is given an audition on the stage of the Festspielhaus in the presence of Wolfgang Wagner.

Setting aside the obvious prerequisites – a voice that reaches the standards required by a house, at a fee it can afford – the criteria applied in casting vary according to the practical circumstances and artistic priorities of the individual company. Glyndebourne, for example, lays more stress on the singer's physical suitability for a role than many larger, less intimate houses where visual shortcomings are not brought as forcibly to the audience's notice.

A problem faced by all those in charge of casting, irrespective of house, is the issue of colour. Despite the growing number of black singers and the conspicuous success of artists like Jessye Norman, Grace Bumbry, Shirley Verrett, Leontyne Price, Kathleen Battle, Barbara Hendricks and Simon Estes, the colour of a performer's skin is still an issue in casting and will remain one as long as it is felt to be degrading for a black singer to 'white up' in the same way as a white singer would black up for roles such as Otello and Monostatos. In some operas – and particularly in productions aiming at a high degree of naturalism – to have a black singer in a role where the text, or the context, specifically suggests a white one

OPPOSITE Shirley Verrett as Carmen (Covent Garden, 1973).

is felt to impair dramatic credibility. In
1984, for example, black bass Willard
White was said to have been excluded
from Jonathan's Miller's production of
Rigoletto, set in New York's Little Italy
in the 1950s, on the grounds of colour
– presumably, though this was not made
explicit, because a black *mafioso* was considered unlikely and destructive of the
illusion the production was working to
create. It is difficult to prevent a certain
literal-mindedness creeping in: while a
white Macbeth and a black Lady Macbeth, a white Norma and a black
Adalgisa, a white Rodolfo and a black
Mimi present no problems, a white
Rigoletto and black Gilda, a black
Daland and white Senta can, initially at
least, be distracting; and Brian Dickie
adds, 'I don't think we'd have a black
Fiordiligi and white Dorabella – which
is not to say we wouldn't have a black
Fiordiligi and a black Dorabella.' Given
the visual conservatism of many operagoers, let alone the prejudices inextricable
from a pronounced sense of nationality,
there are some roles in which it is probably more difficult to cast black singers
than others – Hans Sachs, say, or Peter
Grimes, Falstaff or Baron Ochs where the
black singer would very likely be at much
the same disadvantage as the thin one.

The question of bulk is itself controversial. Within the opera profession
there is a faction, composed principally
of conductors and singers, which believes
that an artist's shape is irrelevant and that
it is part of the producer's job to find in,
or coax from a singer of whatever proportions a *persona* somehow suited to the

Kathleen Battle as Zerbinetta in *Ariadne auf Naxos*
(Covent Garden, 1985) with actor David Machin.

role. Claudio Abbado, for example: 'I don't mind if sometimes you have a fat soprano. You can try to find the right kind of character in your singers – use what they've got.' Some producers would agree, though by no means all, and many of those active on the international circuit have become extremely adept in making the most of a mediocre to poor job. Audiences, however, accustomed to seeing in theatre, film and television, performers who are the right weight, height, age and colour for the characters they are supposed to embody, seem to be becoming less tolerant – of the more grossly-overfed Bohemians at least, along with the late-middle-aged corseted Siegfrieds, Teutonic Carmens, the Ebolis and Turandots whose '*don fatale*' poses the most minimal of threats.

Not surprisingly, producers (and audiences) are very much more inclined to overlook, or look beyond, a singer's physical incongruity if it is counterbalanced by the ability and will to act. While some of the world's fattest singers are among the world's least-committed actors, the fat singer is not always the undramatic singer and to a producer the capacity to feel and convey emotion on stage may be worth far more than the authentic face and figure of a courtesan or toreador or wood nymph. The emphasis an administrator will place on dramatic ability depends to some extent on the piece he is casting, as Lord Harewood explains: 'There are certain pieces, like perhaps *Trovatore*, where even if you're not at all a good actor or actress you may well get away with it, if you've got an absolutely stunning voice and a lot of energy. . . . In other operas, like Mozart's – if your only attributes are a stunning voice and no ability to do anything other than not knock over the furniture, you'll be absolutely useless.'

Even more important will be the priorities of house and audience. It would be rare, say, for English National Opera, a house which on principle performs opera in the language of its audience, to engage a singer who had no interest at all in communicating dramatically as well as musically. Mark Elder, in endorsing the policy – 'What I'm interested in is to find the singers who want to speak to the audience directly' – is prepared to accept the need occasionally to compromise musical standards in the cause of dramatic honesty. 'Casting is where David Pountney and I rub up against each other quite often. I'm really thinking of *la voce* and he's thinking of all the other side of it. There may be a wonderful candidate for a role who would do it marvellously from my angle, who is absolutely unacceptable to him. They *are* compromise decisions in the end, unavoidably. Anyone who tries to make out otherwise is not telling the truth. But the decisions are, ultimately, *operatic*.'

In the eyes of any casting director, reliability and congeniality are virtues highly prized. What people outside the profession describe half-admiringly as 'temperament', those within it call 'being difficult' – cancelling performances for psychical rather than physical reasons, manifesting nervousness in tantrums and power plays rather than petrified silence, refusing to deal with the wardrobe mistress, the voice

OPPOSITE Leontyne Price as Leonora in *Il Trovatore* (Covent Garden, 1970).

coach, the armourer, the press officer or anyone below the rank of General Manager. Such foibles impose a severe strain on the time, patience and energies of the administrator and his staff who will, if at all possible, sidestep the problem, as British bass Richard Van Allan explains: 'People will prefer to book someone who *isn't* difficult, all things being equal – or even slightly unequal: a marginally less able person might well get booked in preference to an awkward one.'

In a profession as competitive and alarmingly insecure as opera-singing, it is sometimes hard for performers to resist the suspicion that the odds are loaded against them and that hidden forces are at work to prevent their success. Perhaps understandably, they feel occasionally that they are being, or will be, discriminated against – for their colour, their height, their looks, their politics, their age, their agents. . . . Beverly Sills is vehement in her disapproval of favouritism on the grounds of nationality: 'We do have a tendency to pigeonhole people. If the name is Italian, of course it sings Verdi better than if it's American – if that were true, poor Leontyne Price, Shirley Verrett, Sherrill Milnes – and poor Placido who isn't Italian either. If it were only the Germans who could sing Wagner, you would never have heard Nilsson, Flagstad, Melchior, Vickers, Traubel. It's so silly to pigeonhole as if God said, "These people who live here are going to sing Donizetti and Bellini very well, but these people over *here* – just forget it, they're only going to be into Mozart." What are we talking about? These are God-given talents, and God doesn't live geographically'.

Other artists are more concerned that their sexual preferences leave them at a disadvantage. The opera world contains a higher proportion of non-covert homosexuals than, say, quantity surveying, and some heterosexual singers find this sinister. Stuart Burrows: 'It's always been true of the theatre and the music world, but it's never been at as high a point as it is today. The norm is now the homosexual and not the heterosexual person, that's a fact. It's a great tragedy. . . . If you have this element of homosexuality going through opera, heterosexual singers are not even considered. . . . You can count the heterosexual singers in many opera houses almost on one hand.'

To the outside observer, however, the world of the opera singer would seem to be the ultimate meritocracy. Abuses (invariably well-publicised) do occur, in the form of a unilateral decision taken by administrator, conductor or star singer to introduce a less than adequately equipped *inamorata* or *inamorato* into a cast. But opera-singing is a profession that carries a built-in safeguard against nepotism in that the deficiencies of the unjustly favoured are bound to be revealed almost immediately, and in an exceptionally humiliating fashion, and it is hard to credit that many artists, however ambitious, would subject themselves repeatedly to the ordeal. If genuine talent is lacking, in the long term there is little that the singer can do to conceal the fact; equally if genuine talent is there, the opera world at large is unlikely to let it remain concealed.

II

THE SINGER

5

Building the Voice

The kind of publicity campaign which enables a select band of international opera stars to appear with the Muppets and compete with Mel Brooks and Barbara Woodhouse on breakfast television has distorted the popular image of the opera singer, less because of what it says about the stars than because of what it conceals about the rest of the opera world: it makes opera-singing look easy.

It is true that the genuine talent by which an opera singer stands or falls is in its essence a gift for which the owner can take no credit. But while the gift itself is beyond the singer's control, what he (or she) makes of it is not. The effort required to develop a natural asset into a full-time career is extraordinary. In the words of Beverly Sills, 'If God gave me the pipes, I had to play them, and it hasn't been easy.'

Singers are late starters in the music profession, and their training is protracted. Where most instrumental musicians would expect to have a fairly advanced technique by the age of sixteen, the singer has almost none at that stage; and while by the age of twenty-five the average violinist would hope to be earning *some* kind of living many singers, even those destined for stardom, have yet to collect their first professional fees. Where a virtuoso pianist, cellist or violinist would hope to carry on performing with his powers practically unimpaired at sixty or even seventy, singers can usually expect more or less rapidly diminishing returns in their fifties.

During the twenty or twenty-five years which may constitute a performing career, the pressures which beset the singer, both from within and without, are ferocious – the stress of constant competition in a grossly overcrowded field, the ever-present threat of illness, the fear of public failure and condemnation. The opera audience is in a curious way both the most doting and most aggressive of audiences, capable of violent enthusiasm and the most offensive criticism. The relationship of performer to audience is much more like that to be found in a sport than in any of the other arts. The singer cracking a top note suffers a disgrace as instant and unequivocal as the skater falling over in mid-double-axel – a different order of experience from the actor giving an indifferent performance; and the Bayreuth audience which stays for thirty minutes after curtain-fall to boo resembles nothing so much as a contingent of British football fans lingering to tear up the terraces as an expression of disappointment in their team. Booing is a feature of boxing, ice hockey, all-in wrestling and opera; it is not commonly found at the theatre or the ballet, at concerts, art exhibitions or literary award ceremonies.

Audience behaviour along these lines is a stimulus which opera singers rarely need, so intense are the stresses they are capable of generating for themselves. Every performance requires an effort of will. Backstage in the principals' dressing-rooms, the half-hour before curtain rise is revealing. A pale and clammy skin which resists make-up betrays the singer who has been physically sick with fright; the tantrums, appalling joviality, shrieks of laughter or unnatural calm of others tell much the same story. Nervousness can either be localised – the bottom C in the first act of *Der Rosenkavalier* for an Ochs, the first 'Hojotoho' for a Brünnhilde, 'Che gelida manina' for a Rodolfo, 'Celeste Aida' for a Radames – or general. The singer may be worrying about things that went consistently wrong in rehearsal, about negotiating the scenery or looking laughable in his or her costume; it is often assumed that an artist who looks totally wrong for a part either does not know or does not care about the incongruity – neither is true. During the run-up to the first night, even the prospect of illness can impose intolerable strains. Four days before the première of Gluck's *Alceste* Robert Tear, cast in the crucial role of Admète, detected an impending cold. Because no replacement was available, he was persuaded against his better judgement to sing the first performance – and within the first five minutes of arriving on stage found himself almost voiceless; he finished the performance miming, with an understudy singing from a score in the pit. 'It was a funny thing: having had the most hideous tensions up till the moment I got on the stage – I was so tense for four days I couldn't speak to anyone, I looked as if I were gazing into a pocket of blackness – once the worst had happened on stage, I went absolutely cold, perfectly calm. But two days later, watching television, I went totally blind in my left eye, just as things were getting back to normal. It shows the kind of tension we can impose on ourselves.' And many singers find themselves getting *more*, not less nervous with age; whatever they gain in experience, they lose in confidence that the voice will do what they require it to do. 'Even the most wonderful singer is at the mercy of his cords', as Sir Charles Mackerras puts it. Every singer knows the horror stories about voices apparently in their prime which have simply withered and died for no discernible reason and many, perhaps most singers established for a reasonable length of time (artists of the stature of Hans Hotter, Luciano Pavarotti, Maria Callas) have themselves had temporary vocal crises which they cannot be sure will not recur, this time for good. . . . It is perhaps the insecurity of not knowing how long the voice will last which explains, and to a large extent excuses, both the displays of temperament and the apparent compulsion to accept any and every offer for which many leading singers are criticised.

The health of the voice is a constant preoccupation for the singer from the moment when he first begins the long-drawn-out business of shaping it into an instrument. The violinist, pianist, oboist are all supplied with the tools of their trade ready-made, each with a determinate range and an in-built physical capacity to make sounds. The singer has to create his own compass from inside himself, pitch, match and balance his own notes, develop his own capacity to make sounds through his breathing, voice production and so on.

Again the sporting parallels hold, fanciful though they may sometimes seem in the face of portly performers who are no longer young. Opera singers dedicate a considerable part of their lives to developing, training and maintaining certain muscles – throat muscles, the intercostal muscles of the rib cage, the all-important diaphragm; delicate, but muscles nonetheless, and the athletic feats performed with them require a comparable degree of strength, stamina and control. Certainly the singer must be as careful as the athlete not to perform when unfit; Norman Bailey defends the apparent capriciousness which so often disappoints audiences: 'The average person with a cold can do his job – but a singer singing with inflamed vocal cords is like an athlete running with rheumatism. A runner who runs with an only partially healed hamstring injury – if it goes again, it may be the end of his career. In certain circumstances, if you sing with inflamed vocal cords there's the possibility of growths on the cords or blood clots, which may have permanent effects. . . . It *can* just be nerves – but one mustn't underestimate nerves, they have a reflex action and one effect is dehydration. . . . If you've ever had a nasty shock, you find you can't spit, everything's gone dry. The singer can be in this situation through nerves – the actual membranes, the vocal cords, dry out.'

Some singers are inclined to battle on – Beverly Sills was once dubbed 'the Iron Lung' for her determination to ignore minor ailments, on the basis that the audience would rather hear the scheduled performer in mediocre form than a healthy but less distinguished substitute. In some theatres this is unlikely to be the case, as James Bowman explains: 'If you're ill while performing in Germany, you mustn't sing – the audience will boo you. If you appear on stage, they assume you're well enough to sing your best.' And Stuart Burrows takes the opposite of the 'Iron Lung' line: 'You owe it to the public to cancel if you're ill. *I* wouldn't pay thirty-four pounds to hear somebody with a bad throat.'

Almost everyone can sing a little, just as most people can run or jump or throw a little. But how is the natural attribute turned into the professional instrument? In the initial stages at least the transformation is in the hands of a singing teacher – and many singers continue to consult teachers all through their careers, partly for moral support, partly for advice on the maintenance and repair of the voice as it matures and changes. Generally speaking, what the singing teacher provides are the technical resources which the artist needs in order ultimately to create a performance for himself; together they will build the instrument which later he must learn to play in his own style.

Of vital importance at the start is for the young aspiring singer to develop breath

Dame Eva Turner, who first sang the title role in *Turandot* in 1926, coaches Gwyneth Jones for the same role in Covent Garden's 1984 production, conducted by Sir Georg Solti, with Placido Domingo as Calaf.

control, mastering the technique of breathing from the diaphragm as opposed to clavicular breathing from the upper chest which is all that is used for ordinary speech. A robust physique is an undeniable asset for an opera singer; displaying an interesting set of priorities, Caruso once defined the great singer as one with 'a big chest, a big mouth, ninety per cent memory, ten per cent intelligence, lots of hard work and something in the heart.' The slighter singer, however, can to some extent find in diaphragmatic breathing a source of the strength and stamina which the Nilssons, Dimitrovas and Domingos possess naturally by virtue of their build. Breathing from the diaphragm, the singer can generate volume without harshness and it is an essential, if not the most essential means of controlling the voice; by providing support, it facilitates the steady *pianissimo*, the *legato* deserving of the name, and is a vital ingredient in true *bel canto* style. 'In *bel canto* singing', according to Dietrich Fischer-Dieskau, 'the breath must be expelled steadily so that as little air as possible emerges with the sound. You must be able to sing without extinguishing a candle held in front of you.'

The technique is not developed initially without a conscious effort. In the days when she was appearing regularly at the Albert Hall, Dame Eva Turner evolved an exercise which she could practise as she walked to rehearsals across Kensington Gardens: twelve paces breathing in, twelve with bated breath, twelve paces breathing out. But diaphragmatic breathing must eventually come to be second nature, a reflex action, (one which can occasionally be detected in singers' ordinary conversation). Josephine Veasey elaborates: 'When you go round in the daytime, do you think of your breathing and how you're speaking, and whether your lungs are working and what your diaphragm is doing?... If you stand there thinking about what you have to do with your breathing, you've already locked every muscle, the flow of breath will automatically be inhibited.' The whole airway from diaphragm to mouth must be open, the throat relaxed, the tongue flattened – which in itself can cause problems for the young singer, as Dame Kiri te Kanawa explains: 'I found when I was starting that the lower part of my tongue got in the way for nearly everything; I had to learn how to flatten it so that it didn't tickle with the vibration and make me choke.'

With breath control established, the teacher's next task is to help the singer extend the compass of the voice. Most people have a natural untrained voice of between five notes and an octave which require no particular effort to produce. To sing the operatic repertoire, the singer needs a range of at least two octaves and frequently more. The role of Fiordiligi, for example, spans two and a half octaves, Ochs also two and a half, from a low C to a high G sharp inside the baritone range, and the Queen of the Night almost three octaves – a punishing set of demands rarely equalled in either *Lieder*, for which about one and a half octaves are usually enough, or oratorio, in which sopranos rarely have to go as low or mezzo-sopranos as high as in opera.

The teacher will establish the existing 'length' of the voice and give the singer exercises to perform which will extend it gradually at either end, one or two notes at a time. This is a process which must not be hurried; Dame Kiri te Kanawa remembers her teacher constantly reining her in. 'My voice still retains the quality it had when I first started, at fifteen; my singing teacher just learned to use that and never forced me to sing louder or higher than I should. Anything that was an extreme, one always cut back by one or two notes.' The consequences of forging ahead regardless can be very serious indeed, according to John Streets, pianist, vocal coach and for some twenty years head of the opera class at the Royal Academy of Music. In particular, if the maturing voice is stretched too hard too soon, a crack may appear which, if the singer persists in forcing the part that is not yet natural, will become a break, and this may remain a scar on the technique for the rest of the singer's life.

The aim is to build an instrument that moves smoothly and uniformly through its entire range of notes without jerks or involuntary variations in volume or tone.

Singers' voices tend naturally to change between registers (sometimes called the 'chest', 'middle' and 'head' registers), and there is usually a point, common to most singers, at which it becomes necessary very slightly to alter the method of voice production in order to progress up or down. This change of vocal gear is known as the *passaggio*, and in extending the voice the singer has also to learn to bridge each *passaggio* as it is opened up. Failure to master the technique can lead to the eventual destruction of the instrument, as Birgit Nilsson explains: 'I don't like registers, or those singers who pull one out like an organ. . . . After a while you hear the breaks in the voice, because you get holes there. When you go from second gear to third there is a little break that gets bigger and bigger, and after a while you have a big hole and you cannot touch that note from either above or below.'

In developing his range, the counter-tenor is a case apart. James Bowman is insistent that what distinguishes the voice is its artificiality as 'an acquired falsetto technique, and don't let anybody ever tell you any different. . . . It's something which the tenor can do in overdrive, at the top of his range – put notes into a head voice. My head voice is more developed and goes down further – I've taken that overdrive and brought it down throughout the whole stave. . . . If you decide you have the facility for singing in a falsetto voice, you must start working at it straight away; you mustn't let your ordinary voice develop after puberty – you can't do both, it's bad for your voice. . . . The nearest analogy I can think of is the harmonics of a violin: I never use the natural strings of my voice, I use the harmonics and I use them so much that I've turned the harmonics into a natural voice in their own right.'

Teacher and singer together will decide when the limits of the range appear finally to have been reached, and it is then possible to attach a label to the voice: soprano rather than mezzo-soprano, baritone rather than bass and so on. Voices do of course sometimes expand or settle downwards. Mezzo-sopranos become sopranos – Grace Bumbry, Kiri te Kanawa and Maria Ewing, for example – and sopranos mezzos: Marilyn Horne began her career as a soprano in such roles as the Merry Widow and Minnie, the Girl of the Golden West. Baritones become tenors, like Placido Domingo and Carlo Bergonzi, and basses baritones: Norman Bailey spent an uncomfortable year or so in his youth as a Verdian bass. Equally, it may become obvious at this point that the singer simply does not have the notes he or she will need in opera. This happens perhaps most often to the tenor who, as Dennis O'Neill points out, tends to work more consistently at the top of his range: 'I was talking to a baritone in San Francisco and he said how glad he was not to be a tenor. Although he only earned about half as much money as he probably could if he were a tenor, he could never cope with the strain of it. The tenor is the only voice that spends about sixty-five to seventy per cent of the time at the top of its register; think of tenor, you think of high notes.'

OPPOSITE Kiri te Kanawa as Xenia in *Boris Godunov*, one of her earliest roles with the Royal Opera, Covent Garden (1971).

The very top of the tenor voice is in fact a danger zone – not an entirely natural voice, and one that is easy to wear out. The high C is traditionally taken as *the* tenor high note (hence the tag 'King of the High Cs' attached to Luciano Pavarotti, a *trouvaille* that must have made some publicist's day). This is partly because it is at the extreme end of the range required for the central lyric repertoire, partly because any higher and the voice could almost be described as falsetto (James Bowman's 'overdrive'). High C itself calls for an admixture of the pharyngeal voice, the special technique that takes over from the natural voice for high D and above, making it a particularly precarious note. Suspended between techniques as it is, it cannot always be performed to order, so that there is a peculiar perversity in the accepted practice of inserting high Cs in places where the composer intended none. Dennis O'Neill: 'I can't think off-hand of a single high C that Verdi actually wrote; they've all been put in ... Verdi didn't *like* the high Cs. He went to a good deal of trouble *not* to make it difficult for the tenor. In *Traviata*, for example, in 'Di quell'amor', the 'misterioso magno' phrase goes up to an A, which Alfredo sings on stage. When he sings it *off* stage, the key has changed from F to A flat, and *if* the phrase were repeated exactly, the high note would be a C. The phrase *isn't* repeated exactly, and to my mind there can be only one reason for it – because Verdi wanted to make it easier for the tenor. It must have been pretty infuriating when tenors started doing the opposite, *and* spending half an hour sitting on the high note, while the poor soprano, whose aria it interrupts, remains alone on stage and has to wait for all the nonsense to end.' Placido Domingo adds to the indictment the high C in 'Di quella pira': 'Tenors sweat blood over it, develop ulcers because of it. Yet ... Verdi wrote a G ... a note that any tenor in any glee club is expected to be able to sing. Manrico is not a high role: the highest note written by Verdi is an A, not even a B flat. Sometimes productions of *Trovatore* are avoided altogether simply because a "high-C tenor" cannot be found. One unwritten note has turned a middle-range part into one of the most difficult roles in the repertoire.' Both, however, acknowledge the appeal of interpolated top notes – Dennis O'Neill: 'The fashion is changing, becoming much more puritanical – but it will take a long time to get rid of interpolations because they are very successful and immensely thrilling, given a certain amount of taste. ... There are some I like and some I don't. *Rigoletto*, for example – in 'La donna è mobile' that high B is absolute nonsense, but I like it, it's very exciting and it doesn't do any harm. Whereas the one at the end of 'Questa o quella' is *ghastly*.'

For the instrumentalist able to afford a fine violin, clarinet or harpsichord – and possessed of a reasonable technical competence – beauty of tone is virtually assured; the singer, on the other hand, has with great pains to manufacture the tone of his instrument himself. It is for the teacher to explain how to make best use of every region of the voice in the search for warmth and richness of tone

OPPOSITE James Bowman as Oberon in Britten's *A Midsummer Night's Dream* (English Opera Group, 1969).

– how to avoid a 'white' tone, bleached of all harmonics, by using the lower regions of the airway, for example; and he will show how to exploit to best effect the various resonators which modify the sounds issuing from the throat – the larynx and mouth, the nose and sinuses. He will help the singer to 'place' the voice well forward in the mouth rather than leave it recessed in the throat. Ileana Cotrubas considers it an immense advantage to have been naturally endowed with a forward placement which has ensured that her voice, though small, projects easily; and Beverly Sills once commented on Rosa Ponselle's similar good fortune: 'Her face is extremely broad between the cheekbones – the area that singers call the "mask" – and her whole voice seemed miraculously to sit up in that mask.'

Evenness of tone throughout the range is a principal feature of traditional *bel canto* training – something by which Linda Esther Gray sets great store: 'You learn to make, say, an F sharp and the B above ring in the same way so that you can sing them soft, loud, *mezzoforte*; and when you have to go up to the octave above, there's not a great heaving.' The singer must also develop a precise sense of pitch and a technique for placing the notes accurately; much of Dame Eva Turner's teaching consists in helping the singer to balance and fine-tune the voice – 'The singer must have a very keen ear to what we call "matched tones", to get a beautiful uniform line of vocal emission.'

In all this the teacher is indispensable not only as a guide along the way, but also as a critic of the resulting sounds which the singer himself cannot always hear clearly. As Dame Eva points out, 'The ear is posited *behind* the source of the sound and if the singer is projecting as he should be, he ought not to be able to hear it perfectly; if he *can* hear, because the sound is resonating largely within the cranium, he probably is not projecting sufficiently.' Gwynne Howell expresses the dilemma from the singer's point of view: 'There's how I feel about it and what other people tell me about it – we're talking about two versions of the same voice: what I hear in my head and how it feels singing, and how they hear it. I can't feel the effect it has, I can only feel the emotion and what I try to put into it.'

In tandem with this shaping of a precision instrument out of an untrained voice, the singer has also to develop the capacity to enunciate intelligibly the syllables in which those accurately pitched, matched and supported notes are framed. Good diction is an attribute some artists never acquire. 'With some it takes a few bars to determine the language, let alone the words', according to Michael Langdon, head of Britain's National Opera Studio. Different singers have different problems; some find it hard to produce undistorted vowels, some choke on consonants, others make a conscious effort to obliterate their own regional accents – with the occasional exception, including Welsh and Rumanian accents, which are held by their possessors to be halfway to Italian. The challenge is to convey each language distinctly without destroying its individual character and reducing it to the homogeneous slurry of deformed vowels and interchangeable consonants that is international 'opera-ese' in which, for example, 'hop', 'hope' and 'hoop' all come out as 'hawp'. Italian is universally acknowledged to be the easiest language to sing, with the purest vowels and the fewest consonants. German combines a wealth of diphthongs with compressed, often clipped vowels, as Robert Lloyd explains: 'It's something you have to develop as a purely vocal skill: how to sing a word like "nichts", getting the juice out of the vowel.' English vowels, on the other hand, are uncomfortably open and a much bigger proportion of words end in consonants.

Nor can the young singer rest there. He may now be able to make himself under-stood, but can he make himself felt? After all, 'Singing is not a sentimental telepathy, but a deliberately and carefully organised physical process.' David Franklin's point is that communication of emotion requires technique, and as the voice extends, strengthens and becomes more flexible, the young singer will look to the teacher for instruction in the various techniques which will be a necessary part of his or her operatic armoury. How to sing *legato*, how to sing *staccato*, and to do it lightly or heavily at will; how to graduate dynamics over a phrase or line or aria, or on a single note; how to handle eighteenth-century *recitativo secco*, or Straussian *parlando* or twentieth-century *Sprechgesang*; how to control vocal leaps, or, where appropriate, to bridge them with the technique of *portamento*, literally 'carrying' the voice up or down the scale from one note to the next without a break in the sound, to provide an easier approach to a note and to save the voice. In all this, the singer's aim is to develop enough technical proficiency to be able to sing without consciously considering technique at all.

Style is another matter – after basic technique the most important thing a singer can cultivate, in the opinion of Marilyn Horne. With every technical accomplish-ment secure, to become an artist the singer still requires an intellectual understand-ing of differences in style and an instinctive sympathy with the individual nuances of each – how singing Monteverdi differs from singing Handel, or Handel from Mozart, Mozart from Weber, Weber from Wagner, Wagner from Strauss, Strauss from Berg; the variations in style between Rossini, Bellini, Verdi and Puccini.

It will be for the teacher to distinguish between 'style' and 'tradition' and, prefer-ably, to impart the one without handing on the other. Practically nothing of what John Streets teaches is tradition. 'One starts from the notes – I'm an anti-traditionalist in that sense. I don't believe in a "tradition" of Verdi or Donizetti singing. In the case of Verdi, all you need is in the score; every single bar of *Aida* has something over it that Verdi wrote, and if you can just do that, you get jolly well near a performance. Most singers don't get anywhere near. . . . One can't stop the kids, because as soon as they're told what the opera for the term is going to be, they immediately go and buy the record, and they pick up all the awful tricks and you have to spend two or three weeks getting rid of them. . . .'

In one sense the building of the voice continues all through the singer's life, because the voice, being a function of the body and not a separate entity, is affected slightly but perceptibly by every change the body as a whole undergoes: as Dame

Kiri te Kanawa puts it, 'The problem with my instrument is that I can't unscrew it out of my throat and leave it on the mantelpiece and walk out. It's got to go with me.' The singer's training and career is delayed precisely because of the relation between body and instrument which no other musician shares: the singer must wait until the vocal cords are adequately grown – a process which, incorporating the breaking of the voice, takes rather longer in men than women. The male singer, therefore, having already had one major voice change by the time he starts his training, throughout his career is liable to lag slightly behind the female singer in terms of physical development of the voice; the soprano voice may be fully developed at twenty-six, say, whereas the tenor or baritone may not be mature until twenty-eight or thirty. The bass voice would seem to be the slowest of all to develop; it is interesting that three of Britain's leading basses – Robert Lloyd, Gwynne Howell and Richard Van Allan – entered the profession as a second start in their late twenties, the full potential of their voices having only then become apparent.

For women the physical phenomenon influencing the voice most directly is the menstrual cycle (although its effects vary widely and, while it may be an acceptable plea in mitigation against a murder charge, pre-menstrual tension is not yet an announceable reason for cancelling a performance). In later years, the change of life can have serious, even conclusive consequences for the voice – vocal difficulties may in fact be the first indication of the menopause for a singer, with the voice suddenly vanishing and just as suddenly returning for no apparent reason. Obviously, many singers survive the change of life vocally; for others it may mark the point at which the voice no longer needs to be built, but rather shored up against decay.

6

Building the Performer

Building the voice is largely a matter for the singer and his teacher, working in private. Learning to use the voice as part of an ensemble, on the other hand – a crucial process for the would-be performer – necessarily involves other people. Since the decline of the independent touring companies it has largely been the business of opera schools and departments and classes in major musical institutions to see the young singer through this stage of his training.

Matters are usually well-advanced – some four or five years spent building the instrument – before there is any indication of whether or not the voice is likely to be suited to a career in opera. Opera courses are therefore almost invariably arranged to begin towards the end of undergraduate studies, or specifically as post-graduate studies. To join the Voice and Opera course offered by the Opera Training Department at the Juilliard School in New York, for example, applicants must be over twenty-one with at least three years of general voice-training behind them. The Indiana University Opera Theater, the largest opera school in America, will only take on students from the university's music department once they are halfway through their course there. Similarly, the Royal College of Music's Opera Department caters largely for graduates of the General Performers' course, plus a few singers from outside with professional experience but no formal training; and the Opera Class at the Royal Academy of Music is a part-time course which voice students may not add to their curriculum until the third and fourth years of their general studies.

A further stage of training exists in both America and Britain for those most likely to make a career in opera, during which learning is largely through performance. The American Opera Center for Advanced Training at the Juillard exists, according to its Director, Erica Gastelli, 'to provide young singers with the performance experience they need between final training and a career. It is devised for the young professional who has mastered vocal technique and other basic studies, and the curriculum concentrates on opera production in all its facets'. The National Opera Studio in London pursues broadly similar aims under Michael Langdon, who puts the emphasis less on voice-training than on an understanding of musical style, on stage geography, movement, acting and characterisation.

In Europe, and in most Iron Curtain countries, a different system has evolved, with conservatories attached directly to opera houses; La Scala, for example, now has its own opera school, as do most German houses. The system has considerable practical advantages: students have access to a fully professional stage, costumes, orchestra and sets and they work in the context of a performing house and not in academic abstraction.

Advanced training aside, wherever they may be, most schools cover similar ground in the courses they offer young singers. On the music side, besides individual vocal coaching which continues uninterrupted throughout the three- to five-year course, singers will discover how to hold their own in ensemble work – how to co-ordinate breathing, regulate volume, adapt the pitch and tone of their voice to others, how to work to timing other than their own and, almost as important as technical competence, how to preserve and assert their individuality. Dame Kiri te Kanawa explains the special contribution that opera school has to make: 'College is useful because you *should* be up against your peers; you have to measure yourself, because competition is always going to be a major part of your life. Learning how to break away from your anxieties, and shyness about working on stage; learning to cope with a difficult young tenor; learning to work as a team; learning to cope with the egos . . . '

A rather more concrete asset that the young singer stands to gain from these years is help and encouragement in the matter of building up a repertoire. As the voice settles and the *Fach* is established, the learning of single arias on a fairly random basis is replaced by the systematic assemblage of whole roles – arias, ensembles and recitatives. By the time he leaves, a singer may have no more than three or four roles in the armoury: priorities are to learn accurately (an attribute which in Michael Langdon's view is both rare and guaranteed to impress the music establishment) and with intelligence. To help with the interpretation of roles, many institutions employ seasoned professional coaches to whom students can take the music for private instruction. Both the Royal College and the Royal Academy, for example, employ as consultants Norman Feasey and Arthur Hammond who between them have some 120 years' experience of training the voice and of opera performance. Arthur Hammond, for many years principal conductor with the Carl Rosa Opera Company, explains the function they fulfil: 'My work with singers is to try and make their vocal work *theatre*. They do the vocal work with a singing teacher – but really what they're building is the instrument. I'm concerned with playing it . . . with giving them the ability to phrase and interpret, to take music and *convey* it to an audience.'

As for opera as drama, the degree of attention paid to it varies from school to school. At New York's American Opera Center, drama-training accounts for about one third of the course; and London's Guildhall (as the Guildhall School of Music *and Drama*) is similarly geared to producing a new breed of actor/singer.

OPPOSITE A master class on *Der Rosenkavalier* at the National Opera Studio, 1985; Jady Pearl is coached in the role of Annina by Michael Langdon, playing Baron Ochs.

It is in fact the only school in London to give its singers systematic drama coaching; neither the Royal Academy nor the Royal College offers a separate drama course (though the Royal Northern College of Music in Manchester does). For Bryan Drake, head of the Royal College's Opera Department, it is a matter of priorities. 'In the long run when they go out and do an audition, they'll get a job if they can sing well; nobody's going to ask them too many questions. It's the sound of the voice in the theatre that matters.' Many singers would support his decision, though for quite different reasons – Robert Tear, for example, objects to formal drama-training on artistic grounds, believing that the only way to translate feelings into actions is spontaneously: 'As soon as you've *learnt* something, in many ways you've lost your immediacy. . . . It's instantly secondhand, you've been propagandised.'

All the schools, however, offer some sort of tuition in the various forms of stage movement, including mime, dance and fencing. At the American Opera Center, the aim of drama coach Norman Ayrton is to develop in his singers an organic physical response to the music. 'Voice teachers tend to encourage them to stand still; my job is to get them to move. When I audition an applicant for the course, I blot out the face and see if anything else is happening there.' (Again, some singers dispute the need for elaborate training in how to move – Linda Esther Gray, for example: 'I don't think acting is about moving, it's about thinking.') The National Opera Studio devotes a good deal of attention to the practicalities of stagecraft – how to see and be seen, how to position yourself so that you can act convincingly *and* sing out through the proscenium arch, how to avoid blocking other performers or crossing in front of them while they are singing. The Royal Academy has recently begun sending selected students for instruction in stage techniques at English National Opera, and most courses now include classes in stage make-up.

All schools also provide language-teaching, aiming more at correct pronunciation and increased comprehension than at any degree of fluency in the languages concerned (German, Italian and French in British and American schools, and occasionally Russian). Some also offer speech coaching for dialogue, an integral feature of *opéra comique/Singspiel*.

For a variety of reasons, a few conservatories are beginning to feature musical comedy; the opera world is becoming increasingly overcrowded, while the musical is enjoying a boom, and many year-round houses (more perhaps in Germany, Australia and America than in Britain, Italy or France) carry such pieces as *Oklahoma*, *West Side Story* and *Fiddler on the Roof* alongside *La Fanciulla del West*, *Roméo et Juliette* and *La Juive*. In Britain the Guildhall was the first to introduce a course in musicals, and in 1984 the Royal College followed suit; from now on each singer to complete the opera course will have at least one song-and-dance routine prepared – 'a bit of a lifeline', according to Bryan Drake. 'In the long run we are responsible for producing people who can go out and get work . . . and a lot of modern musicals are far more complex musically and dramatically than a lot of opera; it requires a lot of skill and preparation to put them over.' (It is perhaps worth noting that Tatiana Troyanos made her first stage appearance not in opera but on Broadway in the chorus of *The Sound of Music*.)

Perhaps the most important training an opera school can offer is in public performance, and most gear their courses accordingly. The Royal College, for example, schedules two major productions (in English) every year, and two or three 'informal' performances of excerpts. The Royal Academy presents three full operas (in the original languages) and three workshop productions. American Opera Center students work on various scenes and vignettes which they tour round schools, and on three full productions a year – one of a standard work, one a twentieth-century piece, and one a rarity of some sort. (In the 1984–5 academic year, for instance, they performed Puccini's *Trittico*, Dominick Argento's *Postcard from Morocco*, and Handel's *Xerxes*.) The Indiana University Opera Theater offers the most intensive experience under perhaps the most luxurious conditions; the theatre combines a stage almost as big as that of the Met (ninety feet wide and sixty feet deep) and a pit big enough for an orchestra of ninety players with an auditorium (seating around 1500) which, unlike many American theatres, is not oversized for the student voice. Every year IUOT students present six major productions and two minor, all double-cast and all in English; in thirty-six years they have done a thousand performances of some 220 operas, including twenty world premières. Their productions have been on public television, and in 1981 they rented the Met to give the US première of Martinů's *The Greek Passion*.

Obviously an operation on this scale is less restricted in its choice of repertoire than the smaller schools. At the Royal College, say, with an annual intake of twenty to twenty-four singers, an imbalance between the different voices almost always tends to rule out the nineteenth-century core repertoire; as Bryan Drake explains, much as one would hope for an intake of six sopranos, six mezzos, six tenors, and six baritones and basses, what one usually gets is eight sopranos, three mezzos, two tenors and four baritones and basses – and many nineteenth-century operas need a predominance of men. (Poulenc's *Dialogues of the Carmelites*, with thirteen female principals, is a boon to opera schools, as is Suppé's *Zehn Mädchen und kein Mann*.) Few schools can attempt chorus operas or the heavier dramatic works; Wagner's operas, though well-written for the voice, are uniformly exhausting for young singers simply because of their length, and much of Verdi's writing is too demanding for developing voices.

Whatever the repertoire, however, to have appeared in a range of three or four productions before braving the paying public has obvious advantages for young singers. They develop confidence on stage, discover how to sustain a performance over a whole evening, learn about working with producers. This last can serve them in particularly good stead once outside, since most schools prefer to use professionals – often quite distinguished – rather than students. The performances also provide direct exposure to critics and agents, and help to develop audition technique – both the practical skills and the protective shell needed by the salesman whose product is himself. Perhaps most importantly, these early appearances will help to establish whether the student has what it takes to graduate from simply singing in public to becoming a stage performer. In an extraordinarily competitive field, the right temperament is essential – this is generally agreed to consist not merely of a willingness to work and an average allowance of ambition, but also of a single-mindedness that can verge on the ruthless. Character is more of an imponderable, though. Some observers consider a certain simplicity an asset; Josephine Veasey, for example, believes that a very complex personality may well be reflected in the voice, not always to its advantage, and baritone/producer Peter Knapp would agree: 'You've got to have a certain type of personality to stand up there and vocalise from your deepest feelings . . . It's a disadvantage to be too intellectual about it, to allow a mental process to get in the way. . . . The great singers are pretty straightforward people. . . .'

Certainly a considerable degree of extroversion is vital, as Robert Lloyd points out: 'The biggest single enemy of good singing is inhibition. Opening the voice up and extending oneself is quite an adventure for an Englishman.' For Scots-woman Isobel Buchanan, the question never arose: 'I found that being on the stage came absolutely naturally – it's either something you're born with or you're not. You can teach somebody how to kick off with the upstage leg rather than the downstage one, and not to cross over badly, and how to hold a fan . . . but if you haven't got that in-built desire to get up there and show off. . . .' In the greatest performers, a stage presence is almost tangible, a magnet for the audience's attention. Michael Langdon calls them 'the natural stage animals. It's personality, it's charisma – it's the Placido Domingo, the Boris Christoff thing – they just grab the audience.' An instinct for the stage is by definition something that cannot be taught, but even in these early years it can be identified and developed and, when it is strong enough, it can be made to compensate for almost any failing, as Ileana Cotrubas found out: 'I have never had a big voice; I have always had a big temperament.'

OPPOSITE Grabbing the audience: Boris Christoff (*Boris Godunov*, Covent Garden, 1971).

7

Building the Career

'How do you build a career? Well, first you hope you're going to have one' (Dennis O'Neill). The years immediately after leaving music school are unlikely to be easy for a singer. Even for those who go on to post-postgraduate training (at the National Opera Studio or American Opera Center, say), there may still be a hiatus between the educational system and the professional world, between learning and earning. At twenty-four or twenty-five an opera singer can be trained as comprehensively as he or she needs to be, and still not be ready to take on professional work. This is most apparent in the young bass, as Martin Isepp, head of Glyndebourne's music staff, points out, because of the nature of bass roles: 'All the parts are either *buffi* or old men, very hard for young chaps to portray. Rarely are they the hero. How can they survive until their voices are ready?'

The young singer fresh from music school will rarely have very much money; every penny of grant will have been exhausted simply in reaching this stage, and the private lessons which many singers may still be taking are expensive – in the USA in 1985, as much as a hundred dollars per hour. Nor, unless their student careers have been quite out of the ordinary, will singers have either reputation or agent. In a time of financial stringency for the arts, agents need artists who already have a market value. For 'patron' read 'agent', and Doctor Johnson's famous rebuke to Lord Chesterfield would sit well on the lips of most successful singers: 'Is not a patron, my lord, one who looks with unconcern on a man struggling for life in the water, and when he has reached ground, encumbers him with help? The notice which you have been pleased to take of my labours, had it been early, had been kind; but it has been delayed till I am indifferent and cannot enjoy it . . . till I am known and do not want it.'

It is in these first would-be-professional years that many singers accept that they are not going to make a career in opera – either because they lack the temperament to endure the stress of constant auditions, constant vying for favours; because, as they contemplate their counterparts in other branches of music making an acceptable living, they are not prepared to make sacrifices which seem both inevitable and unreasonable; or, simply, because vocally the competition is too hot.

Some will leave the profession altogether, or teach, or go into light music, or pursue a career as a singer outside opera, though to make a living purely as a recital artist has itself become extremely difficult. Some will join choruses, occasionally with a view to pursuing a solo career at a later stage. A few choruses are recognised as stepping stones in this direction – the Glyndebourne Chorus, for example; others – notably those of the major houses – are not, and many teachers are reluctant to recommend entering them straight from school. But they offer, among other benefits, a security which is hard to find elsewhere in the profession.

The most popular amongst the various options is that of joining a year-round company on contract. This may be seen either as an apprenticeship – Placido Domingo, for instance, spent what might be described as his formative years, between the ages of twenty-two and twenty-five, with the Hebrew National Opera in Tel Aviv – or as an end in itself. Not that such posts are easy to secure: while there are now more opera performances than ever before, possibly even more companies, proportionately the number of openings for contract singers has not increased. In Italy, where most cities and some towns used to boast their own permanent ensemble companies, the short season and the international guest are now far more usual. In America few of the companies founded in recent years can offer singers either a full year's work or a regular living wage. Germany, with its multiplicity of small companies, has traditionally been an excellent hunting ground for British and American singers anxious to acquire performing experience and build a repertoire in relative seclusion under ensemble conditions; in Britain the Carl Rosa Opera Company for many years fulfilled a similar function, to a lesser extent. Now, however, German union regulations limit the intake of foreign singers to fourteen per cent; and the Carl Rosa, forced out of business by the rising costs of touring and the withdrawal of its government grant, has not, as such, been replaced.

Broadly speaking, there are two levels at which a solo singer may be invited to join a company – as a principal or as a *comprimario*, literally 'accompanying the principal'; it is not unusual to join as the one and become the other. The label of '*comprimario* part' is most usually attached to 'character' roles, small but juicy, such as the Idiot in *Boris Godunov*, M. Triquet in *Eugene Onegin*, Annina and Valzacchi in *Der Rosenkavalier*, Benoit and Alcindoro in *La Bohème*, Berta in *The Barber of Seville*, the Emperor Altoum in *Turandot*, and others. To extract the full mileage from a short role without turning it into a demonstration of coarse acting is an art in itself, and a skilled *comprimario* player is an invaluable asset to a house. Equally important, however, is the nucleus of bit-part players who can be relied upon to give high-class support to the principals in less rewarding but nonetheless indispensable roles, and may in an international house be the main source of continuity and cohesion.

For some artists the small part is no more than the natural and necessary first step on the freelance ladder; Dame Kiri te Kanawa, Dame Joan Sutherland and Jon Vickers all spent several early years on contract to Covent Garden, James McCracken to the Met, playing Ladies, Heavenly Voices, messengers and heralds. For others it is a peaceful way out of the profession, a less painful method of retiring than the clean break. Many singers, however, make *comprimario* playing a full-time career, either as freelances, or on permanent contract. If the latter, the houses by whom they are employed use them very flexibly to play a wide variety of small parts, to understudy larger parts and, on occasion, to perform these larger parts. The Met, for example, is required by the singers' unions to employ seventeen or eighteen contract artists (which is less than they used to have, but probably more than they need). Longest-serving of these is tenor Charles Anthony, who made his Met début in 1954, and in 1981 was the first singer to receive the Metropolitan Opera Company Service Award. In the 1984–5 season, he appeared in eight of the twenty-two productions – as the Sergeant (*The Barber of Seville*), the Young Servant (*Elektra*), Riccardo, esquire to Don Carlos (*Ernani*), a Noble (*Lohengrin*), the Lamplighter (*Manon Lescaut*), Zorn the Pewterer (*Die Meistersinger*), Roderigo (*Otello*) and an Esquire (*Parsifal*). The Royal Opera House employs from year to year some fifteen singers on salary for a fixed number of performances (approximately fifty a year, understudying counting as one third of a performance). Roles are not specified in advance and are often allocated at quite short notice; and since appearances are spread through the season, singers need permission to take work elsewhere.

To play small parts in a big house has the advantages of bringing a singer to the attention (however brief) of that particular management, administrators elsewhere, a high concentration of critics and agents and a cosmopolitan public. There are those, however – Thomas Hemsley, for example – who would argue that to play large parts in a less prestigious house is more effective in consolidating the young singer's confidence, stageworthiness and technical skills. Contract principals, engaged on an annual basis to play all the season's leading roles in their particular *Fach*s, are the mainstay of the smaller German houses operating on the ensemble system, and many international careers (especially those of American singers) have been founded on five or more years' intensive exploration of the repertoire in, say, Detmold or Düsseldorf. Barbara Bonney, for example, served for several years as a principal soprano on contract to Darmstadt, appearing as Gretel, Blonde, Cherubino, Manon, Adina, Gilda and Lauretta, before proceeding to Munich, Frankfurt and Hamburg to play similar roles and in 1985–6 to Covent Garden, the Met and La Scala as Sophie and Pamina. Marilyn Horne's international career effectively began in Gelsenkirchen, Helen Donath's in Hanover, Barbara Daniel's in Kassel, James King's in Berlin; and between 1968 and 1971 Frankfurt housed both Agnes Baltsa and Ileana Cotrubas.

Outside Germany and Austria, contract principals tend to be employed on a looser basis. Welsh National Opera, for example, keeps some dozen principal singers on an annual salary without either guaranteeing or requiring a specified number of performances, and the composition of the roster varies from one year

OPPOSITE Barbara Bonney (*right*) as Sophie in her Covent Garden début, with Anne Howells as Octavian, in *Der Rosenkavalier* (1985).

to the next, depending to a considerable extent on repertoire plans: some seasons may call for more baritones than tenors, others *vice versa*, and it is very rarely necessary to keep a mezzo-soprano on contract, given the scarcity of principal mezzo roles and the company's policy of giving small and middle-sized parts to the chorus. New York City Opera employs some principal artists for specified performances, others for specified periods. Jerry Hadley, for instance, has in recent years been on contract to NYCO from June to October (after which a similar commitment to the Vienna State Opera calls him away). During this time, as Beverly Sills explains, the company may deploy his services over a wide field: 'I can put him in *Lucia, Manon, Pearl Fishers* – move him around constantly, so long as he has three or four days in between and has a chance to be sufficiently rested once the rehearsal periods are over.'

 With the ensemble system no longer the norm and the guest freelance proliferating at every level, the practice of hiring singers on contract is beset by difficulties. There has always been the risk that the singer's contract will outlast his or her usefulness; if they are not going to attain stardom, people want security and under some systems it cannot be denied them – after fifteen years a contract singer in a German house, for example, is on the payroll for life, a humane but expensive arrangement. Conversely, it can now be as much of a problem to retain the singers whom the company *does* want. This has been brought home forcibly to Mark Elder in his first five years as Music Director of English National Opera: 'The company and the company singer have changed. . . . We're really trying to sustain something in this company that is gradually being eroded by speed and by the twentieth century. . . . Because of the jets and motorways; because it's now possible to go and do a job in America for two or three weeks with very few rehearsals and few performances and make a lot of money – people don't want to stay. It's put a great pressure on us. Here in the middle of a metropolis it's very hard to sustain a twelve-month loyalty. . . . You get a young singer on contract, and they do three or four years with you – and then they come to you and they say, "I've been turning down all this work – what am I going to do? Don't you think we could have a little more flexibility? Couldn't I have gone and done that thing in Amsterdam?" We say, "We'd like you to sing elsewhere, it reflects well on the company and it broadens your experience, gives you a chance to sing in original languages" – which *is* important, it's good that they get other experiences. So then we have a different type of contractual relationship: we put them on a kind of guest contract where they give us certain periods each year, agreed in advance.' This, he acknowledges, is often the thin end of the wedge. 'Singers know that their future is limited, their days are numbered. A conductor will go on conducting till he drops, but a singer's voice will reach its peak, and in that peak they will want to feel that they're getting as much money and acclaim and success as they can. We've got to face the fact that we come somewhere down the list. We're on the list, but some way down it. So they say, "I've had an invitation to go and sing on the West Coast of America. It's terribly important to me, I haven't sung there before, I must go." So I say, "You mean you want to come out of that project that you and I talked about for two years' time?" and they say yes, but they won't let you down about the *next* thing. . . . Many singers prefer a small part in Italian up the road with the red velvet to a really major role here in English. They'll put Covent Garden above us because of what Covent Garden means in career terms. It's very painful to accept, but it's true.'

For some the freelance career is first choice – those singers 'born' freelance, in possessing talent which gives them the power to pick and choose; some achieve it as the fruits of long service in a company; whilst others, in trying and failing to get into a company, have it thrust upon them. Combining maximum freedom with a high degree of risk, the freelance career can be accelerated by various means, some attributable to luck and some to good judgement.

Singing competitions, in ever-increasing numbers, offer useful exposure both for the winners and the leading also-rans (provided that the competition does not become a way of life; Jonathan Friend warns, 'I very seldom pay much attention to the credentials of people who have won seventeen prizes if they seem to spend all their lives winning prizes and never actually getting up on the stage to perform'). Dame Kiri te Kanawa came to London to study on the strength of repeated successes in competitions in Australia and New Zealand; Georgian bass Paata Burchuladze first became known outside the Soviet Union after winning the international competition for *Voci Verdiane* at Busseto in 1981; and it was Ileana Cotrubas's victory at 'sHertogenbosch in 1965 which produced her first important roles in the West. (If competitions have helped in the past to lure singers out from behind the Iron Curtain, one might perhaps see the recent striking success of artists from the People's Republic of China as a pointer to a future market.)

Particularly valuable is the prize which incorporates a performing opportunity. As first prizewinner at Busseto in 1971, José Carreras was able to make his Italian début in Parma; and the Achille Peri Prize brought Luciano Pavarotti his first Rodolfo, in Reggio Emilia. In recognition of the impetus given to his career, in 1980 Pavarotti helped to found the Opera Company of Philadelphia Luciano Pavarotti International Voice Competition 'in order to give young aspiring singers a chance to launch their career by making their débuts with the celebrated tenor Luciano Pavarotti and the Opera Company of Philadelphia'.

Another time-honoured shortcut to success lies in stepping in for a well-established artist at the last moment. Joan Sutherland saved the day at Covent Garden in 1952 as a substitute Amelia in *Un Ballo in Maschera*, and Kiri te Kanawa made her début at the Met in 1974 replacing an indisposed Teresa Stratas as Desdemona at very short notice; while she would in any case have taken over the role in a matter of weeks, the sense of emergency gave an edge to the occasion which transformed a sure-fire success into a triumph. To be adopted as a foil by another singer can be just as effective. José Carreras has never failed to acknowledge with gratitude the help provided by compatriot Montserrat Caballé when he first decided to abandon chemical engineering for singing. Likewise, Luciano Pavarotti's career was consolidated by his association in his mid-twenties with Joan Sutherland and Richard Bonynge. (Apart from the beauty of his voice, Dame Joan was impressed by his height; at 5ft 8½ins. herself, she much prefers tall tenors.)

Until securely established, the freelance singer obviously has far more need to sell himself on a day-to-day basis than the company member, and in this an agent can be indispensable – provided that he does not have on his books half a dozen other singers in the same range, all of whose claims he will advance with a fine impartiality. In America a significant distinction is drawn between 'agent' and 'manager'. In the view of Matthew Epstein, Consultant to Columbia Artists Management and Artistic Director of Carnegie Hall, the agent is he who waits by the telephone for work to come in and then negotiates the fee; the manager goes out and generates employment for his artists. 'It's the difference between fielding with the glove at center field, and standing at the plate and hitting bat.' He can guide the singer in his choice of roles, having first ensured that he *has* a choice; and he can prise open doors against which the singer alone might batter until doomsday.

The manager/agent is also a useful scapegoat. At the beginning of a career, a serious hazard faces the gifted freelance singer – not so much the shortage of work as an excess of the wrong kind of work. The greater the early success, the more frequent the offer that must be refused – the role that is too high for the voice, or too low, or too heavy. José Carreras reports that the first result of his winning the Busseto Verdi competition was a crop of invitations to play Don Alvaro in *La Forza del Destino* or Manrico in *Il Trovatore* – roles which could seriously have damaged the voice that had just been given the prize. Verdi has been dubbed 'the Attila of the voice' for the havoc his writing can wreak on the mature instrument, let alone the evolving voice; *tessiture* are generally high, breathing irregular and the singer is required to use full voice a lot of the time. (One vocal coach reckons that a heavy role like Azucena can knock a hole of about six notes in a developing mezzo register.) The young singer who essays a major Wagnerian role is also taking a chance, as Placido Domingo discovered when he performed Lohengrin at the age of twenty-seven – not on paper an alarming-looking role, neither especially heavy, nor with many high notes; but it is one – Hoffmann is another – which lies awkwardly much of the time in the *passaggio* between middle and upper registers, in the Es and Fs and F sharps. 'If a part lies basically lower in the range, it does not matter that one has to go up even as high as B flat now and again. What really taxes a voice is a concentration of middle-high register singing, and that is exactly what the role of Lohengrin – which never goes higher than an A flat – contains.' In retrospect he feels that the experience unquestionably harmed his voice, and while the damage was, patently, reparable, it was sixteen years before he attempted the role again – at the Met in 1984.

Another pitfall for the young singer is the offer of the right role in the wrong house. Opinions differ as to whether the size of a house need affect a performance in musical terms. American houses in particular tend to range from large to huge:

José Carreras as Nemorino with Geraint Evans as Dulcamara in *L'Elisir d'Amore* (Covent Garden, 1975).

San Francisco and Dallas, with over three thousand seats, and the Met with almost four thousand are not untypical. Many singers maintain that by sensible use of the voice it is possible to cope with any size of auditorium; while it may be a question of 'turning full-frontal and getting on with it' – James Bowman's phrase – the well-produced voice need never be forced. 'It's not a question of pushing harder, it's a question of focus. If you push, it diffuses the sound and you get nowhere. If your voice is focused, it'll ping across.' But these are mature voices and seasoned performers; the young singer may have neither the experience nor the technique to avoid forcing and hurting the voice.

Even the right roles in the right houses can be ruinous if they present themselves too frequently. The pressure can be killing – too many performances and too much travelling; singing when unfit for fear of wasting opportunities which may not come again; too little time to prepare, roles not sung into the voice, and the consequent strain of living through each performance on one's wits. In an ensemble company the young contract principal may be hypersensitive to vibrations from the chorus behind him – 'Why him and not me?' – an uncomfortable predicament which is shared by the inexperienced guest brought into a principal role over the heads of house artists. English tenor Graham Clark, as a new David at Bayreuth, had the additional handicap of having to perform in front of a chorus composed of professional Wagner singers from all over Europe – 'the one role in Wagner where he explains the nuances of the German language and German singing. . .'

Damage to the voice at this stage may set the singer back years, as the teacher delves far into the technique to repair it – assuming repairs are possible. And even if the voice itself survives, the performing temperament may not. Norman Bailey, having evolved from a bass into a baritone in approximately eighteen months, was encouraged to tackle Verdi too early: 'It created certain nervous problems, stage fright, which stayed with me for a long, long time, till I swore I wouldn't do any more Verdi baritone roles, and stopped for about five years.' For Isobel Buchanan, it was a critical crisis of confidence that precipitated near-disaster. Under the auspices of Richard Bonynge, she was propelled to stardom as a lead soprano in Sydney, where by the time she was twenty-two she had already sung Pamina, Micaela and Fiordiligi, to huge acclaim. After two or three happy and triumphant years, she returned to England to a terrific build-up from agents – and the instinctive suspicion of critics. Audiences continued to applaud her performances, critics less so with every production; and when their comments began to be directed not only at her singing but also, by implication, at her personality and professionalism, she began seriously to question her future. 'I began to lose confidence, because I hadn't had this build-up through small parts for the critics to get used to me. I began to question myself – "Can I really sing this? Is this the right noise? How did I do that?" . . . And then I thought, "I don't want to sing any more" . . .' Though Isobel Buchanan's career has since taken off once again, as a homily on the perils of early success her story could hardly be bettered.

It is easy enough to cast the agent as the villain in this situation, blaming on his greed the fatal over-extension of the young singer; and in many cases the charge will be justified. Equally the irresponsible administrator or music director eager to solve an immediate casting problem regardless of the long-term consequences has much to answer for. But it is not *always* the agent who is grasping or reckless, ambitious or impatient. Matthew Epstein pleads in their defence: 'Sometimes the managers *are* at fault. But if you get to know singer personalities very well, a very ambitious singer is not to be reined in. They're unstoppable – and when they do these things to themselves and get into difficulties, then they blame the manager. But while they're getting into difficulties and doing stupid things, they are very headstrong and very difficult, and honestly you just can't tell them no. Rare is the singer who has the smart to say, "I have twenty years – I can do that part five years from now." Most of them will accept all the parts they've been dying to do as fast as they come in.'

Many singers do in fact acknowledge that ultimately the artist must take responsibility for his own mistakes. Dennis O'Neill: 'You plan your career in what you

Dennis O'Neill as Alfredo in *Die Fledermaus* (Covent Garden, 1983).

don't sing. You're going to get offered things, some of which will suit you and some won't – and in the end you're the only person who knows.' When offered a part, the singer will look, obviously, at the *tessitura*, to check that the notes are actually within the right compass; at the orchestration, its weight and colour, to see whether the voice will make itself heard; at the other artists who have assumed the role, and their relative success or failure in it; at the personality of the character, as well as the notes – is it intelligible? translatable? risible? And if on any of these grounds the singers have misgivings, they must have the right, and the strength of mind, to refuse the offer. Stuart Burrows is very decided on this subject: 'The greatest gift a singer can have is the ability to say no. . . . I've been threatened with being sued for turning things down. . . . But after all the fanfare, the rehearsals, the publicity, the razzmatazz, there comes the moment when you walk out on to that stage, and it's entirely up to you.'

One means of monitoring the development of the young voice and shielding it against abuse is the apprentice programme or Young Artists scheme, which a company may operate through privately-sponsored altruism, or as an investment for the future. These schemes are much favoured in America, where they have the additional advantage of stemming the exodus of young singers to Europe. The first apprentice programme was introduced at Santa Fe to run conjointly with the festival – that is, for two months in the summer – since when programmes of varying lengths have been set up in opera centres such as Chicago, Houston, Cincinnati and Miami, and New York City Opera is considering something similar. At present the principal year-round apprentice scheme is organised by the Met – the Metropolitan Opera Young Artists Development Program. Its administrator, Larry Stayer, explains its origins: 'About five years ago it was our sorry observation that many of the young people coming through the National Council Auditions would come on stage and we'd think, "That voice will be interesting for us in another three or four years." By the time they got back to us, something had happened with the talent, the voice had gone.' The Development Program was established to accommodate a maximum of six singers a year for a two- to three-year period, during which time they are effectively paid *not* to work; in being given an annual stipend – in 1984 it was $18,000 plus the costs of their singing lessons – they are protected from the necessity of taking unsuitable jobs in order to live, and have the opportunity instead to continue their studies in voice, language and drama. In addition they act as understudies and are offered small parts with the company. Originally opposed to the apprentices singing small roles – 'So many apprentice programs use it as slave labour' – Larry Stayer now believes that the benefits of the experience outweigh the risk of exploitation; they are paid a fee in any case, over and above the stipend, and have the right to refuse roles that do not appeal. Conversely, the Met administration is entitled to veto any unsuitable offers they may receive from outside.

Such good husbandry can only pay dividends when these fine young voices mature – and as guests, not contract singers, 'a stable of young American leading role singers at the Met – like Malfitano, Shicoff, Quivar, Battle. We're not looking for a Flora in *Traviata*.' This perhaps explains why the annual quota of six has yet to be filled. The apprentices are overtly, and efficiently, groomed for stardom: 'From the time we bring them into the program we have an eye to where we think the career is going and what slot they may fit into in the theatre. Our casting is done so far in advance that we are able to leave, say, two performances of Rodolfo and seven covering opportunities open on the off chance that this young tenor will be *in* in two years' time. . . . All the singers have débuted during the course, some in smaller roles than others [Ravel's *L'Enfant et les Sortilèges* has been a godsend to the apprentice programme, with its multitude of cameo roles, each with its short aria], but all are earmarked for major assignments.' Soprano Marvis Martin, for example, made her début on tour as Pamina, and by 1985 had sung in New York Xenia in *Boris Godunov*, the Princess in *L'Enfant*, the Heavenly Voice in *Don Carlos*, Almirena in *Rinaldo*, and Clara in *Porgy and Bess*. But as Larry Stayer points out, this kind of cultivation does not suit every temperament: 'They have all to be a specific kind of personality that will allow us to mould their career, in a sense, and their way of thinking. There has to be a malleability, or there is no point in their being here.'

Singers who survive these early years and establish themselves securely will probably be on the threshold of a successful career at thirty. In purely vocal terms, most reach their prime in the mid- to late thirties when the voice should still have all its bloom and more strength and character than in the first flush of its youth. Opinions differ as to how much it is possible during this peak period to structure the career. Bryan Drake, for example, sees little scope: 'You've got to be prepared to be the victim of luck. It's not notices often that make the difference but meeting people. You've got to be ready to take the opportunities. . . . There's no structure to it – it's a series of blind dashes from one thing to another.'

Without being quite this fatalistic, many singers are guided more by their five-year diaries than by an overall game plan for a career. In considering an invitation, given that the role is a suitable one, the questions they ask themselves are most likely to be 'Am I free on those performance dates? Can I do those weeks of rehearsal? Do I have time to learn the role beforehand?' Unless supremely confident that the offer will be repeated at a more strategic time, the singer may well take a role 'out of order' in terms of the conventional wisdom, rather than risk never performing it at all; thus Donald McIntyre's début at Bayreuth (an invitation accepted against the specific advice of Glen Byam Shaw) was as Telramund, vocally the most difficult of the Wagnerian *Heldenbariton* roles in his opinion. And the career of a singer within a company will be shaped more by the company's needs than by an individual strategy; on this basis Birgit Nilsson in her early years as principal soprano with the Royal Stockholm Opera sang Sieglinde and Brünnhilde before Elsa, Venus before Elisabeth.

Nevertheless, there are some decisions which singers can, and perhaps must, make. Are they to confine themselves exclusively to opera? – and many do, saving the occasional Verdi *Requiem* – or to intersperse their operatic appearances with *Lieder*, oratorios and other concert work? The mixed career is perhaps a more typically British phenomenon than a French or Italian one: many of Britain's leading operatic performers (Dame Janet Baker, Robert Tear, Philip Langridge, Anthony Rolfe Johnson, Gwynne Howell, Benjamin Luxon) have come into opera from concert-singing and relish the differences between the two. To a certain extent, opera requires a separate technique. Elisabeth Schwarzkopf talks in terms of channels – one for singing over an orchestra on stage, and another for small-scale singing with piano accompaniment. Anthony Rolfe Johnson distinguishes different types of singing on stage: 'One can explain it in a backwards way by saying that sometimes one is told not to be operatic when singing on the concert platform. Projection has to be much fiercer for opera, larger than life. . . . You've got such a lot more people to reach individually, and they have to be involved in a total drama rather than only a musical experience.'

The performer can usually choose how often he or she will sing. The most prolific average at the peak of their careers between sixty-five and eighty performances a year; José Carreras, for instance, makes about seventy appearances annually, Placido Domingo now slightly less (although he has already given more than twice as many performances – by 1984, some 1750 – as Maria Callas totalled in her whole career). Others ration themselves more strictly: Tatiana Troyanos, for example, rarely commits herself to more than forty or fifty performances a year – 'The public expects a certain intensity from me, and it's exhausting' – and Ileana Cotrubas prefers to do fewer still, between thirty-five and forty, partly because she is not very robust, partly because she does not enjoy doing more: 'I think you become a kind of machine. An artist works with emotions, with something very special, very difficult. . . . You should always have the feeling that each performance is the very first one, that you are creating something afresh. . . . You are not a *fonctionn-aire*, you're not working at the Post Office, coming in at eight and leaving at five and rubber-stamping things. . . . In the arts you have to express so much, you are working with something very sensitive. I had a bad experience when I sang too many performances in a short period – and I decided if I don't have pleasure in what I do, it's not worth doing it.'

While most singers do accept roles in the order in which they are offered, there is a sequence in which, all things being equal, they might prefer to sing them. At the highest level artists may have the power to order their roles within a season depending on whether they prefer to work from lighter to heavier, or *vice versa*; Sir Rudolf Bing considered it took longer, for example, for a soprano to scale her voice down from Aida to Violetta than to build it up in the other direction. Certainly most singers will be reluctant simultaneously to rehearse a low role and perform a high one – Richard Van Allan for one: 'I want to sing the voice in high and keep it there, and not be grovelling away the next day or two days later on a low *tessitura*. You can move the voice about, but if you start stretching it between two extremes at the same time, it can be dangerous.'

And over the whole span of a career, a natural order asserts itself to some extent. Some roles are patently better suited to youthful voices and looks – pages, shepherd boys and other 'trouser' roles, maids and other *ingénues*: both vocally and dramatically Sophie, say, should be lighter than the Marschallin. Others it is hard to play without a certain weight of voice – Otello, for example – and an understanding which some feel can only come with age. Sherrill Milnes sees Simon Boccanegra as a part better suited to the mature artist, or at least one old enough to be Amelia's father; and Norman Bailey, tackling *Lulu*'s Dr Schön in his thirties, found it hard to conceive or simulate the mentality of a fifty-year-old man. The vocal resilience, physical stamina and technical expertise required for some of the major roles take years to develop. Ochs, 'the bass's Grand National', combines a generally high *tessitura* with length and a greater degree of physical activity than is usually demanded of basses. Hans Sachs is marathon-running where Verdi baritone roles count only as a short sprint – Dietrich Fischer-Dieskau was fifty when he first attempted it. A Falstaff must be sufficiently weathered to be convincing, but fit enough to bear up under the punishing costume and action. Placido Domingo singles out Arrigo (in Verdi's *I Vespri Siciliani*) and Huon of Bordeaux (in Weber's *Oberon*) as roles which only a voice toughened by experience should undertake; and Chénier, Radames, Manrico and Enzo (in *La Gioconda*) are all parts which Luciano Pavarotti thought it prudent to postpone until later in his career.

Generally speaking, the voice progresses naturally with age from lighter to heavier roles (one might expect a *Heldentenor*, for example, to move from Lohengrin to Walther to Parsifal and then on to Tannhäuser, Siegmund and Siegfried), and some think this process is irreversible – that the vocal cords perhaps thicken with more strenuous use so that in singing, say, Radames you coarsen the voice for Nemorino and having performed Wagner repeatedly, you cannot return comfortably to Handel. As Luciano Pavarotti puts it, 'The voice is like a sheet of rubber: if you pull it one way, it loses something in the other dimension. If I push my voice into heavy, dramatic roles, I would risk losing the quality of the top.' This is why many singers pick their way with the utmost caution, Anthony Rolfe Johnson amongst them: 'I suppose what I'm looking to do . . . is to try and reach out a little every once in a while and extend my experience, extend my voice, extend my ability – always with this feeling of coming back into safe water. . . . For my peace of mind, I like to be able to feel that I can move outwards all the time towards my limit – and still sing Schubert, Schumann, Wolf, Purcell, all that end of the weight range. . . . If you go too far down the path, make too much of a diversion, you can't come back.'

Perhaps the most far-reaching decision the singer can make is whether or not to specialise – in Italian rather than German repertoire (as to a large extent both José Carreras and Luciano Pavarotti, as opposed to Peter Hofmann and Siegfried Jerusalem, have done); in eighteenth-century and *bel canto* opera, rather than Verdi or Puccini (Marilyn Horne, for example); in Mozart (a bevy of British sopranos, including Felicity Lott, Margaret Marshall and Isobel Buchanan); in baroque music; in contemporary music.

From the practical point of view, specialisation has distinct advantages – Matthew Epstein regards it as conferring a certain visibility, a sharper profile: 'It is very fine for an artist, once they've achieved international acclaim in a specific repertoire, to expand into lots of other things – very healthy, they get bored otherwise. But in order to *make* a real big name internationally. . . . I have a quiz I always use for proving this point; I always say, "Think about Nilsson, what is she famous for?" and people say Brünnhilde, Isolde. "Think about Sutherland", and they say Lucia. A singer should be famous for a few – five or six – roles. Think of Gobbi, or Callas – Scarpia, Tosca, Violetta, Norma. The careers of singers who don't focus themselves on specific roles tend to be diffused. . . . What a manager is supposed to do for a singer is to look and see what their strengths are and maximise them, and to eliminate from their repertoire parts which expose certain weaknesses – give them a sense of how they can best promote themselves. Take Shicoff or von

Stade – when I first came into contact with Neil, my sense of him was that he could do a certain kind of passionate romantic part more in the French or Russian mould than in the Italianate, though he does Italian roles very well. I pushed him to sing Lensky, Werther, Roméo and Hoffmann because I thought that the combination of his physical presence, his stage qualities, the kind of voice he had, and also the fact that there weren't too many people who could do those roles at that time, would make him move forward better. With von Stade, one created a whole special repertoire which no one really has ever had, which combined some of the repertoire of Berganza, some of the repertoire of Ludwig, some of the French parts – a special kind of thing. And also one realised that von Stade had a special affinity for French literature; so one looked for unusual operas that she could do – from Rameau all the way through to the fact that she was the first mezzo to sing Mélisande.'

Specialisation will not always be voluntary. The counter-tenor, for instance, is inevitably confined to the extremities of the repertoire – baroque or mid-twentieth-century works (Britten, Tippett, Aribert Reimann). James Bowman complains that even within this narrow range he is often typecast: 'Extra-terrestrials – you're always used for the supernatural or other-worldly effects. . . . The sound lends itself more to unusual characters. I can't very well play Germont *mère*. . . .' And other voices in any way striking or unusual may find themselves similarly stereotyped, but by

Peter Hofmann in the title role of *Parsifal* (Covent Garden, 1980).

Frederica von Stade as Elena, the Lady of the Lake, in Rossini's *La Donna del Lago* (Covent Garden, 1985).

administrators rather than composers. Lucia Popp originally made her name very largely as a matchless Queen of the Night – but it was a role she came to find increasingly upsetting and inhibiting: 'I found I was suffering too much in it. I had terrible nerves in the end. . . . It restricts you in your other repertory, if you want to keep all those high notes. Your whole life is circling round them and that role. Nobody would let me tackle lyrical parts at the same time.' Any singer skilled in a role which few can master will find themselves forced to 'specialise' in it by eager administrators anxious to keep *Siegfried* or *Turandot*, *Norma* or *Salome* in their repertoire. At one time Josephine Barstow was asked to step in as Salome so often that she toyed with the idea of making her livelihood with it: 'I decided that the thing to do to be a big international artist was to have one's dance ready, and then when you were rung up, you packed your veils, and off you trotted. . . .'

Specialisation may make a singer more marketable – but is it healthy in artistic terms? Apart from the risks of vocal ruin or emotional exhaustion inherent in a career devoted exclusively to the dramatic roles of Verdi or to Wagner, say, the principal hazard of specialisation might appear to the outsider to be boredom. If, on Matthew Epstein's reckoning, artists can make a career with no more than five or six roles, and if they average seventy performances a year over twenty-five years, they are likely one day to find themselves delivering their three-hundredth Tosca or Lucia or Werther; the most avid Puccinian operagoer would surely balk at thirty *Tosca*s in a lifetime, let alone three hundred, and to the rest of the audience the prospect of repetition on this scale would seem absolutely intolerable. Not so, according to singers, as long as the purely musical challenges remain. Dennis O'Neill, who is planning in future to sing less Verdi and Puccini and to concentrate more on the *bel canto* repertoire, explains: 'Dramatically the *bel canto* operas are far less satisfying, but musically they're beautiful, and the technical demands are enormous. At that level you *can't* get bored, because every evening you have to go out and sing something like *Puritani* or *Sonnambula*, huge virtuoso pieces – you can never be good enough to feel, "Oh, just *Sonnambula* again"; you're continually walking a tightrope, no matter who you are.' Dame Kiri te Kanawa agrees: 'Puccini I might get bored with – there's nothing much you can do with it after a while. But not Mozart or Strauss. You can always perfect your technique – get most of it right, for a start!' And José Carreras, who in 1983–4 was singing the same roles (Don José, Rodolfo and Andrea Chénier) very often indeed, maintains: 'Every performance in every different house in different parts of the world – it's a constant challenge, a constant fight with yourself. You want to prove to *yourself* what you are able to do.' It is the element of unpredictability, the near-impossibility of the perfect performance, that for the performer makes the 210th *Carmen* not only endurable but enthralling. Carreras again: 'If one day I arrive at a routine – the day that going to the stage becomes like going to the office – then I'll seriously consider stopping. For me, to perform must be the most exciting point in my life – every time.'

Without electing to specialise quite as narrowly as Matthew Epstein proposes, most singers would accept the importance of finding one's *Fach*, not merely in terms of the range and timbre of the voice – these the singer cannot choose – but also in terms of what suits the personality and holds the interest. Michael Langdon observes: 'I think it's important for an opera singer to find out as early as possible what he does best; nobody does everything equally well. . . . I'm thinking more of the make-up of the person – not so much how they sing, but what their personality is. Some people are naturally better with comedy, with outgoing parts, others with the very still, dramatic parts. It doesn't mean one is a better singer than the other, it means one is a different type of person.' He himself felt more attuned to the comic bass roles – Ochs and Osmin – than the stately ones – Pimen, the Grand Inquisitor, Sarastro. Dennis O'Neill detects a similar tendency in himself: 'I like clowning around, I enjoy it. I wouldn't want to do *Cenerentola* again, but I'm certainly going to do the *Barber*. . . . I *could* do Radames, I've got all the notes – but in the end it's not me, it's not the right personality.'

Many singers for various reasons find themselves out of sympathy with Verdi – Felicity Lott, for example, because of the degree of self-projection which many of his leading roles entail: 'It's not natural to me, I'm not an exhibitionist, I don't know how to just stand up and say, "Stop and listen to what I can do with this" . . . If I've got anything to offer, it's through a character, through somebody else.' For Robert Tear, it is the intellectual (or, rather, the *anti*-intellectual) mould in which much Verdian drama is cast: 'When it comes to Verdi, I don't like the obvious one-to-one romantic relationship. If I'm talking about *romantic* opera, I love Russian opera, whereby it's a kind of generalised trouble. What I can't accept, as I can't accept it in novels of that time, is this *personal* "hero-and-heroine" thing. I find it quite false, it makes no sense to me.'

To ignore or override temperamental likes and dislikes of this kind can be unwise; what one does or does not enjoy doing is closely related to, often synonymous with, what one does or does not do well, and Robert Tear owns, 'Not liking the Verdian hero, I can't actually sing him. I don't know which comes first: my voice is not really meant to sing that stuff – it's not in my spirit, either the feel for it or the singing of it.' (Nor, he adds honestly, does he feel he looks the part: 'I've always looked like a Loge and Shuisky and Galitsin.' On a similar basis, Dietrich Fischer-Dieskau has always declined to perform Papageno or Rigoletto.)

Graham Clark is another tenor who has discovered with experience that the Italian repertoire is neither what he does best nor what he finds most interesting. 'It's only as I've been working that I've found my voice is perhaps most suited to North and East European music [Alexei in *The Gambler*, Herman in *The Queen of Spades*, Albert Gregor in *The Makropoulos Case*, Matteo in *Arabella*, David in *The Mastersingers*] – and oddly enough I've found at the same time they're the kind of operas that interest me most, because they're more substantial. The Southern European stuff is generally aria-quartet-duet, stop-sing-back into the action, a stop-start situation. The German and Northern European and Eastern European is a continuum, dramatically more substantial.'

A growing number of artists could be said to specialise in roles with a higher specific gravity, dramatically speaking. Graham Clark again: 'The only roles which interest me are roles which have some sort of individual character response – a very clear psychological interest. I was asked to do the Duke in Jonathan Miller's *Rigoletto*, but not only did I feel that I didn't have the right voice for the music – I think to sing early Verdi you have to have the Italianate sunshine and warmth in your voice, and I don't think I have – but also I find the Duke a very boring character. . . . He goes through the opera in exactly the same personality, he starts a bastard and finishes a bastard. . . .' In much the same spirit, Robert Tear prefers

David to Walther, Pedrillo to Belmonte, Loge to Lohengrin. And Josephine Barstow states categorically, 'If I'm considering a role, it has to be interesting dramatically, otherwise I don't really want to do it.' Roles like that of Adina (in *L'Elisir d'Amore*) – a part far more interesting for its vocal than its dramatic potential – hold very little appeal for her; abstract beauty of sound, as she is the first to say, is not the single most important constituent of her performances, and this kind of role is best left to the singer whose principal, even sole asset is a lovely voice. 'It seems very important that whatever level you're at, you have to understand your instrument. You have to understand what you've got to offer.'

Throughout the middle years of a career, the voice will often change without deteriorating. There may be much talk, for instance, of a lyric tenor voice becoming 'darker' or 'richer', moving perhaps nearer a heroic tenor. This will not necessarily entail a lowering of register (though Placido Domingo, for example, has seriously contemplated singing Don Giovanni, by no means the highest of baritone roles, at some time in the future). For every singer, however, there comes the time when the voice does, by objective standards, decline. Diaphragm, throat muscles and vocal cords age and slacken in sympathy with every other muscle and membrane, and the voice loses some of its power, smoothness and bloom, its top or bottom notes. Vibrato often increases, and breath control may falter.

It is pointless to try to put an exact age to the last stage of a career. Each voice will deteriorate at its own rate (one of the incalculables which make advance-planning so treacherous), though many critics – Harold Rosenthal, for example – believe that the jet-fuelled life style of the successful singer today will generally accelerate decay. Some artists decline while still in their forties, and it is rare for either the male or female voice to survive the fifties unscathed. This is not to say that the singer is not still giving a good deal of pleasure – in Placido Domingo's words, 'Any competent artist will be more interesting to listen to at forty-five than at twenty-five' – and some sail easily into their sixties: Joan Sutherland, Carlo Bergonzi, Birgit Nilsson and Alfredo Kraus are obvious examples. The Met's roster for 1984–5 included six ladies who made their débuts in the house between 1950 and 1959 and continue to take roles like Elsa, Clytemnestra and Lady Macbeth.

When the signs of wear and tear are unmistakable, singers can still prolong active life by choosing their remaining roles carefully – selecting those, for example, where an imposing stage presence, a flair for comedy, or sheer style of delivery can more than compensate for vocal deficiencies. It behoves them to avoid roles in which, while the voice may convince, the looks simply cannot. Less and less is it acceptable for sopranos to appear older than their purported fathers or romantic leads to resemble paedophiles; Cio-Cio-Sans rarely look anything like fifteen, but they need not be permitted to look fifty. Not long before her retirement, Beverly Sills faced facts squarely: 'It once took two and a half hours to make me up as Elizabeth I in her sixties and only a half-hour to turn me into a seventeen-year-old Manon. Now it's the other way round. . . . That's the way the cooky crumbles.' Baritones are luckier in this respect, as Norman Bailey points out, than either sopranos or tenors: 'As a baritone you start off in your twenties playing men of fifty or sixty, and there comes a point in your life when you grow into it. . . . The tenor is going the other way: he is usually playing the romantic hero, and there comes a point when time is fighting against him – same for the soprano. Whereas time is working for the baritone. . . . There comes a point when you fit the roles and, if one's been sensible, the voice has survived and one can give the ideal combined performance.'

To go out gracefully is an art (one which some singers seem determined to master by long practice), and a wise and compassionate manager who can assist in this process here earns again every percentage he has ever taken. Matthew Epstein: 'You try to advise them to be conservative about what they do, so that they don't expose their weaknesses, and when it's really at the end you try to make them finish their career in a distinguished way, as opposed to a way that is going to debase them. A big mistake is for a singer to return to the stage ten years too late in a role they sang with great fame twenty years before. Better for them to do something new that is perhaps a little less demanding and do it with distinction and then say farewell while they're still on a high level.'

III

THE CONDUCTOR

PREVIOUS PAGE Otto Klemperer holding a rehearsal for *Fidelio* on the stage at Covent Garden (1969).

8

Conducting Opera

The qualities which go to make a good opera conductor are much the same as those which make a good symphonic conductor. He needs on the one hand inspirational insight into the meaning of the music backed up by a thorough grasp of the methods by which it has been expressed, and on the other hand the personality to communicate these discoveries to other musicians and the technique to control their re-expression – allowing for the fact that in opera some of these musicians are actors as well, and the technique required to manipulate them is rather different. Not surprisingly, therefore, many of the most eminent opera conductors are also distinguished symphonic conductors – Carlos Kleiber, Claudio Abbado, Riccardo Muti, Sir Colin Davis, Herbert von Karajan, Sir Georg Solti, James Levine and perhaps half a dozen others. Every opera company, given a choice, will opt for these names and many go to considerable lengths to secure them as guests. Claudio Abbado: 'I invite the best. To get Carlos Kleiber to conduct at La Scala, I changed my plans twice. We were going to do *Otello* with me and *Tristan* with him, but I saw he wanted to do *Otello*, so I quickly offered him *Otello* and decided to conduct something else myself – it was more important for the opera house to get the best conductors.'

Unfortunately like star singers, 'star' conductors are in short supply and acute demand. Most have time-consuming commitments – as music director or principal conductor – to symphony orchestras; and there is the added disincentive that opera is financially unrewarding for conductors – 'an absolutely non-profit-making occupation', in the words of Raymond Leppard. They are generally paid, like singers, per performance; a week spent rehearsing one opera, or even a week in which there are two performances of an opera, pays considerably less than a week in which, as freelances in the symphonic world, they might undertake three concerts with six hours' rehearsal each and four recording sessions.

Given the difficulty of ensuring a constant but varied succession of distinguished guests, responsibility for maintaining high musical standards rests ever more heavily on the house's permanent music director. If a much sought-after artist is to tie himself to a single house, he is likely to expect to be able to exercise his own tastes and talents – which entails a partial surrender of the general manager's autonomy (a sacrifice which Sir Rudolf Bing, for one, opposed on

principle). Claudio Abbado makes no bones about the appeal of the post of music director: 'First, you can plan for many years in advance; and second, you can plan works you like.' For La Scala, where he has been Music Director since 1972, this has meant festivals of Mussorgsky – in 1981 – and Debussy (planned for 1986), and the injection into its repertoire of an unprecedented proportion of twentieth-century works – not merely those which are already recognised as classics (*Erwartung*, *Lulu*, *The Rake's Progress*, *Oedipus Rex*), but recent works by Stockhausen (*Donnerstag aus Licht*), Berio (*La vera storia*), Ligeti (*Le Grand Macabre*), Penderecki (*Paradise Lost*) and Nono (*Il gran sole carico d'amore*). 'I think we have a duty to play modern music – not just because I like it! – just as in the last century it was important to play Beethoven and Verdi. The difficult thing today is to identify who will be seen as the great composers in fifty years' time. It's easy today to say that Berg or Stravinsky or Bartók are great, practically classic, composers: thirty or forty years ago it wasn't so easy.' For Vienna, where he takes up the post of Music Director in the 1986–7 season, Abbado's taste for experiment will mean the introduction of some of the lesser-known French and Italian repertoire, previously neglected in favour of German opera and the most popular works of all nationalities.

Early in his association with the Met, James Levine, frustrated by his meagre influence as a guest, was clear that he wanted the post of Music Director, as without its authority he could not hope

Sir Georg Solti, 1985

to have any real impact on the house's musical identity. Since his appointment to the position in 1976 (and particularly during the years of his collaboration with John Dexter, Director of Productions from 1976 to 1981), he has put his own stamp on the Met's somewhat conservative repertoire with pieces such as *Rise and Fall of the City of Mahagonny* and *Dialogues of the Carmelites*. On the other side of the nineteenth-century core repertoire he has added *Idomeneo* and *La Clemenza di Tito* to the Mozart works usually performed, and made way for Handel opera to appear at the Met for the first time in a hundred years. Almost more remarkable, in a house that is particularly sensitive to the time of curtain fall (with stage crew and orchestra eligible for substantial overtime, and an audience anxious to get cars out of car parks and still get home before midnight), he has established a convention that major works, however long, shall be performed uncut – *Parsifal, Don Carlos, La Forza del Destino, Die Meistersinger* – and in editions as authentic as may be established. At Covent Garden, the fifteen years of Sir Colin Davis's tenure have seen productions (most of them new) of virtually all the major works of the three composers with whose music he is perhaps most closely associated – Mozart, Berlioz and Sir Michael Tippett.

But while choice of repertoire undoubtedly helps to characterise a house, many Music Directors see their prime concern, whatever the works being played, as the calibre and consistency of orchestra, chorus, contract singers and, indirectly, the guest singers to whom invitations are extended. Within the limits of the money allocated, the physical facilities of the house, the rehearsal time available, and the union regulations which govern the working of chorus and orchestra, each Music Director tries to create a permanent musical framework of the highest possible quality within which soloists may be displayed to best advantage. In the larger international houses, which tend to have their principals in common, the quality and character of orchestra and chorus may be the main distinguishing feature.

Every Music Director is responsible for the direction of musical policy (including repertoire and casting), the administration of musical activities, the preparation of orchestra, chorus and singers, and the overall standard of musical performance in his house. In determining policy he confers principally with his General Administrator and, where available, the Director of Productions. In his other duties he works through a team of administrative and musical assistants without whom he would have the time neither to prepare the operas he himself conducts, nor to supervise preparations for those conducted by others.

Companies may vary slightly in their musical organisation, but generally speaking every Music Director will have one or more administrative assistants responsible for the detailed scheduling of the house's musical preparations. In some houses music rehearsals and production rehearsals are interspersed, running parallel to the point where the conductor's and producer's efforts *must* be combined – rehearsal on stage with the orchestra. In other houses, and perhaps more usually, music rehearsal largely precedes production rehearsals. In broad outline, a typical rehearsal schedule for a new production might run:

TYPE OF REHEARSAL	VENUE	PRESIDING	ACCOMPANYING
MUSIC (individual, ensemble and chorus)	rehearsal rooms	music staff (& some-times con-ductor)	music staff & piano
PRODUCTION	rehearsal stage or rooms	producer	music staff & piano
PRODUCTION	stage	producer	music staff & piano
SITZPROBE (a full reading of the score without staging)	stage	conductor	conductor & orchestra
ORCHESTRAL STAGE	stage	conductor (producer present)	conductor & orchestra
PIANO DRESS	stage	producer	music staff & piano
ORCHESTRAL DRESS	stage	conductor (producer present)	conductor & orchestra
GENERAL DRESS	stage	conductor (producer present)	conductor & orchestra

Etiquette (and practicality) demands that rehearsals on stage with the piano are the producer's, but that once the orchestra is present, the conductor is in control.

The Music Director will also have a musical support staff responsible for the implementation of the plans. Many have a corps of staff conductors at their disposal – junior, usually younger, conductors whose function is largely one of filling gaps: preparing the orchestra for guests whose time at the house is limited, conducting less prestigious revivals, and stepping in to take isolated performances which the principal conductors cannot fulfil. In 1984 Covent Garden announced for 1986–7 the creation of a post roughly intermediate between the Music Director and the staff conductor: as 'Principal Conductor', Jeffrey Tate will regularly be available to the house for far longer (sixteen weeks a year) than the average guest. But

having assisted Solti, Boulez, Levine and Kempe in the course of his six-year career, he can offer more experience and expertise than any apprentice, and will expect and be expected to conduct both revivals and new productions. (He will already have conducted his first new production at Covent Garden by the time he takes up his appointment – Strauss's *Ariadne auf Naxos* in June 1985.)

The music director generally administers the orchestra through an orchestra director, and the chorus through a chorus master. The bulk of the musical preparation of soloists, both guests and company singers, he achieves through his music staff – usually trained pianists, with additional experience of voice-training and conducting, who have a variety of duties wide enough to qualify them for the title of 'musical odd-jobmen' around the house. But the surest way for the Music Director to monitor the standards which he has set for orchestra and chorus is for him to conduct a high proportion of performances himself. Sir Colin Davis, for example, contracted to conduct twenty-five performances a year at Covent Garden, regularly conducts between forty and fifty – between a third and half of all the performances put on in his house. Failure to conduct anything resembling that proportion has contributed significantly to the ill-feeling (press, public and governmental) which has effectively removed successive *Generalmusikdirektor*s of the Vienna State Opera; until his resignation in 1984, Lorin Maazel was paid considerably more than a quarter of a million pounds a year to conduct approximately an eighth of all performances in Vienna (whereas Claudio Abbado has agreed to conduct a minimum of two new productions plus twenty-five other performances there, and to forego conducting opera anywhere outside Vienna for the duration of his five-year appointment). James Levine, on the other hand, is sometimes accused of monopolising performances at the Met. In the 1984–5 season, for example, he was scheduled to conduct three out of the four new productions, and ten out of the total of twenty-two productions (including all the Wagner and Berg, and none of the Puccini or Strauss). His critics complain that he offers little scope or incentive to guest conductors of the highest quality; his riposte is that it is his duty to spend two thirds of his time in New York, giving his virtually undivided attention and guidance to his company – the only safe prescription for consistency.

With the best will in the world, though, not even James Levine could conduct all the performances under his aegis – which brings the opera house full circle to confront the original problem, the one that the creation of the post of music director was in part designed to solve: how to ensure the musical quality of its performances given the difficulty of procuring a steady flow of good guest conductors.

It is ironic that even were year-round houses invariably able to secure the world's greatest conductors, they would be unable to make use of them in more than a

OPPOSITE Sir Colin Davis in music rehearsals for *La Traviata* (Covent Garden, 1985).

fraction of their productions. The problem is one of time, and the circumstances in which performances often take place in international houses. The Orchestra Director of Covent Garden, Bram Gay, remembers, for example, Carlos Kleiber telling the players, 'There are two versions of *Otello* – one you can have this evening, the other takes three weeks to rehearse. It's a different approach from us both.' Neither Kleiber nor any of the half-dozen other most sought-after opera conductors will ever settle for the approach which produces quick results. Most will insist not only on adequate (lengthy) rehearsal, but on having considerable discretion in the choice of singers, producer and designer and all will stipulate that the whole cast, including international stars, should be present throughout the rehearsal period. From the beginning of his career, Claudio Abbado has set his face against working under the conditions imposed by the deadly combination of the repertory system and the exigencies of the star singer's overcrowded schedule. 'When I was a young conductor, they asked me to conduct with two rehearsals, only seeing the singers at the last moment. I always refused. It was difficult at the very beginning. I got maybe two concerts and one opera in a year, and I had a family with two children. So I had to teach in a conservatory. For that time I didn't have enough money for my family – but I got time to study. . . . I don't accept the star system – I don't like it. It could be one of the reasons I've never worked with some of the famous singers who have marvellous voices but no time for rehearsals. Domingo, Pavarotti or Carreras will work for weeks with me on a new production – or if they won't, I don't accept the job.'

That Claudio Abbado should choose to make a stand over this issue is thoroughly understandable. But only a festival house, or one with a season of no more than four or five operas, could afford to give each work rehearsal this thorough. As Sir John Tooley points out, if he attempted to meet the needs of an Abbado, a Muti, a Kleiber, a Solti, simultaneously or in quick succession, 'the system would collapse'. A considerable proportion of performances must be put on with more or less limited rehearsal, in conditions under which the eminent maestro will not operate and, at the other end of the spectrum, the young and inexperienced conductor, however gifted, *cannot* operate. (The present scarcity of opera conductors has a good deal to do with the fact that music colleges have offered little systematic training specifically for opera, and that unless the aspiring conductor is prepared to follow the long and laborious route of the répétiteur, opportunities for 'on the job' training are severely limited.)

So for these productions the administrator must look to the kind of conductor who is both willing and able to walk into an orchestra pit, pick up the baton, and conduct an orchestra, chorus and soloists whom he has not chosen and has rehearsed little if at all – a task he often carries off not just to the satisfaction but often the delight of a paying public. Some of these are distinguished musicians who genuinely enjoy the 'one-off' occasion, others are most often referred to as *routiniers* – competent professionals who can be relied upon to produce a respectable performance under virtually any conditions and are rarely expected to do more.

Either way, without them the opera world could not survive: the 'instant opera' on which the bigger European repertory houses primarily subsist requires skilled technicians, not interpreters whose profundities take weeks to crystallise. At the Bayerische Staatsoper in Munich, for example, for an isolated performance of a production that has been in the repertoire for some time, the principal guest singers are required by their contracts to arrive the day before the performance for a three-hour rehearsal in the morning (largely devoted to the music), and another in the afternoon (largely devoted to the staging). Both will be in the set, on a rehearsal stage, but neither will be with the orchestra or chorus, since nightly performances and the rehearsals for new productions account for virtually all the man-hours permitted by union rules.

By rights, performances this hastily assembled should be disastrous. But Sir Charles Mackerras – who as First Conductor for three years at the Hamburg Staatsoper (one of Germany's largest and busiest companies) and Music Director of Sadler's Wells/English National Opera from 1970 to 1977 has had wide experience of the problems of casting conductors – makes a persuasive case for their worth. 'Incredible as it may seem, these performances can and do attain absolute greatness. I'm often impressed by how little difference there is between well-rehearsed performances and unrehearsed performances. It is all a question of the chemistry or atmosphere generated. Success depends on each and every one of the participants knowing what he or she is doing on the night. Singers will often know the standard roles so well, and so fixedly, that rehearsal will make little difference to their performance. 'A good baritone or soprano can walk into the standard production of *Don Giovanni* and give his or her interpretation of Giovanni or Donna Anna or Elvira without any difficulty, musically or dramatically. . . . I have conducted performances of *Don Giovanni* in Hamburg which had absolutely superb casts, in which there was no proper rehearsal; they rehearsed the ensembles and the production the day before, they "marked" the arias, sorted out the tempi and the breathing. . . . You can write a lot of things into the score – you'll find my scores of *Butterfly* and *Pagliacci* and *Don Giovanni* have people's names in them – "Slower for X" or "Hold that phrase for Miss Y" – lots of name-dropping in my scores . . .' Ideally the conductor would

Sir Charles Mackerras during rehearsals for *Semele* (Covent Garden, 1982).

prefer to have had the chance to blend their voices perfectly beforehand, but as
Sir Charles points out, this is not always possible even with ample rehearsal time,
given that many singers prefer not to use their full voice until the performance
itself. He might also prefer the singers to have tested the acoustic of the auditorium
before the night itself; for a Radames to make his first entrance and immediately
have to sing 'Celeste Aida' in an unfamiliar auditorium is unquestionably an ordeal
– but it is one that would be only marginally alleviated by rehearsal.

Similarly, an experienced opera orchestra will not necessarily need rehearsal for
every performance. 'Lots of operas play themselves. . . . For a standard opera, an
opera about which there is no argument as to the right interpretation, an orchestra
is expected to be able to play it without rehearsal . . . Wagner, Puccini, Strauss
– where there is no doubt about the style – can be done all the time without
rehearsal. In German-speaking places an opera like *Dutchman* which is an easy one
to play, or *Traviata*, will never be rehearsed in twenty years in spite of the fact
that the orchestra personnel is constantly changing. A conductor, if he's good,
ought to be able to get an excellent performance. The special things that certain
conductors bring to certain works can be done by their personality more than
by rehearsal. . . . The conductor *is* still an interpreter in these situations – every
conductor, by his sheer emanations, is an interpreter. If I stand up and conduct
one phrase, it's going to be different from any other conductor conducting the
same phrase. It's that emanation of the personality which is the true art of the
conductor, in symphony or opera, but particularly in opera, his ability to put over
his view of the work by his gestures and without talking. . . . The whole art of
doing opera properly is a mixture, the right mixture of inspiration, idealism and
pragmatism. The total pragmatist fails – and so does the total idealist. The best
opera animal, whether administrator, conductor, player, singer or producer, is the
person with the ideal mixture – setting himself ideals, but seeing what the practical
problems are going to be.'

The major practical problem is exclusive to opera. As the only person who can
see and hear all the other performers, both in the pit and on the stage, the conductor
is the lynchpin of an opera performance, and he requires considerable technical
skill simply to coordinate the forces under his control. Some conductors (Klaus
Tennstedt, for instance) feel that opera is easier to conduct in musical terms because
the text is there to help one form an interpretation, whereas for a symphony there
is no such outside assistance. Few, however, would disagree that opera is technically more difficult – as Sir Colin Davis puts it, 'In the theatre you've got to have
a technique – if a bloke hasn't, there's hell to pay.'

The principal problem is a geographical one – that of bridging the gulf between
stage and pit. Placido Domingo, a relatively recent arrival on the international
conducting scene, graphically describes the sensation: 'It's like being a Roman
gladiator with one leg in one chariot pulled by a hundred horses in one direction,
and the other in another chariot pulled by another hundred horses in a different
direction!' The situation is made no easier when the orchestral 'horses' are not

Don Giovanni, produced by Ruth Berghaus for Welsh National Opera, with an on-stage band providing the music for dancing at Don Giovanni's house (1984).

only pulling in different directions, but widely scattered to start with; the conductor may on occasion be required to synchronise the orchestra in the pit, musicians back-stage, and an on-stage band or bands, the counterpoint between the various forces being crucial not only in musical terms but also to the drama. In *Gloriana*, for example, the formal *coranto* played and danced on stage to celebrate the reconciliation of Essex with his Queen after his appointment as Lord Deputy of Ireland is gradually drowned by an ominous swelling orchestral accompaniment which more accurately reflects his ambitions and the doomed nature of the relationship. This kind of additional complexity has been eased by the advent of closed-circuit television which has revolutionised the art of backstage conducting by enabling the offstage conductor, with the principal conductor's image on a screen before him, to face the musicians he is directing rather than crick his neck to peer sideways through a strategically-placed slit in a curtain or flat. Nevertheless it still requires considerable concentration, as Martin Handley – now Chorus Master at English National Opera but once himself a *répétiteur* – explains: 'It gradually dawns on you that you have to beat in advance of the conductor because of the time-lag between pit and stage – and how much in advance depends on the conductor. Any orchestra will play for some conductors on the beat, for others after the beat, because of their stick technique.'

Mark Elder, Music Director of English National Opera, conducting a rehearsal of *Mazeppa* (1984).

In earlier times, the conductor squared up to the challenge from the position now occupied by the prompt box, right up against the stage and facing the singers, with his back to the orchestra for all except the overture and the purely orchestral interludes – and at times conductors might wish this were still practicable. In such contentious areas as the duration of high notes or the degree of *rubato* (or rhythmic freedom) that is desirable, it can be difficult for the conductor at the back of the pit to communicate his wishes if the singer prefers to evade his eye. The conductor must both curb and cater for his singers without neglecting his orchestra and the detail of the orchestral contribution to the score. Orchestral players not unnaturally resent being treated as little more than a collective rehearsal piano – and more importantly, the full wealth of the piece is not exploited if the conductor concentrates too closely on the voices.

Unlike a concert programme, an evening of opera is an organic unity, and the conductor must manipulate it accordingly. Jane Glover: 'You're not doing a bit of this, that and the other – you're pacing something from seven-thirty till ten-thirty, you are actually structuring a whole evening. You can be an architect as well as a painter.' And within the overall framework, he (or she) must know how to pace the music from moment to moment, often in accordance with non-musical criteria, amongst which Nicholas Cleobury lists the speed with which the drama is unfolding, the evolution of character and the mechanics of performance – the time which is physically necessary to allow a character to make his exit, or a dress to be tried on or a duel fought convincingly. Constructing a ballet sequence requires a particular discipline from the conductor, since a dancer can remain airborne for only so long. The moulding of a whole evening demands remarkable concentration and stamina, emotional and physical; one medium-length Wagner opera is the equivalent of two and a half concerts, and Sir Georg Solti has complained about Wagner's tendency to save his most passionate climaxes until near the end of the evening, when the conductor has already been exerting himself for four hours.

Perhaps most importantly, the opera conductor has not only to lead, to provide the pulse of the performance, but also be able and willing to accompany – to use the orchestra sensitively and unselfishly in support of the singer and not in competition. Linda Esther Gray comments: 'I think the conductor's job is to make the orchestra give the flavour of the piece. He should go in there to paint the colours that I need for you to understand Isolde.' To accompany the voice, the conductor needs himself to understand what it can do and what it cannot – and it is here that experience as *répétiteur* or accompanist can be invaluable. Many conductors will breathe the roles with their singers, so as neither to rush nor overstretch the vocal line, nor punctuate the accompaniment with breaks or pauses in conflicting places. The exigencies of different languages must be acknowledged; generally

OPPOSITE The conductor's beat is relayed by closed-circuit television from the pit to the off-stage band during a performance of *La Traviata* (Covent Garden, 1985).

speaking, Italian and French may be sung more quickly than English and all three more quickly than German – Italian *secco* recitative, for example, will probably have to be slowed down if the words are sung in translation. Much as the conductor might wish, for the sake of naturalness and authenticity, to aim at the tempo of the language in which the opera was written, he must always make allowances for singers struggling with awkward consonants and diphthongs. Even where the opera is being sung in the original language, he must be prepared for the fact that a non-German may not be able to negotiate the hurdles of Wagner's German with as much facility as a native Bavarian.

The conductor must be able at any given moment to balance with the orchestra voices that may be moving round the stage, to regulate the volume of the orchestra so that the singer is free to interpret the role with as much subtlety as he or she wishes. This may be simply a question of holding the orchestral sound down, or encouraging it to play more softly sometimes than the marking in the score may indicate, but without any loss of expression – not an easy task, as Sir Charles Mackerras points out, particularly for the brass: 'Playing with the kind of accentuation and verve which you use when you see *forte*, but actually playing *piano* in terms of decibels is part of the art of operatic orchestral playing.' He adds that the conductor himself may unwittingly sabotage the orchestra's efforts at restraint: 'The conductor can really make a difference in performance to the balance and the loudness of the orchestra by not getting worked up, by maintaining a very calm stance even if the music is very passionate. . . . So many modern conductors really overdo it, throw themselves around and overconduct. No wonder the orchestra frequently plays too loudly'. Certainly Gwynne Howell finds that it does, and has learnt to modify his approach accordingly: 'In a concert it's all focused on the voice – you can use a tremendous range of technique. In the pit the conductor is very near the whole sound of the orchestra, it all gets a bit exciting, and the arms go a little bit broader, and the sound goes up another twenty decibels. . . . If the sound is down, you can do things on top of it. If it isn't, you're not aiming for too much subtlety, there's less room for it.' Hans Hotter once said that only under Rudolf Kempe could he start Wotan's monologue in Act Two of *Die Walküre* in a whisper.

Equally, achieving good balance may depend on creating an orchestral texture that is easy to sing through or over. Some instruments are more difficult to sing against than others – and not necessarily the louder ones. Sir Neville Marriner points up some interesting coincidences of timbre: 'Of a contralto you might say that the cellos and violas eat up her sound – cellos, violas, bassoons, clarinets, horns – very dangerous. They're all in the same part of the spectrum. You can have violins up at the top – no problem; and basses and trombones down at the bottom won't interfere. But all this stuff thick in the middle – it wipes the voices out.' (On the same principle, Andrew Lloyd Webber avoided scoring for violins in his *Requiem*, where the treble line is prominent.)

The other principal requirement of the opera conductor as accompanist is flexibility. Without losing control of the overall shaping of the piece, he must give his singers their head in some of its detail. José Carreras describes his ideal conductor as 'somebody who knows exactly what he wants, somebody who leads – but at the same time is flexible enough, and sensitive – that's what *I* want. To communicate with me, to give me the opportunity to communicate with the audience. To do music together – not to impose on each other.' This kind of empathy entails coming to terms with the fact that each performance may well be slightly different – obvious enough but not, in Linda Esther Gray's experience, as readily recognised as one might think: 'It has to be a *performance* – there's no point getting up there and singing it the same, night after night. With German conductors you have to adopt a different attitude – "Yes, sir, three bags full, sir, thank you very much, sir", and you do what they say. But in the end they're the losers because I'm not freed to give more than a crotchet-quaver performance. They all rehearse you to the nth degree to get it pretty perfect – but then the good ones let you go'. Sometimes it takes excellent reflexes to follow a singer's lead – 'boxer's reflexes', according to Sir Georg Solti. It is one of opera's occupational hazards that the singers are working from memory and are therefore more prone, under pressure, to skip bars, or miss cues, or run out of breath. Moreover, as an awesome quantity of anecdote testifies, there is an indefinite number of physical misfortunes that can befall the opera performer – scenery that buckles or totters or fails to enter or exit on cue, costumes that burst or snag or go up in flames, props that break or simply refuse to co-operate. As Mark Elder puts it, 'It involves the general life of the theatre . . . as opposed to the concert hall, where everybody is *still* and concentrating solely on an exclusively musical experience. You're dealing with the perverseness of the theatre.' Every opera conductor has to acknowledge and, if he can, accept the limitations of the medium – Claudio Abbado: 'I know they are trying to do their best, but it's usually about eighty per cent of what I look for. Maybe twenty per cent you have to forgive, no? You have to understand.'

9

Preparing the Music

When a conductor – Music Director or guest – commits himself to a new production of an opera, he begins to fulfil his responsibilities well before rehearsals start, because it is principally for him to determine the performing edition of the work. The scope of his responsibility for the notes which are actually performed is often surprising, extending as it does even to so-called standard works. Most composers – including those from the nineteenth and early twentieth centuries, let alone from the more distant past – have left at least one work in a form which requires some exercise of discretion. They have had second thoughts themselves, or have been required by popularist managements to make revisions, or have died leaving acts to be finished by others.

Is the conductor, for example, to prefer the first version of *Simon Boccanegra*, which Verdi considered 'monotonous and cold', or the 1881 revision stage-managed by Boito? Is he to perform *The Flying Dutchman* in its original condition, or in the rescoring which Wagner made three years later to bring the work into line with the thicker, lusher sound he had by then adopted? Should he honour Puccini's original intentions for *Madam Butterfly*, or abide by the judgement of the 1904 Milan audience that the piece did not work in two acts and that Pinkerton was excessively unsympathetic? Were Italian managements right to ask Verdi to reduce the five-act *Don Carlos* to suit audiences grown shy of the sheer scale and display to which nineteenth-century Parisians had been addicted? – and if they were, should the conductor follow Verdi in leaving out most of the first act, or evolve his own compromise? As Andrew Porter comments, 'Once the clock, local circumstances, or weaknesses and strengths of the original performers – rather than the composer's wish – are held responsible for aspects of an abridgement, the way is open for anyone to propose his own edition compiled from the surviving materials.' Thus for *Carmen* the conductor must decide whether he wants spoken or sung dialogue, and may choose between versions of *The Tales of Hoffmann* which differ in length, the number of acts, the order in which they are arranged, and the musical material of which they are constructed.

When it comes to opera of the baroque period, the conductor who is preparing his own edition is faced with far more radical and creative decisions. The works of Monteverdi and Cavalli, generally speaking, survive only as a vocal line or lines plus a bass line for realisation by continuo instruments – and opinion as to how precisely the accompaniment should be realised differs widely and passionately. Some musicians, most notably Raymond Leppard, believe these pieces should be adapted to present performing conditions and modern audiences; others do not. Whichever dogma he espouses, the conductor/editor must decide literally what notes should be played to support the vocal line, whether the harmonies should be major or minor, and what combination of instruments should be used.

Even where the notes themselves are not in doubt, as in Handel's operas, there remains the question of the voices best-suited to sing them: should the castrato be replaced by a counter-tenor? or by a mezzo-soprano? or even a tenor or baritone transposing the part? And the conductor must also formulate his views on ornamentation, unless (which is rare) he trusts his singers to decorate their own lines with skill and taste and in a consistent fashion. (Andrew Porter has written bitterly of ornamentation taken to the lengths of 'Mad Scenes from *The Messiah*'.) He need not necessarily work out and write down the details of every *appoggiatura* or trill, which can largely be determined in rehearsal with the singers, but the issue of whether or not the music of some composers (Mozart, for example) should be decorated at all is still hot enough to necessitate its being settled in advance.

In many operas where there can be no argument about either what composers wrote or what they might have hoped to hear in performance, traditions have grown up of disregarding their indications and cutting or altering the music they left. Cuts may be made in deference to less expansive modern tastes – with Handel and Donizetti as prime candidates – or 'for the sake of the drama': the arias of Marcellina and Basilio are almost always omitted from Act Four of *The Marriage of Figaro* on the grounds that they do not advance the action. Ferrando's aria 'Ah, lo veggio' is often cut from *Così fan tutte* for the rather more basic reason that it is long and difficult, one of the highest pieces Mozart ever wrote for a tenor. A less drastic, and less readily detectable solution to the problem of dangerously high *tessitura* is transposition. While it is no longer particularly respectable, it is by no means uncommon for a guest principal, especially a soprano or tenor (though, for example, the baritone role of Mandryka is regularly transposed) and especially in Donizetti or Bellini, to require that a whole aria be transposed down a semitone, even a tone, to avoid an uncomfortable top note. Probably only those in the audience with perfect pitch or tuning forks will notice, but any member of an international opera orchestra can tell you which singers have still got infallible top notes and which have not: the degree of the singer's popularity will determine the extent of the orchestra's indiscretion. In a slightly different category is the type of contemporary work where the composer has allowed for a certain leeway. Hans Werner Henze specifically provides for an element of improvisation in some of his opera and music-theatre work; and John Barker, head of Covent Garden's Music Department, has described the task of preparing for the Royal Opera House's production of Stockhausen's *Donnerstag aus Licht* as less one of establishing an edition than of drawing up an order of events.

The growing insistence in musicological circles on *Werktreue*, or 'fidelity to the work' has made it unfashionable in recent years to permit cuts or transposition. Another area of conflict between pragmatists and purists is that of instrumentation. Some of the most successful composers for the theatre were often impractical or careless in their scoring. Sir Charles Mackerras has commented on Janáček's tendency to score for high strings and low brass with little in the middle registers – an exciting sound, but one that is hard to sing through, and he will retouch the instrumentation if he thinks it will improve the balance in live performance. Even worse offenders, in his opinion, are some of the Italians 'who you might think would be the great lovers of *bel canto*. You'd expect Wagner with his immense orchestration, or Strauss, to be the difficult ones, but in fact Donizetti is the most difficult of all to balance – great thick blaring masses of brass. Normally one doesn't like to change a composer's work, even if in some cases it's mistaken, but I sometimes prune Donizetti because his orchestration is fairly primitive.' Sir Neville Marriner agrees on the need both to do it and to do it with circumspection: 'Most composers were aware of how to write for the voice – it means knowing exactly what the problems are. The soprano may be very happy working around the top of her voice but suddenly, for musical and dramatic reasons, the composer will drop her down an octave and a half – most sopranos will be groaning around

in the depths, with very much less sound. Usually composers will orchestrate accordingly. If they haven't – if they're a bit routine, Donizettis who weren't expecting much out of the pit anyway – you may yourself have to change it. It's one of the very small basic responsibilities. Take out, say, one bassoon, one cello, one bass. . . . If you look through your scores, you'll find quite often the composer has written '*A due*', 'both' – both bassoons are playing the same line just to get a strong sound. If it's not going to work in the theatre, take one out – you still get the same composite sound but softer. . . . You wouldn't change the dis-

Sir Neville Marriner, 1985

position of notes, though; you wouldn't give a bassoon line to a flute. Even though you *can* improve on a composer's scoring in practical terms, as soon as you do it, it doesn't sound like the composer any more – you've lost it. You can make it work, but it doesn't sound right.'

The conductor may equally become aware of his responsibility for safeguarding the authentic voice of the composer where a piece is to be performed in a language other than the original, because in a house that puts a high premium on dramatic impact and intelligibility, it may be considered necessary to alter the music to fit and serve the translation. Some musicians regard any such interference as quite unacceptable, another good argument for performing operas only in the original; while a less extreme school of thought concedes that altering note-values to mirror the scansion of a word can sometimes be necessary, but would limit this to recitative and would certainly not contemplate tampering with pitch. But the most dedicated advocates of opera in translation, like Mark Elder, assert: 'We should be prepared to make much more radical changes to the Holy Writ of the composer than is generally held to be the case. There is nothing worse for me than to be told by translators, as I have been in the past, "There it is – and I haven't changed a single note", as if that is the acme of achievement in translation. My heart sinks. The public couldn't care a damn. What they want is something that they can respond to and be moved by, they want naturalness and honesty and truth – they don't care if it's two semiquavers or three. . . .' When performing *Pelléas and Mélisande*, for example, Mark Elder was confronted with the problem of reproducing in English speech rhythms which in the original French were both natural and conversational, and subtly poetic. 'What we had to do was to produce an entirely new vocal score. Almost every bar there were major changes to the music – mostly in the rhythm, but sometimes in pitch once the rhythm had been changed.'

If the conductor is preparing for a production at a house which has a music department, he will have been conferring from the outset with the head of music. At Covent Garden, John Barker describes his job as one of informing the conductor of the edition which the house normally uses, finding out whether he intends to use this edition and, if not, establishing what he *is* going to do. It is then his responsibility to ensure that, well in advance of rehearsals, the conductor's full score, orchestral parts, vocal parts and choral parts are all consistent and clearly marked up.

The actual music may be supplied from a variety of sources. When the changes the conductor has made to a work are extensive and thoroughgoing enough to constitute his own edition, he may supply both full score and parts himself. (In recent years, for example, Jesus Lopez Cobos has produced his own edition of *Lucia di Lammermoor*, and Sir Charles Mackerras an edition of *Don Giovanni* for Welsh National Opera in 1984, the latter incorporating long-held views on Mozartian ornamentation.) The house obviously receives the benefits of any discoveries the conductor may have made and the novelty value of a new edition; but this arrangement has the practical disadvantage that copyright in that edition of the piece now rests with the conductor and when his run of performances is finished, he is entitled to take the music away with him or to require that a fee be paid for its subsequent use. In the circumstances it may be simpler for the house to revert to the edition it has used most often before. Covent Garden, for example, revived *Lucia di Lammermoor* in 1985 with Dame Joan Sutherland, and Richard Bonynge reverted to the more familiar Ricordi edition of the score.

Where a visiting conductor is Music Director of another opera house, he may bring that house's musical material with him, already marked up to save time; Claudio Abbado has occasionally travelled with La Scala's music, for example, and Sir Colin Davis with Covent Garden's. Alternatively, he may ask the house to hire from the publisher the set of parts that he used last time he conducted the opera, wherever that might have been. Otherwise he will give instructions for the marking of the house parts, which may be either owned or hired. Most year-round houses will have invested in their own materials for any work in the standard repertoire that is out of copyright, but a significant proportion of the operatic repertoire – including some works out of copyright – can still only be hired. (Vocal scores with piano reduction may be on sale, but not the full score, nor the orchestral or choral parts.) Some publishers – Ricordi, for example – may reserve a set of material for one company's exclusive use so that its markings need not be put in anew every time, but will nevertheless retain ownership.

Once the music has been procured, the music librarian and his or her staff take over. Cuts must be indicated, and the singers notified before they start their preparations for their roles. Where a translation is being used, this must be copied into the vocal parts and the consequent adjustments made to the music. All the material must be checked for accuracy, in particular the choral parts which are often in old-fashioned editions, carelessly printed: some give just the individual section's line, and offer only word cues for the other lines with no indication of pitch. Some conductors will require bowings and phrasings to be written into the music in advance, and may send a set of the first-desk string parts with markings to be copied into the rest of the material. Others prefer to evolve these and other details, like tempi and dynamics, in the course of rehearsals by consultation with the players. Sir Colin Davis: 'That's part of the fun of rehearsal. After all, they do play the fiddle slightly better than I do. . . .'

Throughout all these preparations, conductor, music department and librarian, in international houses at least, have to face the fact that all their efforts may be negated at the last moment by bad luck. If the house is using anything other than a standard edition of a work and one of the principal singers falls ill and is unable to perform, it is all too likely that their replacement, having learned the more familiar version of the part, will be unable to meet the conductor's requirements. Music lovingly restored to a work after seventy or 170 years of neglect will have to be cut again at four hours' notice to suit the incoming soloist, and messages left on every stand to notify the orchestra that tonight it will be business as usual. . . .

10

The Orchestra

The unilateral decision to alter the music two or three hours before a performance is just one of many minor indignities which threaten the self-esteem of the orchestral player in the opera house, fostering the feeling that his contribution is secondary – an evaluation that Bram Gay is quick to refute: 'I don't believe it's possible to have first-rate opera with a second-rate orchestra. As Riccardo Muti says, "The score is all that the composer left us, everything else we make up – and the score is with *us* in the pit. If it's good here in the pit, assuming a minimum level of casting they can't spoil it up there. If it's bad down here, they can't save it."'

The pit, however, can pose problems. Working, as it were, 'below stairs', largely unacknowledged by a public intent on stage, stars and lights, itself depresses many musicians coming from symphony to opera, and their gloom is often deepened by physical discomfort. Space may be cramped – Glyndebourne, for example, on a Strauss night – and the players are vulnerable to dust and splinters dislodged by the performers overhead, or props accidentally scattered from the stage: any producer who makes great play with liquid in his staging, be it water, blood, champagne, whisky or milk punch, is likely to be unpopular with players who have valuable instruments to protect.

Sound in the pit is inevitably 'boxier' than in the concert hall, and there can be problems of balance and ensemble within the orchestra. The arrangement of the players usually differs from the conventional symphonic placings; at Covent Garden, for instance, the brass section is split, with the trumpets and trombones on the extreme right of the conductor, horns on the extreme left (all facing inwards, so that the full force of their sound is not directed straight into the auditorium). While the double basses and percussion provide a rhythmic link across the pit, few of the brass players can hear each other clearly in these conditions, and precise ensemble is hard. On occasion the players may not even all be within the pit – the offstage trumpet player who heralds the arrival of Don Fernando in *Fidelio*, for example, or the tuba who represents the foghorn in the third act of *Peter Grimes*.

An almost more serious threat to morale is the element of monotony which it is hard for the most adventurous of companies to avoid. Any orchestra in a year-round house is bound, even on the *stagione* system, to repeat certain works for box office reasons from season to season; in a repertory house it may be from month to month. It is not inconceivable that a player who has been in an opera orchestra for twenty-five years may be on to his four- or five-hundredth *Carmen* or *La Traviata*. For an inexperienced or mediocre conductor that can be a boon – Bram Gay explains: 'The players know their job, they know the pieces, they know the house, they know the cast, half of them could sing the works. . . . The orchestra could get a complete idiot through quite a lot of operas provided they liked him – and provided they thought he wasn't coming back. They wouldn't encourage an idiot if they thought Covent Garden would give him to them again.' An orchestra which has played Puccini under twenty different conductors and with fifty different casts is thoroughly accustomed to his persistent use of *rubato* and singers' methods of dealing with it, and will be at least as quick as the conductor in fielding a piece of spin-bowling from the stage. For the players themselves, however, constant repetition can deaden their response to the music to the point where only the most distinguished conductors can overcome their indifference.

Professional indifference is often maintained to be an inevitable corollary of union-isation in the performing arts. Many of those in the 'upper' echelons of opera – administrators, conductors, producers, etc. – occasionally feel that their efforts to achieve the highest artistic standards are undermined by organised mercenariness and a stifling insistence on the letter of union law. John Schlesinger is particularly disturbed by what he sees as the prevalent attitude: 'There is a huge difference between the film business and the opera world on the administrative side. I can't see the technicians in a film ever turning off the lights because it's one o'clock. I find it absolutely ludicrous that you're on the last page of an act – and suddenly the musicians have packed up and gone because it's lunch time. Absolutely appall-ing, unthinkable.' Sir Charles Mackerras, while acknowledging the readiness of managements to take advantage of a sense of vocation unless checked, regrets the vehemence of the union counterattack: 'I think the trouble with unions in artistic ventures is that they tend to give conditions of work greater priority than the work itself, which can't help but reduce standards to a certain extent.'

As far as the opera orchestra is concerned, unionisation has two consequences that undoubtedly affect artistic standards. Union members have fought for and secured a degree of job security which ensures that some players are retained past the time at which, in an open market, they would have been replaced. The problem is perhaps at its most pronounced in Germany where many opera orchestras have effectual life tenure; at the Deutsche Oper in West Berlin, a heavily subsidised house, orchestral musicians have the virtual status of civil servants, entitled to work in the house until retirement – and the Intendant, Götz Friedrich, estimated in 1983 that his orchestra contained some ten per cent of 'dead wood'. It is a prob-lem he shares with his American counterparts, obliged since the legislation of the

OPPOSITE Giorgio Zancanaro takes his curtain call over the heads of the double-bass section of the orchestra at Covent Garden after a performance of *Andrea Chénier* (1985).

Carter administration on the retirement age to accord tenure to orchestral musicians until they are seventy years old.

But it is the limits imposed by union regulations on the orchestra's working week that have produced the most bizarre effects – resulting in many houses in a system of rotating players from rehearsal to rehearsal. Most year-round houses need to schedule more sessions per week (rehearsals or performances) than any one set of musicians is permitted to play. The solution is to have at one's disposal more players than will be needed on any one occasion and to call different players for different sessions. The Met, for example, with a basic orchestra of about ninety-two, has a pool of about two hundred extra players available, some hundred of whom are called upon regularly. New York City Opera, with an orchestra of fifty-nine and ten extras, rotates its players principally at weekends when a total of five performances in three days often proves too taxing, particularly for the brass section. Both houses, however, abide by the principle, enforced with varying degrees of rigour, that the musicians who play the performances of a piece should have attended a reasonable proportion of the rehearsals. This practice, however obviously desirable it might seem, is not always followed in the busier repertory houses, particularly in Germany and Austria, with predictable results. The consequences can be particularly dire for contemporary works where the orchestra is not merely rehearsing but learning the piece, as Nicholas Maw discovered when his opera *The Rising of the Moon* was given its German and Austrian premières. 'In Austria and Germany each player only has to do six sessions a week, as a result of union agreements. You can't put on an opera every night and then rehearse new productions if you only have eighteen hours playing out of your orchestra, so you have to have two sets of players. But do you have a separate orchestra A and orchestra B? No, you do not, you have a terrible mix-up of the two, so you never know who you've got in the pit. They may have learned it, or they may not. . . . At the dress rehearsal I was practically in tears, I'd never heard such a mess – and bear in mind that I was lucky to have the same orchestra for the dress rehearsal as I was going to have for the first performance. This is exactly the kind of situation described by Berlioz 140 years ago.'

These are all problems which can to some extent be alleviated by the conductor. At the most severely practical level, he can insist that the orchestra remain consistent enough throughout the rehearsal period to receive and transmit his interpretation as a unified body. Carlos Kleiber, for example, will not countenance any rotation whatsoever, and will expect precisely the same players at every rehearsal and at all the performances. One of Sir Colin Davis's most significant and durable achievements at Covent Garden has been to make this luxury available to every visiting conductor, not merely by using extra players on a temporary basis but by enlarging the regular orchestra to the point where it can offer both opera and ballet companies a constant force for each production. This has been expensive – it has entailed, for example, the addition of an extra desk of two players at the top of each string section and the doubling of principals in the wind, brass and percussion – but in terms of artistic standards, the investment has already shown returns.

To improve morale and counteract the *longueurs* of repertory, the conductor may encourage his players to undertake as much non-operatic work as they can combine with their duties to the opera house. For the orchestra of La Scala, for example, Claudio Abbado has formed the Scala Philharmonic Orchestra which plays a number of symphony concerts every year as an independent entity. He has also encouraged the orchestra to play as much chamber music as they have time for: when he first went to La Scala there was only one string quartet within the ranks of the orchestra – now there are several, plus quintets and octets, for brass and wind as well as strings.

Abbado, who for several years actually taught chamber music in a conservatory in Parma, believes very strongly that the chamber music approach should be applied even to music-making on the largest scale, and wherever possible welcomes the collaboration, and not merely the obedience, of his players. 'The players in the orchestra are good musicians, and one can always find something good to learn. I like it when they suggest musical points. . . . It's the same kind of collaboration as in a quartet' – an attitude likely to transform even the most routine of rehearsals for an orchestral player.

But ultimately the quickest way to an orchestra's heart may be to avoid over-rehearsal. Protracted rehearsal will obviously be acceptable if the piece is unfamiliar, or if the conductor has a completely novel conception of it, or if the orchestra considers him in some way extraordinary. Sir Reginald Goodall, for example, prefers an exceptionally long period of preparation, both vocal and orchestral, for his Wagner productions and most orchestras (though not necessarily most managements) are happy for him to be given as much time as he needs. Where none of these conditions applies, however, the orchestra may well feel with some justice that a lengthy rehearsal period is more for the benefit of the conductor than for themselves, and the extra time will not necessarily be productive. Some of the most experienced conductors prefer to take the risk of a short rehearsal period, in the expectation that improvements can be achieved just as easily during the run of performances with players who have not been staled by rehearsals they consider superfluous.

This much the conductor can do – but beyond a certain point the quality of an opera orchestra's life and the standard of its performances depend heavily both on its members' talents and on their attitude to their job. The Music Director can control the technical proficiency of his orchestra by recruiting players of the highest quality available. It has traditionally been assumed that the best players are most often found on the concert platform and not in the pit; no coincidence that the opera orchestra most often cited with awe, the Vienna State Opera, is a symphony orchestra (the Vienna Philharmonic) in another guise. In recent years, however, opera orchestras have sought out, and been preferred by, players of an increasingly high calibre. By the second year of his reign Sir Colin Davis had made a considerable number of changes in the Covent Garden roster, and since 1968 Claudio Abbado has replaced almost eighty per cent of La Scala's musicians. Comparison with symphony orchestras is, in any case, largely meaningless, because what is required of the opera orchestra is a difference in kind, not degree.

What makes a good opera orchestra? A great tradition is obviously an advantage, and a feeling of identification with the music. This may be a sense of national identity: it could be argued that a German orchestra will always play Wagner better than a non-German orchestra, an Italian orchestra will be unrivalled in Verdi, and an English orchestra in the music of Britten. To the extent that an intuitive understanding of the language of an opera, a sensitivity to its nuances, and the capacity to match words with sounds are crucial to the finest operatic interpretations, this must surely be true. Claudio Abbado is convinced of it: 'I once heard Karajan conduct *Bohème* at La Scala – a great performance. Then I heard him do it with the Berlin Philharmonic. You could say that the Berlin Philharmonic is a better orchestra than La Scala, but they don't play *Bohème* like La Scala because they don't have the feeling, they don't follow the words like an opera orchestra, like La Scala can follow Italian opera.'

The good opera musician is one who *likes* to accompany, knows how to do it, and takes pride in it – a matter of aptitude as well as attitude, in Raymond Leppard's view: 'If you get an opera orchestra that wishes to be a symphony orchestra, forget it. They've got to have accompanying ears.' Martin Isepp elaborates, 'They have to learn about not being the soloist – I think it's the same as the difference between a solo pianist and a good accompanist. You don't actually sacrifice anything of your integrity as an instrumentalist, but your attitude to the music becomes different if you know that you're actually part of something else.'

These are players who enjoy attention to detail, relish the opportunity to concentrate on a single composer for a whole evening, and refine their performances over a series of evenings, reasonably spaced. They are players who accept the stricter discipline that the pit imposes, trusting less directly to their own ears than to their view of the conductor and *his* sense of timing. Bram Gay describes them as responsive to command: 'If you need a unanimous attack, then the opera orchestra, unlike the symphony orchestra, will wait for the conductor to move.'

The ideal opera musician appreciates the extra dimensions that theatre can add to music-making, and revels in the feeling of being part of an infinitely complex and exotic whole: Hugh Maguire, co-leader of the orchestra of the Royal Opera House – 'In a concert you're totally absorbed in the music, that one thing – outside things are a distraction. If the conductor comes on in a green shirt, he's immediately suspect – "What's he up to? He's not thinking about the music". . . . Here there are an awful lot of people involved who are not the orchestral musicians – a chorus of about eighty, all the technicians, thousands of people who move scenery around, the people who do the lighting, and the production staff, the front-of-house people, the booking office, the library, the people who run the wardrobe, paint the scenery, bring the horses on and the parrots, a great mix of people. It's a sort of fairy tale, a dream land. At seven-thirty when the lights go out, you get a wonderful feeling of something magic being created. There are enormous numbers of people apart from the musicians doing absolutely their best to make it work, all focusing on one point in the middle of the stage – the orchestra focusing with their music, people up in the roof with their lights – all focusing on this magic moment. That's the captivating thing.'

Above all, the opera musician needs to love the voice, understand how it works, and derive his enjoyment from working with it. 'The orchestral musician is interested in more than his own line,' maintains Sir Colin Davis. 'The viola part in *Traviata* may not be too difficult even for *me* to play – but if you've got a good singer, it's of infinite interest. And you've got the human voice the whole time, which is the basic instrument from which we all started. You're always coming back to the breath, the sound, the line, the *legato* – everything we all practise and dream about on the other instruments.'

This sensitivity to what is happening on stage can cut both ways. You can depress an orchestra to the point where it will play even *Aida* badly, and an unsatisfactory vocal effort *will* depress the players who have to accompany it. Hugh Maguire recalls the preparations for a production of *Otello* during which the tenor made little attempt to sing at all until the first night. 'Really rather irritating. . . . Rehearsing an accompaniment alone makes *some* sense, because you've got to learn how to play the notes and how to perform the mechanics of it – but you can't really put a suit of clothes on nothing, you've got to have the body there.' Sir Charles Mackerras adds: 'I used to do endless performances in Hamburg of *The Magic Flute* with different casts every time. If the singers were not good enough, the standards of orchestral playing would become slovenly . . . There is a big reaction in the pit to the standard on stage.' An extraordinary performance from the stage, however, can be the catalyst for the kind of musical event that no one forgets. Sir Neville Marriner believes that 'most musicians genuinely wish to be involved in a good performance. I don't think any of them go out to perform expecting to be bored. Some of them give up, because they know the conductor's an idiot or the soloist is a disaster, and that's very discouraging. But under most circumstances everyone wants it to be a success, and if suddenly they see all the things that have been rehearsed coming off and the conductor can generate enough excitement to make them suddenly, instead of very good, *spectacular* – then you're beginning to get a performance. It doesn't happen very often. . . . Good singers can do it to an orchestra – just as I've seen it happen with instrumentalists. Someone like Denis Brain could be taking part in a very ordinary performance, and he'd suddenly play one phrase and the orchestra would think "My God, what are we doing – this is *something*. . . . Something's happening", and everything changes. . . .'

11

The Chorus

The chorus attached to an opera house may be a major artistic asset or, in administrative terms, its principal bugbear – or both: in any event it requires careful and expert handling. Until production rehearsals begin, the conductor will tend to communicate with the chorus at one remove, through the chorus master. Where possible – and it is *not* always possible, especially in an international house with a non-resident conductor – conductor and chorus master will meet before chorus rehearsals begin, to discuss the overall musical interpretation and style of the piece and the potential choral contribution. The conductor will also make his suggestions as to the distribution of choral voices – not merely how many sopranos, tenors, etc. he wants altogether, but how many soprano cigarette girls he wants in the first scene of *Carmen* and how many gypsies in the second act, how many tenors will be dragoons and how many smugglers. (If the work to be cast is a revival, he will probably be offered guidance on this question by a wardrobe department conscious of the fact that it already possesses fifteen dragoon costumes and only six smugglers). It will usually be for the chorus master, knowing his singers best, to say *which* sopranos should be the cigarette girls. If it is a new production, though, he may have to contend with the producer who might also have ideas as to how many choristers should be on stage at any one moment, and what he wants them to look like, which can greatly complicate the chorus master's task. People who have always sung first tenor expect to go on doing so, generally speaking: to be moved to second tenor in order to be cast as substantial burgher rather than fresh-faced apprentice is often taken amiss, and resentment compounds the difficulty of learning a new line.

But after these initial negotiations, the conductor will often have no dealings with the chorus until the stage rehearsals. The chorus master thus has, very properly, considerable leeway in the initial preparation of a work. Peter Burian, Chorus Master at Covent Garden since 1984, believes 'the chorus master should also put his handwriting on the score as far as breathing is concerned, and phrasing and articulation'. His primary responsibility, however, is to teach the choristers their notes, since as full-time employees they are not required, nor do they have time, to learn their music by themselves in advance of production rehearsals. Very occasionally, for the more complex works, the chorus master will work with choristers

Chorus master Peter Burian and language coach Maria Cleva rehearsing with the chorus (Covent Garden, 1985).

individually or in small groups; but more often he will prepare one section at a time or, where schedules are tight, he may simply rehearse ladies and gentlemen separately. Sight-reading at first, eventually without copies, each group learns its own line, incorporating as many instructions in the way of dynamics, tempi and co-ordinated breathing as it can reasonably absorb. Each section will also be discovering how its own line relates to the others, learning cues and recognising harmonies in anticipation of the next stage, when the chorus is rehearsed as a whole.

At the same time, occasionally with the aid of a language coach, the chorus master must teach his singers the words. The problem is threefold: to memorise the words (and with some languages this is extremely difficult – Russian, for example, has to be committed to memory virtually syllable by syllable), to pronounce them correctly and to enunciate them intelligibly. To Peter Burian, this last is the most crucial: 'The basis of choral-singing is the clear delivery of the text – the right placing of consonants and vowels. A well-defined final consonant in a word is both the key to the understanding of that word – until it is closed, it will remain vague – and a springboard to the next.'

With the learning of both words and notes well-advanced, the chorus master can begin work on ensemble and balance. Accuracy – in entries, in breathing, in the lengths of notes – now becomes crucial, almost more so for the chorister than for the soloist, according to Martin Handley, Chorus Master at ENO: 'If a soloist mucks it up, changes a breathing and then forgets and breathes in both places, the only people who know are probably him and the conductor. If the chorus does it, you've got a mucky phrase.' Simultaneously the chorus master has to impart the style of singing that is suited to the particular piece: *Tannhäuser* demands a different style from Handel's *Samson* or from *La Traviata*.

It is at this stage that the conductor generally encounters the chorus. While his presence at those rehearsals given over to learning the piece might have been inhibiting, he will usually try to do some work with the chorus once the chorus master considers it presentable and before the production rehearsals begin. For the chorus it means the chance to get used to a new beat; for the chorus master, the advantage of another pair of ears assessing what he has already achieved; and for the conductor it is an opportunity to establish a rapport and to begin to communicate some idea of his overall aims for the piece before the chorus's attention is absorbed by the demands of the staging.

For some operas (and for many choristers) it is easier to learn the music in combination with stage action, when a phrase or line can be associated with a move or a situation. Philip Glass's *Akhnaten* might be taken as a case in point, with its choral contribution consisting often of a hypnotic, monotonous rhythmic pulse, much of it on the same note, occasionally going up or down a fourth, with words in ancient Egyptian, Akkadian and Hebrew – far more readily committed to memory in conjunction with production rehearsals.

Once the opera has gone into production, the chorus master no longer has the choristers to himself and his role shifts to that of reminding them of what they have learned musically and helping them to combine it with what they are being told to do dramatically. He will, if he thinks it necessary, take it upon himself to persuade the producer, on the choristers' behalf, of the need to serve the music as well as the dramatic concept in his positioning of choristers on stage: sight lines to the conductor will also be a constant concern. And even when the conductor has joined them for stage and orchestra rehearsals, the chorus master has an important part to play, working on balance – internal, and with the orchestra and soloists. Martin Handley: 'This is the crucial stage, this is building up to the first night, getting the runner ready for the off: to hand it over to the conductor would be like the coach deserting the runner in the practice rounds in the Olympic stadium. You must be there, and obviously there.'

This concern is carried over into the performances. On most evenings the chorus master will be in the wings. In the most complex pieces he may cue difficult chorus entries with a torch – though some large houses (La Scala, for example) have a separate prompter for the chorus; more often his official function is to conduct off-stage singers or instrumentalists. He will certainly be listening to the performance with one ear open for mistakes, and at subsequent music calls during the run he will give notes on what needs to be corrected. However, his presence is at least as necessary for the positive reason of maintaining morale. Martin Handley: 'The backstage part is important – the geeing-up, the Beecham technique of telling them a funny story before they go on and sing something full of boundless joy. And people do want to know how something has been, they'll come up and ask you. That's one of the good things about the job – to a certain extent the chorus are singing for you. . . . It's one of the great pleasures – not so much an ego trip as a feeling of community.'

This feeling of community may actually be an essential prerequisite for success as a chorus master, since his other main responsibility is to act as the representative and champion of their interests against all comers – a role that is demanding in proportion to the strains under which the choristers themselves operate. And these can be very considerable. Within the profession a clear distinction is drawn between 'career choristers' and others, and between 'career' choruses and those regarded as a stepping stone to higher things. Festival choruses are the most obvious examples of the latter – the Bayreuth chorus, for instance, offers singers an excellent opportunity of learning the Wagnerian style at source. Similarly, the Glyndebourne chorus is perhaps the single most valuable source of employment for young singers building a solo career in Britain, as a small chorus singing in a small house with a light repertoire which presents no dangers to the developing voice. Glyndebourne also offers opportunities by casting small parts from the chorus, and by using chorus members to understudy principal roles – actually sending them on if the singers they are covering do fall ill. And since the foundation of Glyndebourne Touring Opera in 1968, the management has in addition been able to guarantee a certain number of choristers performances as principals outside the Festival. In consequence, as Martin Isepp comments: 'The chorus does tend to be a collection of the best young singers around in England at any given moment, rather than the kind of singer who's decided that this is as far as they're going to get. The difference between the two attitudes is just the world. . . . It's always had that connotation of not being a chorus, and therefore being kosher. . . .'

Martin Isepp's remarks, though not unkindly meant, illustrate the problems that face the other kind of chorister. In the large year-round houses (such as the Met, Covent Garden, ENO, La Scala and Vienna) and in the repertory houses of Germany and Austria, the majority of choristers are permanent, salaried and free to take on only a limited amount of outside work. (At ENO, for example, opportunities to accept external professional engagements are granted on a 'first come, first served' basis.) Conditions in a 'career' chorus are far from easy, and the onus on the chorus master to watch out for his charges is correspondingly greater. The average chorus member will sing a far greater number of pieces in a year than any principal or *comprimario*. He will sing in different languages, different vocal ranges, different styles, on successive days or even on the same day. Most permanent choruses work between eight to twelve sessions a week, about half of which are performances; on most days they will expect to be rehearsing one piece, performing another, possibly even attending staging rehearsals for a third. (Even within the one piece a chorister may be asked to assume more than one character; the soldier listening aghast to Azucena's horror story in Act One of *Il Trovatore* may well find himself a gypsy singing the 'Anvil Chorus' in Act Two.) In a repertory house, chorus members may be required to carry as many as forty or fifty different operas in their memories for use during the season, the majority of which will have to be pulled out and presented with a minimum of rehearsal: Sir Charles Mackerras, a Janáček specialist, is in German houses given no more than an hour with the chorus, not on stage and not with orchestra, to revise a work as difficult as *Jenůfa*. The music a composer gives the chorus to sing is not necessarily much easier than that which he gives the principals, and Martin Handley feels that its technical demands are too often underrated: 'If a lot of the principals had to sing with the precision and attention to detail that the chorus need all the time, they would very soon realise how difficult it is. You see this in, for example, those of the Verdi operas where the *comprimarii* are all singing along with the chorus. . . .'

Members of a chorus work irregular and unsocial hours, they are not particularly well-paid and there can be by definition little sense of individual achievement in their work; it is the chorus master's job to iron out any voice that is clearly audible above the rest. In short, to be a career chorister ideally requires a sense of vocation – which not all of them have.

It is by no means true, as infuriated producers and jaded administrators sometimes like to think, that all choristers are failed soloists. Choruses include a fair proportion of singers who have realised at an early stage that while vocally equipped for solo work, they are temperamentally unsuited to it; and they attract many people who enjoy the variety of repertoire and the companionship usually denied to the soloist. Equally, no chorus is without its quota of members for whom a career as a chorister is quite simply second-best, and the equilibrium of the chorus as a whole may depend on how these people adjust to their situation. The sense that there is a stigma attached to the career chorus can make its members hypersensitive, aggressive, petty and militant on the finer points of union law. (The chorus at La Scala claim extra pay whenever they are required to wear armour.) And however precarious the relations between chorus and management, they can always be worsened by the insensitivity of administrators who openly subscribe to the 'once a chorister, always a chorister' philosophy.

Members of the chorus in *Peter Grimes* (Covent Garden, 1984).

The chorister's principal compensation is security. Many houses – Vienna and La Scala, for example – offer their choruses life contracts and pension schemes; Covent Garden's choristers, technically hired on an annual basis, can in practice count on permanent employment provided they acquit themselves adequately in auditions held every three years. (In 1983 their average age was forty-five.) Some houses audition more frequently than this, others less: Australian Opera, for instance, re-auditions its members every two years, Scottish Opera every year, while ENO does not re-audition at all.

The practice of employing choristers until retirement age inevitably means that a significant number will be working long after their voices have passed their best, and a few will have obvious vocal problems. Mere loss of power in a voice will not necessarily mean that its owner should not be retained, particularly if he or she still has something to offer dramatically; it is when a voice acquires an ugly wobble or in some other way sticks through the texture of the overall sound that problems arise. To locate the source is not always easy, as those most likely to be in trouble are often the most seasoned professionals, best able to disguise what they are doing. Having identified singers who are struggling, it can be very difficult to remove them; La Scala has armed itself with a clause in each contract giving the management the right to dispense with the services of anyone whose voice is no longer satisfactory, but in Britain it is necessary for Equity to agree that there is 'cause for concern', a process which can be extremely protracted. Nor will any chorus master be eager to make redundant anyone whose principal incentive in joining a chorus may have been precisely the prospect of guaranteed employment until retirement age.

Perhaps the most valuable contribution a chorus master can make to the welfare of his choristers is to treat them as individuals and encourage others to do the same. *En bloc* the chorus can be intimidating, as Martin Handley confirms: 'As far as one can tell, choruses are made up of very nice individuals, but stick them together as a unit and they seem like a totally uncontrollable monster with no human feelings whatsoever. If you start treating them as a unit, firstly they sense it and resent it, secondly you get terribly paranoid.' And ultimately no house can afford the disaster of an uncooperative chorus. John Dexter, who makes great use of the chorus in his stagings, makes the point forcefully: 'The chorus should be the heart of the opera house: when the circulation isn't running, you're in trouble.'

12

Working with the Principal Singers

Unlike the actor, the acting singer is customarily expected to arrive at the first rehearsal knowing his part. But, as Lord Harewood ruefully acknowledges, this is not to say that he (or she) always does, to the vexation of the management which in cases like this is helpless : 'Nobody can do more than exhort them to come knowing their music. If they don't, what do you do? Fire them? Kneecap them? Or just don't employ them again? But what if there's nobody else? . . .'

Assuming that the will is there, the way in which a singer learns a role is a matter of personal taste and capacity. Some play the piano well enough to teach themselves the music – Placido Domingo, for example; others, like Dame Kiri te Kanawa, prefer to have a tape prepared by a vocal coach, consisting of their vocal line plus piano accompaniment and the relevant entrances and exits of others. Unlike any other professional musician, however, the opera singer is not required, and is sometimes not able, to read music; it is the voice, the physical instrument and not the intellectual or musical capacity sustaining it, by which, with very few exceptions (and Maria Callas is the obvious one), the singer can primarily expect to be judged. Some conductors are rather bracing about this: 'Singers are not all noted for intelligence, it must be said. I think it's the air pressure on the brain – on the principle of the blown egg. . . .' Sir Charles Mackerras is more charitable: 'Some singers are not musicians. That's not to say they're bad singers or sing unmusically, but many of them can't really read music and have to be taught everything. On the other hand, many, of course, are first-class musicians who also have the gift of a voice. Singing opera can be a different thing from being a musician.' This may result from deficiencies in their early training – Claudio Abbado comments: 'It is true, especially in Italy, that many singers have good voices but don't know how to play the piano or even to read music; they have no all-round musical education. That was one of the reasons for forming the school at La Scala.'

The professional opera world has long been geared to this apparent disability. Many singers learn by ear and in some this facility is so highly developed that it can pose problems of its own; one international tenor, for instance, has so immediate and retentive an aural memory that he will assimilate mistakes if they are played to him even once. For similar reasons, opinion is divided on the advis-

Maria Callas with the conductor Carlo Felice Cillario watching a rehearsal of *Tosca* on stage (Covent Garden, 1964).

ability of listening to recordings while learning a role. Placido Domingo does it, sees it as instructive, and frankly disbelieves singers who affect to avoid the interpretations of others as a matter of principle. Dame Kiri will listen to recordings once she has almost finished work on a role, always taking care to use more than one recording, so that no single interpretation sticks. Where there *is* only one interpretation available, and that a distinctive one, the risks of involuntary plagiarism are obvious; in learning the part of Gustav von Aschenbach in Britten's *Death in Venice*, a role created and recorded by Sir Peter Pears, Anthony Rolfe Johnson took the obvious precaution: 'If you listen to him once, it's crept into the ear and it's there to stay. . . . I didn't listen to a single note, piano, orchestral or otherwise, before I studied and learnt it entirely myself.'

However a singer chooses to prepare a role, it must be thoroughly 'sung in' to the voice – it is for this reason that most performers arrive for rehearsals with the notes already committed to memory. 'Singing in' a role is not just a question of *knowing* the notes, they must be 'placed' in the voice, sung over and over again until they feel comfortable there and the technical difficulties have been identified. Matthew Epstein: 'Any great singer you talk to will tell you this – the singing in of a role is the crucial thing about this role. Physically knowing how the voice has to function through the role – here comes the high note, here comes the low note, here comes the long phrase – knowing how to do it, having it thought through.' For this reason, it requires considerable effort for a singer to move the voice from one role to another, the more so if the roles are markedly different in style. As a counter-tenor, James Bowman tends to oscillate between the extremes of the operatic repertoire and this frequently entails subtle 'gear-changes' in the voice. 'The baroque style is in many ways a bit sewing-machine – very stylised, very formal, very disciplined; you're stuck in the same rhythmic mould. With modern music, there's none of that; it's much more spread, more *legato*. I found going from *Midsummer Night's Dream* to *Julius Caesar* this summer [1984] quite tricky, to get the baroque feel back into my voice again.'

One of the first tasks for the singer approaching a role is to work out how best to breathe it. James Bowman: 'Some composers tend to make phrases a little on the long side, more like an instrumentalist's phrase, and you often have to have little places in reserve where you know you can sneak breaths if necessary. It's much easier in a baroque context, because it's more sequential and you can split words more easily. In a modern thing, it can be very difficult, you have to do it terribly subtly, fade a note out, and fade in again.' Verdi, as Rodolfo Celletti points out, is more like the moderns in that his phrasing for the voice more closely resembles the pacing of ordinary speech than the regular formulaic rhythms of baroque or *bel canto* writing, and in consequence the breathing of his music is irregular.

In many cases the singer's psychological grasp of a role anticipates his or her mastery of its technical problems and the interpretation of character may be well-advanced before rehearsals start. Linda Esther Gray, in particular, makes good use of all the musical clues dropped by the composer: 'I just sit at the piano and play the harmonies – it tells you an enormous amount about the character. . . . You get a tremendous flavour of Puccini or Wagner from the kind of chords that they've put under something. There's really no argument as to whether that's a straightforward lie she's telling, or the truth as she sees it – the chord underneath will tell you.'

All that is contractually required of artists, however, is the notes of their own roles; and once they arrive at the opera house, a good deal of help is available to them, primarily from the music staff – in Martin Isepp's phrase, 'the conductor's hit men', through whose initial efforts singers are brought to a state of musical readiness where they can be used by the conductor in the forging of his interpretation. Several *répétiteurs* will be allocated to each opera in a house, and several singers to each *répétiteur* who will ensure that they are perfectly familiar with their notes, their words and their cues. This he does by literally 'repeating' the role – taking the singer through every bar over and over again, filling in on the piano as much of the accompaniment as is necessary to the singer's performance and supplying the other voices where required – a virtuoso display, very often wasted on a singer too preoccupied to appreciate it. As anyone who has ever tried to play a Lisztian opera paraphrase will testify, it is virtually impossible to represent on the piano everything that is in a score, and the *répétiteur* must select the elements he will emphasise from moment to moment, tailoring what he plays to the changing needs of the singer who will sooner or later have to find his bearings unaided, on stage

Martin Isepp, Head of Music Staff for Glyndebourne Festival Opera (1985)

in front of an audience. The orchestral line which may at any one point sound predominant to the listener in the audience might be less helpful to the singer than a concealed motif or phrase elsewhere in the texture from which he can get his cue. Donald McIntyre, for instance, faced with the expanse of Wotan's music, frequently focuses on phrases in the woodwind – armed, however, with alternative cues elsewhere in case the first oboe has an off-night.

The music staff are looking in the singers' 'repetitions' for mistakes in the notes – not mistakes in voice production (these are for the voice teacher to correct), but faulty intonation, inappropriate colouring of a note or phrase, unevenness of tone, imprecise rhythm, the wrong words attached to a note and, simply, notes of the wrong length or pitch which, while they occur most frequently in new works or lengthy tracts of sung recitative, may bedevil the 'big tunes' as well: Glyndebourne's music staff speak of 'laundering' a role for a singer, turning a general impression once more into a detailed grasp.

Their counterparts as far as the words are concerned are the language coaches. Most houses performing operas in the original languages have coaches – Covent Garden has two for Italian, one for German, one for French and one for Russian – who will sit in on rehearsals throughout the production period. Their first task is to check that the singers actually understand the lines they utter – not in paraphrase, but word for word; even quite proficient Italian or German speakers may need an interpreter for the archaic language of some of, say, Bellini's libretti or the more convoluted of Wagner's 'wordplays'. (The language coach can also be indispensable, or irritating, to a producer working in a foreign language, by

Alicia Nafé working on her role as Rosina with the conductor Gabriele Ferro at a music rehearsal of *The Barber of Seville* (Covent Garden, 1985).

pointing out concealed meanings in the text – ironic or sarcastic inflections, for instance – which may invalidate the construction put upon it in the staging.) Meaning once established, the coach must check that the singers are pronouncing every syllable correctly. Each language has its pitfalls for other nationalities; in the experience of Maria Cleva, one of Covent Garden's Italian coaches, Italian vowels pose problems for English-speaking singers because of their brevity – 'a' as in 'abet', rather than 'table' or 'half', 'e' as in 'bell' rather than 'before' – but also for Germans because they are not as tight as German vowels. Sometimes the singer may even be required to simulate a particular dialect, as Graham Clark found when he went to Bayreuth as David: '*Meistersinger* is basically *southern* German, a softer accent than the northern German, nearer the dialect of Nuremberg than that of Hanover, *Hochdeutsch*; the audience would be aware of these things, so they were constantly making me soften my consonants.' Accurate pronunciation is especially hard to maintain if a singer is having to perform in different languages alternately: 'Russian

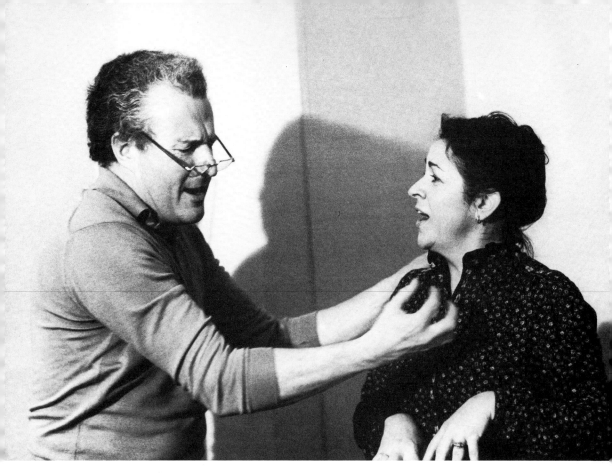

Sir Colin Davis at a music rehearsal with Ileana Cotrubas, preparing the role of Violetta in *La Traviata* (Covent Garden, 1985).

and Italian don't go very well together', according to Maria Cleva, 'because Russian is all the way back in the throat and Italian is very forward.'

How much else the music staff will do with the singers depends principally upon when the conductor chooses to arrive. If he arrives late (i.e. only for the start of orchestral rehearsals), the music staff may well already have begun to impart notions of style and even interpretation on his behalf. Most leading conductors, however, prefer to communicate their ideas directly and will arrive near the start of the music rehearsal period in order to be able to work with the principals individually – Riccardo Muti, for example, or Claudio Abbado, who himself rehearses his singers at the piano (a practice which used to be widespread but is now, according to singers, all too rare and, some say, a significant factor in the passing of the Golden Age). Sir Reginald Goodall invariably coaches as well as conducting his operas and could not conceive of working in any other way. Sir Colin Davis, if he has not worked with singers before, always tries to start individual rehearsals with them at an early stage. In his view, as important as the conductor's own attempt to penetrate the composer's mind is his ability to elicit his fellow musicians' efforts; he attaches great importance to the process – which may take time – of getting people into the frame of mind where they can do their best. 'It's very difficult to work with singers if you don't know them at all, until you've had time for the shyness and awkwardness to rub off. They've got to get over that before you have the freedom to say what you need to say. A strange person comes into the room, a musician who's as nervous as hell. I'm not exactly *inhibited* by that, I just want to be careful with the person so they don't get put off, wounded and destroyed – give them time to relax, sing a little bit. The person begins to feel some confidence that nothing awful is going to happen. And *then* you can start to work.'

As singers see it, the exchange with the conductor during this period should be reciprocal. Isobel Buchanan fears it no longer is, blaming the change on the new age: 'One of the unfortunate things about opera in the jet-set period is that nobody has enough time to get to know each other – dramatically, musically, personally. If I had had more time with some of these people, they'd have got to know me better vocally. Instead of that, it's "This is the way it's done."' With the evidence of the composer's markings before them – pitch, rhythm, volume,

Placido Domingo with the conductor Giuseppe Sinopoli at a rehearsal of *Manon Lescaut* (Covent Garden, 1983).

expression – singer and conductor have less scope for argument where interpretation is concerned than, say, actor and producer wrestling with a text in the theatre; but some room for manoeuvre remains. Josephine Veasey regards tempo in particular as a matter for the individual singer to decide, not merely a metronome marking. 'It's a pulse within the person. It's different with ensembles, but with an aria there's a certain pace for every singer, without overindulgence, which is perfect for them. It's where they get their words out properly and where they can sing a phrase really beautifully, interpret it properly.' Quite obviously if the singer's preferences are not inconsistent with the general principles of the conductor's interpretation, it is in his interest to accommodate them. Where there *is* a significant difference of opinion, all but the most resolute 'star' soloists will usually defer to the conductor – Dennis O'Neill, for example: 'I know what tempo suits my voice – I like either extremely slow or very fast. I love "Questa o quella" very fast, for example – not a lot to do with what Verdi marked it, mind you. If the conductor likes it, he'll agree to do it like that; if he doesn't and points out what Verdi actually said, naturally I'll go along with that.' The concession, however, can make life more difficult for the singer, as Robert Tear explains: 'If it is going a little bit slower or faster than you would think ideal, then your interpretation has to change slightly. Physically it *must* change; if something is going quicker, then the body somehow will react in a different way.'

In the first two or three days of music calls, singers will have been rehearsed on their own, by the conductor and/or the music staff. Soon afterwards ensemble calls begin, and it is here that many see the conductor as making his most crucial contribution – in the integration of individual performances to create a harmonious and dynamic whole. At the most fundamental level, the voices must be balanced against each other (and here sensible casting can help). Singers can, given an unselfish disposition, make some adjustments themselves, largely by intuition, but they are not in the best position to hear exactly either what they themselves are doing, or even what their colleagues sound like from a distance – a difficult thing to judge objectively from only a few feet away. An external arbiter is needed to pronounce not only on relative volume, but also on intonation and vocal colour.

Breathing in ensembles must be co-ordinated, if not synchronised – Richard Van Allan: 'There are places where you have to breathe mutually, where the ensemble demands it, but there are also places where you want to get the effect of it just going on for ever, so you all nip a breath at the places where you're most concealed by the other voices – where you can best afford to miss a couple of notes out on a less important line going underneath. . . . Particularly when you get a long patter-type line, say in Mozart or Rossini, where it's impossible to sing it all . . . you look and see where the thickness of the other voices is at its greatest. . . . Animal cunning rather than a deliberate musical effect. . . .'

And the conductor must also impose some uniformity of style. International

singers will all have been working in completely different environments and styles
– some in enormous venues in America, or open-air arenas in Italy, where the
'stand-and-deliver' approach is hard to avoid, others in near-chamber conditions
in Wexford or Glyndebourne. Some may have become accustomed to the Vienna
style of playing Mozart, for instance, others to the more robust and dramatic style
generally favoured in Britain. In these and other matters the conductor must make
plain his tastes – *rubato* or *portamento*, say, ('dragging' and 'scooping' to some,
invaluable aids to expressivity for others), interpolation or decoration – how much
and in what mode.

Once the producer takes over and staging rehearsals begin, the conductor and
his staff, far from relaxing, must if anything increase their vigilance because musical
standards will at this point inevitably deteriorate. Suddenly there is twice as much
to concentrate on – where and how to move, how to manifest emotions physically,
how to react to the gestures of others – and much of what the singers have been
so carefully taught in the way of style, dynamics, ensemble, (even the notes, in
the more problematic passages), they will simply forget. Martin Isepp has toyed
with the idea of scheduling production rehearsals first and getting them over with;
Sir John Pritchard would rather have music rehearsals, especially ensemble calls,
interrupting staging rehearsals throughout the preparation period to maintain
musical standards – the system employed at Bayreuth. Usually conductor and producer contrive to work out some sort of compromise; the music staff may, for
example, barter early music calls for access to the singers during what are technically the producer's rehearsals – Martin Isepp's favoured solution: 'I've now found
by trial and error that if we're putting on a Strauss opera, say *Arabella*, it's counter-
productive to have an enormously long music rehearsal period. That sounds crazy
because it's so difficult, but in fact . . . the sooner the singers can relate moves
to the various musical points, the quicker they will memorise the whole thing.'

The singers' performances will be affected again when they work with the
orchestra for the first time. It is not always easy to adjust to the altered texture
and timbre of the accompaniment; a cue that they have grown accustomed to hearing on the piano sounds quite different from the orchestra. What is more, the
tempi will almost certainly have changed from those agreed at piano rehearsals –
Martin Isepp: 'The thing about every conductor is that the tempi he does with
the piano differ quite a lot from the tempi he'll do with the orchestra – it's just
a fact of life. Funnily enough, the variation isn't consistent. Basically it's slower
with the orchestra – it's more unwieldy to take with you than ten fingers. But
sometimes you get a double-take – the conductor is so aware that there's a chance
of it being slow that he overcompensates.' Balance has obviously become far more
complex to monitor for the conductor, who will post members of the music staff
in different areas of the auditorium to listen and report back, but interestingly
the physical effort for the singers is often less despite the greater weight of the
sound they have to contend with. 'It's usually a great step up', according to Martin
Isepp, 'because however well you play a score on the piano, it doesn't give the

buoyancy and support that an orchestra will give you. . . . The advantages are huge, because most singers find they can float over an orchestra, whereas they really have to work with a piano.'

Throughout the production rehearsals, the task of the conductor and his staff is complicated by the phenomenon of singers 'marking' their parts in order to save their voices. Josephine Barstow defends it as a necessary preventive measure, to forestall complete exhaustion: 'Marking isn't sublimating the music, it's sublimating the physical energy that it requires to perform the music so that you can use your body to do the discovering process about the role. . . . Obviously one marks in order to save the voice, but you can also mark in order not to have to produce that physical energy.' Sir Charles Mackerras also approves the practice, for in certain repertoire at least, it can be dangerous for artists to sing full out all the time: 'If singers didn't mark, they would not be able to get through the work they do get through. Good singers are in constant demand, and during a gruelling lot of rehearsals if they're asked to give too much, they are frequently so exhausted physically and emotionally that they are too tired to do a good performance. That's why very often at least one of the most important singers may suffer vocal exhaustion during the last few days of rehearsal, thus endangering an important production.'

The conductor must find the happy medium between letting too many inadequacies (wrong notes, imprecise dynamics, poor intonation) pass uncorrected, and wearing his singers out. Otto Klemperer was, as his biographer Peter Heyworth remarks, frequently guilty of overworking his casts; for his notorious production of *The Flying Dutchman* he forbade any marking at all. Herbert von Karajan, on the other hand, has singers rehearsing to a prerecorded tape, usually but not always of their own voices, a practice which Placido Domingo considers equally hazardous in that it may entrench bad habits and lull the singer into a false sense of vocal security.

The singer must find the marking technique which both suits him or her, and satisfies the conductor. Some will transpose the line or the top few notes down an octave, some sing in a personal brand of falsetto, others will simply sing softly or even mouth their words. But to offer less than one's prescribed contribution cannot be helpful, and may be positively distracting for other singers, depending on the skill with which it is done. Where illness, actual or incipient, is the cause, marking is naturally understood, but the more advanced the rehearsals, the less forgivable it becomes – and the harder for the singer himself to bridge the gulf between rehearsal and performance. Anthony Rolfe Johnson, interviewed when about to undertake Massenet's Des Grieux for the first time, was seriously distressed at having been forced by a bad cold to mark throughout almost the entire rehearsal period. 'I've not really been able to sing, so I don't know if I can do it. . . . Knowing the music is only about a third of the whole thing, you relearn the music considerably when you come into production. It's an entirely different piece, so you need to be able to sing out. . . . There's the Saint-Sulpice scene where he sings, "Ah, fuyez, douce image" – bad enough when you sing it just on its own, but sing it after you've sung two acts already, then you find out whether you should actually be doing the piece – *and I can't find out.*'

Not every production is prepared under ideal conditions, of course – with all the artists and the conductor present and performing, with enough music staff on hand, and enough time to rehearse unhurriedly. The system is all too easily shortcircuited by the artists themselves, either failing to turn up for rehearsals or presenting themselves but not singing. Because international guest singers are paid per performance and not per week or month spent working on a production (though the *per diem* idea is gradually gaining ground), it is more profitable for them to pack in performances elsewhere than to engage in unpaid rehearsal which, if the role is one they have done frequently before, they may additionally feel to be boring and unnecessary. Administrators in international houses, faced with complaints from conductors, producers, other singers – and, where the artist's detachment from the proceedings is perceptible, from the critics – make their best efforts to hold singers to their commitments. Contracts stipulate the length of the rehearsal period required and the fact that during this time singers will not be permitted to declare themselves 'not available', in order to fulfil engagements elsewhere, and performances are made conditional on singers having attended rehearsals. But when a singer arrives late, and the administrator is unable positively to prove that he or she has been working elsewhere, he tends to accept the excuse offered with reasonably good grace for fear of offending the singer and losing his services. Bernard Lefort, director of the Aix Festival (once himself an agent, and thus familiar with singers' ways), has successfully sued top-rank singers for failing to honour contracts. But few administrators have his nerve.

International singers get away with cutting rehearsals, and with bad behaviour generally, partly because of market forces, partly because stars have always done so and it is now part of the myth of the artistic temperament. Other 'lesser' singers do not share this fascination with the famous. *Comprimarii*, who do attend every rehearsal, in no way acknowledge the principals' freedom, as superior beings, from the same obligations. As one administrator points out, 'No singer thinks of himself as less important than another; if they didn't have confidence in themselves, they wouldn't be doing what they do.' Nor do other principals, finding themselves without support at rehearsals, necessarily condone this kind of high-handedness – 'operatic' in the worst sense. Ileana Cotrubas for one, disapproves: 'This is not a concert, where you are alone. . . . In an opera you have to be a team – the result is not your own result, it's the team's result. I can't sing, say, *Traviata* without Papa Germont, Alfredo, the chorus, the orchestra, the conductor, costumes, lights – it all involves so much work. I think it's very un-serious to arrive three days before the première as some tenors do. He may say he's done the opera so many times in other new productions and he knows it. But he doesn't know the conception of this producer – and what help will he give to the other singers? In four weeks of rehearsal, you grow from day to day in the parts, your personalities develop. You learn how he is reacting to your phrasing, and your emotions.' From the other point of view, as a romantic lead required to ingratiate himself with female counterparts who arrive at the last possible moment and perform, necessarily, *in vacuo*, Dennis O'Neill complains, 'Of course you can't perform well with them, not your best. You can get away with it, and you can get a lot of applause, but no. . . . If I'm singing "Di quell' amor" to someone who's not even looking at me, what hope is there?'

The grand entrance three days before the final dress rehearsal also means that conductor and orchestra of necessity become accompanists rather than collaborators. Sir Neville Marriner sees in this situation a parallel with that of the symphony conductor confronted with elderly instrumental soloists whose interpretations of popular pieces have evolved over thirty or forty years: 'Maybe they have played this concerto fifteen or sixteen times that year. They come to you the day before the concert – you're not going to change their performance in two rehearsals. If you invite them, it is a foregone conclusion that you are going to accompany them, make the orchestra complementary to them. It doesn't mean you have to lose orchestral detail doing this, but it means that tempi, dynamics, phrasings are very much theirs. This is what happens if you invite one of the iron-clad stars to join your opera production three days before the first performance. You are not going to influence their performance one iota. The only thing they have come to do is find out where the entrances and exits are.'

Nevertheless, in some operas of the 'concerto' type, to continue the instrumental analogy, good individual performances may do some justice at least to the composer. Not all operas are by nature *Gesamtkunstwerke*; in some, consisting largely of virtuoso solo set pieces, the orchestra's role *is* primarily to accompany – in Sir Neville Marriner's view, 'Donizetti is the equivalent of Wieniawski or Vieuxtemps, these people who wrote virtuoso concertos for one instrument. They're *not* conductors' pieces – even the Chopin piano concertos are fairly typical of the dullest musical activity that an orchestra or conductor can be involved in. Nothing but pianism all the way through, you just hang around waiting to put down a chord or fill in a harmony.' In other words, the co-operation required between the star soloist and the other performers is less detailed and more intermittent, and the big *bel canto* operas (of Bellini, Donizetti, *et al*) perhaps suffer least from the soloist who effectively opts to go it alone.

Even in operas with a lower proportion of purely solo work, outstanding solo performances can certainly satisfy an audience – somewhere like Vienna, say, where the dazzling individual display is above all what is required – and may even satisfy the critics. Martin Isepp: 'If you've got people coming in to sing *Tosca*, to get it the way you *should* have it (like with Callas and Gobbi), the two people have to know each other, have to have worked together and be on a wavelength. But you *can* just get away with a *Tosca* that's wonderfully sung by each individual. . . . I'm not saying it's ideal, or what should be done, but it still has a great deal to offer.' Dennis O'Neill, while far from admiring the 'instant opera' syndrome, is prepared to distinguish between works more and less suited to it: 'There are some pieces that I could go on and do rather quickly. I'd sooner do *Ballo* in an afternoon than *Traviata*, although Riccardo is a role that's three or four times as long as Alfredo. I don't know why – it seems that it's a very obvious piece. That's not to decry it, it's a very complex composition, but it's a piece that is very direct and very safe. . . . I could watch the conductor and get through. I most certainly wouldn't do that with *Traviata*.'

It is where ensemble is of the essence that the consequences of missed rehearsals will be most apparent and most damaging. Martin Isepp states outright that a Mozart performance which has not been rehearsed for ensembles 'is simply a travesty, and has no sense to it. Even the big houses will set aside more time if they do a Mozart piece than if they do Donizetti or Bellini' – though some singers may still be found, Stuart Burrows amongst them , to defend 'instant opera' in this context: 'If you've got the highest level of singers for Mozart, you don't need them for an eternity to practise with anybody for musical ensemble.' In response Raymond Leppard, whilst not volunteering himself, half-seriously advocates a system of 'relegating a certain number of operas to the canary-fanciers. . . . Give as good as you can on the least possible rehearsal so that they're *almost* a disgrace, saved entirely by the good voice you hire who comes in and just sings the odd performance' – whereby one saves enough time and money to give the remaining productions of the season festival treatment. 'I think attempting to have the same time scale for everything is a mistake; you should be quite cynical about it.' In many companies operating on a tight budget, this policy has in effect been covertly adopted, particularly where revivals are concerned. There are others, however, who cannot honestly countenance the abuse on any terms. During his truncated reign in Vienna, Lorin Maazel made a practice of informing singers who failed to attend rehearsals that they were assumed to have withdrawn from the production. But it may be simpler for the conductor himself to withdraw, or at least to take evasive action. One of the reasons given by Carlo Maria Giulini for retiring from opera in the late 1960s was the present-day singer's unwillingness to devote enough time to rehearsal, and Sir Colin Davis concludes: 'When you get to the top of the profession, the problem of singers not turning up to rehearsals is quite considerable, and it's insoluble. . . . My inclination now is to keep out of grand opera and work more in the pieces in which it doesn't matter if you haven't got big stars.'

13

Working with the Producer

'*Prima le parole, dopo la musica*' – the wrangle on this issue between poet and composer in Strauss's *Capriccio* finds its modern counterpart in the relationship between the secondary creators, the producer and the conductor. Ever since the producer emerged in opera as a force to be reckoned with, this relationship has been a delicate one, and when it goes awry it can generate emotional scenes in the best operatic tradition: a recent production of *Boris Godunov* in Geneva by a young Rumanian producer ended with the (Russian) conductor not merely joining in the boos of the audience, but turning to face them and kissing the score.

On behalf of the composer-as-musician, the conductor – as guardian of the score – will assert the primacy of music, following Erwin Stein's tenet: 'The whole drama is in the music if it is adequately rendered. Anything else – acting, movements, décor and lighting – should appear as functions of the music.' Even if they were allowed equal status, the other aspects of an opera should certainly never be allowed to *interfere* with its music, and the conductor will resist anything that threatens the complete and correct delivery of the score. The music should rarely be cut, for example, simply on dramatic grounds: James Levine has been quoted as saying, 'If a producer tells me that performing a certain cabaletta in a Verdi opera is undramatic, my answer should be that Verdi was a man of the theatre *par excellence*, and knew more about the theatre than a hundred of you. Your job is not to change it but to make it work!' Nor should the demands of the drama be permitted unduly to distract the performers' attention from the musical sounds they are making. The most extreme proponent of this view, one of the more distinguished Verdian conductors of today, is reputed to have said, loudly, 'When I conduct, nobody moves', and many other conductors, given a free hand, would be inclined to follow him at least part of the way towards the concert-performance style of opera production.

The producer, on the other hand, is likely to contend that there is no reason to view an opera as being any more akin to a concert than to a play. He may quite convincingly present himself as the representative of the composer-as-dramatist and argue that he must be free to express the work's dramatic meaning

OPPOSITE Carlo Maria Giulini

with *all* the means at his disposal – which include the music, but are not confined to it; he must be free to work as well through movement, gesture, colour, shape, speech, dancing, acting – through a physical setting for the piece and the behaviour of characters within it. Carlo Maria Giulini is spokesman for that school of conductors who feel that in asserting their theatrical rights, producers neglect, or swamp, the music: 'This generation is getting all its intellectual experiences only through looking. . . . Television and the cinema have affected the young producers, who now pander more to actions than to anything else. They have forgotten that in opera the actions have to be done to music. The visual part has become so important that the music of *Traviata*, for example, becomes like movie music – a comment, not the central issue.'

One way for a conductor to ensure that the music is given the emphasis it deserves and the necessary attention to detail, is to produce the opera himself. During his time as Music Director of the Kroll Oper, Otto Klemperer wrote, 'Opera is in my view a unified organism in which the orchestra and the stage must be in precise accord. As, however, it is in the first place a *musical* art, in so far as everything should flow from the music, I consider that the conductor is artistically justified in also taking charge of what happens on the stage' – beliefs on which he acted, taking charge of costume, lighting and production for many of the Kroll's first productions. Herbert von Karajan reaches the same conclusion from the opposite direction, arguing that the conductor should be in charge of production in order to *form* his musical ideas; in his own case at least, the effort to conceive the work in visual terms often gives him insight into its musical significance.

Rarely, however, has the attempt to combine conducting with producing been an unqualified success. Klemperer was much criticised for his 'tyranny' over every aspect of the *Fidelio* with which the Kroll inaugurated its first season in 1927, and similarly Karajan has regularly been accused of failing to give the stage equal weight with the pit – by Andrew Porter, for example, commenting on his *Ring* at the Met in 1974: 'Up on the stage, often behind a heavy gauze, the singers and the scenery provide a series of large, beautiful illustrations subordinate, even at their most spectacular, to a drama conceived principally in instrumental timbres.'

Most producers would probably consider this kind of failure to be inevitable because they not unnaturally see producing as an art in its own right – 'not just something you do with your left hand', in Jonathan Miller's words. 'It simply is a highly expert job, conceiving and directing a drama on the stage, just as complicated as the job of the conductor. I like conductors to recognise that.' To be a producer it is not enough simply to have a conception: it is also necessary to have certain practical skills in order to implement the conception and make it work in terms of the theatre. Raymond Leppard acknowledges, 'I haven't got any technique of stage direction. . . . I have a *musical* theatrical instinct, but I don't have a *movement* theatrical instinct. I can look at a stage action and see that something is wrong, but I can't analyse what it is. Whereas I *can* analyse if a fiddler plays in a certain way – I can say, "Either take three bows to articulate that phrase, or do a different fingering" . . . I can reduce that to technical lingo, which is what a pro must use in any profession.'

Producing also requires a sure visual sense – and there is no reason why musicians, however gifted, should have this sense, either by instinct or by training. Certainly in Jonathan Miller's experience, the majority do not: 'You get extremely traditional conductors who have no visual sense at all, and are constantly interfering with the design and cannot actually see the way it relates to the music. Their sense of colour in relationship to tone is often very derelict. On the whole musicians are not very visual people – I've not found them to be so, anyway.' Even for the conductor who does have a natural eye for the beautiful, striking or expressive image, it is not always easy to know how well these images will translate in stage terms: John Dexter emphasises the difficulty of 'reading' a model of the set and grasping the intricacies of scale and perspective, as complex in its way as reading a score and not an art that many conductors have had occasion, experience or training to master.

For the conductor who is neither self-confident enough to stage the work himself, nor eminent enough to dictate precisely what the producer should do, it is often easiest simply to ignore his work – the conductor having the advantage of controlling most of the later rehearsals and all the performances. Sir Peter Hall condemns this practice in no uncertain terms: 'They come in at the last moment and make music which has absolutely no bearing on the drama or on the interaction of the characters, and means something quite different to what the producer has decided it means with the singers. The singers are left high and dry, really crucified between the conductor and the producer – it happens very, very often in opera houses, and is one of the greatest sins. Totally uncreative – a function of inadequate rehearsal time and bigheaded conductors who don't see it as a collaboration.'

Fortunately for producers, and for the cause of the truly integrated opera production, many conductors sincerely believe for practical as well as ethical reasons in the virtues of collaboration – Claudio Abbado: 'I sometimes have ideas as a producer, but I've promised myself never to do it. I think with a good producer you can always find something better. Like using a soloist for a symphony concert – I can play the piano, I was a pianist, but with a good pianist you can find something better. The producer, the soloist – I know they know better than me. I may suggest things to the producer, and if he likes it – good. With collaboration you can always find something better for the music and for the opera.'

In ideal circumstances the conductor and producer would collaborate throughout the gestation of a new production, to evolve an interpretation of the work in tandem. This is, however, only really possible in a festival situation or where they work together on a regular and frequent basis. (Mark Elder and David Pountney, for example, are at a considerable advantage as respectively Music Director and Director of Productions at English National Opera, with the opportunity to communicate on a day-to-day basis about their work together, current or future.)

Elsewhere the chances to meet and make plans are more sporadic, but conductor and producer will aim if at all possible to confer before either has elaborated an independent interpretation in too much detail. This may be months, even years before the work goes into production: Raymond Leppard and Sir Peter Hall will be discussing a joint project for Glyndebourne at least two years in advance, and even in the less leisurely world of year-round opera Claudio Abbado prefers to consult his producer months ahead, while they are still free from the pressures imposed by a tight production schedule.

If the dual controllers of a production can reach genuine and ungrudging agreement at this early stage, it can be very fruitful for both. The conductor can work out how best to use the musical resources at his disposal, voices and instruments, to implement the producer's conception during music rehearsals – and the more guidance the producer can give him at this stage, the more minutely detailed the support his interpretation is ultimately likely to receive. Mark Elder: 'Really what I'm asking a producer to do . . . is to tell me how they want every line inflected; I want a play-reading with the producer really. What I'm interested in working with the singers on is clarity of intention, thought, colour, text . . . getting them to colour the words, getting them beyond the crotchets and quavers and the complexities of the music into the thought behind the music' – an excellent description of a process which is traditionally believed to be the producer's responsibility.

Even if conductor and producer enter rehearsals aware of each other's intentions in general outline, there is still a great deal of detail to be resolved jointly. Pacing, for example: while they will probably have discussed how the overall musical structure of the work relates to its dramatic structure – where the high points are, where the moments of light relief, and so on – they will only find the pace of the piece act by act, scene by scene, working through it together and achieving their results, so Colin Graham believes, through the operation of an invaluable system of checks and balances: 'The conductor's perfectly within his rights to say, "I really feel the scene should flow and build to this great climax, and what you're doing is splitting it up into little short sharp movements." He should be able to see that and feel that and tell you – just as you should be able to say, "If you really take it as slowly as that, then the audience will have forgotten what the last word is before you get to the next one and we've lost the flow and the wonderful tautness of it, you're dissipating it." '

The eventual positions of the performers on the stage may equally be subject to negotiation. The conductor will want to ensure that the singers are not so far upstage, or off to the sides, or above or below the level of the stage that balancing voice against orchestra becomes impossible. He will want to be confident both that the singers can see his beat, directly or in a television monitor in the wings, and equally that they are not forced to rely on sight alone – most important in Sir Neville Marriner's opinion: 'If an ensemble is to be worthy of the name, the singers have to be well-placed. They have to be close – they don't necessarily have to sing into each other's faces, but they have to be within, as it were, vibratory

Jeffrey Tate and producer Jean-Louis Martinoty in a rehearsal for *Ariadne auf Naxos* (Covent Garden, 1985).

distance to know exactly what's going on. You cannot expect an ensemble to hold together *just* by watching the conductor.' They should be close and, ideally, they should be roughly on a par; to have one of the participants very much further forward than the others, or higher, or in any other way overshadowing them, can quickly convert what should be a sextet into a quintet plus soloist.

All the problems of placing are naturally compounded when it comes to the chorus. The conductor will generally resist any tendency to relegate the chorus to the edges of the stage as a frame for the stage picture, and he may well also disagree with the producer on the question of grouping: should choristers be deployed for scenic effect – tallest at the back, prettiest at the front, and so on – or strictly according to voice, sopranos all together, etc.? In a work of exceptional musical difficulty, like Schoenberg's *Moses und Aron* with its double fugues for the chorus, it is perhaps prudent for the voices to stick together. And for certain types of concerted movement – the procession of the Grail, for example, in *Parsifal* – grouping may produce a better effect. But usually with professional singers it does no harm for the producer to mix up the voices on stage and, if done sensibly, it may even result in a better-integrated sound. Certainly there must be consultation – and some producers are more vehement than others in asserting their right to choose between the various options open. Jonathan Miller is emphatic: 'If there is a question of musical coherence, then you have to listen and sort the chorus out so that the sound balances are right. There are certain mechanical requirements which obviously have to be observed. . . . But sometimes the conductor will want something a little bit too stolid in order to keep the orchestral and choral sound correct. I'm all in favour of keeping it correct, but there are lots of ways of skinning that cat and I think that they have to leave that to me, that's my job.'

When it comes to co-ordinating music with movement on the stage, it is again the chorus who are most likely to be caught in the crossfire between conductor and producer. Conductors are prone to disapprove if a chorus is expected to begin singing before all its members have arrived on the stage; it is far easier to achieve tidy musical ensemble if they have had time to establish themselves on stage and draw breath. Exits pose problems for chorus and soloists alike, as conductor Julian Smith observes: 'Producers want singers to go upstage with a marvellous exit – and the conductor needs their eyes to take them off the final note.' It is movement *during* the music which infuriates Sir John Pritchard, who calls for 'a more positive acceptance of the validity of the great concerted ensemble as an intrinsic (and mainly static) ingredient of opera; perhaps, even, an encouragement to accept the set pieces at face value, in need of no accompanying distracting stage movement either by swaying, rocking or marching.'

Monitoring the suitability of the stage action for the music is an area where the conductor can be very helpful to the producer if he is allowed to be; he can, for instance, point out the reappearance of a significant motif (the motifs of renun-ciation or compact in the *Ring*, for example) in a form which might not be apparent to the non-musician, information which may well influence the way the producer conceives the scene. He also can, and will, oppose any action which actively con-tradicts what he believes the music to be saying or which simply interferes with its performance, and singers (particularly young singers confronted with an influential producer) look to the conductor to protect them from requests to sing bent double, immersed in water, or swinging from the flies.

The conductor may feel less entitled though equally tempted to intervene when

OPPOSITE Raymond Leppard and Sir Peter Hall rehearsing *L'Incoronazione de Poppea* (Glyndebourne Festival Opera, 1984).

the actions or effects devised by the producer are not obviously incompatible with the music, are in fact intended actively to support it and intensify its impact. It has become quite a common device, for example, to 'produce' the overture and the orchestral interludes in an opera by accompanying them with projections or mime, sketching the story so far, or adding extra scenic detail that the set cannot provide – a practice that Andrew Porter has consistently opposed throughout its progress from innovation to cliché. Where the music was intended to carry the full weight, he argues, it should be allowed to. To elaborate on it is unnecessary: 'The charm of the prelude to Act Three of *Tosca* lies in its aural depiction of a whole city waking, stirring into life around the actual scene that we look at; it would not be enhanced by adding a movie travelogue of Roman *campanili* or by bringing the shepherd boy and his flock across the stage.' And it can be damaging; orchestral interludes are sometimes a deliberate variation of the dramatic mode, and this effect is lost if the dividing lines are blurred.

Some of these problems can only really be solved when the performers are on stage with the orchestra in the pit. Others can be identified from the start of the production, and conductors of a particular type (Claudio Abbado among them) are increasingly eager both to invite the producer to early piano rehearsals with individual singers and to be present themselves at as many production rehearsals as possible. Raymond Leppard regards these last as the matrix 'where the opera grows. The two people most in charge have to be there together all the time.' Some producers, equally, will not rehearse *unless* the conductor is present – Visconti, for example, would not hold staging rehearsals for *Don Carlos* at Covent Garden which conflicted with Giulini's rehearsals with the orchestra.

It is perhaps, after all, a non-question to ask 'Who is ultimately in charge?' Where once many would have answered, without hesitation, 'the conductor' (Wolfgang Wagner, for example, once stated that fifty-one per cent of any production belongs to the conductor), now, with much talk of the 'age of the producer' and the primacy of eye over ear, it is less easy to quantify power and responsibility. To have an Intendant who is himself conductor or producer can make a difference – one might argue that the Met and Munich, with James Levine and Wolfgang Sawallisch at their heads, are more conductors' houses, Berlin and Cologne, with Götz Friedrich and Michael Hampe, producers' houses. Companies which boast both a Director of Productions and a Music Director, like Glyndebourne or ENO, run less risk of being categorised as either. In the end, however, the balance of power in this relationship, as in the opera world as a whole, depends on the force of the individual personalities, the relative status of the people concerned, and the inclinations at that particular moment of the singers they must control.

IV

THE PRODUCER AND DESIGNER

PREVIOUS PAGE Andrei Serban during rehearsals for *Turandot* (Covent Garden, 1984).

14

The Producer's Job

Though this is often heralded as 'the age of the producer', it is still hard to define the producer's job, or the aspect of a performance for which he can legitimately take credit. Some producers like to assume responsibility for the intellectual content of the work, which would doubtless surprise the original creative partnership of composer and librettist. And in fact, as John Schlesinger admits, the opera producer, working within an immutable musical framework, has far less personal control over the ultimate shape, structure, workings and meaning of the piece than the film director, who in the course of editing will cut dialogue, eliminate whole characters and sub-plots, and change the order of scenes to make the work say what he wants it to say.

Other producers, ceding to the conductor the responsibility for everything the audience hears in the opera house, claim the credit for everything it sees on the stage; most designers and lighting designers would politely demur. The producer's individual contribution is hard to isolate because now, more than ever, he works as an integral part of a team – with designer, lighting designer, singers and conductor – without whom no evidence of his own creativity would exist, and by whom, as Götz Friedrich says, it is invariably influenced. 'My ideas are filtered before they come to the audience – a thousand times, by everybody I work with. I may have a strong idea in the beginning, but it is filtered – sometimes corrupted, sometimes developed'. When the team changes, the stimuli change and the producer's own input changes; and some producers acknowledge this in a constant search for fresh collaborators, particularly vital if – as often happens in opera – they are confronting a work they have produced several times before.

One of the difficulties of defining the producer's job and assessing an individual producer's qualities, is that his contribution is made at several levels. At the most basic, he translates what is on the page into movements on stage, co-ordinating what happens physically during the opera much as the conductor co-ordinates what happens musically. At a deeper level, however, his function might seem to be to offer an interpretation, 'spectacles' through which to see the piece – simultaneously a statement of the work and a comment on it. The growing emphasis on this second aspect of producing was foreshadowed in the straight theatre, particularly in Shakespearian production, in the 1960s, as Michael Billington – theatre critic

Götz Friedrich with Kiri te Kanawa and Placido Domingo during preliminary rehearsals of his production of *Manon Lescaut* (Covent Garden, 1984).

of the *Guardian* – suggests: 'Quite clearly, in the 1950s, Shakespeare was dominated by star actors, and producers were mainly there, it seems to me, to clear the stage more general, and more profound, relevance. Wieland Wagner, for example, has with every role given weight and power, was very rare, almost nonexistent. . . . The attitude to Shakespearian verse was often that of some singers to arias – it was warbling, the sort of thing you sang rather than thought. Peter Hall was the visionary who changed the face of things in Stratford in the 1960s, partly by creating a company, partly by putting great emphasis on meaning. . . . I would have thought that by the same process something of that sort is now going on in the best of the opera productions I see. You don't just drum up another *Madam Butterfly* or *Rigoletto*, you ask what the work is about and try to get the meaning across to the audience.'

But what degree of licence does a producer have in the search for the meaning of the piece? How far should he be constrained, in offering his version of the work, by the intentions of its originators? Should he concentrate on bringing out what the composer meant? or something else that he himself perceives within the piece? or both? One school of thought holds that generally he should confine himself to realising what the composer had in mind – the same sentiments, in the same period setting, accompanied, where these are known, by the same manoeuvres on stage, same gestures, same props, even the same type of designs: in other words, both his general intentions and his specific operating instructions for the piece. Carried to its logical extreme, this principle has produced the *riesumazione* – the 'exhumation' of the original sets and costumes, or their reconstruction in accordance with the original designs. In Verona in 1983, for example, a production of *Aida* was mounted in the original costumes from the première in 1871, with sets that were replicas of those used for the first Verona *Aida* in 1913. Elaborate lengths to which to go in pursuit of authenticity, perhaps, but it would not have displeased Verdi who is known actively to have resented the notion that every performance is a fresh creation. 'This is a principle that leads to exaggeration and artificiality. . . . I want to have one single creator, and all I ask is that what is written down shall be performed simply and accurately.'

Letters, reminiscences and scores (printed and in manuscript) often furnish information both as to what the composer wanted and what in the event he got. In the case of Verdi, for several of his later works (*Simon Boccanegra, I Vespri Siciliani* and *Otello*, for example) 'production books' survive – documents compiled during rehearsals, setting out bar by bar, move by move, staging ideas which Verdi either initiated or approved. Of the *Otello* production book Andrew Porter has written, 'It provides for the staging what the score does for the singing, and to observe it should be no more "inhibiting" to artists than it is to observe the composer's printed notes.'

On both purist and practical grounds there would appear to be a strong case for absolute fidelity to the composer's express instructions, where they survive. It should – theoretically – make it easier for the producer to serve the spirit of the work, by reducing the risk that he will contradict the music in his staging or introduce distracting anachronisms. And a traditional approach is better-suited to the short rehearsal periods which bedevil the producer, particularly in the United States, forming an existing foundation of common knowledge on which he can build quickly, without debate.

Nevertheless many, perhaps most producers these days argue vigorously against attempting to recreate the past. As Liviu Ciulei, Director of the Guthrie Theater in Minneapolis, points out, audiences and performers have changed over the years. So has the producer, and his conception of a work can only ever be a view of the original through a prism, not through a magnifying glass. The present cannot but affect the way we look at the past – Peter Brook: 'It is rare for a historian or a philosopher to escape from the influence of his time, and for the worker in the theatre, whose livelihood depends on his contact with his audiences, this is impossible. Consequently, however hard a producer or designer may strive to mount a classic with complete objectivity, he can never avoid reflecting a second period – the one in which he works and lives.'

The current climate – social, political, aesthetic, philosophical – will have a more pronouced impact on some works than others. Elijah Moshinsky: 'Take Wagner's anti-Semitism – there's what he meant by it, and what it means to us after the Holocaust. When you have the undercurrent of all that pomposity and tribal senti- ment and soul-stirring Aryan myth-making, can it mean the same thing now? Can we be so innocent? It's well-nigh impossible to think as if the Holocaust hadn't existed. . . . Operas are part of cultural history and the history of ideas, and I don't think they necessarily exist in a kind of uncontaminated world which doesn't have a morality; all life has a moral basis of some kind, and you can't say that operas exist in a moral free zone.'

To some producers, it is something of an abdication of responsibility *not* to obtrude the present; to insist on what is specific about a piece – amongst other things, the way in which it was first produced – may be to obscure what is of more general, and more profound, relevance. Wieland Wagner, for example, has reasoned: 'It is no denigration of Richard Wagner to say that he was a true child of his time and that what he left behind is perhaps nothing more than a consummate interpretation of his own epoch. . . . There are elements, valid for their time, which may appear to be an indivisible part of the work as a whole, but which in fact rather obscure what is of permanent human significance.'

Peter Sellars, Director of the American National Theater in Washington DC, is a leading campaigner for the cause of making the theatre of the past speak to an audience now; and rather than reconstructing, painstakingly and literally, the visual imagery and modes of thought and gesture of another time, he will recast each work he produces, play or opera, in the cultural vocabulary of the twentieth century. Partly he feels this makes it easier for the performers to articulate the ideas contained in the original: 'They can feel free to do things that they understand completely, rather than existing in some nether world which they're pretending to understand. . . . By the time they've exhausted themselves in the effort of imagination of what it was like to live in the sixteenth century, they have little mental space left for the primary issues of the play.' At the same time it makes these issues easier for the audience to ingest; a novel can be read and re-read, a piece of live theatre is seen once in the space of two or three hours and then it is gone. 'I think a very important function of drama is to operate in images that are so immediately buried in the audience's daily experience that there's not that initial leap that has to be made to get at the material. . . . Frequently operas are written in code. They are written in a code that a previous audience has under- stood, both in terms of a musical language and also in terms of a series of images . . . Our task is to crack the code, and recast it in systems of reference that have the same heightened possibility of meaning and connection to a sense of national, historic and individual identity for today's public'.

As an American, five years out of Harvard, Peter Sellars has worked almost exclusively for an American audience and his references have largely been those of the American twentieth century – an *Armida* set in Vietnam; a *King Lear* whose principal decorative motif was a Lincoln Continental; an *Orlando* whose action was divided between Cape Canaveral and outer space; a *Così fan tutte* which unfolded in a 1930s-style quick-and-filthy Despina's Diner; a version of Gorky's *Summerfolk* set in counterpoint with a dozen Gershwin songs. (He freely admits that he does not feel as fluent in the image-languages of other countries.) This is not the same, however, as literal updating, which might be defined as straight and complete transliteration of a work into another, more modern, period; its aim is almost always to be veristic and updaters have no hesitation in altering words and production details to fit the chosen setting. A *Norma*, for example, whose Druids have been replaced by Middle European partisans in and after the Second World War; a *Forza del Destino* set in the Spanish Civil War (or the present conflict in El Salvador – wars, universal in horror, being considered pretty well interchangeable); a *Madam Butterfly* set in the Nagasaki of 1938–45, in which Cio-Cio-San's fruitless hankering for Pinkerton is presented as a would-be-mordant *exposé* of the twentieth-century American Dream, and her suicide is staged, with frightful predictability, against the explosion of the second atomic bomb. In the last ten years certain settings have become particularly popular – the Roaring Twenties, the French Riviera (preferably in the Edwardian period), the British Raj, Fascist dictatorships.

This trend Peter Sellars despises: 'I *hate* updating as a gambit, I resent it actively – it's cheap and vulgar and obnoxious and not the point. My productions are never updated.' Updating for him simply replaces one set of limited images with another, and falls foul of one of his first precepts – that the audience should never be told precisely what to think. 'Any time an image narrows the field and says "This means *this*", a circumscribed level of meaning, that's a catastrophe. Rather than narrowing a field of possibilities, I try and make my images open.' In consequence, though he uses everyday modern images, there is no need to obliterate all trace of the original period; past and present can coexist on stage, as they are *not* permitted to do in an updating. 'In this Gorky/Gershwin evening I didn't change the lyrics of the songs so they would fit into the Gorky play, and I didn't change the Gorky play so it would fit the 1920s. I left every word of both intact. . . . There were lyrics that were clearly of the twenties, a play that was clearly of 1905. I made no attempt to join those corners and smooth them off. . . . Most directors, when they update, clean up the mess and the result is that the play has to lose things to fit.' He took an equally firm line with *Così fan tutte*, compromising Da Ponte's Italian libretto not at all to accommodate quintessentially American stage pictures.

In Sellars's productions diverse ideas from different periods, different contexts, different cultures coexist, not peacefully but productively. 'It's the old Eisenstein thing – we work by montage. By juxtaposition, combined with a ferocious exactitude, you can have two ideas which you get at terribly precisely, and by putting them next to each other, a chemical reaction results which is extremely stimulating and puts a number of other ideas into the air. It's building up these little detonator points. . . .' A plurality of images, often deliberately incongruous with each other and sometimes apparently at odds with the text, can be confusing but it is also a rich breeding ground for ideas: 'The best way to show up a text is not to mirror it, because then you see the same thing twice. . . . Seeing the same thing twice doesn't make you think twice, it makes you think less than once because you don't have to work so hard. I like to set up a visual counterpoint.' He packs in Noh drama, music-hall turns, Victorian barnstorming melodrama, deaf-and-dumb sign language, television commercials, contemporary politics. The jigsaw can then be assembled in innumerable different ways: 'I leave huge room in my productions for the audience to enter and participate and make it happen. . . . What they bring to the theatre is three quarters of it. . . . If you have a hundred readings, you know you have something truthful. The minute you have one reading, you have something fascistic.'

The results often seem to stray very far from the original, but Peter Sellars feels he is attacking only the *inessential* instructions of the composer – the operating instructions, the physical trappings of the piece, not its intellectual core. 'Why does a composer go to all this trouble of writing an opera? Not, ultimately, because of preoccupations with notions of style or a predilection for certain types of costume. The central issue is always subject matter. . . . I don't care what period a production is set in. Ideas like setting *Così* in a diner are a dime a dozen, I don't set much store by them. . . . What I care about is that the things which are happening between those people are happening and they could be happening in any other set. It just happens that the diner gives me some language that I can use. It could have been an ocean liner.' He is anxious to demonstrate the irrelevance of external form and style – and in the process to make a point about the commercialism of twentieth-century American society. 'I invite all this materialism on stage to its funeral, to frustrate it and to thwart it and to humiliate it with anachronisms, and to break down finally the lie that anybody's life is based on what they're wearing or the furniture they're sitting on.' Towards the inner content of the work, however, his attitude is avowedly one of respect. His aim is to convey, by using tools with a sharper cutting edge for our time, the composer's essential arguments with as much force as they had when the piece was first performed – 'to recreate at some level the opening-night experience for the very first audience. I want the things that surprised Mozart's audience to surprise this audience.'

This impulse to serve the composer – 'Stravinsky said all directors and conductors were second-class creators, and I really do believe that I'm a second-class creator and not a first' – is what Peter Sellars has in common with many ostensibly more conservative producers anxious not to assert themselves at the composer's expense. It does not mean that they, any more than Peter Sellars himself, are necessarily prepared to limit themselves to following the original production to the letter

– the manner and direction of exits and entrances and other movements, the relative positions of characters on stage, details of dress, equipment and setting – as though the meaning of the piece were immanent in the operating instructions which, as Elijah Moshinsky firmly insists, it is not. (On the other hand, there are stage directions and stage directions: there are those simply appended to the libretto and superimposed on the score, and those which are built into the score. The latter, in Jonathan Miller's view, you ignore 'at your peril – like the place where Verdi quite clearly intends someone to enter a garden, as in *Rigoletto*: probably it would be unwise not to observe that strange change of key, and the relaxation of the tempo to go with the moment when he enters this peaceful garden where he thinks of himself as at home. In the same way, when Susanna exits from the closet in *Figaro*, there's a moment when the music builds up to a tension and then quite suddenly there's a change in tempo and she comes out. . . . If you listen to what Mozart is actually saying, not in what he or his librettist writes in the score as stage directions, but what he actually writes in the notes, you can generally tell when someone must turn, when someone must enter, when someone must embrace. There are phrases which melt, phrases which restrain. . .')

Nor do these producers accept that there is only one 'correct' perspective on a piece. Most works of any complexity have meanings which the composer has not acknowledged. Jonathan Miller argues that creators do not always have determinate images or explicit ideas in their heads when writing imaginative works, and that no work with any degree of depth should be capable of precise paraphrase, but should have the capacity to deliver versions of itself which the author did not necessarily anticipate. 'If you insist on a single canonical interpretation, you turn opera houses into churches and audiences into congregations.' Elijah Moshinsky elaborates: 'If opera is to be alive . . . it has to be what Shakespeare has become at the Royal Shakespeare Company – you can perform *Much Ado* five times in five different ways, and each time it becomes another fragment of the endless meaning of the play.'

Nevertheless in bringing out supplementary or alternative interpretations, these producers tend to feel it vital to stay within the composer's 'field of meaning' – to reproduce something at the core of the work which he, being a reasonable man, would recognise. For John Dexter, it is a case of identifying the emotional centre of the work – for himself initially, but if he discovers this to be too far removed from what he perceives the *composer's* emotional centre to be, he will not produce the work for fear of distorting it. For Jonathan Miller, it is a case of searching for 'a metaphor which lies at the heart of the work'. Metaphors can be applied very freely, and the more general the theme, the greater the scope for interpretation. *Fidelio*, for example, treats of the universal issues of married love and the right to freedom of belief; to express its message on stage in terms of other crusaders for freedom – Christ, Gandhi, Che Guevara – may rarely be convincing in the execution, but in principle it is valid. To recast a court jester in an Italian city state as a barman compelled to entertain a Mafia boss and his mob, or to rephrase the unimaginably long and mysterious sea voyage of Tristan and Isolde as the flight of a spaceship between distant planets is to present situations which, though beyond the cognisance of the composer, are recognisably equivalent to those he has depicted and, in this sense, within his field of meaning. Exactly what constitutes exceeding the composer's limits is largely a question of degree and a matter of opinion; but there would probably be general agreement that in presenting the same three operas as treatises on conjugal prison visits, student promiscuity, or drug abuse, the producer would have done it.

In extreme cases such as these, the producer could be accused of having failed to produce genuine instances of the works in question, and of having wasted time, effort and money in the process. There is, however, another school of thought which considers a concern for the composer's intentions to be only one aspect of the producer's responsibilities – which are those not merely of a re-creator, but of a creator in his own right. In this context Anthony Besch has remarked, 'If a director asked Harold Pinter what his plays were about, particularly the earlier ones like *The Caretaker*, he would never, never answer. He'd say, "It's what you make it." Quite acceptable in a creative artist.' If you can use the materials the composer has provided to express something other than what he expressly directs, the argument runs, then you may (some would say, must), if the results are going to have greater force and truth for an audience *now*. Götz Friedrich: 'You have to recognise that you're not playing the opera for the time when it was written. . . . Look at *Fidelio*. We know Beethoven wrote it, but the time that has elapsed since he wrote it has *also* written it, the 170 years since it was written have co-written it, have written how we approach the work today. It must have a particular interest for our time if people are to extract the message, appreciate the artistic structure and the aesthetic marvels of the work.'

For him there can be no question of being 'unfaithful' to the work, because it has no single, independent objective existence to be either mirrored or sullied. Every piece of live art – opera, play, ballet, symphony or song – has two existences: one in the composer's head or on paper, the other in performance – the one essentially just a blueprint for the other. 'An opera only truly exists when it is performed . . . and no two productions will be the same. This is opera's fate, to change – and its opportunity, to assimilate more and more with time.'

Friedrich believes implicitly in the need to know what the composer intended – 'We have *always* to go back to what the authors wanted, although we don't have to *do* everything on that basis'. He never alters a note or word of the original (which is more than can be said of many less 'radical' producers), and he makes it quite clear that he feels a dual responsibility – not just to himself and our time, but also to the composer and his. Nevertheless, belief in the producer as a creator in some sense on a par with the composer has opened the door to others who acknowledge no obligation to the composer at all. Sir Peter Hall: 'There's a kind of surrealistic school of direction current now, particularly in opera, but also in the European theatre, where it seems that the director's function is thought to be that he reads the text of the play, or listens to the records of the opera, and whatever images come into his head he puts on the stage.'

At its worst this approach leads to the producer producing his own psyche and nothing more – his own impulses towards violence, his own sexual fears and enthusiasms, his own feelings about marriage, parents, children, death, some doubtless subconscious, others patently self-conscious, all with a more or less appropriate musical accompaniment. The result may or may not be interesting, but it tends to bear no relation to the original work. A more calculating form of deviation from the composer's wishes is the use of his work as a vehicle for political statements – most commonly Marxist and made by German producers, either in Germany (a land, in critic James Helme Sutcliffe's words, 'where seriousness of purpose is a perennial substitute for fidelity to the work as written') or in other European houses where the administrators suffer from what Rodney Milnes describes as 'post-Imperial guilt'. Applied uniformly, the politicised approach is not only a denial of the individual genius of the composer – each work becoming a similar-sounding quotation from a larger thesis – but also tends to undermine the individuality of the producer. Jonathan Miller, for one, claims half-seriously that German productions of a certain sort could virtually be computerised: feed in the same ingredients – 'pieces of publicly-owned apparatus' such as alienation effects and phallic symbols – and if you can work the keyboard, you can make a production.

So diverse are the aims which different types of producer pursue, and so dissimilar their perceptions of the producer's job, that generalisations are rash. But for any producer, whether he considers himself an unfettered creator, a literal recreator or something between the two – most could perhaps best be described as unfettered recreators – there are certain basic criteria which have to be met if a production is to be successful.

Firstly, is the producer's conception of the work an organic whole? Is it generative? Does the idea, in Jonathan Miller's phrase, have a 'topographical entirety, from which the production detail can be mapped'? For Franco Zeffirelli, the inspiration for his production of *Cavalleria Rusticana* was a single mental image – 'You don't need many ideas, you need one. In *Cavalleria* I have always seen the core as a wide white street going uphill in a Sicilian village, that and the sky. At night the wind blows, and a tiny figure with a black shawl comes down running, closing under her shawl her pain and sorrow.' The hazard is the shaft of inspiration which throws dazzling light on one aspect of the work – but fails to illuminate the whole. For Jonathan Miller, for instance, the world of *Rigoletto* could be generated complete in the setting he had chosen for it; that of *Don Giovanni*, he discovered, could not. Though he was greatly tempted to express what he saw as the work's surrealist side through the visual imagery of Giorgio de Chirico – 'statues and strangeness' – the two worlds, he perceived, intersected only at this one point; to have applied the same references throughout, ignoring both

what is funny and what is overtly rather than latently sinister about *Don Giovanni*, would ultimately have done more to obscure than elucidate. Some of the least successful productions occur when a producer is unable to resist the appeal of the isolated brilliant idea, pads it out with less brilliant fellow travellers and ends up with a 'Christmas stocking of notions'. Elijah Moshinsky: 'I think there's a new "high camp" opera production style – and that is gimmickry, gratuitous and meretricious invention, striking images hauled in to entertain – almost like a circus entertainment at times. It has a starting point, but no rationale.'

Even more important a question – is the concept intelligible to anybody besides the creative team of producer and designer? For if it is not, it makes very little difference how original, striking or unified it is; as Walter Felsenstein stressed: 'Even in productions tackled honestly the intentions, while they are valid and could be put into practice, are only partially recognisable. Not enough for the public to understand, though enough for the public to misunderstand. And this is a state of emergency.' Peter Sellars takes good care to hedge his bets by issuing a manifesto. 'Every show I do, the program is just crammed. I never leave that sort of thing to chance. Of course people come with expectations, and it's our responsibility to cope with that and to shape them. People say "Isn't it cowardly to have reams of program notes?" – no, all I want is for people to get it. You just want to share as much information as possible, so nobody feels they are on the outside of it looking in, so people feel included.'

Some have argued that the imaginative impact of the producer on a work is what is keeping opera alive. Jonathan Miller: 'Most of the works in the existing operatic repertoire had their death rattle on them, all these works of art have got the risk of dying; it's only now that we have the same attitudes to works of art that we have to patients. We endlessly believe that they've got to be resuscitated, given heart transplants. . . . It's a very peculiar feature of modern times that we do keep them going and these transformations are probably the only way in which we will keep them going.'

More positively, Elijah Moshinsky believes, 'The theatre generally is not necessarily a place where serious ideas survive without the help of a producer. . . . The composers had the depth; now that they are dead, it is for the producers to keep their moral seriousness alive' – and to do this in the face of strong competition. In the 1960s Wieland Wagner put the rise of the producer in a practical perspective: 'Have [the older generation] not grasped what difficulties are involved in maintaining the dramatic and operatic stage against these new mass media [radio, gramophone, cinema and television] and in keeping them alive in the changed social conditions of today? The increased importance of the producer is certainly attributable to this necessity.'

OPPOSITE Franco Zeffirelli rehearsing Amy Shuard as Santuzza in his production of *Cavalleria Rusticana* (Covent Garden, 1959).

15

Evolving the Conception

'Having a conception' of a work means vastly different things to different producers. To one it may entail complex and detailed reference to a specific religious or philosophical system, social or political theory, literary or artistic background; to another it may mean no more than a vague resolution to stage the piece in modern dress, or a conviction that the setting should be outside rather than in. For Ronald Eyre it is 'a matter of finding a little way into a work which isn't an arbitrary expression of self-satisfaction or self-aggrandisement, not a self-congratulatory thing – trying to find some little series of keys with which you can open the doors that are already put there in the music and libretto'. And the conception will not necessarily be fully formulated by the time production rehearsals begin – many producers Elijah Moshinsky included, find the rehearsals themselves a necessary part of the creative process: 'Sometimes you come to a production realising how you want to find it, but you need the rehearsals to *actually* find it . . . to bring the interpretation out within the framework of what you've prepared'. But the producer is likely, at whatever level of detail, to have some sort of 'fix' on the work, to have channelled and ordered his initial responses clearly enough to provide a basis for action.

Hans Werner Henze once wrote, 'The real producer is always the same, namely the musical score', and some producers, in full agreement, derive their conception of an opera primarily from its music (though not all can actually read a score – the expansion in the recording industry having opened opera to producers with no musical training at all). Sir Peter Hall, for example, one might expect (though he reads music) to work first and foremost from the libretto, given the fervour with which he has always subscribed to F.R. Leavis's doctrine of 'textual seriousness', and his insistence on elucidating the underlying meaning of a text. But in opera, for him, the music is the text – 'The primary expression that the audience receives is musical, not verbal. I have the same feeling towards the music in opera as towards the text in literature', and he starts from the score.

For John Dexter the style of a production is dictated at the outset by the music, elucidated by the text. Similarly, each of Andrei Serban's conceptions has been founded on 'a response which comes from listening to the music itself, not the story – an emotional response, out of which the whole logic of why, and how, and in what period has to come afterwards'. His production of *Eugene Onegin*, stylised and set largely in the open, grew in this way: 'Tchaikovsky's music evoked for me this Russian endlessness, there's no horizon to the field, it's a field which just goes on forever. I could see Tatyana walking in the field while she was writing her letter. There was no way I could see her locked in her room, sitting down writing this letter. I could see her responding in movement to the emotional states provoked by the night and the open space of the field, the smell of the field. . . .'

For other producers, however, the emphasis is rather different. David Pountney, for example, argues: 'The motivation of the music is on the stage and not the other way round. The Count's aria is a vigorous aria in a certain key because the Count is in a certain temper, because of what is happening dramatically, not because Mozart wanted to write an aria in a certain key at that point. . . . It is *dramma per musica*, as the phrase goes, drama through music, not music through drama'. This is not to advocate simply producing the libretto, which is always to be examined in the context of the music, but many producers derive much of their inspiration directly from the text and its associations, and research into its background – historical, personal and literary – will constitute a major part of their preparations.

'Historical background' may be construed in two quite different ways. For some operas, the producer will choose to concentrate on the historical context in which the works are actually set – Tudor England, Czarist Russia, Republican Rome, France during the Revolution, Vienna in the Biedermeier epoch. Colin Graham describes his approach in such cases: 'I do as much historical work as I possibly can, to find out about the people involved . . . compare various writers' opinions of the protagonists – whether Don Carlos was a drivelling idiot, as some say, or whether he was a neurotic, rather deprived young man as others say. Then find out about the conditions of life at the time, all facets of life. Then compute all that along with what the composer and librettist have done, find out what choices they have made and what emphases they are making. . . . Very often those historical operas are about the private person in a public position. . . . The composers are very interested in what happens to the characters (ball scenes, say, or street scenes) at the moment of a particular event, but not terribly interested in the historical aspect of what was really happening in the country at the time, socially and politically. Inevitably the composer will go for the emotional impact of a story, because on the whole music is emotional. As director and designer, you can point up these things with a social and historical context.'

Where the work's setting is less immediately evocative ('Italy, fifth century AD', 'mid-seventeenth-century Bohemia', 'Ancient Greece'), the producer may find more to interest him in the historical background to its *composition*. Götz Friedrich, in fact, considers that the atmosphere and values of the epoch in which a piece was composed *must* be taken into account: 'It is first of all necessary to read what composer and librettist have written, and to study what it meant in that time – in terms of its social implications, their artistic aims, any personal relevance it may

have had for them. . . . Every artistic work is a combination of the subjective and the objective – in the subjective expression you find a mirror for the objective circumstances of the time. . . . When I did my *Freischütz* for Covent Garden, many people were horrified because it was so *dark* – but it was written just after the Thirty Years' War; it is necessary to understand what they must have had in their minds when they wrote just after a chaos like the Thirty Years' War. . . . To tell a story of men means looking at the history of Man.'

Simply on artistic rather than on ideological grounds, the producer may feel that a piece is more revealing about the time in which it was written and performed than that in which it is set, and will try to put *both* on the stage, concentrating his researches on the composer's milieu and using this as a filter through which to view the action of the opera. (It has become something of a cliché, for example, to cast the chorus as an on-stage audience contemporary with the composer, observing from a distance of centuries the protagonists of the drama.) Because the settings for *opera seria*, for instance, are often deliberately remote and rarely

Nicholas Hytner's production of *Xerxes*, designed by David Fielding, with Valerie Masterson as Romilda (*centre*) and Ann Murray as Xerxes (ENO, 1985).

integral to the plot, these works are often felt to say more now about the convention of *opera seria* itself and the time in which it flourished – a line taken by Nicholas Hytner in his production of Handel's *Xerxes*. Intricate and pointless goings-on in ancient Persia were mounted firmly in a frame of Handel's London: in one act, a miniature three-dimensional Persepolis at the back of the stage was seen through the perspective (literally) of the Vauxhall Gardens downstage, with the Roubiliac statue of Handel overlooking the proceedings, and the chorus cast as *habitués* of the Thames Embankment rather than the shores of the Persian Gulf. The production made no attempt to convey the feel of the ancient Middle East, as a traditional production of *Don Carlos*, say, might try to evoke Spain during the Inquisition, and was far more instructive on the subject of what amused fashionable eighteenth-century pleasure seekers. The programme was full of references not to Xerxes or the bridge of boats across the Hellespont, but to Dryden, Pope and Addison, Orientalism rather than the Orient, antiquarianism rather than antiquity itself.

Occasionally the circumstances of the composer's life may provide an insight into his work. Producers have drawn inspiration, for example, from the fact that Mozart, in love with two sisters, could marry only one (Sir Peter Hall in his production of *Così fan tutte*); from the suggestion that Puccini was haunted by the suicide of a young serving girl, precipitated by the implacable harshness of his wife (Tony Palmer, in his version of *Turandot*); from the knowledge that Janáček was capable of exploiting ruthlessly even the most painful and personal material in the cause of his art – he is known to have noted in music his daughter's dying sigh – as the composer Živny is made insistently to do in David Pountney's production of *Osud*.

More often, however, the producer contents himself with pulling out and applying an idea or ideas from the composer's social or intellectual environment. Dvořák's *Rusalka* was premièred in the year in which *The Interpretation of Dreams* was first published, and Freudian symbolism dominated David Pountney's staging of the work, set not in the glades and pools of Bohemia but in a Victorian nursery where an adolescent Rusalka is tormented by sexual feelings awakened only to be repressed. Mesmerism was all the rage in Vienna in 1790, and for his St Louis production of *Così fan tutte* Jonathan Miller took an isolated reference to Mesmer's discoveries – the magnet with which the 'Doctor' revives the insensible 'Albanians' – and extended it to embrace the work as a whole. The set (designed by John Conklin) was constructed as a room within a room, on the model of a 'Mesmer box' – a wooden box divided up by a maze of partitions, into which mice were dropped and from which they could only escape if they executed specified manoeuvres in a certain order; in much the same way, Jonathan Miller suggests, Fiordiligi and Dorabella, Guglielmo and Ferrando are trapped in a situation from which they can free themselves only by performing emotional acrobatics of Don Alfonso's devising.

It is not uncommon for Jonathan Miller to find his 'generative idea' in this way, in the climate of thought surrounding the composition. After familiarising himself with music and libretto, he explains: 'I'll read as much as I can about the composer to find out what sort of things he was up to, look at letters, diaries, whatever there is about him and what he said about his work, what *he* thought he was doing.' Then, in search of a metaphor, he will begin to think about 'all sorts of background stuff – not necessarily associated with the music'.

In the case of Janáček's *The Cunning Little Vixen*, lateral thinking took him a long way from the traditional stagings: 'I immersed myself in all sorts of folk material from Czechoslovakia – peasant costumes, woodwork. . . . Then I began looking at things like animal furs and skins, and I got the idea that they looked somehow very like uniforms. I began looking at Hungarian and Czechoslovak Hussar uniforms – and I began to get the idea that perhaps peasant costumes and uniforms were akin to animal skins, which are also uniforms of one sort or another. Gradually a metaphor of uniforms in relation to animal species sprang into existence. . . . I knew I wasn't going to make a kind of Disney spectacular, I had to find what Janáček was on about, and it seemed it was a metaphor *about* Nature, rather than Nature itself. Nature, it seemed to me, represented a sort of *ancien régime* as compared with the human beings, who had changed with history in a way that animals don't change with history; human beings have a history, animals don't – animals merely have a past. Therefore I wanted to get something that was pretty traditional for the animals; whereas the humans were dressed in rather drab early twentieth-century clothes, the animals were bright and colourful, wearing the traditional peasant costumes of the area. I think it was *that* that Janáček was trying to pull out – some kind of distinction between a woodland world of antiquity and a world of drab everydayness that was the humans.'

Where the opera is based on an already existing work, the producer has an additional reservoir of information to hand. Ande Anderson has always considered it of paramount importance to understand how the composer has used his sources. After listening to the score to discover precisely what the composer has done in the music, he goes back to the source – poem, novel, play – to find out *why* he has written the music in that particular way, 'which part of the source he has caught in which passage of the opera: why he has written *this* phrase in *this* way over *these* words'. Whether or not the composer has represented his source faithfully, the comparison is invariably instructive. Elijah Moshinsky, for example, felt that Verdi, unlike nineteenth-century commentators such as Bradley, *had* captured the essence of Shakespeare's *Macbeth*, seeing it as a study of the nature of evil, in microcosm (within Macbeth himself) and in macrocosm (manifest in Nature); he presented the piece accordingly as 'a murder with metaphysical ramifications', and felt the experience greatly to have enriched his understanding of the play. Jonathan Miller, on the other hand, studying Henry James's *The Turn of the Screw*, came to quite different conclusions from those drawn by Benjamin Britten and his librettist, Myfanwy Piper. To credit the ghosts of Peter Quint and Miss Jessel with an independent existence (by implication, since in Scene Eight they talk directly to each other with no one else present) was, he felt, mistaken. They are far more likely to be mere projections of the Governess's repressions, since it is she who is the principal catalyst of corruption. This view, rooted in his reading of the novella, he considered to be corroborated by the discovery that Henry James had contact with the eminent neurologist Hughlings Jackson and could through him, therefore, have become familiar with the symptoms of temporal lobe seizure (the 'turn') clearly manifested by the Governess (the children's warder, or 'screw').

The conception is both the first step towards a production, and the last the producer can take unaided. From now onwards he will be at least partially dependent on others to translate the 'concept', the 'metaphor', the 'emotional centre' into a stage setting in three dimensions and make it public.

16

Working with the Designer

Ours is a predominantly visual age, in which we tend to have been conditioned by television and film to base judgements primarily on what is seen and only secondarily on what is heard. Any opera production makes its initial impact, and sometimes its lasting impressions, through its design – people not infrequently criticise a production when what they dislike is the set; and the casting of the designer, the man who in Ronald Eyre's words must 'help to create the world in which the work can live – can be born, live its course and die', has become in consequence crucially important.

Designers, like any other creative artist, shrink from typecasting. Nevertheless, unless extraordinarily versatile they will tend to be associated in the minds of others with one, or at the most two, particular styles and the producer will be careful to choose a designer (this being a privilege he will almost always claim) whose general approach he expects to be compatible with the piece and the conception he has in mind. John Copley: 'I'm not going to choose someone to do a baroque opera if they can only do dustbins and plastic bags.' In making his choice the producer will these days have a good deal of scope. As producers have claimed more and more licence in their interpretations, the range of designers working in opera has widened correspondingly. With some notable exceptions (at the Kroll Oper, under Klemperer, for instance), design in major houses tended even as late as the 1970s to be predominantly naturalistic and decorative – but an increasing number of producers no longer feel constrained to operate within this genre. For example, when originally evolving his conception of *I Vespri Siciliani*, John Dexter abandoned the idea of a literal, period approach. What he saw at the heart of the drama was the figure of Elena centre-stage calling for blood and, tragically, getting it when she no longer wanted it – a situation redolent, he felt, of Greek tragedy for which a formal and abstract approach was required, and he invited Josef Svoboda to provide 'something I could do Oedipus on'. Fifteen years ago the resulting set – almost entirely black and white and consisting principally of a monumental flight of steps – was given a luke-warm reception at the Met as 'insufficiently evocative of Palermo', but it was a harbinger of the attack that has since been launched at all levels of the opera world on unbridled naturalism and decoration.

Many have pointed out that there can be no such thing as absolute realism in the context of the theatre. Jonathan Miller argues: 'There's no realism in art. Even if you look at the so-called realism of Courbet, it's always a realism which is seen through an imagination. In the same way, a designer who works with realism does it within the framework of the artificiality of a theatre. It's always notional realism, stage realism.' And in the opera house any semblance of reality is under-mined still further by the presence of the orchestra which makes it impossible to sustain the illusion of the 'fourth wall'. But logical impossibilities notwithstand-ing, the tradition of naturalism has grown stronger as the means of simulating reality have developed – as painted flats have largely given way to three-dimensional scenery and construction materials have become ever more varied and flexible – and for many, 'bravura realism' remains the acme of opera design. Evoking a powerful illusion of reality, bravura realism is rooted in a shrewd under-standing of what an audience is looking for and how much it in fact sees. Desmond Heeley points out that the designer has it in his power to focus audience attention wherever he wants it. When designing *Manon Lescaut* for the Met he took consider-able pains with the furnishings for Manon's dressing table in Act Two, demanding absolute clarity of detail in order to crystallise an image and evoke by implication an ambience of splendour; with this achieved, the rest of the room could actually be slightly blurred. For Act Two of *Tosca*, Franco Zeffirelli lit Scarpia's apartment from the fireplace on one side, with light falling principally on the wall opposite. Against that wall he placed solid busts; on the back wall, not directly lit, and in shadow, he had busts created by *trompe l'oeil* painting.

Following on but distinct from this approach – a truly theatrical mixture of built scenery, perspective painting and minutely detailed props, some fake and some real – is a more thoroughgoing photographic naturalism perhaps best repre-sented by the designs of Julia Trevelyan Oman, in which everything *is* precisely what it seems, meticulously recreated with every period detail correct, in the style of television costume drama. For her designs for *Eugene Onegin*, Miss Oman flew to Leningrad to examine the originals from which Lensky's pistols were to be copied. The challenge of this type of design is making actuality serve the theatre.

There is no question but that both these brands of naturalism – one dependent on illusion, the other on facsimile – are still popular with audiences. They can be very beautiful, they rarely contradict audience expectations and they are almost never controversial. But within the profession, objections are increasingly voiced. From the practical point of view naturalism, requiring a good deal of detail, tends to be expensive; 'poor theatre' has its advocates on economic as well as ideological grounds. Equally, 'naturalism', like 'authenticity', is a relative and not an absolute term. When devising a production of *Macbeth*, is the designer faithfully to recreate *our* view of eleventh-century Scotland? or Verdi's? or Shakespeare's? In any case, some would argue, by settling upon any one specific scene and recreating it exactly, the designer can narrow the field of meaning unnecessarily; he (or she) should avoid what Jonathan Miller calls 'a hideous determinacy of image', the type of design which, replete in every detail, restricts rather than stimulates the imagination. For *Rigoletto* he sought from his designers (Patrick Robertson and Rosemary Vercoe) a version not of 1950s New York itself, but of Edward Hopper's paintings of New York from which detail had already been bleached by the artist, leaving room for the play of imagination.

For many professional theatre designers, making simulacra of reality is not what theatre is about. Theatre is not essentially a medium for the conveying of information – Stefanos Lazaridis: 'There's so much television and film – people can get all that visual information from there. When Puccini wrote *Madam Butterfly*, how many people had been to Japan? Everybody knows or has an idea of what Japan looks like today – why go to the opera house to see what Japan looks like?' The theatre's *forte* is the effect that is outside or beyond daily life. Sir Osbert Lancaster, with a good deal of elegant and highly stylised painted scenery to his credit, remarks: 'To have everything built into three dimensions is not just a waste of time, it means you lose a lot of the magic of theatrical effect. To have real trees on stage – too dotty . . .' John Conklin elaborates: 'We are so tied to prose, to anecdote, to realism or naturalism in our society. . . . All the words like "melodramatic", "operatic", "theatrical", "rhetorical", "extravagant" are all words of disrepute. Opera is "false". I don't accept this. In its rhetoric, in all the things that are "wrong" with it, lies what makes it so interesting. . . . We've missed the lessons of *Wozzeck* and the lessons of Shakespeare, and tried to extract from them something which *isn't* their best feature – we've turned away from what is mysterious and artificial about them, and insisted on what is "true" and realistic in them, pinned them down to meaning just one thing. . . . We're constantly trying to demystify art, to *understand* – we feel that our duty with things is to understand them. What fascinates me about opera is that it is basically un-understandable.'

Realism is also under attack because so much of its detail is purely decorative, existing only for its own sake and serving no purpose in terms of the drama. The audience's involuntary gasp of appreciation at the prettiness of it all is the designer's reward and often, it might seem, his sole objective. Taken to its extreme, this approach – dismissed by its opponents as 'interior decorating' – can suffocate the drama, casting the design as principal protagonist of the evening. (A current rash of German designer-producers is particularly liable to reverse priorities in this way.) It is not, however, simply the 'realists' who are vulnerable to this criticism, which is often levelled at fine artists coming into opera, few of whom could be described as naturalistic. Although the revolution in ballet design in the 1920s and 1930s effected largely by fine artists was never consistently emulated in opera, individual artists have always been attracted to this particular branch of set design. The Kroll made a principle in the thirties of employing young artistic talents such as Giorgio de Chirico and Laszlo Moholy-Nagy, since when artists as diverse as John Piper, Marc Chagall, Barbara Hepworth, Victor Vasarely, Sidney Nolan, Salvador Dali and David Hockney have all worked in the opera house.

Verdi once wrote: 'In order to do sets for the theatre, one must have painters for the theatre. Painters who would not have the vanity to value their own technical brilliance, but serve the Drama.' Critics continue to suggest that painters are too used to working entirely in response to their own imaginative dictates to be able to serve another master – that the 'pure' painter can never turn himself into an 'applied' painter, and too often his efforts to do so produce little more than a 'calendar' effect, or series of images, often beautiful but not a coherent expression of the drama. John Bury, Head of Design at the National Theatre, comments: 'I don't think there are many people who are totally fixated on canvas painting who ever really make the transition well. It's usually high-class gimmicky managements who try it, get a famous sculptor or painter to do a set. . . . It's not a real theatre thing, it's an art trick. It can work in its own context, and it's normally better with lesser works.'

It has perhaps the best chance of working in cases where the style of the artist is organic to the producer's conception of the work. John Dexter was attracted by the element of pastiche and caricature in David Hockney's work which he felt was ideally suited to a piece such as Ravel's *L'Enfant et les Sortilèges*, which itself makes ingenious use of parody. Elijah Moshinsky, elucidating his ideas for a production of *Samson et Dalila*, wanted it to have 'a painted feel . . . I didn't want it to feel as if it was happening in a kind of Royal Court reality. . . . It was all aimed at a particular sensuality – I deliberately wanted that sensuality to occur through paint, and through a rather profound painter, not a fussy stage decorator . . . Since I'm an Australian, Sidney Nolan's paintings always meant a lot to me in terms of barbaric myth-making and I thought that was what one needed for the Saint-Saëns.'

There are various ways in which a design may serve the drama. It must, as Götz Friedrich points out, 'create the artistic, aesthetic environment in which the wonders, the miracle of the story-through-music happens. The set has to build a special area – it cannot be the real world, or even a slice of the world, it must always be a special world existing by itself, a microcosm.' It must also support and, if possible, clarify the way in which characters behave on stage. John Bury: 'The audience are not there to look at the scenery, they're there to believe in what the singers/actors are saying. . . . One has to reinforce the actors' motivation the whole time, that's what one's job is.'

Increasingly in opera designers are adopting a reductive approach, influenced (though not all would call themselves Brechtians) by Brecht's view that 'whatever does not further the narrative harms it'. As John Bury puts it, 'always go for the minimum possible to create the image you need', without competing with the drama for the audience's attention. This has tended to mean avoiding naturalistic or decorative clutter: if the drama calls for a table, provide a table and not

OVERLEAF Patrick Robertson's set for Act 3 of *Rigoletto*, reflecting the composition and balance of Edward Hopper's *Nighthawks*. Jean Rigby (Maddalena) and Arthur Davies (the Duke) in the bar, John Rawnsley (Rigoletto) and Valerie Masterson (Gilda) outside (ENO, 1985).

a table, a tablecloth, a vase with flowers, candlesticks, knives and forks, a chandelier overhead and a dog in a basket beneath it. But in the view of Elijah Moshinsky it also means resisting the temptations of the other form of 'high camp' – a design style dominated by proliferating technology, omnipresent machinery which, though neither 'realistic' nor particularly decorative, is just as likely to distract from the human performers. The *Ring* seems especially susceptible to the 'high-tech' treatment. Moshinsky feels that two recent *Ring* cycles – those of Götz Friedrich for Covent Garden and Sir Peter Hall at Bayreuth – were alike, if in little else, in that both expressed the drama by means of a central mechanism, and in the process reduced it: 'It took away from the performers. . . . Their ideas and relationships were overshadowed by where they stood on the tilting platform.'

The importance of reducing sets to their bare essentials is that it liberates space which is a crucial component in design. Sally Jacobs describes the stage as 'a dynamic space', and talks of the need 'to use the space, as a sculptor uses space, in a way that serves the piece' – an approach influenced by John Bury, who speaks of 'editing' the physical production with light and space. (This is the kind of design that now interests John Copley, himself trained as a designer. 'I've *done* scenery. Actually, I haven't used it now for a couple of years. I don't do it any more – no more great big solid sets. Not interested. I've got to find another way of using the space.') There are, of course, limits to the minimalist approach, more apparent in opera because of the size of the theatres involved. As Jocelyn Herbert explains, commonsense prevents the designer from paring down too far: 'You can't put just nothing on stage, because the stages are so big. Think of somebody sitting about a mile away up there, with one little figure on stage . . . Personally I think it would be marvellous if there was nothing there, but the audience would feel cheated, they'd feel they hadn't got their money's worth. Even at the Royal Court in the late fifties when I did *Sergeant Musgrave's Dance* with minimal scenery, the lights went down and a voice behind me said, "Oh Lord, it's one of *those*." I know exactly what she meant.'

The important thing is that however much or little he puts on stage, and whether it is realistic or stylised or wholly abstract, the designer is working towards a visual expression from an integrated concept of the drama. Stefanos Lazaridis is clear about his priorities: 'I never start from the visual. . . . The stage picture has to follow from the *idea*, as an inevitable consequence of it. . . . You don't do a framed picture and then place the actors in it and say "You stand there" and do groupings and aesthetics.' But how precisely does the designer move from idea to image?

Sometimes his route is largely mapped out for him by the producer. Jonathan Miller tends to lay down quite detailed guidelines: 'I have very clear ideas about what I want – the tone, and the resources, and the references that I want used. . . . I know exactly what I want in the way of visual images. . . . I'm a designer *manqué* myself. I can't draw things out, and I'm not a very good engineer, but I have a very intimate feeling for the actual appearance of things.' Thus, 'I started *Rigoletto* knowing that I wanted Edward Hopper's paintings. I knew the colour and the tone and the architectural structure I wanted, and I put all the books and images and the pictures in the way of the designer, and I sent him off to New York to photograph the streets I wanted.' Sir Hugh Casson had experience of this kind of direction when designing (as only his second opera) the world première of Sir William Walton's *Troilus and Cressida* – 'a hugely prestige thing, produced by George Devine and conducted by Malcolm Sargent – and I was frightened out of my wits, I crawled about like an earwig. . . . Devine was very clear in what he wanted – he wanted people to be at certain levels at certain moments, he wanted a ramp for soldiers to march down, he wanted the soldiers to appear on the citadel over the back. It was almost an architectural problem in that he told you where he wanted the people, and you tried to work it out in a way that was simple, practicable and visually interesting.' Equally, force of circumstances can largely take over – Ronald Eyre reasons: 'If the singers you've got to work with are immobile, well-known a-dramatic voices, I think it would be a mistake maybe to give them a simple platform and hope that you're going to be the lucky one to crack the drama out of them. Because what has not been done by nature and life hitherto is unlikely to be your privilege. In that case you have to see that

Jocelyn Herbert and John Dexter

your contribution and the designer's contribution may be a setting in which they can be still – a waving, fascinating surround for an immobile centre.'

More often, however, the designer's role is far more creative. The same sources from which the producer has drawn his ideas can help the designer towards his visual realisation. Some rely almost entirely on the music – Beni Montresor, for example: 'Designing for opera is translating the music in visual terms. I listen to the music before I know what the story is about, to get the music under my skin. . . . I've just spent a week listening to *Rigoletto* – going back to it after many years, I was really moved: to an Italian it's like drinking your mother's milk. It's such strong music, specially at this time when everything is so weak and feeble, without energy, without life – this sounds like the earth, rich . . . I'm very emotional, my approach is not mental, I don't read books, just the music will tell me.' For others, the intellectual exploration of the work is equally important; Stefanos Lazaridis, for example, will research the literary and critical background just as intensively as the producer – the biography of Dvořák for *Rusalka* (and not only Dvořák but Janáček and other Czech contemporaries), *The Golden Bough*

Stefanos Lazaridis with the model embryo, a central component of his design for *The Midsummer Marriage* (ENO, 1985).

for *The Midsummer Marriage*, and so on. Jocelyn Herbert sums up simply: 'The words give you the story and the place, and what's needed in terms of props or furniture. The music gives you the mood of the scene. . . . I think if you don't *like* the music of an opera, it's very difficult to design it.'

Where the producer's own conception is not totally determinate, the designer can make an invaluable contribution. Whenever Sally Jacobs has found herself well-matched with a producer, their close working relationship has proved very exciting indeed: 'The director must have a need for the particular way the designer will manifest the visual elements. . . . And the designer must have a need for the particular way the director will delineate and call for certain kinds of theatre. They feed off each other. . . . It's at a very deep level, that understanding – so that you can make the poetic leaps at the same moment. . . . You know together that the work is going a certain way – "*This* is right . . . *this* is right . . . *this* is right" – and at this beat something must change. You come to that beat together.' Andrei Serban (with whom Sally Jacobs worked on *Turandot*) comments: 'It's a question of exchanging ideas. . . . It's not clear who did what, it's not even important; it's an open exchange – that's what's so extraordinary about live performances, live art.' Or as John Bury puts it, more irreverently: 'It's very difficult to decide who thought of what. There are absolutely clear germinal phrases, but we're all too polite to remind the other parties that we said them first.'

At an early stage John Bury likes to establish the terms of reference with his producer – in the case of *Carmen*, for instance, which he designed in 1985 for Sir Peter Hall, 'whether we're going decorative, picture-postcard Seville, or back-street Salford Seville – the social milieu, the plush factor.' Occasionally the designer and producer will start with identical terms of reference in mind. Stefanos Lazaridis and Graham Vick, for example, reached the conclusion independently that *Madam Butterfly* is no sentimental cherry-blossom romance, but at heart a profoundly unpleasant story centred on a neurosis, the kind of emotion that can drive someone to kill themselves for love, rooted in the suicide of Butterfly's own father years before. Taking this as their point of departure, they felt that the emotional outbursts from Butterfly which punctuate the opera had to be explained, not simply taken for granted, and their conception was built around the notion of contrast – the contrast between what Butterfly needs to believe in, an idyllic American existence with Pinkerton, and the reality of her life in a Japan rapidly industrialising. The two were presented in counterpoint by split-level staging – her fantasy projected on a screen across the top of the stage, the foreground reality the once-romantic little house set in an urban wasteland 'pouring with water and sludge, like a Tarkovsky film'. Originally intent on hemming in this desolation with towering new buildings, Lazaridis and Vick in the event found it enough simply to sketch their presence, 'setting up a tension the more profound for being rooted in suggestion rather than literal, brick-for-brick representation'.

Where *Madam Butterfly* was essentially an examination of character, Vick and Lazaridis saw *Don Giovanni* as a piece of ideas, cold at the core, founded on the

concept of moral degradation – not just
Don Giovanni's but, in Stefanos
Lazaridis's words, 'the moral degradation
of every one of the characters *through* Giovanni, with him as the catalyst. . . .
Through him they recognise things in
themselves. . . . It begins to be a little bit
uncomfortable, and they decide to expel
him . . .' Lazaridis's design drew much of
its energy from images of degradation,
'elements of Genet and Buñuel' – Don
Giovanni and Donna Anna copulating on
a coffin; Zerlina's plea of 'Batti, batti' to
Masetto construed in a sado-masochistic
light; Leporello as a pornographer maintaining a Polaroid record, shared with the
audience, of Giovanni's conquests.

Production ideas can be less drastic and
still have a decisive influence on the
evolving design. John Schlesinger's
perspective on *Der Rosenkavalier* was a
precise and gently humorous one: 'There
is something intensely sensual and sexual
about the opera . . . but there is also
something very specifically about social
strata. That's what we're thinking about
in the design – all the minutiae. . . . In the
second act I feel that Faninal is a total
magpie, *nouveau riche*. . . . The books are
fake, you see that at the beginning. . . .
The label still on the antiques. . . . Far
too many flowers, and far too many col-
lections of bits and pieces which he's just
bought as job lots. . . . So one gets the
impression of a position in society that
isn't really genuine.'

Equally, an abstract conception of a

Sally Jacobs's set for Andrei Serban's production
of *Turandot*: with Gwyneth Jones (Turandot),
Robert Tear (Altoum) and (*far right*) Helen Donath
(Liù) and Placido Domingo (Calaf) (Covent
Garden, 1984).

work, with no specific period or milieu to serve as touchstones, can nevertheless generate ideas which conclusively shape the set, as in the case of the *Turandot* on which Sally Jacobs collaborated with Andrei Serban. Sally Jacobs explains: 'We felt there was no way we could say this was a new, naturalistic story – it's a fairy tale, being used by Puccini in order to express certain emotions, things about men and women, and must be performed as a kind of storytelling, a convention of theatrical storytelling with heightened figures going through the tale of Turandot.' The consequences of this initial perception were twofold – the set was to depict an enclosed theatrical space, a stage within a stage; and the chorus was to have a double role, in the tradition of Greek tragedy, as both participants in the drama and observers of it. To express this idea, various existing forms of the on-stage stage were available – 'Look at the Kabuki stage, with the runways coming out; the Noh stage; all Middle Eastern theatre; rural theatre in India – everywhere where people gather round and well-known characters play out a well-known story as a form of drama or catharsis.' The one on which they finally settled was the galleried interior of a Chinese pagoda; this both served as a theatrical space with provision for onlookers, and had the advantage (which the Kabuki stage, for example, would not have had) of continuing the horseshoe shape of the Royal Opera House's interior, underlining the parallel between stage audience, played by the chorus, and auditorium audience. There was no attempt, however, to identify the two – to mirror the plush and gilt theatre interior (as, for example, Massimo Bogianckino's Paris production of Ligeti's *Le Grand Macabre* did, putting the Opéra on its own stage), because this would have prevented the chorus from effectively entering the drama as participants – 'It had to be that the eye goes into the proscenium and at the point at which it crosses that line, we're in China. . . . The chorus is the stage version of us – part of the story in a way that we're not.'

With the general principles formulated, 'the anchors down', details could be developed. 'Once we were sure it had to be a theatre, and that the whole story was going to be illustrated with theatrical devices . . . everything fell into place. . . . The action could be exploded into very heightened theatrical moments where that seemed right, and everything could be stylised.' Ping, Pang and Pong, for example, could themselves embody a theatrical convention, as 'a leftover from the Gozzi *commedia dell'arte*'; and the moon could become an enormous, solid disc, occupying half the stage and dominating it as Turandot dominates her people (the association between them elaborated in the motif of scudding clouds carried from the moon on to her costumes). In introducing devices such as these, quite foreign to traditional productions of *Turandot*, Jacobs and Serban felt themselves to be acknowledging, as Sally Jacobs explains, 'a poetic need every now and again for the unexpected. . . . If you set up a rhythm and a recognisable language, that could create the kind of consistency which doesn't give you the possibility for the kind of surprises that are in the music, the emotional twists and turns. You have to judge where now something else must happen. . . . You have to know how, within the form you've set, to make some change, some shift, so that it goes on serving the narrative. . . . Sometimes it works, sometimes it doesn't; when it doesn't you call it a gimmick, when it does, it's a marvellous piece of theatrical alchemy.'

For John Conklin, working with producer Nikolaus Lehnhoff on a *Ring* cycle for San Francisco, the starting point was the demands of the administration, modified in accordance with their own instinctive reactions to the work. What was required of them was a straightforward, traditional *Ring* without glosses – John Conklin recalls being urged, 'Just *do* it, just do the piece, don't do all that German bullshit' (a reference to various recent modernist *Rings* mounted in Germany) – to which the reply was, 'But the *Ring is* German bullshit, you have to go with it a little bit.' Behind the facetiousness was a serious point; Conklin and Lehnhoff felt that simply to do 'what Wagner wrote' was impossible. John Conklin explains: 'We're not 1870s people. You can't be a virgin again. . . . You *can't* divorce the *Ring* from, say, Hitler now, you just can't; to believe you can is a false naivety.' Their aim became to combine 'simply telling the story' with representing the complete system of ideas that underlies it, 'working out this reasonably complicated intellectual and visual structure that would hold up for the whole piece', at the same time avoiding the overly politicised, or abstracted, or futuristic treatments of which the management – aware of the expense of a *Ring* and the necessity of reviving it in years to come – was in dread.

In visual terms, their structure was founded on the belief that the images conjured up on stage should resemble those which surrounded Wagner; and at the core of the staging, giving the cycle its unity, was the painting of Caspar David Friedrich, chosen because of his concern for the relationship of man to the natural world. 'It certainly concerned Wagner, it concerned Friedrich, and it concerns us in a way that's direct . . . The original sin of the *Ring* is Wotan breaking off the branch of the world ash to make his spear, in order to make law and civilisation. That's the horrible thing about the piece . . . . In some awful way man *has*, in order to live, to break the tree, and the tree has to die.' This romantic-realistic *Ring*, drawing throughout on German Romantic sources such as Karl Friedrich Schinkel, was to end with a straight quotation of Friedrich's 'The Wreck of the Hope', 'the ambiguous symbols of the frozen lake and the iceberg', with the débris of the Gibichung Hall replacing the wrecked ship, and the winter sun coming out.

But however closely the producer and designer have discussed the production, the end result – as the producer will have realised and allowed for in choosing the designer – will to some extent reflect the designer alone: his aesthetic credos, individual tastes in colour, shape and pattern, the particular *métier* in which he works. John Bury remains visibly a lighting man, Sir Osbert Lancaster a caricaturist and watercolour painter, Maurice Sendak a children's illustrator, Sir Hugh Casson an architect, and so on. The producer may involve himself in the selection of images by agreeing the use of 'references', already existing images from a variety of sources – photographs, film, the costume and architecture of different countries, archaeology, anthropology, sculpture and decorative arts, with painting as perhaps the most popular recourse of all: even painter/designers with highly characterised styles of their own refer to those of others in their opera designs – David Hockney to Matisse in *L'Enfant et les Sortilèges*, for instance. This ready resort to the ideas of others is something John Conklin is quick to defend: 'To be a designer doesn't mean you have to make it up. . . . There's a theory that you do a lot of research and then put it all aside – I don't do that. I have piles of books and pictures everywhere all the time, and I'm always looking at them. . . . Research isn't "bad" in some way – I think this is why Jonathan Miller and I worked together well [at St Louis], we share that feeling.' Both consider it perfectly acceptable to make direct quotations of references – Jonathan Miller of Edward Hopper's 'Nighthawks' for *Rigoletto*, for example, John Conklin of 'The Wreck of the Hope'; as he explains, 'There was the feeling that we should absorb Friedrich and Schinkel and make it our own, but I would much rather use quotations. . . . It's not copying. . . . There is an energy in these things – it's using it.'

Once the range of allusion has been agreed, however, the designer may wish to create a personal system of imagery through which to translate the conception in visual terms. Once Sally Jacobs and Andrei Serban, for example, had agreed upon a wide frame of reference – 'We felt we could freely take anything we wanted from the Orient' – Sally Jacobs set about synthesising a multiplicity of Eastern vocabularies into her own visual language. 'I had to digest it all and make my own version, make it unified. It mattered not a bit whether someone wraps their kimono over from left to right or right to left, it's irrelevant; or whether white has a special meaning; or whether she's wearing a Noh mask and he's wearing a Balinese mask – it all becomes meaningless if you can transform all that information into your own unique language. Sometimes I've taken things very literally and put them in straight from the research, sometimes I've changed it.' Thus Calaf's costume is largely Tibetan; Ping, Pang and Pong are a cross between *commedia dell'arte* characters and Chinese monkey kings; many of the dancers' masks are based on the ivory finish of the Noh mask, but for their costumes and gestures Sally Jacobs looked more to Chinese paper cuts of the martial arts and the stylised movements of *tai ch'i*, 'shadow-boxing'. Paintings of a Chinese door guardian helped to build the Mandarin, porcelain figures in the British Museum the sages who oversee the riddle ceremony. The earth floor of the set was derived from a photograph of an archaeological dig in China.

John Bury's approach is more one of synthesising periods than cultures. The designer, in his view, should take cognisance of three periods – that in which the piece is set, that in which it was composed (reflecting, in other words, something of the images which composer and librettist would have expected to see), and that in which he is living himself. None of them need be reproduced literally, but all should make themselves felt in the end result. 'One's got to have nods in the direction of Rome for *L'Incoronazione di Poppea*,' for example, 'but you can't do the thing as entirely Roman, because Monteverdi had no idea of how it looked and all the music is purely Venetian and seventeenth-century; and I'm designing it in the twentieth century, with all the techniques that I have available. I like to think that it's fair game to wander quite happily through that territory taking what one wants from each period, without being anachronistic. One has to throw all these balls up into the air . . .'

One consideration rarely in the designer's or producer's mind is how long the designs will last. It will however loom large in the administrator's consciousness. On the whole the more conventional a set, the less quickly it dates. 'Modernist' or 'futurist' stagings probably date fastest (Josef Svoboda gave express permission for the Giants in the *Ring* he designed for Covent Garden in the 1970s to be re-outfitted in up-to-date spacesuits as necessary). More unexpectedly, totally abstract settings also date quickly. David Ritch, Head of Staff Production at English National Opera, suggests that television, advertising and film somehow cannibalise images and fashions, and only exist by regularly consuming themselves – and audiences, assimilating contemporary abstract images ever more rapidly, demand constant novelty.

Some designers are actually pressing for a far shorter life for their productions. Stefanos Lazaridis: 'I believe in live theatre. One ought to be able to spend as little time as possible – do something which works, and the ideas are very strong, and it lasts for two or three years – and then throw it away, get somebody to do another one.' Sets are not necessarily meant to be definitive: 'At the end of the day we're only interpretative artists. . . . That's why the theatre has a very temporary feel about it, it's for *now*, this season or next – "let's see what this particular opera means for us *now*" . . . If you happen to disagree with my view and you're an intelligent person, that's fine, you don't have to agree; but it doesn't mean that I have to go out of *my* way to please you. I have to do what I have to do. . . . It is my job to do the best I can with what I know and the way I respond.'

And the designer's response can of course change. It may seem to cast doubt on a designer's seriousness that he should be able to design the same piece quite differently several times. This is unfair, according to John Bury, who feels that while it may occasionally happen that one genuinely 'bottoms' a work, more often enough of the components change from production to production – producers, conductors, singers, stages – to ensure that each time the challenge to the designer will be significantly different. 'Changes of scale, say, are very important. You can't just take a small-size production and blow it up into a big-scale production. There are certain factors inside which make the mix quite different.' Apart from anything else, the designer himself has moved on. 'I think I could design *Figaro* every ten years; I've designed a *Macbeth* every five years of my working life, and I've done *Hamlet* about four times.'

Nor can one safely ignore the fact that audience tastes alter. To be too thoroughly in tune with the prevailing style at any one moment is dangerous; the more successful a creative team has been in spearheading an advance, the more difficult it is to signal a change of direction, as John Copley has discovered. 'From about 1970 on, I did a huge amount of work for Covent Garden and English National Opera [some twenty-five productions in ten years], at a time when the public required a whole series of basic repertory pieces done well . . . We'd gone through a period where things were sometimes rather shabbily staged, rather lacking in ideas and visual richness, and a lot of repertoire had been held over for aeons . . . When I did new productions of these pieces, it wasn't the time to do them in what we would call a trendy way. . . . One was unaware in them of an obtrusive directorial hand, that's what I was very much about at that period – much to my cost now, because I've been pigeonholed as being an old-fashioned presenter of the bread-and-butter repertoire in a traditional way. In fact I *don't* do that any more. . . . My visual taste has changed totally . . . but I'm actually not allowed to do those pieces in this country any more because I've been pigeonholed as old hat. . . . It's curious that people assume that conductors improve and develop with age, but that we stagnate . . .'

17

The Sets

Stage design in the 1980s has evolved into three disciplines – set design, costume design and lighting design – which in some design schools, particularly in America, are taught separately. For some productions three designers may be employed, for others only one – opera houses have no fixed rule, and it is up to the producer to decide (and to deal with the consequences, which may include the expense of three commission fees). Occasionally he may elect to tackle one or more of the functions himself: Michael Hampe, for example, like many German producers, generally designs his own lighting. However the responsibilities are allocated, the three disciplines are interdependent, and on the way in which they interact the success of the production will in part depend.

Each discipline demands that the designer be both artist and artisan; this is especially true of set design. 'I thought it was going to be easy,' confessed Sir Hugh Casson, remembering his first venture into opera. 'Good heavens, you didn't have to keep the rain out, you could control where the light was coming in, right or left, so your shadows could be where you wanted them.' But, as he discovered, the stage designer's artistic aspirations *are* inevitably modified by practical requirements as demanding in their way as those made of an architect, because he must meet the needs not merely of the audience but of the performers and of the house itself.

In serving the audience the designer must take full account of sight-lines. In theory, every individual in the auditorium should be able to see everything the audience is intended to see, and nothing else. In practice, this is rarely the case, in older houses at least. While it may be possible at Bayreuth and in the many German houses built since the Second World War with fan-shaped auditoria, in houses with horseshoe-shaped auditoria, like La Scala or Covent Garden, or very high auditoria, like the Met, views from the side and upper levels are restricted in varying degrees. This is acknowledged by administrators in their pricing, and in consequence designers often feel justified in worrying less than they might about the view from the further reaches of the house. But they will generally be encouraged to ensure at least that those features of the design which are crucial to the plot are universally visible. In Jonathan Miller's production of *The Turn of the Screw*, for example, the ghost of Peter Quint was obliged to make his first and most chilling appearance at ground level, not, as the producer had wanted, raised above the stage, where he could have passed unremarked by much of the house since he has at that point nothing to sing.

Sight-lines are also essential to the success of perspective effects, which lose much of their power to convince unless viewed directly from the front. Glyndebourne is for this purpose at a distinct advantage in having a relatively narrow, rectangular theatre; the auditorium is little wider than the proscenium arch, and only a handful of seats command anything other than a head-on view.

On the other side of the proscenium arch, the performers, too, must have an unimpeded view of the conductor or his image on a television monitor; this includes the chorus who at La Scala have a specific union ruling on this point. The importance of the conductor/singer relationship is something designers always have to take into account. In Jocelyn Herbert's experience, 'opera singers just like to stand in the middle and sing when they get to a difficult bit or an aria', not liking, at such a moment, to be put to any awkward shifts or contrivances in order to be able to see the conductor, 'so the centre of the stage tends always to be the dominant part.'

The performer likes also to be able to move easily about the set; crevasses, rocky outcrops, mossy banks, even grassy hollows, can all be hazards. Singers have to be able to get through all doors in full regalia, and on and off stage in the time provided – though cheating, in the sense of repeating bars to provide the necessary leeway, is not unknown. Stairs should be easily negotiable, bearing in mind that the singer's attention is likely to be elsewhere, and sets consisting largely of steps – Josef Svoboda's for *I Vespri Siciliani*, for example – can pose problems. When characters enter from the top, in order not to sing directly upstage those already on the set have to rush up the steps past the new arrivals and then turn back down in a natural sort of way; the performer has perpetually to give thought to the foot on which he will start his next move; and he may spend the best part of the evening, if the steps are narrow, uncomfortably balanced between two steps.

Above all, singers judge a set by its acoustic – and here scrims (thin gauzes on which lighting designers can achieve miraculous effects) are viewed with disfavour because, as Andrew Porter points out, whether or not they do act as a baffle, they at least *seem* to, (though Beni Montresor recalls a decisive vote from Joan Sutherland in favour of the scrims he had designed for *Esclarmonde* – Dame Joan at least is not bothered by obstacles of that ilk). Even worse are sets upholstered in fur or plush – James Bowman: 'You *feel* the acoustic being spoiled, you can feel the sound just dropping dead at your feet' – or luxuriously draped. Richard Van Allan describes their pernicious effects: 'A set surrounded by cloth hangings is very dull to sing in, hard work on the voice; you can't hear your own resonance so you think your voice is going, and then you start pushing to try and make more resonance – and then your voice *does* start going.' The best acoustic is provided by a closed set, like the Valkyrie rock in Act Three of Patrice Chéreau's

Die Walküre at Bayreuth, which Donald McIntyre found provided a virtual sound shell: 'In "Wotan's Farewell" there is a section marked *pianissimo* and I was able to sing it as if I was in a small room.' Where, on the other hand, the sound is particularly woolly, he has on occasion resorted to putting pads behind his ears – cupping them, in effect. (He also remembers Wolfgang Wagner telling him that leather costumes were traditional for Wagner singers because they improved the ambient acoustic by reflecting rather than absorbing sound.)

In catering for the needs of the house itself, the first thing the designer must do is to conceive the set on a suitable scale – which sounds obvious enough, but large houses in particular frequently pose problems which require considerable ingenuity or a great deal of money (or both) for their solution. The Met, for example, as Gerald Fitzgerald explains: 'Jean-Pierre Ponnelle is one of the few directors not to build little boxes on the Met stage. For *La Clemenza di Tito* he used the full height and width of the stage, which already gives you the feeling that it's *not* such a small opera in that theatre: it fills the eye, and the ear kind of fills up too. But not everybody has the budget he has. Sometimes you feel as if you're looking at a little puppet show in the middle of Madison Square Garden.' It was precisely this kind of reaction that Jocelyn Herbert dreaded when she first designed for the Met – of all things, *Lulu* . . . 'a little intimate opera with very few people and no chorus. In this huge space. . . . I'd given up smoking for a year, and I started again straight away in pure terror.' Her solution was not even to attempt to use the whole stage but to mount the set on trucks which advanced diagonally across the stage and out over the prompt box. 'The scene was being thrust into the audience: then of course the performers could sing anywhere on it, because they were way beyond the proscenium arch.'

In houses this size, designers may have to adjust their standards and adapt their notions of style. At Glyndebourne, designers may become accustomed to working with materials of the highest quality – firstly because in a theatre that small the audience is in a better position to be hypercritical and, secondly, because the quantities required are comparatively modest. In houses four times the size, if costs are not to become prohibitive, the designer will normally be discouraged from using either the most expensive materials or those which require long and costly processing, especially since a good deal of their particular effect will be wasted on all but the front stalls. As Jocelyn Herbert remarks, when working on this scale there is little point in being too subtle: 'If you want a pattern to show, it really must look a bit vulgar and over the top in the dressing-room' (though the designer may be permitted to indulge in detail if the production is to be televised).

It may even be necessary for the designer to abandon the medium in which he or she normally works. John Bury, for example, has been impelled in the past to use painted cloths – a *métier* quite foreign to a designer whose training ground was Joan Littlewood's Theatre Royal, Stratford East. 'You've got to go up to sixty feet high on a big opera stage, and you can't do sixty feet in anything except a cloth, and you can't do anything to a cloth except paint it, because it has to be rolled up and if you try to stick things on the cloth it won't roll. So the bigger you get, the more you go back to *trompe l'oeil* painting – and I'm not a scene painter. . . .'

The designer working for a touring company faces a different challenge – that of producing one design to suit several different stages. It is a challenge that John Harrison faces regularly as Technical Director of Welsh National Opera, the world's leading touring company in terms of the number of productions it tours and the number of weeks it is away. Over his first five years with the company, he has become very familiar with the conditions the designer must meet for these purposes. The touring set has to be infinitely flexible, so that components can be added or subtracted at will without ruining the overall effect – the designer cannot as a rule make much use of either trapdoors or stage lifts. It must be capable of fitting on successive nights stages as deep as forty feet and as shallow as twenty, some flat, some raked, and of being built and dismantled in theatres with no wing space at all.

In any house the designer must take into account not merely its size but its technical resources. From the positive point of view, he will be anxious to exploit any special facilities: for his production of *Aida* at La Scala, Franco Zeffirelli took brilliant advantage of the adjoining Piccolo Scala stage as an arena in which to whip up the pace of a horse-drawn chariot which, in the moment of orchestral silence preceding the Grand March, he then released to charge full tilt across the main stage. From a more negative point of view, he must consider whether his sets will be too heavy or too big for the stage crew to handle efficiently. Quick changes are an essential element of a unified and effective programme – Peter Wood argues, 'Opera is a headlong process, and *nothing* should come in the way. . . . Do you ever think what happened with the rise of the novel in the nineteenth century? The effect was absolutely electrifying – for the first time people required of all forms of theatre a coherent narrative, as they never had before; it had not been necessary that one scene should feed the next.' Where the composer himself has engineered this 'feeding' process by covering a scene change with music (*Wozzeck*, for example, has fourteen scene changes, some covered by no more than a few bars of orchestral interlude), even the slightest acceleration of tempo by the conductor can catch out a stage crew wrestling with an unwieldy set. And speed is no less crucial once the performance is over. In most houses the stage is the only possible venue for rehearsals requiring lights and flown scenery, and by the next morning it must have been completely cleared and re-set for a different opera. If both the sets concerned are heavy and complicated, the stage crew may have little time to break between eleven o'clock at night when the final curtain falls on one piece (and curtain calls are often taken to an accompaniment of creaks and thuds as demolition begins backstage), and ten o'clock the following morning when the cast arrives for the rehearsal of another – after which that set in its turn may be removed and replaced by a third, for the evening performance.

Obviously, the more streamlined the technical facilities of a house, the greater

the demands the designer may make. The cruciform design of the Met's stage –
a main stage surrounded on three sides by areas of identical size where whole
sets can be built on trucks and simply wheeled on to the main stage in minutes –
gives it a considerable advantage over Covent Garden which at present has no
side stages at all, making it necessary for all sets to be dismantled *in situ* and hauled
off manually. After redevelopment, however, the Royal Opera House, like Munich,
will have the same number of extra stages even more conveniently arranged as
a square, of which the bottom right-hand quarter will be the main stage, enabling
stage crew and scenery to move from one side stage to any of the others without
crossing the main stage. The ultimate in luxury is the design proposed for the
new Paris Opéra, incorporating no less than twelve extra stages on two levels,
with a railway running from workshops to side stages to the main stage and back
to the storage areas.

A certain degree of mechanisation in a house also enables it to respond the more
readily to the designer's requests, however ambitious: computerisation planned
for Covent Garden will replace the nineteen men at present needed to operate
a single flying cue in *Götterdämmerung* with one man and a button. The financial
advantages of technology to the opera house are obvious; manning levels and
overtime payments to stage crews make up a large part of the budgets of most
year-round houses. And from the artistic point of view, there will soon be no
technical reasons why administrators should not be able to mount operas in whatever combinations they like, and realise designers' most elaborate visions. The
threat is that designers will take this as an encouragement to extravagant behaviour,
that administrators will feel the need to utilise the greater technical capacity and
in effect will be locked into greater lavishness, and the form will become bloated
– unless of course as technology develops even further, huge built sets are supplan-
ted by projections, lasers and holography. In 2010 AD the miniature train travelling
across the dusty acres of the Paris side stages may carry a whole season's sets in
one truck – a few boxes of holographic plates.

With all these practical requirements – not always compatible – in mind, the
designer begins to translate his stage picture into physical reality. Armed with
the specifications of the house, he makes a scale model of each of his sets (or,
if he is purely a painter, drawings or sketches to be converted by others into
models). The scale most often used is 1:25 (in centimetres) or 1:24 (in inches),
as at the next size down (1:50 or 1:48) detail is difficult. John Bury considers
it another drawback of big houses that on the 1:25 scale the model verges on
the unmanageable – 'Peter [Hall] always wants 1:25 size at the Met – it's a huge
problem, because the model is as big as a plan chest. It then has to be collapsible. . . .
I think it was Oliver Messel who said, "Designing is easy, my dear, it's getting
the model into the taxi that's the hard part."'

This point – the model stage – is perhaps the most critical in the life of a production, in practical terms, until production rehearsals begin. From the model, the administrator and the production team will learn for the first time whether the design is actually likely to work – aesthetically, practically and financially. When the designer is commissioned, he is usually given a budget figure – a working estimate prepared by the opera house: Tom Macarthur suggests as a rule of thumb taking the cost of that particular piece in its last production or another of a similar scale, and multiplying it by the inflation factor, computed in the light of the designer's known style and working methods – hyper-realism, for example, is expensive, as is working in metal, whereas painted cloths are generally cheaper. The designer then evolves his conception and makes his models with this budget figure more or less conscientiously in mind. (Glyndebourne adopts a more gentlemanly approach, as its Technical and Production Administrator, Tom Redman explains: 'We try not to restrict the designer and producer artistically, we try to let them give rein to their ideas, whilst monitoring and controlling a carefully planned budget' – a creative approach buttressed by a healthy cash flow and the demands of only two new productions a year.)

Once the model has been submitted, the Technical Director enlists the help of the various specialist heads of departments – scene-building, scene-painting, prop-making, etc. – in calculating the *actual* cost of what designer and producer are proposing. On the basis of the model, they decide what materials each set will

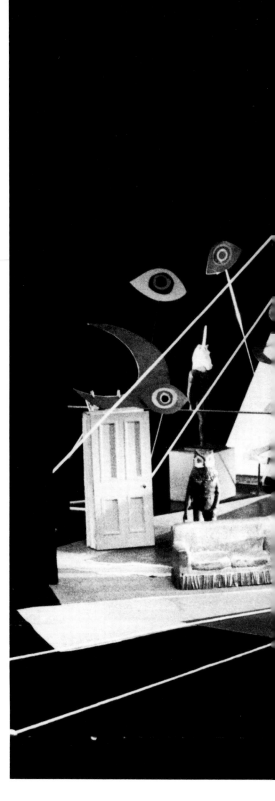

Stefanos Lazaridis's model for Tippett's *The Midsummer Marriage* (ENO, 1985).

be made from, how many pieces it will consist of – generally speaking, the more breaks in a set the more expensive it becomes – and how much engineering skill will be required to make it work. (The designer will almost always have under-estimated the expense slightly, costing only the visual effect and leaving out the 'hidden' costs of supporting, invisibly, what is actually seen by the audience.)

Remaining within the budget figure is partly a matter of experience, of knowing what will be expensive in any particular house – which can be a snare for foreign designers working there for the first time. Jocelyn Herbert remembers, 'Arriving at the Met, you don't know what people earn or what materials cost. . . . Construc-tion is very expensive, because timber is very expensive. . . . Labour is the *most* expensive – what scene painters get in America blows your mind. . . .' (The Met has now closed down its construction shops – sets are made by outside contractors as far afield as Italy.) It is also a question of attitude – an understanding of the financial circumstances of the company and a willingness to make more out of less. Beni Montresor sees this as a challenge: 'I know today there is less and less money – opera is the last madness. . . . If they give me the money, I can spend it. . . . But where there is no money, it can be stimulating to look for what is essential – something different. You don't need millions to make something beauti-ful'. The ability to stick to a budget may be a key factor in the choice of designer, as the exceeding of limits is not considered dashing, but tiresomely unprofessional – especially when coupled, as it often is, with the late delivery of designs, presenting managements with the unattractive alternatives of accepting the *fait accompli* and overspending, or cancelling the production (though the production-sharing habit is making it easier to rent substitute sets and costumes at short notice). Some admin-istrators now offer a bonus of ten per cent of the commission fee to designers who deliver on time.

For the design which is both aesthetically pleasing and financially viable, one hurdle remains – it is physically practicable? There are various questions the Tech-nical Director and his staff still have to consider – will the sets actually fit on the stage, for example? Can they be changed, in view or out of view, without inordinate effort from the stage crew? Glyndebourne, for instance, has space on only one side of its stage, and the designer must have taken this into account when consider-ing how the set would be shifted. Can the stage machinery – the bars for flown scenery, the lifts, the traps, etc. – cope with the demands? Will the sets conform to safety standards – are they a potential fire hazard? Will the stage crew have to work at an unacceptable height? and so on.

On rare occasions, decisions are either accepted without demur or rejected out of hand. Far more frequently, they are accepted on condition that certain changes are made – and here there may be a good deal of horse trading. 'That balcony

OPPOSITE 'Distressing' the surface of a polystyrene wall made in the workshops of Welsh National Opera for the 1985 production of *Norma*.

will require too much hidden support to be economic – couldn't you use the basic stairs we have in stock?' 'You can't have those banisters in brass – would you accept superior gold foil?' 'That revolving disc doesn't earn its keep – you can only have it in the first act if you make it do double duty in the second.'

Once compromise has been reached, the model is analysed into its separate elements – flats, drops, stage cloths, built scenery, props, a kit of parts, as it were – and working drawings of each component are made to scale and sent to the appropriate workshops for realisation. Many major companies maintain their own shops in or near the opera house – La Scala, Covent Garden, English National Opera, the Deutsche Oper, the Vienna State Opera, for example; others, including most American companies, contract out the various manufacturing processes – or simply rent existing sets.

The structural framework of a set and its major built pieces are the responsibility of the metalwork and carpentry shops; virtually everything else constructed in three dimensions is classified as a 'prop' – statues, small furniture, crockery, lamps, food, books, flowers; toads, dragons, swans, harps, spinning wheels, anvils, cobblers' lasts, hoards of gold; laundry baskets, candles, silver roses, magnets, medicine bottles, barbers' scissors, severed heads. . . . Scene painters take charge of the drop curtains, stage cloths and flats, turning their hands equally to wallpaper (real paper is a fire risk), mud, marble, sand, untreated stone; architectural draughtsmanship, *trompe l'oeil* vistas, landscape in the style of Vermeer, Watteau or Cézanne. They are also invited to provide any paintings used as props – Cavaradossi's stab at Mary Magdalen or Marcello's *The Passage of the Red Sea*, or the pastiches of many periods which often adorn the houses of Manon, Violetta, Don Pasquale, the Marschallin, the Countess Madeleine in *Capriccio*. Their skill is put most conspicuously to the test when the designer is himself an eminent and instantly recognisable painter, and they must reproduce not only the style, spirit and atmosphere of his work, but to some extent the technique, down to the effect of his brush strokes. June Dandridge, Production Manager at Glyndebourne in the days when John Piper, Oliver Messel and Sir Osbert Lancaster all made designs for the Festival, much admires the expertise and imagination required to communicate the styles of very different artists – 'not just copying, but conveying from one medium to another. They need not actually *use* the same techniques, but they have to be able to convey them.'

In all these processes, the designer will be involved – sometimes only by 'sampling' (he or she will be offered by the production staff a variety of textures and finishes from which to choose), sometimes more directly. Sally Jacobs, for example, takes an active part in the realisation of her designs, choosing exact equivalents of colours and textures in real materials, and deciding how these materials should be processed – whether wood, if it is meant to look old (as it was for the galleried

OPPOSITE Mime's anvil from *Siegfried* in the 1985 Welsh National Opera production. Moulded in fibreglass, it is hinged so as to spring apart when struck by the sword Nothung.

Reference drawings for polystyrene statue (OPPOSITE) used by the property department in Handel's *Samson*, designed by Timothy O'Brien for Covent Garden (1985).

pagoda in *Turandot*), should be painted, or 'distressed' by chains dragged over its surface or grooved with an electrical drill and then dyed. In the event, she went to the carpentry shop to supervise the grooving of the newly purchased beams herself, drawing lines on the wood where the cracks should run and demonstrating how to taper off the grooves naturally. 'It could come out looking like Mickey Mouse – you know how things are "antiqued". . . . It's a most difficult thing to put a natural crack in a new piece of wood. How *would* it have cracked? Like trying to be God, trying to make trees: only God can make a tree – *you* try making one from scratch.' Long after the designs have gone in, Sally Jacobs maintains the designer has a crucial part to play in helping to co-ordinate the work of the various departments, as the only person capable of generating a unified stage picture – 'If everybody was free to interpret the model and costume designs and make all their decisions – intelligent ones – without me, the whole thing would go off in all different directions. I'm the designer, I'm responsible for the continuation of the thing that I started, so that it all comes out of a single process. . . . It goes on and on and on until you've got it right, and what you don't get right is like a pain. . . .'

Once the set is built, all that remains is getting it into the theatre – a procedure which varies from house to house. Glyndebourne, as a festival house, has the luxury of being able to assemble new sets and try them out on stage in *Bauprobe*, 'building rehearsals', well before the start of the season; the Met will also try to do this for productions due to open in mid-season, when competition for technical time on stage is intense. Covent Garden, with far more new productions than Glyndebourne and a shorter pre-season break than the Met, has to accommodate technical rehearsals within its normal season's schedule, and does so in the form of 'technical Sundays', taking advantage of the fact that there are neither performances nor rehearsals for performers on Sundays. Some four to five weeks before opening night, the 'kit of parts' – which no one has yet seen assembled – arrives in the theatre, and over the ensuing Sundays it is for the technical staff to discover how the pieces fit together – to lay the stage cloth or flooring and mark on it where each piece is to be placed; to practice assembly and dismantling, run through the fly cues, test all machinery and moving parts. As rehearsals progress during the week, the technical staff learn of changes to be made to suit the performers – doorways that are too narrow, steps too steep, beds too high, stools too low, descents too precipitous – or to accommodate the designer's last-minute changes of mind. Motifs bewitching on paper and plausible at the model stage fail to convince on a grander scale, and props made with loving care are ruthlessly abandoned. And while all this is going on, the lighting designer starts his work.

OPPOSITE A scenic painter transposes Timothy O'Brien's abstract design for *Samson* from the scaled plan to a full-size backcloth (Covent Garden, 1985).

18

The Lighting

The relationship between scenery and lights, between set design and lighting design, is symbiotic: developments in the one have consistently gone hand in hand with developments in the other. When scenery consisted principally of painted flats, lighting was even and from the front: shadows were painted in by the scene painter. When built sets began to supplement painted scenery, however, a wider range of lighting techniques was called for, because unvarying front light without shadows flattens out architecture; three-dimensional scenery needs lighting of varying intensity and from different angles for shape and depth and relative positions to be clarified. Advances in lighting technology, which enabled single lamps to be used independently and flexibly, in their turn encouraged even greater extravagance in built scenery, made possible by the development of fibreglass and other lightweight materials.

It is the greatly increased complexity of lighting technology, most noticeable in the past thirty years, which has made specialised knowledge essential; rare is the producer well-enough informed to be able to exploit to the full the almost unlimited potential of modern lighting, and the lighting designer has established himself both as necessary, in terms of technical expertise, and latterly as desirable – a separate creative force and an integral part of many production teams.

In pursuit of creativity, the lighting designer now has at his disposal an enormous variety of lamps, each with its specialised function, ranging from the proletarian floodlight, which produces a wide fixed beam useful for illuminating and colouring broad expanses (such as backcloths and cycloramas – the dawn of *Madam Butterfly* and dusk of *Turandot* would be produced principally by floodlighting), to the aristocratic follow spot. This lamp represents the present state of the science: once relatively crude – of more value in illuminating the Luftwaffe than the Valkyrie – it is now an instrument of extreme sophistication. Follow spots are movable lamps operated by hand, usually from the back of the auditorium (though they can perform an equally valuable function above the stage area). They have an extraordinary technical capacity – projecting beams of varying intensity and colour, sharp-edged or diffused, and of virtually any diameter, down as far as a pencil beam of no more than four or five inches thrown over a distance of a hundred yards. Now the lighting designer's favoured toy, they can be used to achieve the most dramatic

The effect of a follow spot used to isolate Rosalind Plowright, in the role of Elena, in John Dexter's production of *The Sicilian Vespers* (ENO, 1984).

of effects; they can, for instance, be fitted with infra-red gun sights so that performers can take up their positions on stage in total darkness and when on the downbeat the follow-spot operators 'fire' their beams with pinpoint precision, faces leap out at the audience as from nowhere.

The use to which any lamp can be put has been greatly extended by the development of supplementary equipment. Now that colour is no longer all painted on to the set, rather more is required than 'red light for a warm scene, blue for a cool one', and an extraordinary range of coloured filters and gels give the lighting designer his choice of literally hundreds of different shades. 'Gobos', shapes cut out of thin metal and fitted to the end of lamps, enable him to project leaves, clouds, or any other silhouette he wants on to the stage, static or moving; these effects are often used in combination with scrims – clouds, say, projected on to a gauze at the front of the stage, slightly front-lit, with a more brightly lit scene behind, create an illusion of misty distance. Projection – using gobos for shapes, or film or slides to bring an extra dimension – is now becoming an extremely subtle science: Josef Svoboda, for example, has pioneered projection on to different

textures such as string and fine plastic
rods. Another influential Svoboda innovation is the 'light curtain' created by a
bank of parabolic sealed lamps (car head-
lamps, in effect) casting an overlapping
series of exceptionally powerful and
penetrating beams: playing on the dust
in the atmosphere or droplets of aerosol
spray suspended electrostatically, these
give the impression almost of a solid sub-
stance, light become scenery. And
whereas the art of the lighting designer
used to be confined within whatever
effects could be achieved by several pairs
of hands working manual dimmers, the
computerised lighting board has
liberated him to make lighting changes
far more complex, delicate, accurate and,
above all, numerous than could be
achieved by any team of men (though
man – singular – is still needed each evening in the lighting box to trigger off each
sequence of cues as required, the computer not yet having learned to deal with
the vagaries of the live theatre).

Interestingly, with all these resources
at their command many lighting
designers prefer working in opera to even
the most blatant light show on Broadway
or the West End. Opera is more substantial, carries more emotional weight, and
in its lighting is less gimmicky than most
musicals or pop concerts and more
demanding than most straight plays. For
lighting designer Nick Chelton, opera is
very often more highly charged than any
other art form: opera singers, with the
emotional force of the music behind
them, benefit from being lit in a more

A light curtain used to illuminate Richard Van
Allan as Procida in *The Sicilian Vespers*, designed
by Josef Svoboda (ENO, 1984).

overtly dramatic way – 'a painterly or sculptural way'. He finds more outlet in opera for genuine artistic aspiration – which in the final analysis is what distinguishes a lighting designer from a senior electrician.

For John Bury, once a lighting man himself, light must be at the centre of any design concept – to divide set from light is artificial: 'The scenery *is* light, light is what you see. . . . You have to think of the design as all one thing – the scenery's not there to be seen but to be lit. . . . You put scenery in the areas where you want something solid to stop light, or reflect light.' In a practical sense too, his sets are almost always designed round light – 'Light comes before scenery. . . . My sets, because they're a lighting man's sets, always tend to be surrounds – you very rarely find anything in the middle. . . . Like one never wants to put a chandelier in the middle – once you've got a chandelier hanging in the middle of any stage, it becomes quite impossible to light the stage; you have to light everybody from the wrong angle, then they look wrong, the room looks wrong.'

Where designer and lighting designer are *not* one and the same, and the designer feels less strongly about light as part of his initial conception, the lighting designer may be less obviously on all fours with the rest of the production team. Of necessity, he is always working behind producer and designer in the sense that the tangible results of their effort – the sets, and the blocking of per-

Cross-lighting effect used in the opening moments of *The Makropoulos Case* – lighting designer Nick Chelton, designer Maria Bjørnson (ENO, 1984).

formers – must be nearing completion before he can begin to put his own plans to practical effect. This does not mean, however, that he need study the piece any less closely than they do. From the libretto and stage directions, he establishes the basic context within which he will be working – an attic with a north light, in winter; the Nevada Desert; a wooded glade; a lawyer's office; the Forum in spring; the seashore during a storm; a ballroom lit by chandeliers; the bottom of the Rhine; a doctor's surgery – as well as the specific plot features which will require their own lighting effects. In *La Bohème*, for instance, he will note the crackling flames in the stove, stoked by Rodolfo's manuscript; Mimi's candlelight, and the ensuing 'darkness' in which she and Rodolfo hunt for her key, subtly altered perhaps when she sings of the sun; the moonlight specified in 'O soave fanciulla' (*'o dolce viso di miti arconfuso alla luna'*); streetlamps outside, interior light within the Café Momus; braziers for the customs men in a snowy dawn; the shaft of sunlight from which Rodolfo shields the dying Mimi. From the music, its mood and changes of mood, a lighting designer like F. Mitchell Dana may deduce further potential lighting cues, without going so far as to define them precisely: 'Here is a big build, here is a *crescendo* – there should be some upswelling, some change in the light. Here we have a real *ritard* – we should be isolating down on something.' (Dana would never attempt, however, to design straight from the score; in its detail, his lighting design is geared primarily to the production – 'You keep hearing about this aria and that one, this movement has to be pulled up, etc. I think that's an opera buff's way of thinking. I look at it in terms of the movement on stage and what is happening dramatically. . . . When I talk to the stage manager, I talk about wanting cues when they move to stage right, not when they hit the high note.')

At as early a stage as is feasible, the lighting designer discusses with the producer and the set and costume designer(s) their conception and designs, sometimes with the help of the model, offering the suggestions he has formulated during his research and listening to the lighting ideas they have had in mind while designing. This is the moment to agree general principles – for example, is the colour in the design to come from the set itself, or from the lighting (which has the capacity completely to repaint the design)? Some designers resist coloured light – Sally Jacobs, for instance: 'I really don't like coloured light on stage, except for very stylised things – the few moments where we use it in *Turandot* . . . are very heightened moments when action turns into theatre – and I would have been curious to see if we could have done it without those colours. . . . I've had good and bad experiences with lighting designers. You design something and then another designer comes and recolours it. . . . They have to be free to take it on to the next stage, it's not finished till they do their work, but unless they take it on in the way you feel is right, it can wash out six months of work.' In F. Mitchell Dana she found a sympathetic listener: 'I tend to like to use white light and keep things relatively normal-looking. . . . It's a bit of hubris to go smearing everything with colours and changing everything when the set and costume designers have spent a great deal of time sitting down under normal light and working out the right palette and mixture.'

Alternatively the lighting designer can be entirely responsible for the colour, as John Bury prefers: 'I tend to think in monochrome. One has to put a little colour in sometimes – and one gives the whole set a hue: *Così* was all in terracotta, *Figaro* all in brown, *Dream* and *Don Giovanni* all in blacks. But one doesn't go any further than that, because one then has to do the daylight stuff and the night stuff with light. It's terribly difficult to get rid of colour, that's really the point. Take something like *Don Giovanni*, three quarters of which takes place at night. It's absolutely dreadful giving yourself bright green trees and yellow railings and pink bushes and then lighting in heavy blue to try and kill all the colour, then trying to take the blue down so the whole thing doesn't look like the inside of an aquarium bowl, like most sets do at night – you end up defeating your own object. It's much better to start with a black set with black trees, black bushes, black walls – and then you only need to steal a pale blue light on it and it looks like night. Then when you want it to look like day you can bounce in lots of colour and green back light. . . . It will always look a bit sombre, like in *Giovanni*, but it doesn't matter.'

The production team also now isolate specific moments in the drama when they think lighting may be crucial, and pool their ideas. In *Turandot*, for example, Sally Jacobs's setting for 'Nessun dorma' in Act Three was a garden enclosed by high wooden walls into which grilles were let at regular intervals. This garden she had always imagined from the music to be smoky with incense, and from an old post-card of the Le Corbusier Chapelle de Nôtre-Dame-du-Haut, Ronchamp, a dark place riven by streams of sunshine, she conceived the notion that the smoke should be pierced by shafts of light – an effect F. Mitchell Dana achieved by angling a lamp through each grille and pouring smoke through the beam. In Elijah Moshinsky's production of *Tannhäuser*, the notion of a power source centre-stage, alternately attracting and repelling Tannhäuser, was fundamental to the conception, and this found its principal expression in terms of Nick Chelton's lighting. (Producer, designer and lighting designer will not, of course, always be talking the same language. Bill McGee, Lighting Manager at the Royal Opera House, remembers being instructed by an Italian producer to create the effect of 'early morning' and putting much effort into an incomparable dawn, only to discover that what was required was more like 11.15 a.m.)

Once he has studied the opera and been briefed on the conception, the lighting designer translates production and design ideas into his own vocabulary of lighting, and estimates the equipment he is likely to need for the effects he is expecting to have to create; he then informs the theatre, so that they can order any equipment they do not already have – the ordeals by fire and water in *The Magic Flute*, for example, often require special projection equipment. Anticipating lighting needs is part experience – knowing what lamps in which combinations will produce any given effect – and part imagination. Nick Chelton describes the process: 'Take

F. Mitchell Dana's light-and-smoke effect on Sally Jacobs's set for Act 3 of *Turandot* (Covent Garden, 1984).

the beginning of *Tannhäuser* which is mostly done as a red womb – which we originally based on the idea of Bergman's films: I suppose I remembered the obvious images from *Cries and Whispers* and thought to myself, "Well, if I put in two five-kilowatt back lights in red, and if I front-light the cyclorama with about eight power lamps, and if I put some white cross-lighting into it, just in case that's all too severe . . . I've still got the follow spots" – and so it goes on.'

In this way the lighting designer may cover a good deal of the necessary ground in advance, especially if he has worked with producer and designer before – but this is all without doing any actual lighting, for which he needs the set in the theatre and the performers on stage. And for most, F. Mitchell Dana among them, however thorough their preparation and inspired their guesses, the final stage – when theories are put to the test – is the crucial one, albeit the shortest: 'I focus the show – until then I haven't *done* anything.' In arriving at the final lighting plot there will still be some experimentation, some trial and error – but with time now at a premium, the skill of the lighting designer really consists in keeping this to a minimum.

The lighting designer will have had his first opportunity to light over technical rehearsals. Here, as the set is assembled, he can focus the lamps above it, determining the position of each individual lamp (top, side, rear, front of house, in the pit, in the flies, etc.), where on stage it is aimed, how spread the beam is to be, whether the edges are to be sharp or diffused and the colour, if any, of the gel with which it is to be used. Here too he determines the cues – deciding when each lamp comes on and goes off, and its level of intensity throughout its illumination.

A good deal can be achieved at the technicals. The lighting designer can see whether the lighting cues he has proposed to himself actually succeed in 'dressing' the stage in colour, light and shade; if light levels blend; if there are any neglected corners or 'black holes'; if light 'spills' or 'bounces' accidentally on to scenery, or is blocked by it; if overhead light makes obvious circles on the floor which ruin the illusion (this is best avoided by texturing the floor-covering); if light bounces off a reflective surface and spoils other effects; if light dazzles the pit; if 'specials' (any lamp designated for a special purpose – for example, the moonlight shining on Mimi's face) actually serve their purpose. All this is tried out not on the cast but on assistant stage managers or even actors hired for the occasion, walking through the moves without music for hours on end in an empty theatre.

But the lighting designer can really only complete the lighting design, rehearse the completed plot and finally programme the computer when he has the more-or-less-finished production to work with – that is to say, during the stage rehearsals, ideally with full set, cast and costumes. In a very short period, perhaps not more than four or five days leading up to the first night, the lighting designer tries to work through the lighting plot for the whole piece. Now he must judge whether the lamps he has chosen give light of the right intensity – if not, he must suggest alternatives – and whether the colours are as he envisaged them, and satisfactory when seen in combination with the costumes and make-up. Blue light often makes black artists appear unhealthily grey, for example; and the lighting designer may decide to enhance the colour of a particular costume with complementary individual lighting – the traditional flame-coloured outfit of a Méphistophélès, say, with a follow spot plus red filter. (In this gauging of brightness and colour, there will often be an element of serendipity – the unplanned but happy effect arrived at by chance while running quickly, even carelessly through the lighting cues.) The lighting designer will also be anxious to see that he has done justice to the designer's textures, bringing out the contours of carving in wood or folds in curtains, the detail of knotted, crusted, gouged or undulating surfaces. This he may do largely by cross-lighting, whose effect is perhaps best demonstrated by the low evening sun glancing over a ploughed field, catching the peaks but not the troughs, and sharply defining the furrow in light and shade.

He must check that the focusing of the lamps is accurate – that when singers move from A to B, they are constantly covered (assuming that they stay within the light that has been designed for them – and the type of singer who likes to advance to the prompt box tends to do so regardless of the practicalities). If he has devised an arrangement of lamps to underscore a particular dramatic point, he must make sure it is working; in Stefan Janski's production of *Andrea Chénier*, for instance, the lighting designer was required to provide three distinct light sources – moonlight, candlelight and firelight – for three separate characters, to reinforce the point that each was unaware of the presence of the others. In any stage picture the emphasis must be correctly placed, and the lighting designer has something of the power of the film cameraman to focus the audience's attention: where the camera does it by zooming in to close-up, the lighting designer can do it by picking out a single feature and pulling it forward with light. 'Lighting designers have a great deal more to say about what is going on in the theatre', observes F. Mitchell Dana: 'That's why I find it much more interesting than the other media.'

Almost as important as the detail of each separate lighting state is the effectiveness of their sequence. Does each lighting state relate logically to the next? are the contrasts exaggerated or so subtle as to be imperceptible? do the stresses fall in the right place? F. Mitchell Dana explains the problem: 'If you've had a very dark scene that people have been watching for some time, you may raise five lights up one or two points and it will seem like a very big move in light. But if you've had a very bright scene, you may have to raise a hundred lights up from half to full in order to get the same feeling of contrast. You can make things very intense by manipulating what goes before or after. . . . The reason why a little section doesn't work may not be to do with the section itself, but with the things that lead up to it or come after it. . . . It could be something very simple – a light is focused in the wrong way, or it's called in the wrong place . . . so that section sticks out. You have then to figure out what happens with every *other* picture as well.'

Above all, the lighting designer must make certain that his lighting serves the drama – by catching the mood, clarifying the action and, perhaps most important, illuminating the singers' faces: just as, Ande Anderson recalls, the music hall comedian used to be convinced that a joke could only be told successfully if the audience could see his face, so the singer often feels that the impact of the voice is dulled or deflected if it is disembodied by murky lighting. It is in any case virtually impossible, in F. Mitchell Dana's view, to pay too much attention to the singer. 'Take that element out – the set designers will become architects, the clothes designers will become couturiers, the composer will compose beautiful music, the librettist will go off and write novels and poetry – but without the performer standing on stage, there is no reason to be in that theatre.'

Given the amount of nervous energy expended in evolving a lighting design under pressure, it is hardly surprising that the video-recording of operas tends to generate a certain amount of ill feeling amongst lighting designers, since of the changes that will have to be made to the stage production, the majority concern the lighting. The basic problem of commercial opera videos, as opposed to the one-off, one-country television relay, is that the images taped have to be of an exceptionally high quality if they are to survive the transfer from the system in which they are recorded to those of the countries in which they may be transmitted. (The British recording system of 625 lines, for example, is incompatible with the American system, and the pictures must be re-recorded in this system, mnemonicised outside the USA as 'Never the Same Colour Twice'.) The complications all stem from the fact that the television camera is unable to respond even half as effectively as the human eye to the demands made of it in the theatre. It cannot 'see' at all in dim light, it cannot cope with sharp colour contrasts – the lighter colour will 'flare' – and in general its colour range is surprisingly limited; black 'snows', white dazzles and red 'buzzes'.

The aim of the video lighting manager, as described by Chris Bartlett-Judd, a lighting director with the National Video Corporation, is to reproduce the original concept of producer, designer and lighting designer as faithfully as possible; but since the end product is to be viewed through the medium of the camera, the re-production must be in camera rather than theatre terms – and the camera requires, among other things, considerably more light. The lighting manager will invariably have to establish 'base' light in order to provide the cameras with the minimum needed for them to register at all. This is supplied by powerful television lamps imported into the theatre, and the ability to 'cheat' it into the stage picture with a reasonable degree of subtlety is one of the most essential tricks of the trade. Extra follow spots will almost certainly be directed at the faces of the principals (who are, after all, 'where the money is', in Chris Bartlett-Judd's phrase) to service light-hungry zoom lenses used for close focus. Another drawback of the monocular camera as compared with the bin-ocular human being is its tendency to

Aerial view, taken from the lighting bridge behind the proscenium arch, of Marie McLaughlin as the Israelite Woman in *Samson*, showing the effects of cross-lighting (Covent Garden, 1985).

curtail the depth of field in a visual image, and the lighting manager has to compensate for the flattening effect with a pronounced back light, defining the performers' silhouettes and lifting them from the background into which they would otherwise subside (a technique most commonly used, for some reason, on television newsreaders). With so many extra light sources, crucial though they are if the video film is to do justice to the original conception, it is virtually impossible to preserve the mood and atmosphere on the live stage; and it takes a philosophical lighting designer to be cheered by the prospect of future glory on tape whilst surrounded by a live audience, and a livid producer, for whom an evening's theatrical illusion has been spoiled.

19

The Costumes, Wigs and Armour

If it is the artist live on stage who justifies making the journey to the opera house rather than watching the opera on television or listening to a recording, and if the aspect of design most intimately connected with the performer is costume, then it could be argued that of the three elements in design, costume is the most indispensable to a production. It is also perhaps the least controllable, as Janice Pullen, head of Covent Garden's Wardrobe Department, confirms: 'The stage is there, it is forty feet wide and fifty feet deep and it stays there. A hundred people are very different sizes, they have mouths, they answer back, they spill coffee down themselves, they have periods, their husbands die, they break their arms, they break their legs. One person is as much of a problem as one stage. The production team has only got one stage – I've got a hundred people, all answering back and *putting on weight.*'

As a basic preliminary, the costume designer must establish exactly how many costumes will be needed, and of what types, and this cannot simply be done from the libretto; he or she must confer with the producer (and occasionally the conductor) to discover the strength of the chorus (how many men? how many women? how many are to be ball guests and how many revolutionaries, how many Roundheads and how many Cavaliers, how many Druids and how many Roman legionaries?); whether or not there will be any non-singing characters to be dressed, and whether the sets are to be changed in view of the audience, in which case the scene-shifters will have to be costumed; whether the principals change costume for every scene, every act or not at all. Comparing references, they must determine the period of the costumes, and whether they are to be strictly period or to some degree stylised (which many designers prefer, feeling that literal reproduction of a museum piece, say, or a painting can be deadly and artificial, dressing the performers always in costumes, never in clothes). For *Tannhäuser*, for example, costume designer Luciana Arrighi was asked by Elijah Moshinsky for 'Giotto today' – 'We're not doing either a strictly medieval or a Bayreuth-in-the-thirties production, we're doing something that could be familiar, but is based on historical pageant. . . . I have to put this on paper in terms of shapes and colours – stylised, because it's not an exact historic period, you could walk into the street and see people wearing things like it today. I'd like to think that my crowds are very familiar.

It's more creative than being tied to a period. . . . It's also very difficult.'

Quite obviously, the costumes must be carefully integrated with the design for the sets (and here the designer who is simultaneously responsible for both may be at an advantage): Luciana Arrighi goes as far as to claim, 'If you notice the costumes, you've done a bad design; they should be part of the landscape.' The costumes must carry on the intentions of the set in terms of style, colour and texture. Timothy O'Brien's set for *Tannhäuser* was sternly architectural, bold and uncluttered, working in blocks of solid colour; Luciana Arrighi could hardly respond with feathers, frills and lace, and she chose dark, heavy materials – wools, suede and leather – falling in simple folds and straight lines, strong against the burnished gold and royal blues of the set. In contrast, Sally Jacobs was working for *Turandot* largely in silks, chiffons and brocade, and her set – ancient wooden walls and trampled earth floor – provided a sombre background for the flamboyant colours of the principals' costumes: 'Pure colour always lifts out of earth colours very beautifully.'

Principals' costumes must be related to those of the chorus, and those of the chorus blended with each other, bearing in mind that on stage their colours may be continually shuffled and recombined, in different settings under changing light. Because of the numbers of costumes involved, and the need to keep the stage picture constantly in the correct focus, Jocelyn Herbert recommends treating the colour relationship between chorus and principals with restraint: 'Have everybody in more or less the same colours with one or two accents. . . . Look at any painting – Cézanne or Van Gogh, or Manet or Monet: very often they're fairly universal, and then there'll be one little accent, a red cart or somebody in a blue shirt, just a touch that pulls the whole thing together. You can have a far richer feeling of colour with black and white and the odd accent than hundreds of different colours. You don't want to dress the chorus in such a way that they take over. Your accents are your principals – or you can do it the other way round, depending on the story . . . Hamlet in black in the middle of a garish court. That's a *dramatic* fact, a dramatic emphasis, you can use colour for dramatic purposes – that's really how you colour the performers.' In the same spirit of serving the drama, the designer may evolve a costume as an expression of the character of its wearer. This is more positive than the desire merely to conceal weaknesses of age or physique – the short or spindly leg, the thickened neck or waist, the ship's-prow bosom; it is, according to Josephine Barstow, an acknowledgement of personality as an important resource: 'Even if people aren't actors, you've got to use the material, you can't take a human being and obliterate what they've got. . . . If you just put a costume on the stage and expect the *costume* to make the right kind of noise, you've obliterated one of your dimensions.'

Designers have widely differing attitudes to their initial costume drawings. Some, like Luciana Arrighi and Desmond Heeley, see them merely as blueprints, indications to producer, singers and budget controller of what they may anticipate; others expect to see them literally translated into fabric, intact in every detail. But in almost all cases, the transfer from drawing to costume is less mechanical than that from model to set, as each costume is adjusted to its owner to a greater or lesser extent. The drawings go first to the head of the wardrobe department who must assess the expense of the costumes proposed, whether or not the house has its own workshops, and prepare a budget figure. Interestingly, costumes have been far less obviously affected than sets by technological advance. Manufacturing processes remain much the same; and because opera costumes have to be hard-wearing (they generally have to last some ten to fifteen years, being thoroughly cleaned every time they are worn), most wardrobes prefer to use natural materials rather than synthetics, which do not take sweat as well, dye less evenly, and stretch, fade and stain far worse. If the budget is approved, the head of wardrobe will devise a production schedule which both fits in with the other shows due to open in the same period, and takes note of the likely availability of the performers; in international houses at least, costume departments have to bargain on principals who arrive only days before opening night, with little time to spare for fittings. (For this reason, the principals' costumes are usually made last, and are most often the occasion for crises and bills for overtime in the workrooms.)

The first step towards a costume is the preparation of a prototype — an approximation in cheap material, pinned and tacked on a dressmaker's dummy. From this first attempt to get the drawing into three dimensions, the designer and head of wardrobe can see whether the cut is faithful to the design, and whether the design itself is practical and visually effective. It is also a good opportunity to check that the costume will hang and move as the designer wants it to, provided that the material of the prototype sufficiently resembles that which it is eventually intended to use: while prototypes are most often cut in calico, for the sake of economy, a stiff cotton can tell the designer little about how a chiffon or silk jersey will behave, and it is generally cheaper in the long run to find some cheap chiffon, perhaps from a show that has been scrapped, and make one's mistakes on that. The choice of fabric of the right weight and texture is perhaps the single most crucial element in the realisation of the designer's vision, and the head of wardrobe can play an important role at the prototype stage by interpreting the drawing intelligently. Of Sally Jacobs's costumes for Ping, Pang and Pong in the Serban *Turandot*, Janice Pullen remembers, 'It was quite apparent that if the trousers were to be cut as they were in the drawing, with that wonderful huge sag in the girth, they couldn't be made of anything stiff, because it would just stick out . . . Because it had movement in the lines of the leg, it had to be something with a certain amount of weight. And it had got to drape because it had to be able to do all those falls, they'd got to be able to put their legs together and not have great lumps of cloth hanging out of the front and back. That told one the area of material to be looking in – crêpe rather than velvet.'

OPPOSITE A rehearsal break in the televising of Oliver Knussen's *Where the Wild Things Are* (Glyndebourne Festival Opera, 1984).

Chorus prototypes are generally made first. This has become a more complex procedure than once it was, because the old habit of dressing the chorus identically has been largely superseded; without wishing to swamp the principals in too rich a mixture of choristers, designers rarely settle for making them absolutely indistinguishable except if a deliberate statement of uniformity is intended – one might expect soldiers, priestesses or waiters to be dressed the same, but not crowds of the general populace. To secure variety within what is still recognisably a group, the designer may provide basic prototype garments – one standard-design waistcoat, one pair of breeches, jacket, shirt, cloak — but will ask for them to be made in a wide range of materials, and then allocate them in different combinations: one male chorister may be given linen breeches, brocade waistcoat and silk shirt, another silk breeches, linen shirt, brocade jacket and no waistcoat, and so on. The

Luciana Arrighi, the costume designer for *Tannhäuser*, at a fitting with Thomas Allen for his role as Wolfram (Covent Garden, 1984).

audience generally pays so little attention to the chorus that it will register the fact of difference without recognising the ease with which it has been achieved.

Once the prototypes have been approved by the designer, the wardrobe department can start buying the actual materials. Colour indications will have accompanied the drawings – the designer may even have supplied sample swatches – and very occasionally the buyers will find fabric of exactly the right colour ready-prepared; more often they will have to buy fabric of the right texture and dye it. In all this it is prudent to involve the designer as closely as possible, since a colour will rarely appear exactly the same to two observers, particularly when painted colour is translated into coloured fabric whose texture reflects light differently. For chorus costumes, dyeing is done in bulk, along with any other preparatory processes, such as pleating or tucking, that may be necessary; a 'cheap' material (cotton or linen, for example) which requires several processes may ultimately be more expensive than satin or brocade untreated.

With much of the material bought and prepared, cutting, assembling and fitting can begin. Fitting is a crucial stage in the making of a successful costume, and designers will always invigilate at fitting sessions if they can. For the chorus, wardrobe staff will take each basic prototype garment and fit it to a representative group of choristers – Janice Pullen describes the selection process: 'You'll select a small short man, a big fat man, a tall good-looking man and an unshapely man, a short plump girl with a big bust, a tall elegant girl . . . so the designer gets to see what the costumes look like on a good range of the chorus. You can make drawings of costumes on girls with swanlike necks and endless arms, but you've got to see it on stage on a girl who's four foot ten with a thirty-eight-inch bust.' Each of the other choristers then goes into the standard size to which he or she most closely approximates, with appropriate adjustments – waists and seams let out or in, hems taken up or down, sleeves lengthened or shortened.

Costumes are adapted to their wearers in other ways. The opera wardrobe mistress soon learns to accommodate individual foibles and allergies – to feathers, wool, black dye, metal zips, biological washing powder – as well as the likes and dislikes common to all singers. No singer will want to wear anything that covers the ears, or is tight at the neck; collars, ruffs, even breastplates that may rise to press uncomfortably on the Adam's apple, need a couple of inches clearance. The other sensitive area is the chest and diaphragm. Some women prefer a tight corset or bodice to push against when singing, but most dresses, especially those with a low neckline, must be cut so as to allow for a chest expansion which is sometimes truly startling – often as much as seven inches, and many international houses have one lady on their books with a twelve-inch expansion. Excessive heat is another frequent complaint – and one that is much harder to answer. To look natural, costumes must be made of the fabrics that would be used in daily life for garments of that kind – which may, and in much Northern European opera certainly will include wools, leather, fur, brocade. Singing involves fairly violent exertion, often under strong light – a one-kilowatt lamp at full power generates the same heat as one bar of an electric fire, and there can be upwards of 150 lamps ranging from one to ten kilowatts in operation at once. A light curtain can give an opera stage the feel of Horse Guards Parade on an August afternoon; and when a costume is padded – as that of, say, Falstaff is likely to be – the wearer can partially evaporate during a performance.

Before the costumes finally reach the stage, some of the effect so lovingly created must be equally lovingly undone, since it is not always appropriate that a garment should appear in mint condition; as Janice Pullen points out, the chestnut seller in Act Two of *La Bohème* is unlikely to have knife-edge creases in his trousers. A costume like his will be sprayed with aniline dye to give it a well-worn and sooty look; it may be cheese-gratered to grub up its fibres, have buttons torn off and bricks put in its pockets to make them sag. The pilgrims in Act Two of *Tannhäuser* arrived in woollen cloaks crumpled by a thorough wetting (the wool shrinks but the calico lining does not), and sprayed round the shoulders with a thin film of white emulsion paint simulating the effects of a long dusty trek. There can be a certain artistry in the systematic despoiling of a costume. The leather jerkin of a Falstaff, for example – 'What *would* it have down it?', muses Janice Pullen. 'Gravy, beer dribble . . . he has a huge stomach that would hang over the table, a receptacle for everything that missed his mouth.' She adds, with relish: 'We set fire to things if we want something that's *really* ragged and tatty. It's good if it's part acrylic and part wool, because it'll burn *and* fray. You can wipe glue into something to give it a nasty, slimy look . . .' And the designer may connive at an inspired departure from a costume that has been carefully designed and fitted – Luciana Arrighi: 'If a crowd is meant to be poor, I may give people the wrong costumes, swap them around. It's a terrible worry to everyone, but it looks marvellous if it doesn't fit – and it's *effect* you're after.'

The procedure for manufacturing principals' costumes is initially much the same – making the prototype, choosing and processing the material; but the crucial finalising (cutting, sewing, fitting) is squeezed into a shorter period, often under considerable pressure, as it is generally by the quality of the principals' costumes that the costume design will be judged, and each demands a great deal of individual attention. Taking as an example the costume which Sally Jacobs designed for Placido Domingo as Calaf in the first and second acts of *Turandot* (a Tilka jacket worn over black silk trousers and high Tibetan boots): the choice of material for the jacket was straightforward, according to Janice Pullen: 'Turquoise silk – the drawing showed you in its way that it was silk. It was not a dead colour, there was light in the fabric; in actually reading the design you could see that it was textured and that it had sheen and movement.' Because silk is expensive and Domingo was available, the cutter made a calico prototype and fitted it on him before cutting the silk to the same pattern, mounting it on calico with a thin layer of wadding and having it machine-quilted with gold scallops. The quilted jacket was then fitted again to establish the neckline; the design indicated some kind of trim, which it was agreed should be gold russia and black velvet, but with an added refinement: 'Because it had already been decided that for "Nessun dorma" in Act Three he would have a soft red silk shirt, as a little touch just a thin strip of the red silk was put at the cuff and the edge of the collar of the turquoise jacket, to hint at him having that red shirt on underneath all the way through.' And after the first dress rehearsals, only days before the first night, the jacket was changed again: 'We were all aware that there was something not quite right. . . . It had a half-moon sleeve that went right down to his wrist, so you were losing his hands, and he's got wonderfully expressive hands and arms. So I cut the bottom half of the sleeve away at the elbow and squared it off.'

The performer's own reaction to his costume cannot be ignored – and contrary to popular opinion, complaints are motivated less by vanity than by insecurity; James Bowman, having been required as a mythological lover in Cavalli's *L'Egisto* to wear a costume consisting almost exclusively of a short white pleated skirt, maintains, 'If you feel you look silly in a costume, it's difficult to sing convincingly. That costume in *L'Egisto* – I felt a fool. I was livid about it – why should I have to turn up looking like Virginia Wade?' Janice Pullen is a little wry about singers' complaints – 'Sing a bum note – it's the sleeve' – but in practice she accommodates all reasonable requests. And a large proportion *are* reasonable and not capricious, in Sally Jacobs's view. Performers have an acute perception of their own needs in a role (which may change during rehearsal, in which case they will be justified in asking for alterations in their costume). 'They know better than anyone else what they're developing for this performance. They may not understand spatial relationships and the theory of colour and visual phenomena the way I do, but they understand from the inside what is developing. . . . They have got tremendous responsibility on that stage – they've got to be listened to and they have to feel right. Gwyneth Jones has to go on stage as Turandot and do this enormously demanding role; and if the costume is dragging in the wrong way and she feels she doesn't look the part, it's going to undermine the whole performance. It's not a question of indulging them – it's serious, it has to be worked out.' What is more, it has to be worked out afresh to a certain extent almost every time there is a cast change, since as often as not the new singer cannot get into the old costume, even with alterations. This is not just a question of height and girth. Each performer brings a completely new sensibility to a role which must be *included* in the costume; otherwise something which is alive on one performer is a 'dead duplicate' on another.

A costume will almost always need to be complemented and completed by a wig (though since modern fashions have become longer, men can get away with their own hair more frequently). While for a smaller house it may be cheaper to buy or hire wigs, most large houses manufacture their own: Covent Garden, for example, has a long-established wig department, under the charge of wigmaster Ronald Freeman. When submitting costume drawings, the designer will also pass to the wig department a set of wig designs, front and back view, possibly accompanied by design references – photographs, notes on period, colour suggestions, and so on.

The wigmaster takes measurements of each performer's skull, and makes a foundation of wig 'lace' on which he marks the performer's own hairline to ensure it will be covered by the finished wig. He then prepares the hair he intends to use. Covent Garden's wigs are usually made entirely of natural hair since acrylic, though cheaper, soon mats and does not wear well. Some of this is animal hair – yak is popular – used chiefly when an authentic wig of the period would likewise have used it (an eighteenth-century formal powdered wig, for instance). For the more naturalistic wigs, human hair is preferable – mostly Asian, which, being coarser, is better for supplying bulk to a wig; European hair, which is finer, takes curl more readily but is considerably more expensive. Before it is bought, Asian hair will have been bleached and redyed (even where the end result is to be black). The wigmaster then collaborates with the designer in mixing different colours on a hackle (a giant currycomb) to simulate the natural variety of hues in a head of hair: 'grey' hair is in fact a mixture of black, white and brown, and black can be 'warmed up' with strands of red hair, or darkened with blue. (To distinguish the members of the chorus, each is given a wig, individually handmade, in which the colours are slightly differently combined.)

The wig is then knotted, entirely by hand, on the same principle as a Persian rug – a finicky and laborious process which for a long wig may take more than a week. (Long hairs require a wider sweep of the arm, and tangle endlessly.) The finest detail is required at the hairline which will, for example, be very slightly lighter than the rest of the head because, as Ron Freeman points out, 'That's where you get all the sun, particularly in the warmer climates.' Once knotted, the wig is dressed in much the same way as a real head of hair – first cut, then set (with water rather than setting lotion, and a hot evening in the theatre will uncurl it), then dried in an oven for two hours or so or, if it is a period wig, set with irons for authenticity. Facial hair – beards, moustaches and eyebrows – is prepared in the same way on a smaller scale, mostly knotted on lace and clipped to the right length: yak, being more bristly, is good for beards (though the thrifty wigmaster will also use up the clippings from wigs). In cutting, fitting and gluing the lace, he must be careful to make allowances for the vigorous facial contortions which singers cannot avoid. If the face itself is to be altered – with a 'blind' eye, a false nose, a duelling scar – this, at Covent Garden at least, is also the responsibility of the wigmaster.

The male performer – costumed, bewigged, bearded, booted and bejewelled – still has to be armed. Armour may in a small house be hired or faked by the

OPPOSITE TOP Ron Freeman, Wigmaster at Covent Garden, fitting Donald McIntyre with a false nose for his performance as Scarpia in *Tosca* (1984); BELOW knotting hair on to wig lace in the wig department at Covent Garden.

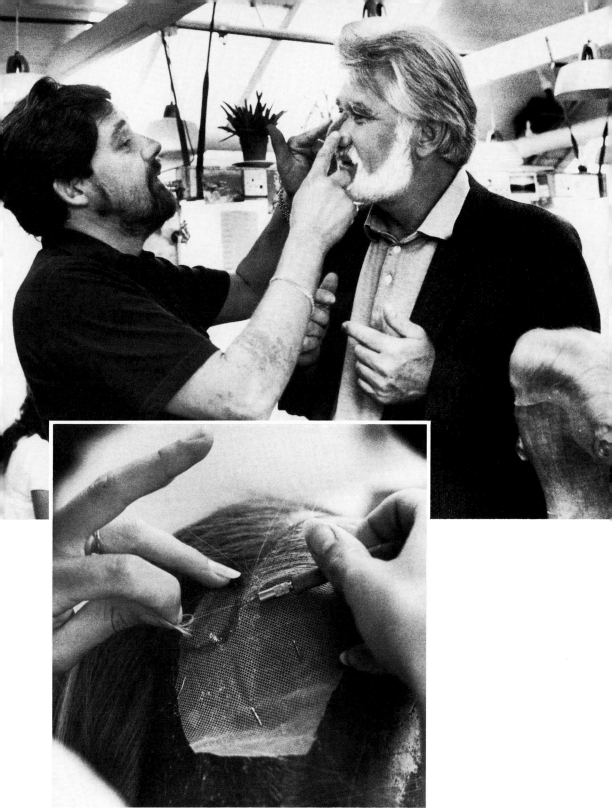

props department. Covent Garden, however, has a superior armoury of its own in the basement, under the control of armourer Terry Keen: all guns, other than those over a hundred years old, are on his personal firearms and gunpowder licence, and all keys to the armoury except his own are deposited at Bow Street police station across the road. The collection, menacing and valuable, includes spears (among them polearms from the Napoleonic Wars, used mainly in *Il Trovatore*); daggers, some with retractable blades, most of them operative; a cornucopia of firearms – matchlocks, flintlocks, rifles, blunderbusses, Brown Bess muskets from the Tower of London; armour – some real, most fibreglass (made off the premises these days, because of the fire hazard and the appalling smell which used to float up the lift shafts into the statelier regions of the house); swords – most real, some cobbled together from stray pommels, quillons and blades, some made from scratch, like the ponderous array of aluminium broadswords specially designed for *Parsifal*, to prop up flagging Knights of the Grail. When a production is being designed, the designer may be invited to the armoury to choose the weapons he or she requires to offset the costumes, or he may ask the armourer to prescribe arms of the right period. Some productions are lighter than others on armour – *Aida*, for instance, 'just a pile of spears', in Terry Keen's phrase, while *Rigoletto*, packed with Zeffirellian period detail, calls for swords, daggers and breastplates all round.

In the Covent Garden armoury, a great divide is drawn between 'armour' (which is old and authentic) and 'props' (which are neither), and Terry Keen wages constant warfare to preserve his best pieces – keeping back the same six rapiers to be used, and ruined, in fights, wiring up rifles so that the performers are unable to tinker with them in rehearsals. Disasters are nonetheless inevitable. Nothung, with a trick release mechanism designed to disintegrate the blade at Siegfried's behest, gets stuck in the scenery at rehearsal and breaks uninvited. Lensky's duelling pistol falls from his nerveless grasp and the stock shatters. ('There's no reason why you can't die and drop down and still keep holding it . . .') The Brown Besses gradually crack and split – 'I watch the performers run off the stage because it's tea break and they've got their twenty minutes – and they *throw* them. I know they're tough, but when you're that old . . .' But in the end he is forced to acknowledge that he is working in the theatre, of which this is an occupational hazard: 'As much as you love the stuff and look after it, it's here to use. I am careful who I give it to, but there are certain times when you can't say no – it's not a museum.'

OPPOSITE Terry Keen, Armourer at Covent Garden.

20

Working with the Performers

The last weeks before opening night, the weeks of production rehearsal, when sets, costumes, lights and singers eventually come together on stage, should be for the producer and designer the fulfilment of months, even years of effort, the moment at which cherished theories and visions are translated into living theatrical reality – and sometimes it works. Almost as often it is a time of disappointment, compromise and even defeat.

It is one of the limitations of opera that by the time production rehearsals begin, the producer has generally committed himself to a specific set and, to a lesser extent, specific costumes (all already made or in the last stages of manufacture), with the result that the drama itself is largely pre-set, tied down to specifics. Sally Jacobs regrets the lack of flexibility at so crucial a period in the production's history: 'There'll be certain locked-in moments right from the beginning, which are dangerous. Anything can happen in rehearsal, it's such an exploratory time . . . Something marvellous may develop that you can't do because the design is rigid at that moment. Most directors want to use the rehearsal period for real discoveries . . . but if the wrong foundation has been put down, it bedevils the whole thing.'

In an ideal world, the order might well be reversed, as Sir Peter Hall suggests: 'The best way to work is to rehearse first and then design it' – something he is occasionally able to do in the theatre, but which in opera, where forward planning is apparently integral to the system, he believes to be impossible. This is one of the aspects of 'establishment' opera with which such experimental groups as Opera Factory take issue; operating at a very much more modest level, they believe it perfectly feasible to evolve designs during rehearsal, sets and costumes emerging from the interaction of singers, producer and designer, conditioned by the drama rather than conditioning it. On the small scale, this approach is often convincing, inventive and practical; but John Bury speaks for many of his fellow designers in warning of the risks attendant on applying it to the large-scale production: 'You tend not to get any set at all. You end up with a set of screens which you move around. . . . If you're just going to play it studio-wise – give them a set of black screens, and they'll all sit there and argue all day long and in the end they find the right arrangement for the screens, and you say, "Lovely, darlings, done it, very clever!" – and that's fine. But surely our job – what designers are paid for – is to do a certain amount of that for them beforehand.'

Trying to find a middle way between the set of screens and the wholly determinate multi-million dollar reconstruction of the Place du Tertres, producer and designer may seek to keep as many options open for as long as they can – a working compromise of which Sir Peter Hall approves: 'I always try to have designs which are flexible enough to admit all kinds of changes. It's like a kit of parts rather than a definite solution.' And for *Turandot*, Andrei Serban asked Sally Jacobs to keep centre stage entirely empty as a space in which the drama could expand – where, in the riddle scene, for example, Calaf and Turandot could express the conflict between them through a variety of metaphors rather than a single image: it could be at one moment a bullring, an arena in which Calaf fights for his life, at the next a courtroom where protagonist (Calaf) and antagonist (Turandot) confront each other before a judge (Altoum) in the conventional three-cornered configuration of Anglo-Saxon jurisprudence.

If the sets can be a constraint for the producer, the cast can be a perpetual frustration, either because they will not carry out his directions or because they simply cannot. In production after production the producer finds himself working with singers fundamentally unsuited for his purposes because in opera – unlike the theatre, where it is axiomatic that the producer should select his own performers – casting is usually done by administrators, with the emphasis on vocal capability, and indeed often before the producer is chosen. What many producers regard as a crucial part of their job therefore becomes a lottery, and the job redefines itself as using to best advantage material provided by someone else.

How a producer uses the production rehearsals will vary in detail from opera to opera, depending upon the nature of the work and his conception of it, the singers and their availability, the time he has been allotted, and so on; but generally speaking, every producer evolves his own characteristic method of working with singers to achieve the desired results in the time. Responsibility for getting the show on to the stage by opening night is ultimately his, and it gives him both the initiative and the right to exert authority. Authority can be exercised, however, in a number of different ways.

The opera producer must have certain basic technical skills. He must know how to wield the stage as a tool, and 'dress' it with the performers; how to build a moving stage picture, consistently balanced and focused with foreground and background related, which will express the music, clarify the story, and comment on the action. At the most basic level, he must be able to 'block' movement on stage so that it is neither cramped nor confused, and he must understand the mechanics of regulating the drama – how to build entrances and exits, how to tighten or relax the tension. He must know how to use every element in his stage picture to best effect – form and line, space and colour, height and width, symmetry and contrast. For a certain essentially disciplinarian type of producer, these skills constitute the greater part of the job, his method being to formulate a conception which he then realises by the application of his technique to the raw material of the performers in the set. Extreme proponents of the 'unilateral' approach to production block every move in advance; rehearsal becomes a form of drill, and success depends almost entirely on the quality of the original idea. If it is a brilliant conception, the performers cannot spoil it; if it is not, they cannot save it.

In some circumstances this approach can be invaluable – when time is severely limited and there is little opportunity to experiment or to canvass opinion, or when the performers are limited and there is little point in doing either. It is also often justified when working with the chorus. The management of chorus rehearsal time is one of the hardest skills for the novice in opera to acquire; when attempting to direct seventy or eighty performers simultaneously, it is crucial to know exactly what you want and precisely how to achieve it – to 'seize the sessions', in Anthony Besch's phrase, 'and squeeze every second out of them.' For the unilateralist, producing the chorus is a question of issuing instructions to be followed, without debate, *en masse*; some of the most visually effective chorus work in opera is virtual choreography.

There is, however, another way of working with the chorus – treating its members as individually as possible depending on the time available. Franco Zeffirelli, for example, has always adopted this approach; and John Schlesinger viewed his chorus for *Der Rosenkavalier* with the eye of a Hollywood casting director, tailoring stage business to the appearance and capabilities of individual choristers. 'Casting gardeners for the second act, we asked, "Shall we have a young gardener, or an old gardener and a boy?" And then thought, "Why don't we have two very aged gardeners who are desperately proud of their hydrangeas . . ."' David Ritch, reviving Jonathan Miller's production of *Rigoletto*, showed the English National Opera chorus *The Godfather, Part II* during a rehearsal session, and subdivided them into Mafia 'families', each with its separate identity and subtext, some laundering money, some running numbers rackets, others overseeing the meat deliveries.

Many producers prefer to share with the singer the responsibility for his or her performance, acknowledging that ultimately the performer will be alone on the stage and to be convincing he must be more than a mouthpiece, must make his own contribution. They reject the 'pre-cooked' approach to producing – some, like David Freeman, on almost ideological grounds, as a feature of hierarchical opera society, others, like Andrei Serban, on practical grounds. The producer who plots every move in advance, calculates every effect, whether he is a traditionalist or an extreme 'conceptualist' in the current German mode, in Serban's view lays a deadening hand on the work. 'It's all written down and it doesn't matter who the human beings are who are there, they have to match the chess situation of his imagination that he's set up at home. To me *that's* dead theatre – really deadly. Theatre is only alive in which there is a sense of giving and taking.'

Those who insist most passionately on involving the performers as collaborators sometimes see themselves as little more than organisers – Peter Sellars for one: 'I'm completely dependent on input from singers . . . I'll spend an afternoon work-

Sir Peter Hall rehearsing *Carmen* with Maria Ewing in the title role and David Holloway as Escamillo (Glyndebourne Festival Opera, 1985).

ing with soprano Susan Larson on an aria, trying to get the physicality of it put together. She will go home and that night for four hours in front of a mirror she will work out how she can do it all *and* breathe . . . I'm just a glorified collator – all one does is organise some of the things which are in the rehearsal room . . . Everyone imagines that the singers are dumb clay and then the director moves in and everything is beautiful. On the contrary, what I have in these people are genuine working colleagues who will say, "Peter, forget it, that's *horrible*."'

The producer's conception of a work may depend to some extent on the properties of the performers through whom he is to realise it. It matters to him what they look like – Peter Brook has observed, 'The vehicle of drama is flesh and blood . . . the vehicle and the message cannot be separated.' Their physical condition may also count: Andrei Serban's perception of Ping, Pang and Pong in *Turandot* was significantly modified by the performers cast in the roles (Kim Begley, Laurence Dale and William Workman): 'I'd no idea they were young and that

Jon Vickers in the title role of *Peter Grimes* (Covent Garden, 1984).

they could move. Usually they would be cast like old ministers, in their fifties . . . It's luck to have three young, willing, gifted singer/actors who could do all these acrobatics and develop the characters much further than I could have hoped other-wise' – as *commedia dell'arte* characters, acrobats, jugglers, jesters. In some perform-ers, force of personality is a factor which cannot be ignored, and may on occasion usefully be channelled: Elijah Moshinsky describes Jon Vickers, whom he has produced in *Peter Grimes*, *Samson et Dalila* and Handel's *Samson*, as 'an extraordinary artist – it's like directing Marlon Brando, because he has a particular kind of indi-vidual intensity. And if you can communicate with him and through him to the work, it's the most rewarding and interesting experience you can have.' If, on the other hand, the producer finds an artist unsympathetic or unresponsive, it may be wiser to forego the whole experience – Andrei Serban: 'The chemistry between the performers and myself is not always the same. It's like an act of love – it doesn't always work.'

A producer like Serban will sometimes go so far as to delay evolving his conception of a work in detail until he has seen his cast in action: 'I never write down a blocking at home. I never come what is called "prepared". Very often in that sense I create a lot of panic in the stage management and administration and the singers – everybody's in corners muttering, "Does he know what he is doing?", because I don't really do much at all at first. When I come, I look at the singers . . . to see what they can do, and then to see what is possible in the situation.' More often the producer arrives with the essence of his interpretation established, but with room within this framework for the singers to evolve the detail of their own performances. The end is his, the choice of means to that end at least partly theirs. Graham Clark speaks warmly of the type of producer who is prepared to incorporate the singers' intuitive responses in his conception: 'People tend to think that opera is stylised, a stylised ritual that one has to go through – if it has a musical framework, there is a stylised ritual. . . . It's not true – and people like Miller and Pountney and Ponnelle have broken right away and pointed out that there are as many different answers as there are in the straight theatre.'

As Jonathan Miller conceives a production, 'There's a strategy, but the tactics are worked out on the floor. . . . You're pursuing a whole series of tactical encounters with people' – some of which are more productive than others: 'These are always the hazards of any work which depends on working with material some of which has got will of its own and therefore talents, and therefore failures of talent. If you're a painter, all the materials are inanimate, and if you're a good craftsman it works because you are already familiar with the limits of its properties. You're not familiar with the limits of the properties of other conscious beings.' And some of the encounters are more closely contested than others. Many leading singers are, not surprisingly, emphatic that they be permitted to contribute: 'Producers expect us to be marionettes. But this is a *Zusammenwerk*, a together-work – they have to accept my personality and my thinking, my preparation for the role. When I've studied the role, he can't just tell me to do things. He's taken me as an interpreter and he has to accept my opinions. As Ileana Cotrubas, coming to interpret Mimi or Violetta, I can bring this and this to the role – my own emotions and potential, my musical possibilities for the part. Nobody can force me to do something which is against my feeling and my preparation' – and producers who have tried have discovered that she is perfectly prepared to act on her convictions by withdrawing from the production. 'I ask all the time why singers accept these nonsense productions. They say I can *afford* to argue and they can't – but I remember that at the beginning of my career I did a new *Flute* in Frankfurt, I was unknown and I still spoke out loudly – and they accepted it. Young singers are too afraid, they won't even discuss, let alone oppose. They won't say they're unhappy, they won't say that they have something to say. They're afraid they won't make a career. It's wrong.' Similarly, Norman Bailey, with some thirty years' professional experience behind him, does not expect to have his performances totally recast: 'I think it's a waste of time and of the opera house's money, to be honest. If you've been engaged to do a certain role, what you're bringing with you is a certain experience and a certain success in that role – to throw it out of the window is a waste of time. . . . There are producers who chicken out, and want somebody who has *not* done the role before, because they're not prepared to face the controversy they'll get with an experienced singer.'

Other performers see the job in hand as being to subordinate their own ideas, however carefully formulated, to the overall conception, and use their talents and experience to serve the producer – Josephine Barstow, for instance: 'My job is not only to explore what the composer has put on the page, but to explore what the producer and designer have had in their minds, and to develop that. . . . Explore it with them, and take it even further than they had thought.' This, however, is not always enjoyable: 'As a professional, one has to stand back from any given performance and manipulate it. Nevertheless, one also has to be involved and commit oneself, and if one *is* committed innately to a work, if it's a piece one loves, it's very difficult to stand back and think, "I don't care, I'll just do it anyway". . . . I can remember one occasion in Germany – I'd given up the Met to do it, which was probably silly – I fought the producer for three weeks because I thought the conception was just terrible (and nobody else fought, because there isn't quite so much of a tradition of fighting for one's views outside Britain). I got to a point where I went back to my hotel room and thought, "Am I going to stay? – in which case I'd better stop fighting and get on with it: or shall I go home?" . . . I find it very difficult to make a fuss and disrupt the whole thing by leaving. . . . But there are people who do, and I think probably they're right. I think there are times when one ought to go home.'

The producer is likely to face his stiffest challenge from those who barely recognise his credentials, let alone acknowledge his authority or sympathise with his aims – singers who prize stagecraft (the art of maintaining some semblance of naturalness on stage whilst watching the conductor and projecting into the auditorium) more highly than acting, and do not necessarily acknowledge any place at all for acting in opera. It is a familiar platform on which to make a stand and there are well-worn arguments to support it – such as those of Luciano Pavarotti: 'It is not as though they [producers] were requesting a supplementary talent that was related to music . . . They are asking you to be accomplished in a totally different performing art, one as difficult and demanding, in its way, as singing. Many Italians feel it is an unreasonable demand and don't make the effort. Others think it is beneath their dignity to try anything that might not be done at the same high level as their singing. They would rather be non-actors than bad actors. . . . You must be believable and definitely "in" the character, but as for pulling emotion from the audience, in opera that is more the job of the music and your interpretation of it. . . . I find that singers who get highly involved in their dramatic performance often allow the vocal part to suffer.' More bluntly, Dame Joan Sutherland remarks, 'I think it is the sound of singing that people want when they come to the opera. If they want a good dramatic performance, they should go to a straight play.'

There has always been a school of thought which rejects the notion that opera is a branch of theatre, on the grounds that both more and less can be expected of it. On the one hand, it is argued, the fact of music takes opera beyond the scope of theatre; singers' priorities are different from those of the straight theatre, their first responsibility is to the score. On the other, opera can never make true drama; it is by nature too stylised and artificial an art form, and is distanced still further by the fact that it expresses itself in words which are either inaudible or, if heard, unintelligible. For both these reasons, producers should acknowledge that in opera they are working in a different medium and that they cannot make the same demands of singers as they would of actors.

It is true that singers are trained, by conventional methods, to express themselves on stage primarily with their voices; concentrating on doing justice to the notes, they feel constraints which few actors share – according to James Bowman, 'Singers don't like being grabbed, or pushed around, because it upsets the diaphragm. . . . And the actor *gives* you far more on stage, the actor is really talking to you at close quarters. . . . Eyes are the secret; if you watch singers, they never look at each other. It's partly because it's embarrassing, partly "Does my breath smell? Am I flat?" – so many layers of inhibitions which actors don't have.' Singers suffer (if suffer is the word) from 'the inhibition of the singing voice . . . a third force to be considered all the time. . . . Perpetual throat-clearing and worries about whether the voice is working'. Undoubtedly a great deal is required of singers besides acting, and many producers are concerned that they should not be forced beyond their capacity. H. Wesley Balk, former Resident Theater Director of the Minnesota Opera, believes that since more has been required dramatically of singers, voices have begun to decay earlier. 'Physical tension of any kind in the body effects a subtle drag on the voice. . . . You put that drag on for ten years, and you have an erosion. . . . We got them into it by asking for acting, and if we don't have the capacity to help them get out of it, then we have no business asking them for it in the first place.' John Copley agrees: 'Look at the singer-cemeteries – vast columns of urns. Such tragedies – and you can see it happening before your very eyes. . . . I love singers – I love the breed, and singing gives me the greatest pleasure of anything. . . . There aren't many of the great singers around, and the last thing one wants to do is waste them.'

It is equally true, nevertheless, that singers' capabilities, generally speaking, are being rapidly extended. Walter Felsenstein, Intendant of the Komische Oper in East Berlin between 1947 and 1975, did more perhaps than anyone to change accepted notions of what could be asked of the singer. If a singer is not encouraged, he wrote, 'to take responsibility for the conception of a role, and to have confidence to interpret it accordingly, he is useless as a creative performer', and he argued for 'the synthesis of singing and acting techniques', to be achieved by specially trained singer-actors through long rehearsal within a permanent ensemble. Opera Factory is one of many groups offering singers the chance to develop their full potential along these lines. 'The aim', according to its manifesto, 'is to develop a genuine ensemble of performers ... who work together over a number of years, who are as highly trained physically and dramatically as vocally and musically.' Training 'based on dramatic and musical improvisation, and physical and mental exercises' is considered an essential preliminary to operatic performance, enabling each performance to be an improvisation in some sense: in David Freeman's words, 'You improvise through a performance with a great deal of information – words, music, climaxes, emphases, plot, etc. – but it's still improvisation.'

Many singers have already reached standards of dramatic expressivity quite comparable with those of the theatre; the familiar and cherished myths of the Lot's Wife soprano, the Neanderthal tenor, the semaphore school of operatic acting, are being vigorously debunked – by David Pountney amongst others: 'I think singers are enormously accomplished. I reckon that on good nights in the opera house, the acting that you see is as good, if not better than the acting that you see at the National Theatre. Partly because actors these days are primarily involved in a kind of suburban performance, they're trained for audiences in suburban living-rooms, round the television ... and when they attempt to appear in a great big epic extravaganza, they can't do it. In a recent production of a French Romantic drama, the Italianate Contessa made her entrance, and she looked like somebody with curlers in her hair – there's no idea of the scale or style of performance needed for that sort of thing.... In that context, singers are much more versatile and in many cases much more able as actors, because they have to act in many more different styles' – a claim indirectly substantiated from the other side of the fence by theatre critic Michael Billington: 'I think voices are less varied and interesting in the theatre than they used to be. When I first went to the theatre – and I don't think this is just juvenile fantasy – I think you did hear a richer range of musicality in the speaking of the English language. It is perhaps a reflection of the times. In the 1980s the English language is in serious decline; our language is becoming duller and blander. A lot of actors, of course, work in television, where the voice doesn't have to be used or projected or trained at all. As people have got bodily more expressive in the theatre, they've got less vocally expressive, there's less colour and less range and less music. They can *do* more – they can swing from trapezes by their heels if you ask them to, they'll do anything physically that you ask them to. I just don't think they have the instinctive musicality of the Gielgud generation.'

Another development which provides the defenders of opera as theatre with ammunition is the interchange of techniques between the two mediums. Much has been made of the incursion of theatre producers into opera, bringing with them (albeit ten or twenty years in arrears) the ideas and innovations of the straight theatre. Much less has been made of the occasions when the process goes into reverse. Elijah Moshinsky: 'I tend to find now when I go to the Royal Shakespeare

Company or National Theatre that straight directors are imitating opera productions – techniques that were first introduced in opera are now being used in theatre. . . . I would say, for example, the recent production of *Mother Courage* by the Royal Shakespeare Company was an operatic production; in its visual approach and its approach to the text, it was closer to the Friedrich *Ring* or the Friedrich *Tristan* than it is to the Berliner Ensemble. . . . Brecht wanted to de-theatricalise the theatre, so you would look at the moral impulse behind people's actions. He played his *Mother Courage* against a white cyclorama under unvarying light so that you would listen. The Royal Shakespeare Company did a production where the lights changed, lights flashed – in a sense, the theatricality expressed the meaning. That kind of approach to theatricality is what you have all the time now in operatic productions.'

As for the criticisms levelled at the art form itself, rather than its practitioners, few of the producers who work regularly in opera would accept that it is in any way inadequate as theatre. To the claim that opera is by nature more artificial and stylised and, by implication, more limited as drama, Jonathan Miller retorts: 'I don't distinguish between the two forms of utterance – they are both artificial. I distinguish between them, obviously, in the same way that I distinguish between verse-speaking in Shakespeare and the prose-speaking of Chekhov, but they're both highly artificial forms of diction. . . . None of the forms of diction that you hear on stage are anything like what we use when talking to one another. They are representations through which one can recognise life, but they are not simulacra of life. . . . The conventions of opera are not the *limits*, the conventions are the constitution. It's what we work with, it's no more a limit than it is for a tightrope walker to have to step this narrow line: that's what you choose to do when you're doing tightrope-walking.' And to the claim that opera cannot communicate as drama because the words are incomprehensible, many would reply that opera is communicating as drama in a different language altogether – a composite, extended language, as Götz Friedrich sees it, of words-and-music: 'The music of the theatre has its own language. Music can explain, give reasons and describe in a way that words cannot. The only true subject of opera is the story that cannot be told only in words. If you agree with this, then you must concede to music a special language that can be understood even without all the words being heard. . . . When you come to the end, to the *Liebestod*, to the final song in *Salome*, to the last ensemble of *Figaro*, you always reach a level where music speaks only with its own language. The words are for the *direction* of feeling. In opera they are only thirty or forty per cent of what there is to understand. . . . Music in the musical theatre remains music, but is not the same as music without theatre. Theatre with music is theatre, but not the same as theatre without music. . . . There are absolutely new and different criteria of judgement when they come together.' It is for the opera producer to penetrate the meaning of this unique language, to help his performers express themselves in it and say with it the things he wants them to say.

*   *   *

Given adequate rehearsal time – four weeks, say – and a reasonable degree of accord between producer and performers, how do rehearsals progress? At a practical level, the producer or his assistant will have devised some form of rehearsal schedule, dividing the time available between the various sections of the work, trying to forecast which scenes will be rehearsed at which point and who will be required at any given moment. This has to be achieved in the context of the house's overall schedule, accommodating music calls necessary during the same period, wig and costume fittings, other producers' demands on the rehearsal rooms or the chorus, technical staff's demands on the main stage and singers' commitments elsewhere. The producer's objective is obviously to ensure that the entire work is adequately rehearsed by the first night; the house's additional concerns are economy and maximum use of resources, and most will have designated one or more staff specifically to deal with scheduling (Raymond Quinn and two assistants at the Met, for instance, and Catherine Lee, solo, at Glyndebourne). The scheduling officer will encourage the producer to avoid calling the chorus, say, for twenty minutes in each of two three-hour sessions for which they must be paid in full. And the quality of the finished production may owe much to the scheduler's agility in juggling the conflicting demands of producers, conductors, music staff and wardrobe to everyone's best advantage.

In Anthony Besch's experience, rehearsal periods tend to fall into three distinct phases – exploration, consolidation and finalisation. 'Exploration' usually starts with the producer outlining his understanding of the piece and his intentions for the production. Some deliver a brisk lecture, some issue the cast with written notes, some begin by inviting questions and suggestions. This opening session is, in part at least, a time for producer and performers to get to know each other before they embark on the process of finding the characters. This itself has a good deal to do with getting to know each other, with the breaking down of reserve. As Ronald Eyre puts it, 'In the first twenty minutes of working with somebody, you do get some notion of where they've been.' Singers have often been used to being puppet-mastered – 'You go to the revival of an opera and somebody takes you by the finger and guides you round the opera' – and some positively prefer it. It enables them to keep themselves essentially to themselves, assuming the character in much the same way as they assume their costume – far less perilous than making an open commitment. 'To survive in opera as it goes on on the grander scale, the singer has to develop a real carapace around him or herself, an asbestos balloon he's got to rehearse with. . . . Otherwise he might find himself overwhelmed by some of the pressures from other people and from the set-up. That sort of hard quality, which is essential, could make people unresponsive, unwilling to take risks, unwilling to be vulnerable. . . . When you're rehearsing a work well, you are dealing with the clay feet of yourself and the performers and the people in the text. . . . A measure of your strength is your capacity to be very straight about it, to sit with the fact of clay feet and not put boots on them. I think that sort of openness, which I find to be brave and upstanding, is difficult to get in circumstances where you're supposed to slam in late through a door in a fur coat. If that sort of timid self-protectiveness is how things go, then it takes a brave and maybe slightly suicidal person to do anything else.'

If the producer fails to penetrate the singer's defences, Ronald Eyre warns, he is liable to be rewarded with the stock performance: 'The extreme cases will bring their costumes from Hamburg, others could bring their mental set-up from Hamburg' – and if all his principals have isolationist tendencies, he will find it exceptionally difficult to foster any kind of ensemble. Elijah Moshinsky's experience is similar. 'If you become too much like Figaro, darting between people making terrible agreements under which they are prepared to get on, you can end up with a very bland product – the lowest common denominator acceptable to all parties.'

Both the search for the characters and the initial plotting of their moves take place in the rehearsal room with piano accompaniment, under the auspices of the music staff; the moves obviously have to correspond precisely with the music, and characterisation too grows out of the score. Sir Peter Hall would agree that the essential content of opera is no different from that of straight theatre, a truth that can be expressed in many ways: 'The human truth, the human emotion inside the performer is the same whether it's a Japanese actor pretending to be a Samurai warrior, somebody singing a Handel aria, Spencer Tracy in close-up or a great Shakespearian actor speaking Shakespeare's verse – the inside truth is the same, and that's what we all respond to.' But, he insists, the journey to the truth is different: 'With modern prose drama you can often start from the inside, from the instinct, and end up with what is said. With formal writing – Shakespeare, Pinter or operatic composition – you have to start with what you're given and work backwards . . . More is given in opera – you're given the tempo, the mood, the atmosphere, even the physical timing.' What is 'given' in opera is the music, and the art of the opera performer is simultaneously to bring out the meaning and honour the music – 'That is the excitement – for an opera singer to be able to emphasise the words to a point where it nearly breaks the vocal line but doesn't. . . . It's a tightrope – a bit like a jazz musician nearly coming out of rhythm' – and the presence of the conductor or music staff helps to safeguard the score. Not that they are its sole defenders: Peter Brook, according to Andrei Serban, makes the singers themselves pay the closest attention to musical detail: 'The orchestra is always a barometer for the inner state of the singer. If the singer would take the time to investigate what goes on in the orchestra, it should affect his posture, his movement, his relation to his body, and to the other singers.'

During the exploratory period, most producers will try to get all the way through the work at least once, roughly blocking every scene and laying the foundations on which performers may construct their individual performances. Consolidation is a matter of working through the piece again, entrenching what is right, modifying what is slightly wrong, eliminating what is seen to have failed – a critical process, in Anthony Besch's view, during which the singer subtly modulates his performance: 'They come to the beginning of Act One again ready to do pretty well what you agreed the first time round – but their subconscious will have sifted that. . . . The middle period is the most important of the whole lot. That's where you actually see what does work and what does not.'

Having found the characters, the singers must find the means of manifesting them – sensitive introspection is not enough, as Michael Billington observes: 'You can have fascinating rehearsal periods where you only discuss your own truths and entirely forget that the art of all theatre is communication. Drama that is only about motivation – "How many children has Lady Macbeth?" – in the end disappears up its own navel. All rehearsal periods are about (a) understanding the meaning of the work in general terms, understanding what you yourself are doing on that stage and (b) finding the technical means of communicating it to an audience.' Character can, and must, be expressed vocally – otherwise, Beverly Sills feels, the singer is selling the production short: 'If the voice remains the same to portray both jealousy and loathing, then all the singer has done is let loose four thousand notes, got paid, and gone to bed.' Singers speak in this context of 'colouring' the voice with shades of feeling, changing with the character's moods – anger, misery, love, longing, bitterness, pride. Josephine Barstow describes the process: 'Some of the colours that you use in your voice are conscious – you apply a colour like a brush stroke to a phrase. But a lot of it comes instinctively because your thought process is right and because your emotional outflow is right – the colour automatically comes into the phrase because you're thinking about the words you're speaking.' This is not the same, she explains, as putting a voice entirely in character – making it sound old, or gin-sodden, or ill: 'Tito Gobbi could do that. . . . When he sang Falstaff his voice sounded as if he were fat. . . . But I think it's dangerous to force the sound into a shape that's not right for it. . . . It's all right doing it for Papagena, when she's pretending to be eighty – she only does it in two or three phrases. If you tried to sing a whole role like that, you'd be asking an awful lot of your instrument.'

Character may also be assumed physically – Josephine Barstow again: 'A lot of the excitement of performing on the stage in a dramatic situation for me is finding the shape of that person, finding how their body fits together and trying to make myself into that – I call it physical imagination. . . . One should never quite walk as one character in the way that another character walks . . . The left shoulder isn't necessarily doing the same thing at the same time on any given evening, but nevertheless the left shoulder is held by that character in that character's own inimitable way. . . . There are certain characters who I'm conscious of as having a long neck, or their arms are held slightly out. I was very conscious of a particular part of my body, the chest and neck, as being Natasha in Prokofiev's *War and Peace* – it seemed incredibly important, the way she always had her

OPPOSITE Michael Hampe rehearsing Thomas Allen as Figaro in his production of *The Barber of Seville* (Covent Garden, 1985).

shoulders. . . . What you're aiming at is that the mannerisms which appear on the stage are the character's mannerisms and not your own.' For Andrei Serban, the physical expression of a role is a question of discovering and developing the unity of voice and body – literally 'embodying' a vocal role: 'It's impossible to believe that singing just comes out of nowhere. The singing comes from the body, the body is involved.' Singers must aim at 'living the music rather than just selling it; being one with the music, the music coming through them so that their bodies are committed to receiving the vibration of the music, rather than egotistically projecting.' Peter Sellars works both by manipulating this largely natural and instinctive type of physical response to the music, and by imposing movement on his performers from without, the latter a consequence of his interest in the vocabulary of gesture: 'We have one theatrical vocabulary which is Cary Grant in a Hitchcock movie . . . We have another vocabulary which is Noh drama – the closest thing we have to Greek drama, what Greek drama might have been like in some of its respects. We have Kabuki or Balinese drama or *commedia dell'arte* or Sicilian *Orlando furioso* epics – all of these things have their specific vocabularies of gesture, and the wonderful thing about living at this moment in history is that we own all of them, we've inherited every single one of them – whether we like it or not, they're on our shelf; if we decide to get them down, there they are.' While searching for an

Placido Domingo rehearsing *Turandot* with the dancers of the opera ballet (Covent Garden, 1984).

equivalent to the eighteenth century's precise repertoire of gesture to use in his production of *Così fan tutte*, he lighted on contemporary Kabuki theatre which, he felt, offered a closer approximation than anything else we have today. In his productions he has used a range of theatrical vocabulary from deaf-and-dumb sign language to the crudely exaggerated mime of the television commercial. He does not necessarily intend meaning or message to be transmitted directly in this way, any more than he wants the sets and props to delimit the field of meaning – enriching the drama, increasing the number of 'detonator points' is what interests him.

Group movement is also an expressive tool for the producer, and one becoming increasingly fashionable as attempts are made to make more inventive use of the opera ballet. This has in the past been much criticised on the grounds both that it interrupts the action (for which the composer, if anyone, is to blame), and that no effort is made to smooth the join by integrating the members of the ballet with their choral colleagues: the corps de ballet is thinner, fitter, younger, coiffed and made up differently, and given to moving, however inappropriately, with the mincing grace of the classical dance. Some companies have now gone to the lengths of actually using choristers to do the dancing – Dame Ninette de Valois has for years advocated including ballet in the training of opera singers. Others settle for reducing the visible discrepancies between dancers and singers – Romayne Grigorova, Ballet Mistress to the Royal Opera, has assembled her dancers accordingly. 'We do prefer slightly more mature people, because they look better against the opera chorus. . . . If they're dancing in *Carmen*, they're meant to be just the same as the singers and must look a little more mature and extrovert than a prim little ballerina.' Some companies make a point of recruiting a proportion of specialists in modern dance and offering them training in acting, martial arts, and other non-classical modes of expression.

With little more than a week to go before the first night, rehearsals move on to the stage. Chalk marks on the floor, token props and the skeleton of a set used in the rehearsal room give way to the full paraphernalia of scenery, lights, props and stage machinery and, with an increased sense of urgency, the cast go through the piece, one act per session, first with piano, and then with orchestra, coming to terms with the acoustic of the theatre and learning to contend with an orchestral accompaniment. Dress rehearsals follow – complete performances, again first with piano then orchestra – with a day's grace before opening night. With the arrival of the orchestra, the situation changes. The producer is no longer in undisputed command, and he must by this time have brought the production to the point where it can be finalised – where theatrical improvisation and experiment must stop, and the drama must be 'frozen' to give the singers the security they need to achieve musical excellence. Even Andrei Serban, prizing flexibility as highly as he does, grudgingly admits the necessity: 'It's a very deadly word, freeze. A corpse is frozen. It's a word that is used all the time – "Let's freeze it now", which means "Let's make it a corpse." I don't fight that word; I have to accept it. They say, "Let's freeze it", and I say OK, hoping it will never freeze. . . . During the rehearsals, as we improvise and vaguely sense the material going deeper and see what talent the singer/actors have, how much they want to bring, how much they want to receive – I know that finally it will become very specific. In the last week or ten days of rehearsal, the scenes are very specific, directed by me. Almost every step is quite precisely scored.'

This account of production rehearsals takes various things for granted – firstly, that the production is a new one, and that it has been given adequate rehearsal time: most new productions get three to four weeks, in Germany perhaps five to six weeks, though singers can begin to balk – Robert Tear, for one, is wary of the effects of over-rehearsal: 'By the time you've got to the first night . . . you're getting stale: not necessarily bored, but the shine is going, it becomes a slightly false shine.' It also assumes that throughout this period all the cast are present, and willing: some producers would find it hard to reconcile the notions of 'physical imagination', 'intuitive response' and 'living the role' with their experience of the professional opera performer. It is quite possible that none of these conditions will apply – that rehearsal will be limited, either through the conscious decision of the administration (Anthony Besch: 'You'd be amazed at the way in which a management can modify its artistic standards to what it chooses to afford'), or because singers are not available to be rehearsed: though contracted, they do not turn up, regarding their presence as unnecessary until the last moment – after all, they 'know' the role. This assumption that it is possible to acquire a role for a professional lifetime is unique to the opera world, as Sally Jacobs comments: 'Actors in the theatre won't say, in the way singers say, "I *have* seventy roles" – that once you've done *Hamlet*, it's part of your repertoire and you'll do it all over the world. . . . When you get Alec Guinness doing *The Merchant of Venice*, five weeks' rehearsal – he's there from the first day and he'll go through the whole run. It's unheard-of that he would come just a week before it opens because he "knows" the role.' Singers' rehearsal time may also be limited through no fault of their own if they are coming into the cast as replacements once performances have started.

Nor can producers expect the luxury of extended rehearsals for revivals, which are the staple diet of most year-round houses and generally take place in a far less highly-charged atmosphere. In ideal circumstances, the administrator would always prefer the original producer to revive his work; but the more eminent the producer, the less frequently is he obtainable. Some refuse to do revivals on principle, finding it tedious to retrace their steps; some refuse because it is impossible to reassemble the original cast and they consider the replacements inferior; the majority are in any case fully occupied with new productions elsewhere. Occasionally the house may invest in a 'restaging' of the piece by the Director of Productions or a junior guest producer, using the same sets and costumes, permitting inexpensive modifications, and taking the original concept as a starting point, though with no obligation to adhere to it in detail. More often, however, for reasons of economy the piece will simply be revived by a staff producer, who will usually have assisted at the original production with this end in view.

The staff producer's job is not entirely enviable. He is generally given less than half the original rehearsal period in which to reconstitute the production with a new cast, within an old (possibly very old) set and with lighting that even if it is computerised can only approximately recapture the original effect, because lighting equipment – filaments, filters, even the basic lighting rig – constantly changes and is rapidly replaced. Perhaps more serious still, he cannot hope to establish the same relationship with the singers as the author of the production. Even within the first run of a production, once the producer has departed singers tend visibly to relax: uncomfortable hats and wigs are subtly adjusted, props discarded, personal jewellery appears – and a staff producer, especially a young one, will find it hard to assert anything like the same degree of authority over a chorus or over leathery international principals stepping into a revival of a piece they have performed countless times before.

In essence the staff producer's task is to pilot his cast through moves devised by someone else. While assisting the original producer he will have prepared a detailed production book, usually a copy of the score interleaved with blank pages, in which are recorded scene by scene, even bar by bar, artists' positions on stage, every entrance and exit, every move and gesture relevant to the action, all the necessary props, scene changes, lighting cues, the numbers of choristers and extras deployed, and so on. (The volume of information obviously varies from opera to opera: *The Barber of Seville*, for example, is liable to generate a far more elaborate production book than a more static opera like *Tannhäuser*.) He may, if he feels it necessary, include notes on motivation, or even attempt to summarise the gist of the conception. But after a gap of several years a production book, however meticulous, can be hard to interpret, especially if the original production was in any way idiosyncratic. (Lord Harewood observes that, for example, Sir Tyrone Guthrie's productions were always difficult to regenerate convincingly, since his stage-placings were usually designed for theatrical rather than naturalistic effect, the product of imagination rather than logic; in Franco Zeffirelli's productions, on the other hand, every move is likely to have a clear and compelling rationale, to the extent where it is extremely difficult to persuade, say, chorus members to vary the stage business allocated to them.) Every time a production is repeated, it tends to become more obviously the property of the house and less that of the original creative team – though they are still burdened with a credit in the posters and programmes.

The staff producer may use other more specialised *aides-mémoire* in addition to the production book. Geoffrey Gilbertson, during his long term as principal stage manager at Glyndebourne, could rely on 'progress shots' taken, then as now, by in-house photographer Guy Gravett throughout the dress rehearsal as a complete pictorial record of every position and grouping of the performers on stage. In other houses, for a production in which ballet or other forms of group movement play an especially important part, a choreologist may be employed. Choreology, or movement notation, records the movements of the body rather as the alphabet records speech; Anne Whitley, the first professional choreologist to be employed by an opera house (Covent Garden), uses the Benesch system, developed partly from music notation (its matrix is a five-lined stave), partly from perspective drawing and scientific disciplines such as cybernetics. On the stave a range of basic symbols shows the positions of hands, feet, arms and legs – bent or straight – in relation to the body from moment to moment, making it possible to replicate exactly in three dimensions every move and gesture made. (Choreologists are employed not only to record stage movement and choreography, but also in anthropological research, and in physiotherapy; film is of less use here because it fails, obviously, to record movement on the side of the body away from the camera.)

Perpetually to resuscitate other people's creations can be frustrating. Occasionally staff producers are given productions of their own, and in some houses they are permitted a degree of creative licence in preparing revivals. At the Met in the 1970s, John Dexter actively discouraged slavish adherence to the production book (partly prompted by a serious warehouse fire which destroyed a large number of sets and costumes, making literal re-production impossible). Other houses, however, are reluctant to tempt fate by allowing the staff producer to interpret his instructions too flexibly – which can indeed lead to friction with the original producer. Either way, the staff producer is long-suffering and the majority, as John Copley gratefully acknowledges, 'are very generous. It's a job that has to be done, and it's a job that has to command respect – and very often it doesn't.'

It is in these less than ideal circumstances that a very high proportion of opera reaches the stage, where much of it is found perfectly satisfactory by its audiences. But too uncritical an acceptance of these conditions paves the way for the type of opera about which drama-oriented producers become apoplectic – 'pig opera', in Peter Sellars's phrase. 'Pigs are fun, and there's a certain thrill you get from true pig opera, sung by true pigs. But that ultimately isn't the future, it's the past – and not even a terribly exact view of the past.' At its best, pig opera amounts to skilfully stage-managed individual performances roughly co-ordinated within a traditional framework: Ande Anderson speaks, not very respectfully, of 'pictorial' producing – the art of creating a moving background round foreground gaps into which the stars may be inserted at the last moment. At its worst, it has very little reason or justification for being on the stage at all. Jonathan Miller's analogy is bovine; he sees its protagonists as pedigree stock, transported to the theatres in slatted trucks, prodded up ramps and on to the stage where they remain long enough for the trucks to be sluiced down with fast hoses, then back, with a thunder of hooves, into the trucks and on to the next arena. Not surprisingly, he does not care to participate: 'I don't like working with these great sacred monsters, virtuosos of the long-distance aeroplane. There's no point working with a practised Concorde traveller. . . . They have obstinate ideas about how they do it, because they haven't got time to negotiate. . . . I can't be working with that. . . . You're a butler, you're simply facilitating their performance rather than working out what is going to be an intriguing and interesting art work of the whole opera. . . . There is a sort of corrupt audience that pays to hear canaries sing. That's fine – but that's not opera, that's just concerts in frocks.'

V

IN PERFORMANCE

21

In Performance

On the first night of a new production – of *Orfeo*, *Rigoletto* or *Wozzeck*, at La Scala, the Wolf Trap Festival or the Astra Theatre, Llandudno – an extraordinary electricity can be generated, if all the participants are willing, which is perhaps peculiar to opera. 'Music', Sir Peter Hall reflects, 'because it has no literal meaning, is immediately emotional. Music immediately charges the proceedings with a sensuality and an atmosphere which is much stronger and more electric than the spoken word. . . . I think that's why people applaud for half an hour at opera, and almost never applaud for half an hour at plays. It's not that the experience of a play is any the less exciting . . . It's just that their adrenalin and emotions are high at opera.'

Adrenalin and emotion crackle not just in the audience but throughout the house as the parallels converge and everyone concerned with the production sees weeks, even months of effort brought to a climax and put to the test. Weeks of planning and counter-planning, bargaining and diplomacy for administrators; weeks of learning and rehearsing for the singers and orchestra; weeks of urging, coaxing, guiding and galvanising for the conductor, producer and their assistants; weeks of design and construction in carpentry shops, paint frames, sewing rooms and on lighting boards; weeks in which a careful press campaign will, it is hoped, have wrought the first-night audience to a high pitch of expectation and excitement – 'educating through enthusiasm', in the words of Katharine Wilkinson, Press Officer to the Royal Opera at Covent Garden.

All the more frustrating, then, for the producer that on the first night the most he can do is watch. After all those weeks of collaboration, control over the interpretation of the piece has passed to the conductor. 'During the performance,' Walter Felsenstein once remarked, 'the conductor *alone* is that evening's producer, responsible advocate for the validity and comprehensibility of that evening's conception, and mentor and friend of each of the creative performers.' And as for what is seen, rather than heard, on the stage, responsibility is now in the hands of the stage manager; it is he (or she) who 'runs' the show which the producer has prepared, and generally speaking, the latter's presence behind the scenes is no longer required.

That evening, before the performance, the stage manager is one of a large team preparing to provide the performers with everything they are going to need on stage – wardrobe staff laying out in the dressing-rooms boots and tunics, wimples and capes; music staff issuing last-minute reminders of rhythm, pitch and dynamics; orchestra tuning in the pit. The job of stage management is to ensure that the stage and everything on it is ready for use by the singers, and in the hour or so before curtain rise the stage manager and his assistants patrol their territory. The stage floor must be swept, perhaps sprayed for dust, and cleared of stray ropes, cables, uneven boards and other traps for the unwary; the marks made with tape or chalk to help in the setting of scenery and, on occasion, to help singers find their positions, must be clearly visible. It is for the stage manager to check that all built scenery for the first act has been precisely set, all flown scenery (cloths and built pieces) correctly hung in the fly-tower overhead, and that the lights are accurately focused without unwanted spill or dazzle on the set; props must be to hand, and special effects – smoke, flames, rain, snow, lasers, strobes, trapdoors, lifts – at the ready. The stage manager will ensure that the television monitors are switched on and in focus – both those fixed inside the proscenium arch and those on trolleys in the wings, manoeuvrable to serve singers on stage or off-stage bands and chorus. Speakers are positioned facing on to the stage, to 'fold back' the sound from the orchestra; on many stages, it is hard for singers to pick up their cues or hear orchestral support from the pit unless the sound is boosted in this way. Fire and security officers make their rounds, the iron safety curtain is checked; and as the audience begins to fill the auditorium, the stage manager puts out the calls over the Tannoy to the dressing-rooms – half an hour to curtain; quarter of an hour; five minutes; and then beginners to the stage.

Once the curtain is up, action is simultaneous on all fronts, and from the prompt corner where the stage manager presides, in contact with the conductor by way of a monitor, and by radiophone and bell-less telephones with other parts of the house, comes a steady stream of instructions – to singers and dancers in their dressing-rooms or fidgeting in the wings, to the lighting board, to stagehands in the flies, to members of the music staff behind the cyclorama waiting to direct off-stage bands. Calls go out to the armoury or prop store to bring up helmets, pikestaffs or rifles for a firing squad; to the wig room for spirit gum to secure a wayward moustache; to the wardrobe to warn them to prepare for an imminent quick change for the chorus. In larger houses, at each side of the stage, assistant stage managers armed with scores and torches to read them by wait to cue on each performer in turn, a practice unheard-of in the straight theatre, employed in opera as a courtesy – and as a safeguard. In a curious way, opera singers are often less conscious than actors of the work as a whole, more intent on their individual contribution to it, and stage management bears a lot of responsibility on the night for binding the units together in an integrated whole. Partly for this reason, every member of the team must read music with ease, and will come to know each score in great detail, even if the music is perceived from the perspective of entrances and exits, prop requirements, lighting cues and changes of scenery.

Otherwise, the principal qualities demanded of a stage manager are a sense of priorities, a sense of proportion and a sense of humour. Most stage managers will make a tour of the dressing-rooms in person before every performance, however routine, but their moral and practical support becomes doubly necessary when a principal cancels and has to be replaced at short notice, frequently less than twelve hours. Ensemble houses will almost always have organised 'covers' or understudies (though occasionally where a role is particularly difficult to cast once, let alone twice, they may take the risk of leaving it without a cover), and will have no hesitation in sending them on. In international houses, however, although covers may have been employed (partly for insurance purposes, partly to lull the first cast into some sense of security), these are rarely singers of comparable standing to those they are notionally designated to replace, and managements frequently prefer to ring round other major houses, or the agents, and fly in more prestigious substitutes on the day. This is an option which is seldom open to American houses, separated from each other and from Europe by six- or seven-hour flights; where most German houses have half-a-dozen sources of alternative soloists within an hour's travel, Sir Rudolf Bing once complained that he 'could call Hartford, Connecticut till I was blue in the face without finding a possible Carmen'.

Every artist will make the run-up to performance in individual style. Some spend the day resting – Luciano Pavarotti, for example, inclines to a morning's painting or reading, talking as little as possible; others prefer to behave as though nothing untoward were going to happen. Some eat virtually nothing beforehand, others need fortification – Josephine Veasey used to favour grilled liver, or two eggs whipped with milk and a little brandy. A few rehearse thoroughly at home, may even run lightly through the whole role; most leave their serious vocalising until they arrive at the theatre and even then there is disagreement as to the advisability of exercising the voice on stage. Linda Esther Gray finds it gives her confidence: 'Quite often if the set's up and there's nobody about, I would go on to the stage and have a wee twiddle. I like to do that anyway – make my first entrance, and make sure there's not a big nail sticking up, or anything.' Elisabeth Söderström, on the other hand, is invariably demoralised by the contrast between the voice in the empty auditorium and the softer, less penetrating sound it makes once the audience is in. Many singers, especially women, like to apply their own make-up, finding it as soothing a way as any of passing the time. Others, requiring wrinkles, scars, tattoos or any highly stylised *maquillage* depend upon the skills of make-up staff permanently attached to the house. These, like the stage management, exposed to the artistic temperament *in extremis*, at the closest possible range and the last possible moment, can have an important part to play in helping the performer compose as well as colour the features he presents to the public.

Settling in on stage is for most singers in the very first moments simply a question of discovering how well the voice is working. 'What you feel,' as Linda Esther Gray explains, 'depends a bit on your entrance. Tosca singing "Mario, Mario!"

The final touches of make-up are applied to Robert Tear as Emperor Altoum in *Turandot* (Covent Garden, 1984).

outside the door is different from starting the Countess with "Porgi amor" – you're listening for completely different things. The Tosca entrance is good, because you're outside the door and you can hear exactly what sound you're making, and you're prepared for what you're going to make when you enter. And it's a quick entrance, which is good. Sitting for the whole prelude to "Porgi amor" is very hard.' With the voice established, its owner can begin to absorb and respond to the atmosphere in the house – an inattentive audience can be identified at once – and make contact with the conductor.

The relationship with the conductor in performance is crucial, though very rarely will singers actually look to him for detailed instruction. The prompter, with no orchestra dependent upon him, can give the singers his undivided attention, and is far better placed – in the wings or in the prompt box at the front of the stage – to feed them their cues; although the pit wall directly behind the conductor will usually be painted white (on the principle of the sightscreen behind the bowler's arm in cricket), for a short-sighted singer his beat may be difficult to discern through the gloom even if it is expansive – and one well-known opera conductor's technique, in Mozart at least, has been described by a singer as 'milking mice'. (Fritz Busch made a habit, as Spike Hughes reports, of taking his singers' spectacles off at rehearsals to find out in advance who would and who would not be following the beat in performance.) And if the singers are positioned well-back on the stage (as they are, for example, in Franco Zeffirelli's *La Bohème* at the Met, because of the monumental scale of the set), even if they can see the beat it behoves them not to follow it slavishly but to anticipate slightly, compensating for the time-lag.

To a considerable extent, negotiations between conductor and singers over the detail of the score – rhythms, tempi, dynamics, expression – will have been concluded at rehearsals. As Linda Esther Gray says: 'I know what he wants me to do – what's the use of his waving at me at the last minute?' What is critical in performance is a more elusive rapport between stage and pit, unanimity of attitude and effort. 'If the conductor is *not* supporting,' observes Andrei Serban, '*not* giving inspiration back, *not* giving feedback to what is going on on the stage, the singers feel it, and what they do on the stage is never quite organic acting-wise, because the singing is not quite right. Something is wrong in the communication, and subconsciously it's felt – there's an immediate subtle change of rapport. There just isn't quite an organic response to the event.'

Conversely, to be in harmony with a conductor eager to share and intensify the spirit of a piece can be extraordinarily exhilarating, as Isobel Buchanan discovered as Micaela in *Carmen* for Carlos Kleiber: 'When I wasn't singing, I used to stand and watch him in the monitor because he beats with such energy that the baton was making a sparkler effect. Stunning. You just got in there with the energy, it was so electric.'

This kind of charge from the pit can be very much needed in that however long the rehearsal period has been, the singer is never more than three quarters of the way to a performance. The first night in an unfamiliar role, as Josephine Barstow explains, can be a moment of truth: 'No rehearsal really approaches the circumstances of a performance, you can't really know what it's going to be like to perform a role. . . . I remember lying on the floor, the first time I did Salome, after the dance, knowing that the final scene was coming up, and thinking to myself, "Soon we'll all know whether I can sing it or not" . . .'

First night adrenalin and the presence of an audience can do much to bridge the gap and screw the singer to performance pitch – when the problem becomes one of control. How completely can the performer afford to empathise with the character he or she is playing? For Robert Tear there can be no holding back:

'If you're at arm's length, even at an eyelash's length from what you're doing it never works. You can act your heart out and it makes no odds at all if you're watching yourself. You do turn it on and off – I begin the role when I go on stage, I certainly don't think about it before, and when I come off, then I drink some beer and watch the telly. But in between . . . it's believing you *are* the character, and also believing that you *are* the notes – as soon as you hear yourself doing it, it's lost. . . . If everything's right, if your technique is working right and if you're in a good frame of mind, then you can only *be* it. As soon as you start interpreting it, you've lost it.'

Michael Langdon, on the other hand, argues vehemently against what might be described as musical 'Method' acting: 'When you're working for films or television or theatre, the more you can feel the emotion within yourself, the more convincing the performance. The more real the tears or the anger, the lust, the more real the performance. But in opera that's fatal. Think – what is the one word used for practically every emotion? – *choked* with fear, choked with anger, choked with lust, choked with sorrow – *everything* affects the throat. If you let yourself feel, you get a lump in your throat, your throat feels bruised because you're trying not to cry. You get so angry with someone you can hardly speak.' To convey an emotion to an audience – and this is ultimately the aim – the singer must leave himself able to do justice to the music in which it is enshrined. 'There has to be a little *Doppelgänger* a yard behind saying "Now watch it, you're giving too much voice there, you'll never get through the next page, you've got two top Cs. . . . Now don't forget, support well here, this is a difficult phrase. . . . Now a bar and a half's rest. . . . Now off you go again" – and all the time you're looking as if it's spontaneous . . .'

Stuart Burrows advocates restraint for a rather different reason: 'You've got to be very careful as individuals – there is so much emotion and love in the music that it's the easiest thing in the world to fall in love with the people you're singing to. Until you get to that emotional state you haven't reached something of what the composer intended, you've got to give yourself in every way. This is the kind of situation where you've got to have a marvellous wife or understanding husband.'

In purely mechanical terms, sustaining a role throughout a whole evening is a considerable achievement; taxed by the words, notes, and moves of a three-act opera, singers' memories may betray them in a variety of ways. Most frequently, especially when they are singing in a foreign language, the right words will elude them – in which case they are well-advised, in Dame Joan Sutherland's view, to find a comfortable vowel sound and hold it, or alternatively – Sir Geraint Evans's suggestion – turn their backs to the audience and sing gobbledygook until the crisis has passed. (One of Sir Geraint's bugbears as far as remembering words was concerned, was Beckmesser's serenade in Act Two of *Die Meistersinger*, whose verses tended to present themselves in the wrong order.) A singer who has sung a role repeatedly in different languages, or two different roles in the same opera (both Guglielmo and Don Alfonso, for example, Leporello and Don Giovanni,

Prompter (John Bacon) and conductor (Sir Colin Davis) from the viewpoint of the singers: Ileana Cotrubas and Norman Bailey during a dress rehearsal of *La Traviata* (Covent Garden, 1985).

Figaro and the Count) may well find himself lapsing into the wrong one.

Less often, singers will lose their grip on the music – Dame Kiri te Kanawa has described Act One of *Arabella* as seeming to go round and round in places – and they may find it hard to recover: Donald McIntyre complains that it is extremely testing to act and count at the same time, and made no easier by conductors who subdivide the beat minutely for the benefit of the orchestra. In extreme cases, where for the moment the music offers little clue, they may even find themselves in the wrong opera – Michael Langdon points to the four-bar prelude to a Verdi aria which 'could be from any one of three of his operas – one baritone once started singing something from *Il Trovatore* in the middle of *La Traviata*'.

To cope with these emergencies, many houses supply a prompter, particularly those in which singers are likely to go on with little rehearsal. Most German repertory houses, for example, employ two full-time prompters – one for Italian repertoire, one for German; known as *souffleurs*, literally 'whisperers', they provide every word of the text in a sibilant stream from the prompt box. In English-speaking houses, prompting is usually one of the duties of the music staff, and tends to be more selective; the singer may discuss his or her preferences with the prompter – it may be agreed, for example, that he will give both words and notes for particularly difficult entries, or that he will only offer a word cue when he receives the glance direct – or may choose to dispense with his services altogether. Felicity Lott: 'I can't use a prompter, I just think I'm late all the time, and I find it extremely distracting. You can't be involved in an emotion if you've got somebody perpetually telling you what it is. And if you've got the chance to have a wonderful silence in a recitative, it just finishes it for me to have the prompter rattling on.' There are particular problems associated with Handel or other operas in which the same sentiments are frequently reiterated (Sir Charles Mackerras: 'The prompter and I devised various ways of showing them whether they were on the first version or the second – I used to draw little pictures in the air of the shape of the phrase'), and in general, inconspicuous prompting is neither easy nor particularly rewarding. Felicity Lott recounts with pleasure the story of the prompter who, after feeding an ill-prepared Tristan every word throughout an evening, is reputed to have hissed vengefully: 'Now *die*, you bugger . . .'

To survive a three-hour opera, singers need both stamina and an intelligent instinct for pacing themselves. In one sense, roles which require constant application throughout are easier to sustain and bring off than those whose high points are widely separated – Isobel Buchanan is particularly wary of Micaela, 'a rotten role because it's really exposed. You've got one very famous duet and one very famous aria and a little bit of ensemble – and you wait for about two hours between the duet and the aria, by which time you've wound down completely.' Long intervals can have the same effect of dispersing a creative head of steam: Janet Moores, one of the Festival's longest-serving administrators, recognises that the seventy-five minute dinner interval, so much a part of an evening at Glyndebourne, is rather less popular with the singers than the audience. And even if the singer survives these hazards unscathed, the close of a performance can bring its own problems, as over the course of an evening the voice may alter subtly. In Dame Kiri te Kanawa's experience, her voice goes up in overall *tessitura*, so that a low passage near the end of a long role may pose more problems than a very high one, and it also goes up in pitch, so she must guard against a tendency to sing slightly sharp.

With so much to worry about, keeping concentration might not seem to be a difficulty, but the distractions for the singer on stage are innumerable. Stagehands may be discussing the next scene change (or the afternoon's racing results) in not-so-muted tones in the wings, lighting men shouting in the flies – La Scala is particularly notorious for backstage commotion. The 'fold-back' requested by one singer for a *pianissimo* passage may, if the speakers are left on, ruin the acoustic for the next when the accompaniment becomes heavier; and an orchestral *fortissimo* can send vibrations through the stage floor. A mistake in an instrumental *obbligato* can be acutely disconcerting, as can an unexpected noise from the auditorium – Gwynne Howell sees a change, and not for the better, in today's audiences: 'If

Tito Gobbi as Scarpia in *Tosca* (Covent Garden, 1964).

someone coughs or clears their throat when everything's quiet, it's like being shot in the head . . . It's a strange insensitivity. I attribute it to a new breed of operagoer: the real operagoer would rather have a heart attack or strangle himself than cough at a key moment.'

Applause, on the other hand, may disturb by its absence. Though purists generally deplore the habit of saluting each 'big number' separately, on occasion it has practical advantages – Placido Domingo points out that a reasonably prolonged burst of applause is essential in *Il Trovatore* after 'Ah sì, ben mio', if the tenor is to catch his breath before launching into 'Di quella pira'. And whether it has its roots in politeness, uncertainty, indifference or a spirit of criticism, silence can gravely undermine the singer's confidence, depending on the nature of the aria it is greeting – Linda Esther Gray: '"Vissi d'arte", for example: I did ten Toscas on the trot. The first night I really sang it quite well and the applause was fantastic.

The second night I don't know how I sang it, but I performed it on a quite different level that meant much more – and not a soul moved. . . . One gave me as much pleasure as the other – but the second was probably right. . . . Other arias are different. "Dove sono" – I would die if I walked off and they didn't clap. Or the Queen of the Night's aria. Or *Fidelio*, "Abscheulicher!" – if you walk off and no one claps, *forget* it. But it's not just clapping in that case; Leonore walks off and she's going to *do* something, she's made up her mind, she's going to go down that dungeon and set Florestan free – that's what you're clapping, not the singing. So you've really missed it if you don't get applause.'

Through the haze of light on stage, it is possible for singers to see the exit signs in the auditorium, doors opening and shutting as ushers come and go, opera glasses glinting, a handkerchief pulled out, faces in the first row of the stalls – that is, if they choose to look. Some performers like to single out individuals in the audience and play directly to them as a means of focusing their performance; Linda Esther Gray finds even the thought inhibiting. 'I never look at the front row – it's the last place a singer would look. You would never sing to the first ten rows; ideally you project it to the front of the dress circle – or if you've got a high bit coming up, to the upper circle.'

On stage, many singers take pains to avoid contact with animals – opera producers are irresistibly drawn to wolfhounds, King Charles spaniels, falcons, donkeys, rabbits, geese, goats and monkeys, usually in pairs, despite their compulsion to relieve or reproduce themselves centre-stage – or children. Isobel Buchanan fondly recalls John Copley's production of *The Magic Flute* for Australian Opera, into which he had inserted, as a mark of respect for his hosts, two kangaroos and a platypus. The latter was portrayed by a child of three, crawling and totally blinded by his bill: 'Every night you could see the SM in the wings beckoning with a torch and whispering "Kevin! Kevin!". One night all the audience could see was this hand appearing from the prompt corner to retrieve one smallish platypus heading straight for the orchestra pit. It stopped the show.'

Singers may, of course, only too easily dislocate their own performances. Luciano Pavarotti sums it up: 'Somebody said, "An evening never recovers from a cracked high note." It is exactly like a bullfight. You are not allowed one mistake.' While this may be true for the audience, it is one of the most important qualifications of the professional opera singer that after a catastrophe he or she should be able to carry on, with total aplomb – conductor permitting, that is. Sir Charles Mackerras is well aware of the conductor's power to make a catastrophe out of a gaffe: 'You have to be so gentle on the one hand and so strict on the other. The tiniest psychological miscalculation on the part of the conductor can ruin a performance. If the singer cracks a top note or misses an entry, the conductor must resist the temptation to scowl. It's terribly difficult to avoid doing it, to avoid expressing annoyance when you've rehearsed with a man and explained something and *still* he does it wrong at the performance.'

Potentially the greatest threat to the focused, concentrated performance, however, is a lack of solidarity amongst the performers themselves. James Bowman observes, 'Whatever people say, there's still a lot of competition', and he points to a significant difference between actors and opera singers: 'Actors are much more egocentric *offstage*. If you say to a singer after a show, "You were wonderful", they'll just modestly shrug it off; say it to an actor and he'll say "Do you really think so? Now tell me, what did you think of the bit where I . . ." and you have to go through the whole thing with a fine-tooth comb. Singers will accept it when they have sung divinely, they just take the money and go! . . . But onstage, actors will sublimate much more to the overall company feel, whereas singers will be jockeying for position. If you upstage a singer – go upstage so they have to turn upstage to sing – they won't forgive you.' (When a performance is being recorded for television or video, pole position near the stage microphones is contested in much the same spirit – though as Roy Emmerson, a sound director for the National Video Corporation, observes with amusement, technological developments like the directional microphone have made this type of undignified manoeuvre entirely unnecessary.)

Almost as unpopular as upstaging, and far more destructive of dramatic effect, is the tendency to 'turn private' – to disassociate oneself from the proceedings as soon as one's solo contribution is completed. Michael Langdon exonerates the inexperienced singer, attributing his offence to a lack of technique: 'A young artist singing an aria will finish a phrase and then has four bars before he sings again – and you visibly see them go out of the part and gather themselves and come back, whereas a Placido Domingo will finish a phrase and start the next and you'll hardly be aware that he hasn't sung for four bars because the thought has continued.' Alternatively, in a more seasoned singer, it may simply be the product of selfishness and conceit.

However smoothly it runs, no performance is ever going to be the same from night to night. The first night will have a unique aura of curiosity, apprehension and excitement, but technically at least it is unlikely to be as polished or fluent as later performances; the singers are often tired after a gruelling final week of rehearsal, and inhibited by nerves from taking the risks which make a performance extraordinary. Few performers expect to reproduce the identical gesture, musical or physical, with the identical shade of feeling from performance to performance; not merely their vocal condition but their emotional state will vary and with it their method of delivering or reacting to a line or aria. Many producers allow for this, even encourage it actively as the most effective means of keeping a production alive once it has ceased to evolve. While he accepts the need eventually to 'freeze' a production for performance, Andrei Serban insists that only the framework is fixed: 'Improvisation on the outside is very little – but the improvisation on the inside should go on continuously. One should always try to do things as if for the first time.'

Peter Sellars similarly builds an element of the fresh and unpredictable into his productions from the beginning: 'The sad thing in opera is that it always tends to happen the same way each night unless an elephant gets stuck. . . . I'm a very firm believer that every performance must be different. I got a strong dose of John Cage in my youth, which is still with me to this day. In every show I put in a series of random elements which means that every night there will be a genuine chemical reaction. It used to be that I would stage *Antony and Cleopatra* in a pool and you could never tell what the water was going to do. It's now much more subtle. After one acquires some craft, it has to do with setting up a series of structures which every night intersect each other at slightly different points. . . . Music-drama is by definition present-tense, unrepeatable – things happening at this moment between you and the people on-stage which will never happen again – a priceless moment of time'. He will also, unlike many producers, stay on after the first night until the end of the run, changing his emphasis and interpretation and reblocking moves until the curtain goes up on the last performance, to accommodate the ideas and personalities of new members of the cast. 'With some directors you really can't tell how imaginative each performer is . . . everybody's doing the director's thing, it's all worked out – any cast can slip in and do this production. I will redo a staging for another cast member. . . . Drama and music are performer-oriented, and should be. We exist to celebrate these performers, who are only on this earth for a certain period of time. We're very lucky they're alive at this moment – our job is to present them as well as possible.'

And for the serious opera performer, the aim is to present the composer as well as possible – Josephine Barstow: 'I don't do it for the applause. I think I do it for the very, very infrequent moments when it works. I've never been in or seen a performance where it's worked all the way through. I think perhaps it's impossible. But there are the odd moments when you feel you've done it right for Beethoven or Verdi or whoever – absolutely wonderful, and I think it's that which keeps me going.'

VI

THE MODERN COMPOSER

22

Why Write Opera Today?

Why write opera? In the 1980s fame is rarely the spur, given that very few works have the instant success of *Peter Grimes* or *The Consul* and the financial rewards, when set against the amount of effort expended, are usually negligible. The initial commission fee, unlikely to be overlarge, must be spread over the whole period of composition which is never the three weeks of a Rossini or Donizetti, more often anything from two to seven years. And performance royalties are almost always small or nonexistent, the composer – as H. Wesley Balk observes – 'being expected to subsist on his gratitude that the piece is being performed at all'.

So why write an opera and take the risk of being excoriated if it is a failure (the grander the scale of the attempt, the more conspicuous the failure), or inadequately recompensed if it is a success? Composers rise to different baits. Some, like John Eaton, see opera as the best medium through which to introduce their music, or developments in their style, to an audience, because words and actions may help to clarify the meaning of new musical gestures and materials. Iain Hamilton adds, 'If *Wozzeck* had been a symphonic work, people would have found it initially much more difficult to listen to purely musically; but they absorb it related to its action.'

For Philip Glass, much of the appeal of opera lies in its trappings – the physical resources that the form has come to require and command: 'To present a work like *Einstein* [*on the Beach*], you need a proscenium theatre with an orchestra pit, wing space and fly space. You could call the piece anything you wanted, but the only place it could play was in an opera house. We have these huge dinosaurs all over the planet, these opera houses with all this neat stuff in them. I kind of accidentally wandered into that world, and for me it's now the most interesting place to be.' Other composers are responding to the urge to write for the voice, which they see as lying at the core of music-making, the instrument for which all others are metaphors.

Essentially, however, the incentive must be the fact of having something to say musically that can only be said in an opera – a message which can only be expressed in *musico-dramatic* form, which would be blurred or only partially delivered as a string quartet, a piano sonata, a symphony, even a song or oratorio. Implied in this, very often, is the desire to work in concrete rather than abstract

Philip Glass, 1985

terms. Music by itself cannot fully or exactly delineate or describe objects, characters or concepts. As Nelson Goodman concluded in his book *The Languages of Art*, music is only metaphorically a 'language' (the acid test being that it cannot be paraphrased, as all true languages can). Musical phrases do not 'mean' anything outside themselves as words do; the 'meaning' of music is constituted solely by its expression, because as Jonathan Miller explains, it is by nature non-referential: 'The thing about music is that it doesn't have this complicated, detailed reference to the world. . . . As soon as you use language (unless you do an e. e. cummings/James Joyce-*Finnegans Wake* trick with language and you deliberately start to deny or to disestablish its linguistic function and merely use it for phonetics), you are instantly referring to recognisable situations; words are so unavoidably referential. Whereas music has to be forced into a referential idiom; you *can* write music like Saint-Saëns's *Carnival of the Animals*, where in fact you can actually hear or see the animals being referred to – but it's an unrepresentative form of music that refers to the world. . . . You can only get music to argue on an abstract level – you can't get music to make assertions about the world. It can have onomatopoeic representations of the world – it can give you trickling water, it can give you thunderstorms, it can give you wolves once you've been told it's a wolf and boys once you've been told it's a little boy – but it cannot make assertions, it cannot say, "Yes, it's raining now and there's a thunderstorm, but this thunderstorm you're hearing now is not half so big as the one you're going to hear in half an hour." In language you can do all that, you can refer to the past, you can refer to what is present, and you can deny, promise, threaten, forgive, apologise – these things are not open to music.'

It is precisely the non-referential quality of music which has been envied by practitioners of other arts; abstraction from the material world seems to imply easier access to an interior world of feeling and imagination, and for some thirty years modernist painters and sculptors sought to emulate the 'purity' of music, itself becoming ever more abstract. Sir Michael Tippett considers that 'all this straining toward music has sprung from the tremendous need of our time to reach further into the interior world as some balance against our social preoccupation with science and technology . . . But music too has been straining towards its own inner world . . . Our century has seen a tremendous collective effort to cleanse musical sound of these impurities [of the outer world] and to make music absolutely abstract. This cleansing has been positive, exciting and salutary.' Unfortunately, as he goes on to point out, one of its by-products has been a certain sterility – 'the appearance of composers who are interested only by abstraction and experimentation. The resulting music leaves too much man out, so it quickly gets boring. I have never been able to forget man in this way.'

Many composers *want* to refer to the world in a specific and detailed way, to present theories, narratives, descriptions, and they turn to opera, where a libretto can supply the detailed references (characters, situations, objects, places) around which, in Joseph Kerman's phrase, 'music is free to indulge its most subtle connotative and expressive powers.' And for those who wish their music, like Tippett's, to concern itself with man, opera is a natural medium, having traditionally concentrated less on the abstract ideal or intellectual theory than on the interaction of human beings, their emotions and what happens to them because of their emotions. While, for example, David Blake's first opera, *Toussaint* (or *The Aristocracy of the Skin*) is overtly 'political', in the sense of confronting the issues of racism, colonial exploitation and black revolution, at its heart, in his view, is the corrosive effect of power on one man's private life; and the music which he feels best expresses his musical personality is that which characterises the relationship between Toussaint and his wife Suzanne.

To David Blake the writing of opera appeals also because it is difficult, perhaps uniquely so, and because the successful amalgam of music, words and stage picture has an impact on the listener in purely visceral terms that is hard to match. To devise the variety of techniques needed to present a living stage drama through music, to combine emotional force with intellectual dexterity, is a challenge he finds irresistible: 'Most of the people who make their living from opera will tell you that what it is good for is gut reaction, surging emotion, simple, archetypal ideas that everybody can grasp and understand with their cockles as opposed to their brains. . . . That's why Wagner is so popular – people don't have to worry about the minutiae of his text or what it's saying – there's a groundswell of irresistibly powerful music coming at them and warming them through. . . . And there's the Puccinian way of going straight to your tear ducts, with a simple tune and a poor girl dying of this or the other – you double the tune in the bass and with a parallel, almost modal harmony in the middle, you can put your finger right on people's heartstrings – and it's very moving, it's marvellous. . . . The challenge to me is to try and do that. To try and marry those very simple gut effects that are so much a part of the opera house to a drama where there are quite complex relations between one man and another in terms of ideas. . . .'

23

Choosing a Subject

Mussolini, Robin Hood, Moses, Marshal Tito, Dreyfus, Lancelot, Casanova, Kepler, Lizzie Borden; space travel, spiritualism, schizophrenia, air pollution, nuclear physics, religious fundamentalism; the Napoleonic Wars, the Crusades, the Gold Rush, the invasion of Mexico – the extraordinary variety of subjects used in twentieth-century opera bravely challenges the theory that the operatic form is particularly suited to any one type of subject matter.

There has always been a school of thought to hold that opera should concern itself only with subjects that are somehow elevated, characters that are larger than life. W. H. Auden's description of opera as 'the last refuge of the high style' is much quoted in this context; and Harrison Birtwistle has made the same point more positively – 'Opera is the one form that can take on the big subjects – it can deal with the theatricality.' Because of the emotion it can generate and the grandeur of the resources it can command, opera undoubtedly lends itself to the portrayal of heights – heights of nobility, passion, villainy, etc. – and because it *can* operate at this level, the argument runs, it *should* do so; to deploy its strengths in any other way is to waste them, using a cultural sledgehammer to crack nuts, or even to debase them – a view to which John Eaton at least partly subscribes: 'Part of my quest has been to restore heroism and nobility, ingredients so needed in contemporary life, to opera. That banal, ordinary persons should sing as the major characters is absurd and misses part of the mission of opera: to infuse into a society, through the powerful means of music and poetic vision, high values and purpose.'

Implicit in John Eaton's remarks is the suggestion that opera must maintain a certain distance from 'banal, ordinary' life. This is the impulse which in the seventeenth and early eighteenth centuries kept composers and librettists writing about gods, heroines, kings, courtiers, nymphs and idealised shepherds rather than the characters and happenings of daily life, which were quarantined as a separate genre and reserved for the rude intervals. And mythological subjects, or historical subjects sufficiently distanced to have about them an aura of myth, continue even now to inspire a significant proportion of new operas. The *Oresteia*, for example, has generated at least eight twentieth-century works – by Richard Strauss (*Elektra*), Krenek (*The Life of Orestes*), Milhaud (*Oresteia*), Marvin David Levy (*Mourning*

Becomes Electra), Havergal Brian (*Agamemnon*), Iain Hamilton (*Agamemnon*), Peter Wishart (*Clytemnestra*) and John Eaton (*The Cry of Klytemnestra*). Tudor England has been a fruitful source (with Fortner's *Elizabeth Tudor*, Britten's *Gloriana* and Thea Musgrave's *Mary, Queen of Scots*), as has the French Revolution (Mascagni's *Il Piccolo Marat*, von Einem's *Danton's Death* and John Eaton's *Danton and Robespierre*).

To many, what makes opera an impossible medium through which to view the humdrum events of daily life is the simple fact of singing, which renders the action instantly stylised and destroys the kind of naturalism for which composers often seem to strive with colloquial speech, modern dress, and casual references to everyday objects barely worth talking about, let alone singing about. The drinking of soup and the 6/8 sewing machines in Charpentier's *Louise*, the endless packing of suitcases and the skat game in *Intermezzo*, the seed packets and secateurs of *The Knot Garden*, mirror and powder puff of *The Midsummer Marriage* – anything *can* be set to music or referred to in song, but such efforts will always jar the ears of listeners who feel that the subject matter of opera must be profound enough to justify the phenomenon of singing. Voltaire distinguished opera from play by 'the intensity of the passion depicted, which drives characters beyond the limits of speech'; if that passion is lacking, if the sentiment does not need music for its expression, singing will be at best superfluous, at worst silly. (The fragility of the convention could partly explain why there are relatively so few successful modern comic operas; the composer may invite the audience to laugh because his music is comic, or because the words he has set are funny, but he must do it without invoking, directly or indirectly, the humour that is inherent in people singing their conversation.)

The difficulty of making a deliberate joke in opera exemplifies perhaps most acutely the problem facing every composer – the fact that the success of his opera will depend heavily on the audience having a reasonably detailed understanding of what is going on. In this context, plots that are already familiar have obvious advantages. If the composer can be sure that most of his listeners have in outline at least a good idea of what will happen, he need not be hamstrung musically by the need to make every word intelligible with a one-note-per-syllable text-setting over a light accompaniment; instead, in John Eaton's words, 'the entire realm of vocal gesture can be liberated and the modern orchestra . . . can be unleashed for intensifying the drama or defining a character'. And his new opera can compete on less unequal terms with the standard works, where both music and plot are known in advance and the audience goes primarily to be moved and to judge the nuances of performance.

Familiarity is another reason for the recurrence of myth as a subject for opera – not just classical myth (though the Oresteia, Oedipus, Orpheus and Ariadne stories are among the most often-used of all operatic subjects) but Norse, Hindu and Celtic myth, fable and fairy tale, folk tale and legend – those of Don Juan and Faust, for example – which often come to have the status of myth. The audience can be expected both to recognise the stories in their traditional forms and to have at least a chance of following the composer and librettist in any glosses they may put upon them. It was this universal quality which attracted Harrison Birtwistle and his librettist Stephen Pruslin to the Punch and Judy story, as Pruslin explains: 'It is immediately comprehensible, yet susceptible to interpretation. . . . The function of a myth is to be transparent, so that each individual can project on to it his own interpretation.' Confident in their listeners' core of knowledge, composer and librettist were able deliberately to manipulate their response to the familiar – '[We] used all the imagery, the trappings and paraphernalia of the original as a departure point [to] enable an audience of adults to re-experience the vividness of their childhood reaction during the performance while allowing enough scope for interpretative speculation afterwards.' Similarly, Sir Michael Tippett wanted in *King Priam* to take advantage of 'the resonances that sound in all of us when we speak of Troy', working within the framework of the Trojan myth to examine the nature of relationships within a family – 'the seedbed for all drama'. More usual in his work than the straight quotation of myth, however, is a mythopoeic process – the creation of a modern and personal mythology which incorporates traditional mythical material (the Fisher King of the Tarot, for instance, or the opposition of Athena and Dionysus) but transmutes it in twentieth-century terms so that 'the human characters in a drama are encountered half-within their mythological archetypes'.

The other natural haven for the composer in search of readily assimilable material is the well-known play, novel or poem. Here the appeal is obviously that of building on a proven success, something that has worked on its own terms. Stephen Oliver, who has himself done some adaptations as well as inventing his own plots, nonetheless sounds disparaging about it: 'Composers obviously feel safer parasiting, burrowing into stories like bookworms. . . . There's a reliable artefact already there, the groundwork's done, and they have all sorts of tropes, decorations they can build in.' On the other hand, he is not blind to the practical advantages: 'Managements very commonly go for titles which they've heard before – in my own case *Tom Jones* and *The Duchess of Malfi* – because they can sell them: "based on the rumbustious tale of lechery", "the famous Webster play", and so on.'

Thus operas have been made in the last fifty years out of novels by authors as diverse as Dickens (Dominick Argento's *Miss Havisham* and Albert Coates's *Pickwick*) and Hardy (Peter Tranchell's *The Mayor of Casterbridge*, Alun Hoddinott's *The Trumpet Major* and Minuro Miki's *The Woodlanders*), Conrad, James, Dostoevsky, Gogol, George Eliot, Saki, Emily Brontë, Poe and Fenimore Cooper (Alva Henderson's *The Last of the Mohicans*); from Saul Bellow (Leon Kirchner's *Lily* from *Henderson the Rain King*) and Graham Greene (Malcolm Williamson's *Our Man in Havana*) to Henry Miller (Antonio Bibalo's *The Smile at the Foot of the Ladder*) and Iris Murdoch (William Mathias's *The Servants*).

As for plays, leaving aside Shakespeare (and in the twentieth century composers have been tempted by virtually all his plays except the histories and, perhaps understandably, *Othello* and *Measure for Measure*), operas have been made with varying degrees of success from assorted classics of the nineteenth- and early twentieth-century theatre, such as *Miss Julie*, *Cyrano de Bergerac*, *Ghosts*, *The Seagull*, *Blood Wedding*, *Murder in the Cathedral* and *Six Characters in Search of an Author*. Some later plays have been similarly adapted – Henry Miller's *The Crucible*, for example, Lilian Hellmann's *The Little Foxes* (converted by Marc Blitzstein into *Regina*), Tennessee William's *Summer and Smoke* and Beckett's *Krapp's Last Tape* – but generally speaking, it is no longer as easy to appropriate a recent or contemporary play as it was for Strauss with *Salome* or Puccini with *Madam Butterfly*. From his own experience Nicholas Maw comments, 'It's difficult for opera to have the symbiosis which it ought to have with the drama of its time', partly because of copyright laws which can allocate as much as one third of the performing rights to the playwright or author of the original text – and this usually has to come out of the composer and librettist's share, not the publisher's (if there is one) – partly because where the gain might obviously be worth the cost, competition can be hot. Nicholas Maw himself lost Ingmar Bergman's *Smiles of a Summer Night* to Stephen Sondheim and *A Little Night Music*, and *Sergeant Musgrave's Dance* to a prospective Broadway offer which in the event never materialised.

The answer might seem to be for playwrights to move, like theatre directors and designers, into opera and collaborate with composers from scratch. Or has contemporary theatre in fact diverged too far from opera for this to be feasible? While the development of theatre has never been exactly parallel with that of opera – one could perhaps trace in opera the outline history of the last three centuries of *music*, but hardly the history of either literature or theatre — there have been significant points of contact between the two: between Weber and German Romanticism, for example, the Italian proponents of *verismo* and the naturalistic theatre of Ibsen and Strindberg, Debussy and Symbolism, Sir Michael Tippett and the English verse drama of the 1940s and 1950s. But because of the direction taken by the theatre in the 1950s and 1960s, correspondences are now few. This, at least, is the theory persuasively advanced by Gary Schmidgall, in his book *Literature as Opera* (OUP, 1977). He argues that playwrights lost their appeal as prospective collaborators when they developed a passion for the plotless and pointless or positively absurd (as did, say, Beckett and Ionesco); a tendency, like Stoppard, to explore language for its own sake, producing verbal intricacies which music could only obscure; or an inclination, like Pinter and Albee, towards advanced cerebration in the realms of metaphysics, linguistics and logical philosophy, to which music has little to add.

While the profundity of a theme or its familiarity may sometimes help to commend it, most often the choice of a subject for opera is simply a question of an individual personal response to a particular stimulus, varying from opera to opera, let alone from composer to composer. A quotation from Joseph Kerman's *Opera as Drama* suggests some of the criteria that may condition that response: 'To make possible the ultimate success, the subject matter must match the opera composer's

dramatic vision and technique as well as his temperament, his time, and his particular musical powers.'

Philip Glass, for instance, was looking (as critic John Rockwell points out) for
a particular kind of theatre – somewhere between wholly non-linear 'performance
art' and the full-blown, carefully plotted narrative opera – when he turned to the
'character' opera, which resembles a pageant or string of tableaux arranged round
a central 'iconic' figure: Einstein, Gandhi, Tutankhamun's father. Harrison Birtwistle was guided more by the state of his musical development at the time when
Punch and Judy was conceived. 'I had to take into consideration the music I was
writing, the actual *material*. The good sculptors are the ones who respect their
material and its properties. That's why medieval carving at its best *looks* like wood,
looks like stone. Victorian carving, when they actually got better at it technically
and things were technically more "lifelike", looks *less* like stone and more like
plastic. For me, medieval carving is at its most wonderful when it is really wood
– and yet it expresses what the sculptor wanted to say.' The kind of music he
was writing at that time was much concerned with ritual, repetition and cyclical
progression (as is evident in his large instrumental work *Tragoedia*, itself a move
towards a kind of theatre music), and these are all present both in the Punch and
Judy story, as he saw it, and in the completed opera – in the reiterated war cries,
riddle-games, passion arias and chorales, the exorcism, fortune-telling and 'black
wedding', and in the construction of the work from four cycles of recurring elements, 'melodramas' corresponding with the changing seasons.

Another composer guided at least in part by technical considerations is John
Eaton. Since the 1960s, he has been preoccupied in his music with the expansion
of the conventional system of pitch by the use of microtones – pitches other than
those represented in the chromatic scale. The purpose of this has been primarily
to facilitate greater psychological expressivity: 'To put it in an overly simple and
primitive way: if a major third is happy and a minor third sad, even the use of
only quarter tones (the pitches halfway between a white and adjacent black key
on a piano keyboard) gives one three more distinct thirds, each one of which seems
to have – or at least can be invested by a skilful composer with – its own distinct
psychological character. Thus, an opera composer has greatly enriched tools with
which to probe the human psyche.' It was the possession of such tools which
prompted the writing of *Myshkin*, John Eaton's first opera, based on Dostoevsky's
The Idiot, whose action takes place entirely within the central character's mind.
Different states and degrees of rationality are portrayed by the exploitation of
microtones – Myshkin's idiocy is represented in music based on sixth tones
generated electronically, his return to greater lucidity in quarter tones played on
conventional instruments. By the same means, in *Danton and Robespierre* Eaton contrasts not two states of the same mind, but two diametrically opposed personalities
– the humanist, realist Danton, in music based on two tempered scales a quarter
tone apart, the cold inflexible idealist Robespierre in a 'just intonational' system
of notes becoming increasingly dissonant.

Sir Michael Tippett at home, 1985

As for Kerman's dictum about temperament, and the importance of a subject evoking a genuine emotional and intellectual response, it receives strong support from a letter of Tchaikovsky's, in which he described *Eugene Onegin* as 'the outcome of an invincible inward impulse. I assure you one should only compose opera under such conditions'. Of all twentieth-century composers, Sir Michael Tippett is one of those whose works bear the most unmistakable signs of the inward impulse. His conception of the responsibility of the creative artist is deeply serious – to offer spiritual nourishment in a materialistic world; and 'in music we sense most directly the inner flow which sustains the psyche or the soul'. In his case it is not a matter simply of offering solace or escape through music, but of something more constructive – the articulation of collective imaginative experiences to bring out their significance and in so doing to activate their power to affect men's lives: 'The drive to create has been so constant through the ages, and is so intense in its operation, that it is difficult for those submitting to it not to feel it as evidence of things beyond the individually personal. So that maybe Jung is right when he says that if once the artistic creator, leaving personal idiosyncracies aside, gives expression to the archetypes of the collective unconscious, then he also speaks

The Midsummer Marriage – with John Treleaven as Mark, Helen Field as Jenifer (ENO, 1985).

with the tongues of millions. . . . I believe that the faculty the artist may sometimes have to create images through which these mysterious depths of our being speak to us, is a true fundamental. I believe it is part of what we mean by having knowledge of God.'

In this context, Sir Michael's 'choice' of subject is not entirely in his own hands. 'The more collective an artistic imaginative experience is going to be, the more the discovery of suitable material is involuntary'; when embarking on *The Midsummer Marriage*, for example, he felt himself to be 'the instrument of some collective imaginative experience' dealing with the interaction of two worlds. The themes that in some way force themselves upon him are not all exalting and edifying – collective imaginative experiences are equally likely to be disturbing, even horrifying – but he feels it his duty to confront the dark side of the unconscious mind as well. 'My fate has been to live within a period of enormous destructiveness, violence, of every kind of division and hostility. This "black" material . . . has always been for me part of the sense basis of my own creative act.' He has tackled themes as bitter as mob violence, sexual violence, terrorist violence, the persecution of dissidents in Russia and of blacks in America – his aim being to offer both an interpretation of contemporary malaises and a means of resolution. 'As to subjects, I can never get away from the conviction that the most immediately momentous thing that is happening is not the exploration of space, but the making of one world on this planet.' Sir Michael subscribes to the Jungian belief that the way to the unification of the world is through the integration of the individual personality – hence the stress throughout his work on the importance of self-discovery. 'There is up-to-date drama to be made out of the innumerable conflicts engendered by our ignorance or illusion about ourselves' – drama, in the shape of *The Midsummer Marriage*, *The Knot Garden* and *The Ice Break*, and a pointer to hope for the future.

Where Sir Michael Tippett is primarily concerned with the individual consciousness, and the relationships between one individual and another, Britten was perhaps more interested in the individual's relationship to (or alienation from) the rest of society – being drawn repeatedly to the themes of the outsider (in *Peter Grimes* and *Owen Wingrave*), and the conflict between private feelings and public duty (in *Billy Budd*, *Gloriana* and perhaps even *Albert Herring*). *Owen Wingrave* in particular grew from Britten's reaction to the murder by troopers in 1970 of students at Kent State University demonstrating against conscription for Vietnam. It made him eager to explore the possibilities of a modern Romeo-and-Juliet story in which the lovers, with different social and political ideas, meet in the context of a war in which they do not believe – and this in turn suggested to Myfanwy Piper the Henry James story. (As another example of a direct response to contemporary history one might consider the climactic Senate scene in Iain Hamilton's *The Catiline Conspiracy*, written during the period of Richard Nixon's impeachment.)

Society as a whole, with perhaps less emphasis on, or interest in the individuals of which it is comprised, is Hans Werner Henze's theme; his 'inward impulse' has become over the years overtly political. Henze shares Tippett's awareness of the responsibility conferred by his art; he has long argued that the artist must not retreat into his interior world, despite the temptation and the apparent artistic advantages, and in *Elegy for Young Lovers* launched an extended attack on the 'catastrophic' notion that the artist has to live in isolation for the sake of his creativity. The artist cannot simply feed off the material which the outside world furnishes; he must confront its problems, alert others to them – 'He should react like a seismograph to what is taking place' – and propound a solution. And where Sir Michael strives towards a moral and intellectual reformation, Henze's objective is political change, specifically the furtherance of socialism.

The cast of his political thought was dictated by his upbringing in Nazi Germany

Hans Werner Henze, 1957

(his father was a Nazi,) his musical education at a time of 'contraband culture', when Hindemith was an 'underground' composer and Schoenberg banned as decadent, and his violent reaction against both. Over the last twenty years he has moved gradually but consistently to the left – in 1965 he was campaigning for Willi Brandt and the Social Democratic Party, in 1967–8 taking an interest in student politics under the leadership of Rudi Dutschke, in 1968 he resigned from the West Berlin Academy of Arts to join the East German Academy of Arts, in 1969–70 he made study tours of Cuba and in 1972 he campaigned for the West German Communist Party – and the political content of his work has developed from implicit (in *Der Junge Lord* and *The Bassarids*) to explicit. Where once he merely lamented social evils in generalised terms, without depicting them, after his meeting with Edward Bond in the mid-seventies he accepted the inevitability of a 'collision of art and reality' in the dramatic presentation of specific events. *We Come to the River*, with its libretto by Bond, was a tirade against war and exploitation with particular reference to dictatorship in Chile and the American defeat in Vietnam.

We Come to the River was premièred in considerable style at Covent Garden, and Henze has since been regularly criticised for a seeming fondness for the bourgeois trappings of musical society, for 'playing the capitalist system'. He argues, however, 'Simply to hand everything over to the system and opt out borders on counter-revolutionary behaviour. . . . One should take advantage of every available opportunity for communication. This also connects with the "Long March through the institutions" spoken of by Rudi Dutschke.' David Blake, who studied with Marxist composer Hanns Eisler in East Berlin between 1960 and 1961, has much the same objectives. Since the mid-seventies he has had a particular concern for the issues of racial oppression, Black Power and Third World revolution, and in *Toussaint* he used the resources of a major opera house to draw attention to them and explore their implications. 'I wanted to take over all the strengths of the opera house – the love of singing and the glory of the human voice and the great excitement when the curtain goes up on a marvellous new set and the orchestra blasts out and the chorus yells its head off – it really is an animal pleasure that we get from that, very fundamental, and I'm not going to sniff at it, I love it too. But I wanted to put all that at the service of something which is a little more relevant to our day than, say, *La Bohème*.'

Opera has traditionally provided a focus for displays of political feeling – most conspicuously in nineteenth-century Italy; as Luigi Dallapiccola has remarked, 'Verdi formulated a style through which the Italian people found a key to their dramatic plight and vibrated in unison with it.' In 1849, it took no more than a phrase or situation which suggested the current political state to act as a call to arms. But whether opera is a suitable medium for conveying political messages directly and undiluted is more debatable. Rodney Milnes doubts that it is: 'Opera is too big for anything as narrow as commitment . . . Music is so subversive, so completely non-representational, it says something different to each person; it works *against* commitment.' Colin Graham, on the other hand, argues that far from undermining an argument, music can be used to insinuate it into the listener's consciousness – in reference to Henze's satire on greed, money and bourgeois behaviour in *The English Cat*: 'There is a way of putting over these criticisms in music theatre which maybe would not alienate nearly as many people as if they were done in a straight play. They're seduced by the music into accepting the ideas. I don't think that's dishonest necessarily – if you can make your point that way and make good music at the same time.'

It is certainly a medium which many have tried to use for the discussion of political issues. The majority of Iain Hamilton's operas (*Agamemnon, The Catiline Conspiracy, The Royal Hunt of the Sun, Tamburlaine*) could be called 'political' in the sense that all are centred on an exposure of the military mind and the corrupting effects of power – but none advances a particular ideological doctrine as do, say, the works of Alan Bush (*Wat Tyler, The Men of Blackmoor, Joe Hill – the Man who Never Died*, all produced first in East Germany) and Luigi Nono, whose *Al gran sole carico d'amore*, on the role of women in revolutionary times, incorporates texts from Marx, Engels, Lenin, Castro, Brecht and Che Guevara. (Another Guevara-inspired work – *Die Verurteilung des Che Guevara* – is due from Mikis Theodorakis, to be produced in Dresden in 1986.)

At the other end of the spectrum, in the sense of being guided by no dogma, nor even a consistent policy in the choice of his subjects, is Stephen Oliver. Many different stimuli have prompted his forty-plus operas and musicals (including *Blondel*, with librettist Tim Rice). A particularly resonant line of verse, for example – 'Take a play like *The Duchess of Malfi*: someone brings a coffin to the lady and says, "Here is a present from your princely brothers, and there's a right welcome, for it brings last benefit, last sorrow" – and there's your musical line.' Or the piquant atmosphere of a whole work – 'I've always had a fancy to write an opera to J. G. Farrell's *Troubles*. . . . There's the Major who opens the cupboard and the sheep's head pops out, and the drunken Chekhovian doctor, and the chorus of women at the hotel – I can still hear the orchestral sound of that hotel. . . . I wrote to Farrell and he said, "You'll be surprised to hear the opera rights have not yet been snapped up", and he gave them to me, which I thought was very good of him . . . I thought it might do very well for Glyndebourne – the right ambience, really. . . .' The physical circumstances of the commission may determine the direction it takes: 'I didn't know what the story of *The Garden* was before I wrote the opening; it was improvised from various points of view. . . . I knew this piece was going to be performed in the open air, in a garden, and I knew the instrumentation: it had been commissioned for soprano, tenor, viol and lute. With a viol and a lute, the only things you can really do are buzz and click. So – insects, summer nights, gardens; already you've got a bit of a story. The garden in summer is going to be a bit of a frightening place with the buzzing; the woman is sitting in the garden – why, if it frightens her? She's sitting in it because she's looking over the corpse of her husband who she's buried there.'

The only important precondition, in Stephen Oliver's view, is that the initial impulse or response to preconditions should be the composer's own; he should resist the temptation to gear himself to what he conceives to be the wishes of administrators or the audience. Nor should he necessarily have too sharp an eye to other composers, past or present; to think of oneself as part of a tradition can be damaging. 'I don't think you can look for guidance from other people. You must just think of the best way to tell the story. If it happens to be Mozart's way, it's probably not the story you should be telling. If it occurs to you to start with a comic duet and someone trying on a hat and someone else measuring, there's something badly wrong.'

24

What makes a Good Libretto?

The good libretto is not a completed artefact, not a container into which music may be poured, but a *potential* work of art, awaiting realisation by another creative artist to whom it offers both inspiration and opportunity for development. What Debussy wanted in a librettist was one who 'only hinting at things, will allow me to graft my dream upon his; who will not despotically impose on me the "scene to be set" and will leave me free, here and there, to show more artistry than he and to complete his work'.

If the work in hand is to be a true opera, and not simply a play with accompanying music, the composer must be able to make the text his own in some way – Sir Michael Tippett, in fact, believes that he cannot avoid doing so: 'The moment the composer begins to create the musical verses of his song, he destroys our appreciation of the poem as poetry, and substitutes an appreciation of his music as song. As soon as we sing any poetry to a recognizable melody, we have at that instant left the art of poetry for the art of music.' The librettist must understand that this will happen, that the music will change his text – not knowing exactly *how* it will change it, because this is hard to predict, but that it may alter the cast of a character, the inflection of a word, the shape of a scene. Colin Graham, librettist as well as producer, indicates some of the causes behind the effect: 'A musico-dramatic shape is different from a purely dramatic shape. There are other elements involved, like suspension of time, and the fact that the orchestra comments.' The music may even make words redundant: 'Librettists always find it very difficult to believe – Britten was always going on about this – that two bars of orchestra can replace eight lines of written text. The composer . . . can say, "I don't need these four lines which say how miserable I feel, I can write four bars full of torment and anguish – far more poetic than singing it at that moment."'

Ideally music will always make the words mean more than they can by themselves, but the transformation is nevertheless painful for their originator – 'a bit like having your baby snatched away and brought up by somebody else', according to Colin Graham. Many librettists have found it hard to accept what can seem like an unrewarding and secondary, even anonymous role. Hofmannsthal, for example, was rarely able to rid himself of the feeling that to be worthy of his name, what he had written should be able to stand on its own, be printed and even performed separately. But the fact that this has on occasion proved possible (*Der Rosenkavalier*, for instance, has been staged without music), while it would have bolstered his self-respect as poet and playwright, does not necessarily reflect well on his achievement as a librettist.

Many composers and critics feel that the writing of the lyric dramatist should be different in *kind* from that of the poet, playwright or novelist. The good libretto is written in language designed to be heard, not read; and because it is to be heard only in conjunction with music, this language must be geared in some essential way to music. Of *We Come To The River*, Hans Werner Henze wrote: 'Edward Bond described his libretto as "Actions for Music", and in fact his libretto and the actions it contains are in many respects inconceivable as a stage play: everything that takes place – and the way in which it takes place – is aimed at music.' Music is in some way part of the fabric of the libretto, integral to it to the extent that the words may mean very little, certainly much less, by themselves. As an example of the libretto which is a non-detachable component of an organic whole, Rodney Milnes advances *Il Trovatore* – 'a masterpiece *as a text written to be sung* – short lines, wonderfully linked. But you couldn't perform it as a play; it's quite abstract' – and in this sense, in his view, far more satisfactory a libretto, if not a piece of literature, than *Der Rosenkavalier*.

Of necessity, the ideal libretto will in any case be too short to hold its own as an independent creation. As Fauré complained when writing *Pénélope*, 'Music makes lines stretch out terribly. . . . What takes two minutes to read takes at least three times as long when it's sung.' The composer struggling to keep his *opus* within manageable bounds can ultimately accommodate no more than what Sir Michael Tippett calls 'an extremely tiny text', and a librettist who displays economy of means in articulating his ideas is an invaluable asset – hence Verdi's enthusiasm for the libretto rich in the *parola scenica*, the single, pregnant word 'that sculpts and makes the situation precise and evident'.

To some extent the success of a libretto may depend on the particular flavour of its language and its fitness for the composer's purposes. The kinds of sound he is himself interested in making and the story he has to tell will obviously help determine the choice of librettist. David Blake, for example, for the libretto of *Toussaint*, which might be described as an 'epic' narrative (in the Brechtian sense) of the war of independence in Haiti at the end of the eighteenth century, chose to work with Anthony Ward, a novelist. Nigel Osborne, for the libretto to be made from Pasternak's novella *The Last Summer* – allusive, impressionistic, kaleidoscopic rather than strictly chronological – turned to a poet, Craig Raine.

Language that is too consciously 'poetic', however, may be more of a hindrance than a help to the composer. Distinctive rhythms or fixed metres have either to be accommodated (which may inhibit the composer's instinctive response to the ideas expressed), or ignored, wasting much of the librettist's effort. Poetic diction is likely also to be less intelligible when sung; what makes for clarity is the short word and the obvious one, and poetry cannot be constrained within these limits.

Tippett adds a rider to this, suggesting that a text which is already richly expressive in its language can also be less stimulating for the composer: 'If you go to a poet or writer who wants to make poetic language, you end up with a text to which all the poetic things have already been done.' If the words do not somehow need 'exaltation into music', the composer runs the risk of simply attaching decorative notes to them.

At the other extreme, the rhythms, textures and vocabulary of everyday conversation also have their drawbacks as material for the librettist. Now that both music and poetry have become less formulaic, less subject to external rules of structure and scansion than they were, say, in the eighteenth century, it is open to the librettist to adopt as informal and prosaic a style as he wishes, in the knowledge that the composer is far freer to match the irregular patterns and shifting emphases of ordinary speech. The danger is, however, that day-to-day conversation rarely has the emotional weight to sustain the impact of music – that it will be projected at a level of intensity that is at best inappropriate, at worst ludicrous.

It is perhaps not surprising that some composers opt for language which is effectively meaningless. Stravinsky, writing about the Latin libretto of *Oedipus Rex*, observed: 'What a joy it is to compose music to a language of convention – almost of ritual . . . One no longer feels dominated by the phrase, the literal meaning of words. The text thus becomes purely phonetic material for the composer. He can dissect it at will and concentrate all his attention on its primary constituent – that is to say the syllable.' Going several stages further, Philip Glass set *Satyagraha* in Sanskrit, devised for *Akhnaten* a libretto couched almost entirely in the languages of the ancient Near East – Egyptian, Hebrew and Akkadian (a language of Assyria and Babylon, now extinct), and in *Einstein on the Beach* gave his performers literally single syllables to sing – numbers and the *solfège* names of notes.

Perhaps most important of all, the good librettist must have a keen dramatic sense. T. S. Eliot once commented, 'While I don't think a really poetic gift is necessary, I do feel that the author of an operatic libretto should have some theatrical gift', and he advised Sir Michael Tippett to consult not a poet but a theatre man during the planning of *King Priam*. (It is here that the producer/librettist is at a considerable advantage, as Colin Graham is aware: 'Rather as a composer has musical ideas in mind, I have theatrical ideas in mind when I'm writing, which I want to build into the story. I build in the production the whole time.') The plot should have a clearly articulated structure; it should not be too subtle, or hinge on finely developed discussions, and it should have pace and momentum. Within the bounds of taste, the successful librettist will be alert to the theatrically effective gesture – the sound of the trumpet signalling release in *Fidelio*, for example, and the horn dictating death in *Ernani* – or what composer Carlisle Floyd calls 'catalytic occasions', backdrops which both offset and contribute to the central drama. 'Imagine if you can the third act of *Traviata* as a lovers' quarrel between Violetta and Alfredo but without Flora's party, or Scarpia's revelation of his intentions regarding Tosca but with no Te Deum'.

Special problems face the librettist who is not inventing but adapting his material from an already existing source (and by far the greater proportion of libretti, in fact, originate in this way). Some originals – plays, poems, novels – are more susceptible than others to operatic treatment. As Gary Schmidgall suggests in his book *Literature as Opera*, Verdi must have been instantly struck by the musical possibilities inherent in *Othello*, with its succession of quintessential operatic moments – drinking song, love scene, revenge pact, prayer, renunciation scene, and its actual musical insert, the 'Willow Song'; *Werther* was in its original state a collection of letters, each an emotional outpouring ideally suited to aria form; and Thomas Mann's constant use in *Death in Venice* of literary leitmotifs, repeated, varied and cross-referred, lent itself naturally to translation in musical terms.

Even these works, however, had to undergo ruthless pruning and simplification, and the problem becomes almost insurmountable with less tractable sources. It takes courage, for instance, to contemplate turning Tolstoy into opera, as Colin Graham has discovered in the course of producing Prokofiev's *War and Peace* and making a libretto for a possible treatment of *Anna Karenina* by Britten. His credo is straightforward enough: 'I think the librettist has a duty to convey the spirit of the whole and the intentions, even if he can't convey the letter of the whole . . . You're not providing just a set of illustrations that you might find every fifty pages in the book.' But the sacrifices required simply to get works as massive as these to the stage at all (and *War and Peace*, well over four hours long, is still considered impracticable by many administrators) are serious, perhaps too serious. Because it is hard for opera to take a didactic line, sustained argument being virtually impossible to set to music effectively, the opera *War and Peace* makes only oblique reference to the theory of history (that it is not the 'great leaders' but the people themselves who shape events) which to Tolstoy was the motive force of his novel.

It is perhaps easier, and frequently more successful, to use the original merely as a springboard, improvising on its themes, rewriting rather than simply reducing it. In the case of, say, *Anna Karenina*, this might be unwise; but with a less venerable and (more important) less familiar original, the librettist has fewer inhibitions. Stephen Oliver, for example, feels no obligation to adhere strictly to the plot of J. G. Farrell's *Troubles*: 'What I will do is start the opera without preparing the libretto, just knowing the book thoroughly, and then invent it, using certain of the eloquent phrases in the book.' And in transforming Ostrovsky's *Artists and Admirers* into his own *Sasha*, he ultimately incorporated no more than two lines of the original text and seven of Ostrovsky's characters, as opposed to twenty-three of his own. 'And Sasha did something quite different in the end from what even I had thought. I thought she was going to marry the Englishman . . .'

The Last Summer itself attracted Craig Raine very little on first reading, but it suggested to him ideas of his own which he could elaborate and attach loosely to Pasternak's framework (itself considerably modified): 'If you think of the Pasternak story as a kind of gymnastic horse, you have to imagine that I come along and concentrate like mad and have white stuff on my hands to get a grip, and I go towards the pommel, but don't actually take hold of it, and I do all these wonderful exercises and end with a somersault – I haven't actually touched the horse, it's a stimulant.'

A skilful libretto should survive translation from one language to another – provided that the translator is sensitively attuned to the individual characteristics of the original and capable of reproducing them accurately. According to translator Rodney Blumer, the well-translated libretto will catch as faithfully as possible the *spirit* of the original. Its language will be heroic where the original language is heroic, florid where it is florid (in Handelian opera, perhaps), colloquial where the original is colloquial, and so on; in *Osud*, he saw and reproduced 'a Pinter libretto – disjointed and elusive'. Its form will normally mirror that of the original; there must be a sound reason for rendering a rhymed libretto into prose, for instance, or for adding three entirely new lines rather than repeating the same line four times, as one is often required to do in a Rossini opera. And the correspondence between original and translation should ideally extend also to the smallest detail; the original text inspired the particular notes we hear, and if it must be detached from them, it should be replaced by something which resembles it closely and, as far as is possible, bears the same relation to the notes. The same word should fall in original and translation on the same note as often as the translator can contrive it. (Elisabeth Söderström, who has performed much of the standard German and Italian repertoire in Swedish, has remarked on the difficulty of offering a coherent musico-dramatic interpretation of a role when pivotal words in the text are detached from the musical gestures which express them.) The same vowel sounds should be preserved on key notes where this is possible, and the translator should reproduce onomatopoeia or consonantal clusters where they have been used to achieve a particular aural effect.

The conscientious translator must also address himself to the question of imagery and how he can most precisely render the point of a simile or metaphor. Where the image is written into the music, it must obviously be translated literally. In *Osud*, for example, where the literal translation of one line would read 'There is a gathering storm – the cockerel hurries home', to the English or American listener a horse might be more natural (or even, with echoes of *Macbeth* in mind, a crow), but the cockerel crowing is in the score. Where the image is not transcribed musically, and is perhaps obscure in its new context, he may replace it: in *Osud* again, a girl separated from her lover is likened to a dried gourd rattling in the wind. 'Gourds are not very big in our experience,' remarks Rodney Blumer, and in his version she is a broken reed, drooping and sighing in the breeze. . . .

25

Composer and Librettist

'Sometimes music seizes violently upon language and crushes it in its embrace, or sometimes language wants to seize upon music; they both can degrade, but also can elevate one another.' As Hans Werner Henze suggests, for a composer and librettist working closely together – for any two creative artists working towards a single shared end – the risk is that neither will be able to realise his individual vision as perfectly as he might if he were working alone and independently; equally, in a sensitive and skilful operatic partnership, the eventual whole will be considerably more than the sum of its parts.

It is generally acknowledged to be most important that the *composer* should be free to achieve precisely what he has in mind – as Sir Michael Tippett sees it, 'Since opera is an art in which music must finally eat up action and setting . . . on the creator of the music is put a greater burden of judgement than on the creator of the words or the scenery.' For this reason, some musicians, Sir Michael among them, have always preferred to act as their own librettists, in order to protect their evolving musical ideas against the impact of the non-musical ideas of others (in T. S. Eliot's phrase, 'brilliant things given to you which are not really your purpose'), which may deflect and disrupt the work's natural growth.

The composer/librettist, with no need to refer to anyone else, has the chance – at least in theory – to develop music and words genuinely in tandem, ideas crossing both ways so that the progress of the music may influence the words in both outline and detail just as much and as often as the words determine the shape and colour of the music. Composer/librettist Stephen Oliver describes himself as 'a start-from-the-beginning-go-on-to-the-end man – words and music at the same time. You might just go ahead one way or the other – you might find that a scene needs musically a very rapid incursion of the whole orchestra, and you must therefore make someone rush across the stage, which will then need explaining dramatically. Or you might find you genuinely need to know for the sake of the drama why Horace is in the lady's bedroom, so the music will have to respond.'

For some composers writing their own words, the words will almost always pull slightly ahead – Marvin David Levy, for instance: 'Normally an aria comes about with a key phrase that can be sung and catches your ear. It may not appear in the first line. Then the text comes, without music. Then the music comes, often at variance with the text, leading you in another direction. There starts the battle of moulding one to the other and judging what's worth saving and what must be changed because the musical idea is more interesting. It's a constant give and take.' For others, the music may sometimes crystallise before the detail of the text; of *The Midsummer Marriage*, Sir Michael Tippett has written, 'When I *saw* that my *prim'uomo* and *prima donna* returned to the level of the stage all armed with immediate experience of heaven and hell, I *heard* them begin to sing, one against the other, in two arias; the soprano's having coloratura and the tenor's being rhapsodic, and this long before any words were there.'

But to generalise is pointless: the symbiosis of music and words cannot be reduced to a formula, nor even necessarily described explicitly, since the composer/librettist's principal advantage, besides simple convenience of working, is that words and music can simultaneously evolve not just consciously but subconsciously as well. Iain Hamilton, for example, finds that though he prepares both synopsis and libretto before deliberately turning his mind to the music, 'What is very odd is that when I come to do the first sketches of the music, having done the rhythms of the words in the libretto, it's all there – not just the setting of the words, but the orchestral textures, the instrumental music, the interludes, they all seem to be basically there in my mind. It's something that if I tried to analyse it too much I probably wouldn't do it any more – but it's largely why I write my own libretti.'

Total autonomy can be lonely, and most composers choose to enter into partnership with someone else, partly perhaps from lack of confidence in themselves as writers, partly for the company and the stimulus of another intelligence brought to bear on the same subject. In these circumstances, composer and librettist usually try to simulate as closely as they can the 'give-and-take' process in the composer's mind – though more often than not the opening move appears to be the librettist's: the drama is planned and words are written first. What varies is the degree of finish which the libretto will have attained, and the extent of the composer's involvement in its preparation.

Some librettists have always felt as protective towards their words as any composer to his music. Their aim is to craft the libretto precisely to their own satisfaction without interference, and they do not expect the composer subsequently to make radical changes. Of his libretto for *Die Frau ohne Schatten* Hofmannsthal wrote, 'Every detail must be present in the imagination clear-cut and definite, succinct and precise and *true* . . . nothing remain in a state of mere unaccomplished purpose and good intention. Once this is achieved, everything will have been made ready for the music, so that it need only pour into the bed prepared for it and reflect in its stream the likeness of heaven and earth.' Occasionally the librettist may appear to get his way: Hans Werner Henze said of his setting of Hans Magnus Enzenberger's *La Cubana*, 'Its craftsmanship is riveted together and solid (permanently joined by springs, pins and human hair) so that composing became more and more like doing a crossword puzzle, as if all I needed to worry about was that everything fitted into the right place, like the toothed wheel of a pianola.'

Iain Hamilton, 1985

Rarely, however, will the composer submit tamely to this kind of discipline. He will normally be intimately involved in characterisation, plot development, dramaturgy, style of language, even the choice of the actual words used. In the case of *Die Frau ohne Schatten*, for instance, a suggestion made by Strauss on purely musical grounds in fact caused Hofmannsthal to modify his 'clear-cut and definite' libretto significantly; Strauss proposed using the smaller orchestra familiar from *Ariadne auf Naxos* to depict the 'upper' world of the Emperor and Empress, reserving the full orchestra for the 'denser, more colourful' lower world of the Dyer and his wife, to which Hofmannsthal responded enthusiastically: 'This stylistically most valuable idea has now taken firm hold on my imagination, and the poetic diction will be made to correspond to it' – in other words, heroic diction for the 'upper' world, colloquial conversation for the 'lower'.

Strauss was in his own way as much a man of the theatre as Hofmannsthal, with shrewd ideas on what was dramatically effective: 'In opera all mass scenes and big ensembles make bad curtains: on the other hand, solo scenes or love duets, either with a jubilant *ff* or fading out with highly poetical *pp* endings, are the most rewarding.' Wilfred Josephs took a similar hand in the structuring of his opera *Rebecca*, based on the Daphne du Maurier novel, proposing – always with musical effects in mind – climactic points at which to break the drama. Act One he felt should end with the arrival at Manderley and the heroine's first awareness of the menace of Rebecca; Act Two with her near-suicide forestalled by shipwreck and the explosion of emergency flares; Act Three with the burning of Manderley. Nicholas Maw's main concern, on the other hand, was for the actual language of *The Rising of the Moon*. Particularly in the passages of interior monologue, he found it extremely difficult to issue instructions on how to convey the exact shades of feeling contained in the music he wished to write; easier simply to translate them into words himself. And more mundane needs than this can necessitate changes in a libretto: in setting *L'Enfant et les Sortilèges*, Ravel asked Colette to alter the origins of the Teacup and Teapot, which she had cast as Auvergnois, to free him from the necessity of writing them a *bourrée*, a dance believed to have originated in the Auvergne. She made them Wedgwood and Chinese – and he wrote a foxtrot.

There are, of course, cases where composer and librettist prefer to keep their distance and work virtually independently. After Harrison Birtwistle and Stephen Pruslin had discovered that their interests in the Punch and Judy story were much the same, and had agreed a scenario in outline, Stephen Pruslin wrote his libretto with little ado and no detailed knowledge of any musical ideas which Birtwistle might have had; and subsequently, without further discussion, Birtwistle wrote the music. As he later explained, 'People who write words want to hear them – and I'm not sure opera's about that. . . . What I'm interested in as a composer is form.'

For those admittedly rarer composer/librettist relationships in which the music tends to anticipate the words, there is a solid precedent. Mozart knew precisely how he wished Osmin's second-act aria in *Die Entführung aus dem Serail* to go and issued instructions to his librettist accordingly, stating firmly, 'The poetry must be altogether the obedient daughter of the music', explaining less dogmatically afterwards, 'I am well-aware that the verse is not of the best, but it fitted in and it agreed so well with the musical ideas which already were buzzing in my head.' (One can only suppose that Hofmannsthal was unaware of the first part of this remark when he invoked the shade of Mozart to justify what must have been to him the slight indignity of nailing words to music which Strauss had already written for the duet between Sophie and Octavian after the third-act trio in *Der Rosenkavalier*.)

What made it practicable for Mozart to pre-empt the librettist and write music in abstraction was the formulaic nature of the poetry with which both were dealing. Likewise Bellini, collaborating almost invariably with librettists who wrote in the '*ottonario*' or eight-foot-verse, kept hoards of melodies in sketchbooks, ready prepared for future use – 'I have composed some beautiful phrases which will be developed according to the piece in which they are played.' The manuscript of *La Sonnambula* in the J. Pierpont Morgan Library, New York, illustrates his *modus operandi* well: first he writes the melody, then tries various different verses to it – and occasionally the one he settles on is *not* the one which appears with that melody in the printed score, turning up instead with a different tune.

These days, now that there is no set verse style, and no formula for writing words to be set to music, it is less easy to anticipate the librettist. Wilfred Josephs, however, emulated Bellini to a certain extent in compiling in advance a book of leitmotifs which, like Bellini's melodies, were roughly interchangeable. 'Some would get joined on to a particular character, but some would just be a situation *motif* or, say, Manderley... Some of the ideas were never used, some more than once.' Josephs, who was writing an essentially through-composed opera, found in this technique one advantage from which Bellini, tied to the 'number' opera, could not benefit: motifs and even whole arias evolved in the book could be suggested and forecast in the score well before they made their formal appearance.

Perhaps the most thoroughgoing practitioner of the '*prima la musica*' method ('*prima*' here in its literal sense) is John Eaton, whose musical ideas often come to him before he has even found a specific subject, let alone a fully articulated libretto. 'Generally my operas have begun as musical-dramatic ideas. I have often had to search for the subjects they fit, although this has not been conscious on my part. Rather, in reading a play or a bit of history or a novel, I'd suddenly feel chills up and down my spine and know I had my next operatic subject.' His next step is to formulate the musical-dramatic line of the whole work, often in great detail; and only then will he talk through the synopsis scene by scene with his librettist. After this, the way is clear for the words and the detail of the music to evolve in parallel: John Eaton is aware from his own experience that to add the words at the end, as mere decorative appendages to the score, is as fruitless as tacking notes that are no more than background music to a self-sufficient text. 'Once I tried to write my own libretto after actually composing the music, with horrifying results. Perhaps the most curious line was one that fit the music beautifully: "O! to chew on the entrails of a bleating goat!"'

26

Setting the Text

If the writing of a libretto is different in kind from that of a play or novel – simpler, emptier, shorter, complementary rather than self-sufficient – is the music of an opera also significantly different from that, say, of a symphony? Must it too be incomplete, or 'impure' – both dependent on and tainted by its literary connections? A remark of Verdi to one of his librettists suggests strongly that music cannot but be affected by the operatic environment – 'It is unfortunately sometimes necessary in the theatre for poets and composers to have the talent not to write either poetry or music.'

Without going this far, David Blake would concede that opera music is not, and should not always be, as concentrated and demanding as 'absolute' music: 'Something very strange happens to music when you theatricalise it or put it on a stage. In a way . . . the rigour of musical thinking just dissipates slightly. . . . It sounds dangerous to say it, but sometimes the specific gravity of your music can be much less – it *has* to be much less, because if you kept the screw on a hundred per cent of the time, as you would in a symphony, say, you'll find that your drama is going wrong. There has to be a very wiggly graph of tension and musical specific gravity in order to make the drama on stage work.' Iain Hamilton would agree that the musical language of an opera should be more open – 'You can't get the dramatic points across if there is such an incredible amount of musical detail'; and for Wilfred Josephs, the means of 'opening up' the language of his vocal works is 'without writing *down* at all, to seek a simpler mode of expression in terms of harmony'.

Few composers of opera now feel that the music should be allowed to develop absolutely freely on its own terms, as it might if it were destined for the concert hall. This is an attitude entrenched by Wagner with the doctrine of the *Gesamtkunstwerk* (the integrated art work) and his early belief that music must serve the drama: 'The vocal melody should . . . follow in close detail the sonorous qualities of this poetry; the harmony should reflect its fluctuations of emotional intensity. There should only be modulations for changes in the dramatic situation.' Support for a less extreme version of this view (and Wagner himself later modified his theories considerably) comes from Sir Michael Tippett: 'While I cannot imagine myself underplaying the formal qualities of the music in opera, I feel that these formal qualities must be endlessly varied and changed to meet the needs of whatever sub-ject one is dealing with.'

Stephen Oliver is keen that the constraints imposed on music by its operatic context should be seen in their right perspective: 'I think you *do* have to adapt to what is a mixed medium – but in an entirely healthy artistic way. The negative way of looking at it is as a compromise; the positive way is seeing how you can combine different artistic values in the same thing – *not* really a compromise. I think you do have to be sure that once you have written the nice bit, it is all absolutely practicable – that all the leads are apparent, and the singers can pitch their notes, and there's nothing ungrateful to sing. . . . But that's not compromise; that's to do with skill. It's a positive pleasure to get that right.' And this type of discipline is in any case, as Thea Musgrave observes, hardly peculiar to opera: 'You're constricted in the same way if you write for a symphony orchestra – you can't just write anything you want. . . . The clarinet doesn't go below written E; the violin doesn't go below G unless you tune *scordatura*. . . . If you choose to write for an orchestra of a thousand, or a piece six hours long, you're not going to get it performed. . . . It's your attitude to the constrictions that counts. . . . There are more constrictions in opera inevitably because you're dealing with more people. . . . But that's what learning how to write an opera *is* – learning how to use the constrictions and turn them to advantage.'

Berg, writing about his ambitions for *Wozzeck*, sums up what the serious opera composer will try to achieve: 'The music was to be so formed as consciously to fulfil its duty of serving the action at every moment . . . At the same time this aim must not prejudice the development of the music as an absolute, purely musical entity.' The music should have a structure of its own, some kind of organic unity that film music, say, rarely has. This structure will naturally relate to the drama, but will exist on its own terms; the piece should have both an overall dramatic momentum and a musical momentum, but these need not move at the same pace. David Blake believes the great operas to be those, and only those, which find a really significant amalgam between the shape of the drama and the shape of the music, and cites *Tristan und Isolde* as one example, where the dramatic theme of love resolved only in death is mirrored in musical terms by a harmonic resolution deliberately and ingeniously delayed through four and a half hours until the B-major chord at the end of the *Liebestod*.

In setting the text of an opera, articulating the drama and bringing the characters to life, the composer needs to be something of a dramatist in his own right. As a bare minimum, he must know how to avoid interrupting the flow and tension of events, resisting the temptation to give the music its head in isolation from the text. David Blake: 'You find yourself continually coming up against contradic-tions. You're faced with something which *could* work musically in a certain way; if it were in a concert hall you could go through that process and know that in purely musical terms, it would make sense and people would follow you. But in a dramatic context, if you were to follow that through, it would not be theatrically

Jose van Dam in the title role of *Wozzeck* with Hermann Winkler as the Captain (Covent Garden, 1984).

effective' – a difficulty that producers sometimes find with Tchaikovsky, according to Iain Hamilton. 'He gets so fascinated with the development of the musical idea that he spins it on for his own delight beyond what the dramatic situation actually calls for' – whereas Wagner, in Hamilton's opinion, knew exactly when to 'change the gears', musically speaking, in order to keep the scene in focus dramatically.

The opera composer must also develop certain basic techniques of which he has no need in the concert hall. Representing action on stage, for example – 'the essence of the difference between oratorio and opera', for Sir Michael Tippett.

'Both use stories. But opera must present the drama, and the characters, in action. While oratorio only refers to the events of the drama in order, having refreshed our memory of them or brought them to our notice, to consider their moral implications.' Opera characters are less static mouthpieces for the words than bodies in motion. Knowing how to present action means, at its crudest, knowing how long to leave for people to climb stairs, fight duels, cross the stage in procession/in tumbrils/on a bier; more subtly, it is the capacity to combine complicated stage movements with complex musical forms such as the ensemble.

Characterisation, partly achieved in the libretto, is also very much the responsibility of the composer; it is for him to fill out and reinforce the personalities that may be deduced from the stage directions and the words which the librettist has put into the characters' mouths. Some composers establish the basic disposition of a character with a broad brush stroke; Wilfred Josephs, for instance, looked for a particular instrumental timbre that would most accurately characterise Favell, Rebecca's cousin and lover and the principal surviving villain of the piece. 'I wanted him to be instantly recognisable even if he wasn't visible. It held me up for weeks trying to find the right sound – I couldn't really cast him. A saxophone was one of the things I had in mind – but after Vaughan Williams's *Job*, where the sax is perfect for the oily, slimy music of one of the comforters, it didn't seem right – more the George Sanders version of Favell from Hitchcock's film, suave and blasé, than Favell as I saw him – a nasty piece of work.' He eventually found a noise made by the harp: 'You press a pedal – say a D to D flat – and pluck the string, and then release the pedal through D to D sharp, and it goes Boooinnnng on a rising note – quite sinister. . . .Once I'd got it, then some of his speech patterns – for instance, this tendency to repeat phrases – came automatically.'

Others seek to pinpoint each passing emotion; of *King Priam*, Sir Michael Tippett wrote, 'If emotions typical to a character return, then the same instrumental gesture returns, for the exact length, however short, that is demanded. And on the few occasions when conflicting emotions are given formal musical expression together, then the instrumental gestures are still, as far as is possible, retained as separate entities.'

Of course, music need not always support and reinforce; it can make its point by contradicting what appears on the surface. One of Britten's strengths, according to David Blake, lay in the nice calculation of musical equivalents: 'Britten takes a poem and tries to identify with the spiritual and emotional position of the poet, to produce a music totally in tune with that particular lyricism.' He himself finds it often more interesting to have the orchestra producing sounds that do not attempt to correspond with the meaning of the words. Rather than simply inviting the audience to empathise with the characters and enter into the action on a straightforward psychological impulse, he tries to elicit a multi-level response, with music pulling one way and words another – the music commenting on the words rather than merely underwriting them – in the hope that the listener will step back from the story and consider its intellectual implications as well as its immediate emotional appeal. In aiming for 'alienation effects' of this sort, David Blake has been consciously influenced by his teacher Hanns Eisler (one of Brecht's principal collaborators). It is, however, a technique which has been used for two hundred years – witness Kobbé's story of the orchestra rehearsing Gluck's *Iphigénie en Tauride* for the first time: it came to a halt at Oreste's aria 'Le calme rentre dans mon coeur', puzzled by the restless, syncopated figure apparently at odds with the sense – at which Gluck cried, 'Go on all the same! He lies. He has killed his mother!'

During the twentieth century, as opera has become less immediately accessible in its music, audiences have tended to look for compensation to the libretto, of which more is perhaps expected than ever before. And as opera has shifted, through Verdi and through Italian *verismo*, away from abstract vocal artistry towards a vocal line intimately related to the stage action, the apt, intelligible and expressive setting of words has moved nearer to the centre of the opera composer's art. Some now feel that the emphasis on the verbal aspect of performance is even exaggerated – Nicholas Maw, for instance, regrets the unreasonableness of English-speaking audiences: 'You never hear them complaining about not hearing the words in *Don Giovanni* or *Die Meistersinger*, because they don't understand them anyway. But if the libretto is in English, they expect to hear every single word. . . . The culture of this country is a literary culture. Its great art form is the form of literature, with painting second, but quite a long way behind. . . . If you think that there are a handful of supreme artists in the world, and one of them is English – Michelangelo, Tolstoy, Beethoven, Shakespeare – the fact that he is a literary and dramatic genius has had an enormous effect on the English way of thought. Literature has a prestige in this country which the other arts do not have to the same extent. (You've only got to read the life of Elgar. . . .) This has a real effect on one's life as a composer – it's very often much more difficult to earn one's living in an art form other than literature. The people who call the shots socially and culturally and economically – their culture is primarily literary. The effect that this has on opera is that the English expect to hear *everything* when the libretto is in English. Really most of them expect – particularly the first time round – to go and hear the libretto; the music should be a nice quiet accompaniment.'

But without pandering to this prejudice, most composers acknowledge the pressing need to set words so that they will as far as possible be heard – which might seem obvious, but it is a facility which many lack. Audibility is largely a question of finding the right balance between voices and orchestra – contriving an orchestral texture which, without being thin, anaemic or dull, lets the voices through and helps them on their way, as Thea Musgrave explains: 'It's not necessarily easier to have everything out of the way and have the voice totally unaccompanied. That can scare the life out of them and doesn't give them anything to rest on, anything to support the voice. . . . There's still something to be learnt from Verdi and Puccini, not necessarily in harmonic style but in the sense of how you make a cushion for the voice which helps it carry, so it's a vehicle for the voice to rest on and to project, not fighting the voice. . . . It depends on the hall, too, how big it is and whether the pit is under the stage. In *Mary, Queen of Scots*, at the opening where her brother James first sings, I had horns – which are notorious for blocking everything out. In the King's Theatre, Edinburgh, where there's no sunk pit, it was hopeless. So I simply cut out a lot of the horns – just gave them a chord and didn't let them hang over, to clarify things for the singer. If it had been in Bayreuth, with everything under the stage, I'd have wanted those horns – you'd need the cushion and the *continuo* function to give a kind of warmth to the texture. And the balance problem can alter according to who's singing – where the weight in the voice is; if they'd got a very strong middle voice, I'd probably leave the horns in.'

But there is little point in exposing a voice if what it then has to sing is difficult to articulate intelligibly. While it is up to the individual singer to develop clear diction, the composer who understands the mechanics of speech production in song – which sounds are easy to sing and which are not – can help considerably. (Here Britten's long experience as an accompanist to singers served him well.) In certain *tessiture*, generally the higher ones, singers find it near-impossible to utter certain sounds without mangling them. Nasal vowel sounds like 'ue' and 'ie' are squeezed out of shape on high notes; equally, round vowels – 'oh' or 'oo' – are easier to sing at the bottom of the range. Generally speaking, key words have a better chance of being heard when pitched low, around the middle of the singer's range and sung neither too fast nor exaggeratedly prolonged.

Whatever precautions the composer takes, a certain amount of the text will inevitably be lost, and the pragmatist will learn to distinguish between those words which he or she considers essential to a proper understanding of the piece, and those which he does not. Expendable syllables or phrases he may deploy at moments which from the point of view of audibility are by nature awkward – in duets, for example, Iain Hamilton will always try to repeat words that have already been heard – and he will avoid ever giving them the unnatural prominence ridiculed by Joseph Addison in the *Spectator* for March 1771: 'I have known the word "And" pursued through the whole Gamut, have been entertained with many a melodious "The", and have heard the most beautiful Graces, Quavers and Divisions bestowed upon "Then", "For" and "From", to the eternal Honour of our English Particles.'

The composer is not, of course, aiming simply to transmit words distinctly, but to colour, weight and animate them, and bring out their meaning. For this he or she must be able to find for each word a note or notes of the pitch and rhythm that will best suit its sound, shape and tone – a capacity which Andrew Porter praises in Thea Musgrave as 'rightness in matching of emotional pitch to actual *tessitura*, a sense of where in the voice to find a particular shade of feeling . . . a mark of the born opera composer'. To be fully expressive, the words must also have time to sink in, both for the benefit of the singer gradually building an interpretation from the text, and for the audience – something which Wilfred Josephs believed Schoenberg failed to allow for: 'I've discovered why he wrote badly for the voice as compared with Berg – because he didn't realise that voices need more time to speak for the harmonies to register on your listener's ear. . . . The trouble is that the harmonies move so rapidly that they become meaningless, you get nothing from them; he treats the voices like instruments – that's wrong.'

The text will often 'speak' more eloquently if in addition the composer has a keen ear for the natural rhythms and patterns of speech – an asset increasingly essential in the twentieth century since the gap between song and speech has narrowed. Rodolfo Celletti argues that Verdi was the first to move deliberately from the vocalised singing of *bel canto* opera (where each vowel in every syllable may correspond to several notes) toward a more naturalistic style in which each syllable corresponds to a single note; since then, composers like Debussy, Janáček, Massenet and Mussorgsky have made great efforts to reflect even more closely the pacing and emphasis of ordinary diction.

Occasionally, for the sake of a special effect, the composer may deliberately set the rhythm of the words *against* the rhythm of the musical line. (The intention may be to demand closer attention to the words, but librettists are rarely convinced: E. M. Forster, for instance, objected forcibly, when Britten carried out an experiment of this kind with Claggart's monologue in *Billy Budd*, that the effect was in fact to obscure the sense.) Usually, however, the objective is naturalness. Sir Michael Tippett recalls that whilst rehearsing *King Priam*, Sam Wanamaker persuaded his cast to declaim their lines, particularly those whose audibility was essential, and asked 'if the natural intonations they had given to these words in speech were changed by what they had to sing. The answer was practically never. This is one of the opera's sources of immediacy.'

As a rule the more contemporary the language, the more casual and idiomatic the expressions, the harder they are to translate convincingly into musical form; street credibility and song tend to sit oddly together (and slang has the disadvantage of dating a piece exceptionally quickly). But the truly 'contemporary' opera is not impossible, according to Andrew Porter, who much admires precisely this quality in Leonard Bernstein's *A Quiet Place*, a piece he considers a model of skilful text-setting: 'It is in absolutely every-day speech – it's as inarticulate as what I'm saying now, everything going off into three dots, and the syntax not rounded and complete. . . . It's an attempt to use a completely realistic text and contemporary dilemmas, and music which is giving form to the incoherence of all that. Art does come into it, you can't just present realities: it's given form by very good music.'

27

Getting New Opera into Performance

'The first time something is done', in Harrison Birtwistle's view, 'it ought to be done the way it's been visualised by the composer. The version for homosexual pygmies can be the next one.' Easier said than done, and the composer tends to discover when he has written the final note that his problems are far from over – that to get the work realised as he has heard and seen it in his mind can take almost as long, and be considerably more frustrating than the process of composition itself.

In Nicholas Maw's experience, 'A lot of opera houses, obliged to work with a composer, would far rather he were six feet under the ground, where he could not be a nuisance. . . . One is not in charge of one's own destiny. You kill yourself writing the thing, and then you are obliged simply to hand it over. . . . Glyndebourne's behaviour was exemplary – but when I got to the theatre in Germany for the third production of *The Rising of the Moon*, they'd cut great chunks out of it simply because the chorus were doing something else that week or something. . . . They cut an enormous piece out of Act Two, and when I said, "This is what the *whole opera* is about", I was told, "Oh, it's too long, the audience will get bored." They then turned to Act Three and turned over about thirty-five, forty pages of vocal score and said, "We want to begin here." This was preposterous, there wasn't even a break in the music, it would sound musically absurd – apart from missing out a huge chunk of the plot so nobody would know what was going on. But it was only about forty-eight hours before the dress rehearsal, and in fact nobody had learnt that bit, so I had no choice: I had to sit down there and then at the café table where we were and, to stop it being a total musical shambles, cobble together a kind of *Vorspiel* of the music going on underneath this scene so there was something to begin the third act with. After experiences like this you say to yourself, "There must be something better to do with one's life. If my work is going to be produced at this level, frankly I'd prefer to be a dentist."' (Dame Ethel Smyth, confronted with similarly insensitive cuts made at the première of her opera *The Wreckers* in Leipzig in 1906, stole score and parts to prevent further performance, and left for Prague.) 'It's so much easier to get a decent standard of performance in the concert hall', Maw concludes. 'The imponderables are so much less, what you have to get together is so much more

The original production team for *The Rising of the Moon*: producer Colin Graham, designer Sir Osbert Lancaster, composer Nicholas Maw and soprano Anne Howells (Glyndebourne Festival Opera, 1970).

focused. Now I've been asked to write another opera – and I've said I'll do it *only* if it's clear from the start that I'm going to be right at the centre of the production. At least then if we make a mess of it, it's my fault.'

Composers have always felt the need to be at the centre of productions of their works – Berlioz, for example: 'An opera house, as I see it, is before everything a vast musical instrument. I can play it, but if I am to play it well, it must be entrusted to me unreservedly.' This ideal, always well beyond Berlioz's reach, Verdi had virtually attained by the time he wrote *Otello* – the fruits of a lifelong campaign to establish the rights of the composer over his own work. Because of the popularity of his operas and the bargaining power this gave him, Verdi could insist on the integrity of his scores; his later contracts contained penalty clauses to be invoked in the event of any alteration whatsoever made by managements for the purpose of censorship or singers for reasons of vanity. He could make his wishes known in the matter of casting – Otello, for example, must have a strong *mezza voce*, so that his dying words might be projected forcefully; Iago must have exceptionally distinct diction as his utterances constituted the mainspring of the plot (and as far as looks were concerned, he should be tall, nonchalant and witty, *not* small, malevolent and instantly suspicious). He coached his singers himself, issuing very specific instructions for performance. Desdemona, for instance, was to produce three different voices in the Willow Song: one for herself, one for Barbara (the maid in the song) and one distinct from both – *una voce lontana* – for the refrain of 'Salce, salce, salce/Willow, willow, willow'. He took an educated interest in sets, costumes (here he favoured historical authenticity) and stage movements, in the organisation of the orchestra and its placing in the pit (he liked a generous double bass section, so disposed as to muffle the more piercing brass sounds and faulty woodwind intonation). He rehearsed and conducted most of his premières himself, and by the time of *Otello* had a contractual right to forbid performance altogether if he considered either production or musical standards unsatisfactory.

From the Verdian position of dominance the composer has steadily declined throughout the twentieth century, largely because of the drastically diminished commercial attractiveness of 'new opera' which leaves the composer, conscious that the opera house is probably incurring a loss on his behalf, more hesitant to issue expensive ultimata, and the administration in any case less likely to respond. His eclipse is also due partly to the rise of producer and designer, often cast in the role of the composer's worst enemies – not least by composers themselves. 'I wanted to leave as little as possible to the new despots of the theatrical art, the directors,' wrote Schoenberg to Webern, justifying the extreme detail of the stage directions for *Moses und Aron*. 'The highhandedness of these mere minions and their total lack of conscience is excelled only by their barbarity and feebleness.' Feebleness could perhaps be excused in any minion confronted with the request that he represent faithfully the stabbing of naked virgins, dismembering of live animals, and idolators leaping into fire and running burning round the stage. But Hans Werner Henze, whose demands are by no means as taxing, firmly seconds Schoenberg, though the tone is less personal: 'Putting the composer's demands to one side is even more damaging [in contemporary opera] than in the case of older works. Whereas with older works the ear (thanks to memory) instinctively defends the music against the eye, when the ear experiences a new work for the first time, it (together with the eye) must take at face value everything that is served up. Whenever the new décor does not match the sound world of the new score or express the same things in colour, style and material, the displeasure of the listener (who is also using his eyes) is naturally directed against the music (we are, after all, at the opera) even when it is suspected that the faults lie with the production.'

The composer's best defence is obviously to form his own company, as both Britten and Peter Maxwell Davies, say, have done in the past with the English Opera Group and the Fires of London. But so extreme a solution really only answers for chamber or smaller scale opera, and for the composer who wishes to use the full resources of the opera house to express his vision, the co-operation of a sympathetic producer is indispensable. It is beoming increasingly common,

Peter Maxwell Davies (*right*) with conductor Edward Downes discussing the score of *Taverner* at rehearsals for its revival (Covent Garden, 1983).

particularly in America, for technical advisers to be enlisted at the earliest possible moment, during the composition of the work; composers are coming to resemble playwrights more closely in their readiness to accept practical guidance, and the musician who completes an opera in unsullied isolation and then sends it out to be produced by a stranger is getting rarer. Not every composer has a natural sense of what is feasible and effective in the theatre, and the producer's role is to advise on what will work in dramatic terms and what will not, what can be achieved technically and what cannot. Sir Michael Tippett was persuaded to consult Gunther Rennert during the gestation of *King Priam* largely by his experience with *The Midsummer Marriage*; the temple from which steps lead both up (to the 'masculine' regions of intellect, chastity and independence) and down (to the 'feminine' regions of instinct, fertility and love) was the starting point for the whole opera, and Sir Michael was so reluctant to depart from it that it became in the end something of a liability in staging terms, inducing too intense a sense of place – a pitfall from which he could perhaps have been saved by the advice of a professional producer during the process of composition.

One of the first composers to involve a producer at the generative stage was Britten, who in his insistence on 'total theatre' placed producer and designer on the same footing with the librettist as collaborators. Colin Graham, who produced the majority of Britten's later stage works, has described the various stages in the process: 'We would discuss the libretto of the passage he was going to write the next day, and he would ask how I would see it being staged – where I saw people standing, and so on: very important to integrate the musical directions with the stage directions. . . . We did a kind of mock-up of the production; then he would go away and write that bit. Then at teatime the next day he would play what he'd written, and we'd discuss that – and then discuss what he was going to write tomorrow, and so on. . . . He very often wanted to get the rough stage designs there, so he had a visual image in his mind, the colour and the feeling. . . . Normally when you're doing a production it has to be the other way round: a sensitive designer will listen to the music and gain the colour from the music. But Britten, if he was working with somebody he very much admired, like John Piper, would like a lot of mental images. John would give him a whole lot of watercolour drawings; they wouldn't necessarily be used in the end, but they were concepts. The ones he accepted Ben would draw from and build into his music, and John would complete the designs later on.'

This kind of involvement with work-in-progress at a very high artistic level was a practical training from which several of the other composers with whom Colin Graham has collaborated have benefited indirectly. Working with Stephen Oliver on *The Duchess of Malfi* at Santa Fe, he helped clarify and enrich characterisation by pointing out, for example, that by the end of an act an emotion crucial to the development of the plot had been left unexpressed. For Wilfred Josephs, it was his eye for atmospheric detail which proved invaluable – the arum lilies, for instance, with which Mrs Danvers insists on decorating Manderley for the fancy-dress ball. In *The Voice of Ariadne*, a major scene change was to be covered by a passage in which the Voice itself is heard; since this was to be generated electronically and played on tape (for unearthly effect), it had to be a determinate length, and Colin Graham was able to tell Thea Musgrave exactly how many seconds of music would be needed to give the stage crew time to make the change.

The advantages of a close collaboration between composer and producer have been apparent so often in recent years that some companies now make it a precondition of new commissions. Glyndebourne, for example, delayed finalising the commission offered to Nigel Osborne and Craig Raine for *The Last Summer* until a producer had been agreed. In Peter Sellars they felt they had found a collaborator who could help them realise their joint conception of Pasternak's novella; in the

Benjamin Britten discusses the score of *Gloriana* with Sylvia Fisher, who sang the role of Elizabeth I
in the 1966 Sadler's Wells production.

event, his involvement seems likely to transform both the conception and the
resulting opera. 'What I can do as a director', he observes, 'is to serve as the focal
point for certain ideas, and keep as it were folding into the batter ideas which
I think may be of interest by the time the whole is leavened, ideas which may
keep the thing from being too single-minded.'

For Peter Sellars the project's appeal lies largely in the extent to which it chimes
with his current preoccupations as a stage director: 'I think the issue right now
in theatre and film and video is, "How does human consciousness function?" What
is the process, and how can one adequately represent two or three hours of consciousness on a stage? At what level can the mind wander? At what level does
the mind zero in on something? In what way does one guide the audience, and
in what way does one allow them to roam freely?' The operation of consciousness,

he argues, is rarely a straight sequence, although this is the way in which it has often been presented by drama in the past – by Aristotle, for instance, who insisted on an unvarying progression from exposition to recognition to crisis and dénouement, a rule followed by dramatists from Shakespeare to David Belasco. 'In fact our daily experience does not function in that way. Nor currently does the shape of history – the way Ronald Reagan makes decisions doesn't exactly have initial exposition followed by recognition. . . .' Literature has long acknowledged this, accepting and glorifying in the notion that events may be presented out of sequence, that references may be oblique, that there is scope in art for abstraction – and in this field Pasternak is one of the great formal innovators. What is more, *The Last Summer* comes from his most innovatory period, when parallel and perhaps related advances were being made in the visual arts by creators like Picasso and Braque. Pasternak's writing, as Peter Sellars sees it, operates 'on that little edge of consciousness . . . Images ring and echo through different valleys, and you can't place where you first saw that image, you can't place why that image reminds you of something. You keep hearing these resonances, there's no escape from them. Pasternak thought of it as a musical structure. . . . It really does operate like a Beethoven sonata in which a little motivic figure, when it is finally reintroduced into the weave at the end, is powerful not just because we've heard it before five times, but because it's gone through a harmonic development, there's more than *déjà vu*.' Pasternak, in Peter Sellars's view, makes thoroughgoing use of abstraction – 'abstraction grounded in images that are terrifyingly exact, overwhelmingly tactile, so intensely seen. There's this level at which the precision of a gaze at a single object finally pushes that object to the outer level of abstraction.'

These discoveries in the sphere of the novel Peter Sellars wants to translate in dramatic terms, reproducing on the Glyndebourne stage Pasternak's discontinuous, allusive techniques for revealing situation and character, evoking rather than informing. The setting of *The Last Summer*, Russia immediately before and after the Revolution, has become what Sellars describes as an 'ikonic' period, 'an important nodal point, one that has passed into the realms of mythology', with its own resonances and associations. He sees his job as being to deploy the 'ikons' as Pasternak deploys them, operating like him on 'that little edge of consciousness', juggling and interweaving images in a fragmented, kaleidoscopic narrative moving freely between abstraction and naturalism.

It was these ambitions which at the first meeting of composer, librettist and producer led to a radical reworking of the existing plan. Craig Raine had produced what he describes as 'a foursquare, essentially theatrical version' of the novella, cast in three acts and broadly chronological (more so, in fact, than the original). Peter Sellars's proposal was that the work should more closely resemble a film than a play, with far more scenes, each much shorter, intricately intercut without a strict chronological framework (in which it would more closely imitate Pasternak). Separate images and scenes could be immediately juxtaposed as they might be in the cinema – by cutting, say, from two people talking in one corner of the stage to another corner and the explanation of what they are saying – giving the librettist a far wider choice of situations and settings and at the same time, by breaking down the single stage picture, destroying the notion that what the audience is watching is a *stage* performance. In the process, the conventions of the stage – unities of time and place, for instance – and of traditional opera, can be discarded. 'Before I was involved in the project', Sellars explains, 'it was laid out like an opera – Scene One: In the railroad station; Scene Two: etc., etc. I said, "This must *go*. We don't need scene-change music and then a new set – that's not the current state of the art. On stage we can be in fifteen different locations in a thirty-second period, if that's what's needed." There are any number of ways of doing it. In the Japanese Noh way, for example, of being in heaven or earth when somebody just tilts their finger. . . . Or by the use of video. What is the *Gesamtkunstwerk*, now that we have video? The questions have to be thrown wide open again.'

As for the composer who prefers to articulate his ideas alone, he must hope to reach some understanding with the producer after the fact – more difficult, particularly once the work has gone into rehearsal and the pressures of money and time are making themselves felt. The producer who has had no hand in the shaping of a work must feel his way into it from the outside – and many find the composer's presence inhibiting as they develop and implement their interpretations for the first time. Anthony Besch, for example, while he will discuss a contemporary work thoroughly with its composer in advance of its production, will usually ask for three weeks' grace at the start of rehearsals during which the composer will leave producer and cast severely alone to bring their work to a state in which it is ready to be seen and discussed.

The degree to which the composer may attempt to influence a production once it is under way will vary. Attitudes to stage directions and their observance, for instance, range from relative *laissez-faire* – David Blake: 'We didn't have stage pictures in our minds all that strongly; producers are so clever these days, so imaginative, that you do rely on them finding an apt way of representing what you've got in your words and music' – to serious concern that the producer should appreciate and respect those directions which have not simply been jotted in the margin of the libretto but incorporated into the music – Nicholas Maw: 'The directions were very important to me in writing the music . . . I would think very carefully about the dramatic situation myself. I can remember thinking. "At this point they'd give each other a look, wouldn't they?", and I'd try to write that into the music. The music mustn't mickey-mouse the dramatic situation, but it must fill it out.'

And this ultimately is what is important to the composer – that the producer should understand what the music is expressing and how it expresses it, and reflect these impulses sensitively in his staging. Sir Michael Tippett, who believes that the music of an opera must dictate the speed both of the characters' emotions and the consequent stage actions, was much impressed and reassured during the

King Priam: Alan Opie as Hector and Robin Leggate as Paris in the revival of Sam Wanamaker's production, designed by Sean Kenny (Covent Garden, 1985).

production of *King Priam* by the fact that Sam Wanamaker asked in advance for a tape of the piano reduction with vocal lines complete in rhythm if not in pitch, to give himself 'an absolute framework within which his theatrical imagination and skill were to operate'. Philip Glass takes no chances, and on his own initiative provides this framework for his producer as a matter of course; when an opera score is virtually complete, he records it on a synthesiser which generates the sounds the orchestra will make. This recording he sends ahead to the theatre, giving producer, designer and conductor a 'real time' sound for guidance, rather than a piano/vocal version which may be played inaccurately and at variable speeds. Not only does this make the composer's intentions immediately plain, it gives producer and designer the opportunity of suggesting any changes necessary on practical grounds before the manuscript is even copied or the rehearsals begin; and Philip Glass sums up well the arguments for collaboration – 'You can spend your life learning about opera; it would be silly trying to do it alone.'

28

The Problem of New Opera

'We are in the position of an art gallery whose most modern pictures are by Sargent, or a library whose newest novel is *The Forsyte Saga*.' For 'Sargent' and '*Forsyte Saga*' read 'Salvador Dali' and '*Lucky Jim*' and Sir Tyrone Guthrie's gloomy pronouncement, prompted by the opera scene in 1945, holds uncomfortably true some forty years later. As the opera boom continues, minor works of major eighteenth-century composers, major works of minor nineteenth-century composers are eagerly dug up and dusted off, baroque works reconstituted from crumbling manuscript sources, operettas and musicals imported into the opera house. There are, however, miserably few *new* pieces entering the permanent operatic repertoire – at least, without a time lapse of approximately thirty years. Only now might such works as *The Rake's Progress (1951)*, *Billy Budd* (1951), *The Turn of the Screw* (1954), *The Midsummer Marriage* (1955), *Dialogues of the Carmelites* (1957) (and, if frequency of performance is a criterion, *Amahl and the Night Visitors* 1951) be considered securely established. Others as old, or almost as old, have a toehold, perhaps no more – Bernd Alois Zimmermann's *Die Soldaten* (1965), Henze's *Elegy for Young Lovers* (1961), von Einem's *Danton's Death* (1946), Egk's *Der Revisor* (1957), Britten's *A Midsummer Night's Dream* (1960), Menotti's *The Consul* (1950), Schoenberg's *Moses und Aron* (1957), Barber's *Vanessa* (1958), Moore's *The Ballad of Baby Doe* (1956) and Dallapiccola's *Il Prigionero* (1950). As for operas written since 1970, it is hard to speak of even the most critically successful (Tippett's *The Knot Garden*, Britten's *Death in Venice*, Birtwistle's *Punch and Judy*, Reimann's *Lear*) as having entered the regular repertoire at all. To some extent the creators of opera, the composers, have been superseded in the public mind by the re-creators – the singers, producers, designers – as the makers of opera.

The problem is not that new operas are not constantly being commissioned, written and premièred. Output is perhaps most prolific in Germany and Austria: many of the smaller houses (Darmstadt, Dresden, Gelsenkirchen) support their local composers; and several of the large ones have declared a particular interest in modern music – Cologne, for example, Frankfurt under Michael Gielen and Stuttgart under Dennis Russell Davies. The Deutsche Oper in Berlin has attached to it a workshop for the nurturing of new work, and Götz Friedrich has appointed composer Wolfgang Rihm as his musical advisor. Christoph Dohnanyi, while

Music Director at Hamburg, proposed a joint venture between the opera companies of the northwest region (Hamburg, Hanover, Bremen, Kiel, Lübeck) to commission and successively present two modern operas every year. A previous Intendant at Hamburg, Rolf Liebermann, himself a composer, achieved more, in Harold Rosenthal's view, in the commissioning of new works than any other single figure since the war, and in 1984 he set up as an incentive to others the Rolf Liebermann Competition for Opera Composers.

In Britain, though administrators are uniformly apologetic, the record is not negligible. National companies, as one might expect, have commissioned work from native composers – Welsh National Opera from Owain Arwel Hughes, Alun Hoddinott, William Mathias and Grace Williams, for instance, and Scottish Opera from Robin Orr, Thomas Wilson, Iain Hamilton, John Purser and Thea Musgrave. (Several of their works were on specifically Scottish subjects – Musgrave's *Mary, Queen of Scots* and Robin Orr's *Hermiston* and *Full Circle*, the latter a piece of Scottish *verismo* set in the Gorbals during the Depression and performed in Glaswegian dialect.) English National Opera has issued considerably more commissions than it has acquired new operas; among the composers who have completed works since 1970 are Gordon Crosse (*The Story of Vasco*), Iain Hamilton (*The Royal Hunt of the Sun* and *Anna Karenina*) and David Blake (*Toussaint*), and the company has in view new works from Hamilton, Blake, Nicholas Maw and, in 1986, the world première of Harrison Birtwistle's *The Mask of Orpheus*. This was originated, it should be said, by Covent Garden which since the 1970s has also commissioned Richard Rodney Bennett's *Victory*, Peter Maxwell Davies's *Taverner*, John Tavener's *Thérèse*, Sir Michael Tippett's *The Knot Garden* and *The Ice Break*, Thea Mus-

Sir George Christie in his study at Glyndebourne, 1985, with Brenda.

grave's *Harriet, The Woman Called Moses* (jointly with the Virginia Opera Association), Aulis Sallinen's *The King Goes Forth to France*, Edward Cowie's *Ned Kelly* and another work (as yet untitled) from Harrison Birtwistle.

Glyndebourne's record has been perhaps the least impressive – Sir George Christie explains: 'Glyndebourne doesn't want to take risks with its captive audience who would probably be shocked by some contemporary pieces, which are ill-suited to the festive spirit in which they may be coming to Glyndebourne. I have no desire whatever to see *Wozzeck* put on here – it wouldn't fit. There's a certain atmosphere here which doesn't lend itself to some dire modern problems. . . . It *isn't* to do with class and élitism – I'd be perfectly happy to do a class-ridden opera here. I just don't want to do an intensely gloomy dire opera on a summer evening, with the interval on the lawn. . . . It's not all of a piece, that's why.' Audience reaction over the years – to Henze's *Elegy for Young Lovers* on the one hand, and Nicholas Maw's *The Rising of the Moon* on the other – bears out his argument; the former provoked the first boos ever heard at Glyndebourne, the second, a lyrical romantic comedy, was well-received and revived. And suitability of subject is still a criterion now that Glyndebourne, at Brian Dickie's instigation, has adopted a more positive and coherent approach to contemporary opera. Anthony Whitworth-Jones, formerly the Administrative Director of the London Sinfonietta, was appointed in 1981 to help implement a new strategy by which new works will be introduced, cautiously but consistently, into the Festival by way of Glyndebourne Touring Opera. The intention is to utilise fully the resources of GTO (the only area of Glyndebourne's operations which is subsidised), and by presenting each new work to perhaps more adventurous audiences in the regions (and, it is hoped, London) to entrench its reputation before it appears at the Festival proper.

The first commission to be merchandised in this way was Oliver Knussen's double bill of fantasy operas, *Where the Wild Things Are* and *Higglety Pigglety Pop*, based on Maurice Sendak's books and centred on his designs. By the time the two operas found their way into the 1985 Festival, they had already been seen on tour, and, in the case of *Wild Things*, at the National Theatre and on television. The double bill was in fact commissioned conjointly with the BBC, which has entered into a similar agreement with each of the other major companies, and can claim a half-credit for Edward Harper's *Hedda Gabler* at Scottish Opera, the Sallinen work at Covent Garden, Ligeti's *Tempus* promised to ENO, as well as future works for Welsh National Opera, Opera North, and Kent Opera. This programme, coming after a decade of relative inertia, could be seen as a continuation of the Corporation's activities between 1945 and 1970 when some twenty operas, mostly one-acters, were commissioned for radio and television – among them Walton's *Troilus and Cressida*, Britten's *Owen Wingrave* and Sir Arthur Bliss's *Tobias and the Angel*.

As for America, the opera scene in 1984 produced a remarkable statistic: during the 1983/4 season, more contemporary American works (261) were performed throughout the USA than works from the standard repertoire (254) – an indication that America no longer relies so heavily on Europe either for its repertoire or for its singers. Encouragement of modern opera is admittedly more systematic than in Britain. Various service organisations offer grants. Besides the private bodies (such as the Ford, Rockefeller and Guggenheim Foundations), money is forthcoming from the National Institute for Music Theater, the National Endowment for the Arts, and from Opera America whose programme 'Opera for the Eighties and Beyond' is into its first phase of 'pre-commissioning grants' – 'Exploration Fellowships' (awarded to encourage administrators to travel in the search for talent), 'Team Building Grants' (towards short residencies by teams of creative artists to stimulate collaboration), and 'Development Grants', for the nurturing of pieces up to the point where they may be given a 'work in progress' reading.

Such readings normally take place in opera workshops, where composer and librettist, working closely with the producer, are given the chance during the process of composition to try out scenes, acts, even the whole work in a semi-staging, to discover what is or is not theatrically and musically effective before the expense and risk of a full production is incurred. The workshop is the equivalent of the out-of-town tryout for a play, and is often an invaluable precaution now that composers no longer have the latitude allowed to Donizetti, even to Verdi in his early days, to learn on the job. It is hardly a revolutionary idea; Offenbach, for instance, would put what were little more than sketches into rehearsal with voices and piano and then make any corrections that were necessary before letting the piece go into full production. (Hence the state of *The Tales of Hoffmann*, which had only reached the piano/vocal stage when he died.) Now, however, workshops are being promoted on a large scale, some attached to companies (like Minnesota and Houston) where they may be affiliated to apprentice programmes, some in universities like the University of Indiana where composers such as Leonard Bernstein and John Eaton (the university's composer-in-residence) have tested and tightened their works. Some have been set up specially – that, for example, at the O'Neill Theater Center in Connecticut, one of the first organisations to focus attention on the practical difficulties besetting the composer/librettist partnership.

There remains, however, the problem of what happens after the initial encouragement. Philip Glass, for example, received grants from the Ford and Rockefeller Foundations and a Fulbright Scholarship to study with Nadia Boulanger in Paris. But despite this investment, all four of his operas were premièred outside America (*Einstein on the Beach* in Avignon, *Satyagraha* in Rotterdam, *Akhnaten* in Stuttgart and *The Photographer* in Amsterdam). Some American companies, however, do take full advantage of the groundwork they have put in. The St Louis Opera Theater regularly gives over one of its annual productions to a new work, and has in recent years premièred works such as Stephen Paulus's *The Postman Always Rings Twice* and Minuro Miki's *An Actor's Revenge*. The Minnesota Opera, after a lull, is reviving its commitment to modern music; pieces that have come through its workshop include Conrad Susa's *Transformations* and William Mayor's *Death in the Family* and in 1985 it premièred *Casanova's Homecoming*, the ninth opera of local composer Dominick Argento. Some of the big companies become bolder. Houston has championed the work of Carlisle Floyd (*Bilby's Doll* and *Willie Stark*) and Thomas Pasatieri (*The Seagull*), and in 1984 the Lyric Opera of Chicago was the first company to appoint a composer-in-residence, William Neil, and give him a workshop facility with the orchestra and the scenic resources of the house. And even the Met (whose first season at the Lincoln Center included a new commission – Marvin David Levy's *Mourning Becomes Electra*) has earmarked part of its Endowment Fund for new commissions, offered so far to Jacob Druckman and John Corigliano.

The problem is, in Edward Dent's phrase, less a decline in the operatic birth rate than an increase in infant mortality. Even those few new operas which please both audience and critics are not always rewarded with a revival, let alone a second production, and in consequence they make no mark whatsoever on the repertoire. During the première run, the composer may well be exhilarated by the unwonted exposure he is getting – David Blake points out, 'I've never had any other piece noticed by the reviewer of the *Lady*'. But once performed even three or four times, the piece loses its novelty value while retaining all the drawbacks of being unfamiliar. With the cachet of the 'World Première' gone, funding is harder to find, and these days there is no network of eager impresarios such as spread Verdi's later works throughout Italy and beyond. Nor is there usually any prospect of a recording to give new work some degree of permanence. Opera, with the huge forces it must deploy, is so expensive to record that it is hard to make a profit even on the *Rigoletto*s and *Tosca*s; the copyright fee of six to eight per cent of the sale price payable on each recording is a further disincentive to the major companies to tangle with the work of living or newly dead composers. The composer cannot even rely on his work being published in full; often the music publisher prints merely the piano/vocal score for public sale, and will copy the full score and orchestral parts only when specially requested for a performance. (Karlheinz Stockhausen now takes the precaution of printing and publishing all his own music.) Though new opera – particularly in America – flourishes in fringe venues, reluctance to incorporate contemporary works as a regular feature of a season intensifies as one moves nearer to the centre. For the administrator attempting to justify himself, it is usual – and convenient – to argue that too little of what is being produced has any real merit – Lord Harewood: 'When you talk about modern music at the board meeting, half the members start to giggle. Very tiresome' – and that other, perhaps neglected works of the seventeenth, eighteenth and nineteenth centuries have stronger claims. Since it took almost fifty years for *Wozzeck*'s true stature to be recognised, it is obviously premature to dismiss out of hand anything that is being written now, and it might be more honest to admit that the objections that many administrators have to contemporary opera are practical and not aesthetic. 'What a director [of an opera house] likes most of all', according to Berlioz, 'is something that keeps his company happy and easily satisfied; something that everyone knows without having learnt it, that does not disturb accepted notions and settled habits of mind, that follows docilely the line of least resistance and wounds no one's self-esteem because it exposes no one's incompetence; something that above all does not require much time to get up. His favourite compositions are the nice accommodating ones, the ones that do not struggle.'

Opera of the 1980s certainly 'struggles', making far greater demands than the traditional repertoire in terms of time, effort and money. David Gockley, General Director of Houston Grand Opera, estimates that a new work costs some twenty-five per cent more to produce than a standard one. Commission fees and the expense of preparing the musical materials account for some of the extra costs, but they are generated largely by the need for extra rehearsals. This is due less to the length of a new piece – *The Ice Break*, for example, with its three acts of approximately twenty-five minutes each, was said to have been commissioned by the Crush Bar at Covent Garden – than to its difficulty. The principals may be able to learn their music in advance, but for chorus and orchestra, learning as they rehearse, deciphering the parts (often hand-copied) and working out complex rhythms, a longer than average rehearsal period is indispensable; Lord Harewood feels that much contemporary music is in fact almost too difficult for a chorus to perform from memory.

The choral and orchestral forces required for a new piece may be unusually large. Stockhausen's *Samstag aus Licht* involved only one vocal soloist but – as performed in Milan – in one scene alone deployed an eighty-piece wind band (used not merely as players but as actors forming on a six-tiered scaffold a giant face, whose features contorted as the musicians moved – the audience, seated on bean bags below, were the bristles of the beard). And it was primarily the vocal and orchestral strength required for Harrison Birtwistle's *The Mask of Orpheus* which for over ten years made it virtually unperformable and hastened its passage from Covent Garden to Glyndebourne and on to ENO. One might compare the remarkable success of Peter Maxwell Davies's *The Lighthouse*, written for a cast of three and a chamber orchestra, which in its first five years had already had some dozen productions in four languages. The value of economy of means was a lesson Maxwell Davies perhaps learned from Britten who, after the efforts involved in getting *Peter Grimes* produced, turned to smaller-scale works.

Producers and designers not infrequently succumb to the temptation to overcompensate visually for what they fear might be the inaccessibility of the music, with spectacle, outrageousness or a welter of high technology. While composers are no doubt grateful for the time and money expended on realising it, the end product can occasionally overpower their original vision of the work. David Blake, for example, would now like to see a barer and more rudimentary treatment of *Toussaint* than that given it by ENO – 'epic' as in Brecht rather than Ben Hur. 'There's a danger that if you come up with something that is so beautiful, so beguiling to the eye, it deafens your ear a bit.'

Casting can pose further problems. There was a time when singers regularly got operas written for them – Grisi, Pasta, Caruso and others. Occasionally this still happens; Reimann's *Lear* was written for Dietrich Fischer-Dieskau, for example, and Placido Domingo approached Moreno Torroba with a commission for *Il Poeta*. But it is a minority of present-day singers who lend the support to contemporary opera which could help greatly to ingratiate it with the public; most are some distance removed from modern music of any description. Up to a point the divorce is involuntary, imposed by the acute technical difficulty of much new music – the extremes of range, the complicated rhythms, the minute subdivisions of pitch, the unfamiliar intervals, all to be negotiated from memory. Andrew Porter is decided on the point: 'I hate to admit it – but I think I would have to say that music has grown away from the voice. It *is* harder to sing Berio than it is to sing Bellini.' And Linda Esther Gray owns: 'I'm no use at it. I did a modern mass and the composer thanked me afterwards, said it was *most* moving, and he looked forward to hearing it with the right notes. . . .'

Singers are not yet trained to meet the demands made by composers over the past twenty or thirty years: they are not taught the means of extending the range an octave above the stave, say, or the technique to leap an augmented thirteenth. Harrison Birtwistle regrets what he sees as the limitations of older singers: 'It's to do with the times, and the generations they came from. They're trained in one way and they can't do anything else. They're like horses taking the milk round – you take them down another road and they don't know where to leave the milk.' Others disagree – Thea Musgrave, for instance, considers a traditional training indispensable to the singing of *any* repertoire, and deplores the emergence of specialist 'contemporary' singers, whom she suspects sometimes to be those with less beautiful voices making the best of a bad job. For her operas she does not *want* less beautiful voices, and believes it is the composer's job to understand what the voice can do and to write within its capabilities, accommodating it as one would any other instrument. 'It's knowing what lies for the instrument. . . . When I rehearsed the clarinet concerto with Gervase de Peyer, I looked at his hands and said, "That looks awfully awkward", and he said, "Well, if you will put the B flat after the A, of course it's awkward. If you put it the other way round. . . ." It was a quick run up to a note, there was no particular reason why it couldn't be the other way round, so I changed it. It was easier, so it sounded better, and it didn't really change anything compositionally, it wasn't compromising artistic values.' Harrison Birtwistle agrees completely as to the futility of making life diffi-cult for the singer: 'I don't set out trying to write against the voice. When I write something, I have to express what I'm trying to do . . . Composing is an interpreta-tion of an idea, and then there's a further interpretation or realisation through the performers. So I don't try to make something which is not going to be realisable.'

Nevertheless many singers remain suspicious, some even convinced that con-temporary music can seriously damage the voice – that angular leaps and extremes of volume or pitch ask too much of an instrument developed with *bel canto* tech-niques in mind. Others begrudge the time spent learning a role which may rarely

or never be needed again. Many singers simply do not care for much modern writing. One member of the cast of Henze's *We Come to the River*, encouraged to move among the audience and extemporise text to music, was distinctly heard to be singing 'Money back at the box office . . .' More temperately, Anthony Rolfe Johnson explains: 'I have this awful sensation when I sing modern music that I spend most of my rehearsal time turning it *into* music.'

Even were singers eager and administrators enthusiastic, the principal problem would remain an audience whose present attitude to contemporary opera ranges from apathy to apoplexy. There is now no popular demand anywhere for the latest work of *any* composer as there once was in Venice for Cavalli, London for Handel, Paris for Meyerbeer, Milan for Verdi. Peter Maxwell Davies is acknowledged as one of Britain's leading composers, and not one of its most obscure or *avant-garde*; in 1983 advance subscriptions for the Covent Garden revival of his *Taverner* totalled five per cent of capacity, while in the same subscription series, Puccini's *Manon Lescaut* was completely sold out months before its opening night. Any administrator programming a contemporary work will usually budget a drop in box office of between twenty-five and fifty per cent.

Why are audiences so meagre? One deterrent could be a change in the focus of opera. If a major element in its appeal has traditionally been the romantic aria or love duet (and one has only to look at the composition of best-selling recordings of operatic 'highlights' to know that this is so), then much modern opera has deliberately turned its back on popular appeal. Solo singing for its own sake, for the sheer beauty of the voice, has become a little *déclassé* among radical composers, and romantic love is no longer invariably the favourite theme of opera. John Dexter, for one, feels that the First World War and Freud between them did irreparable damage to the romantic view of love, and for various reasons other views of love and sex are perhaps more common in modern opera – either distinctly unromantic, in pieces such as *Wozzeck*, Penderecki's *The Devils of Loudun*, Shostakovich's *Lady Macbeth of Mtsensk*, Birtwistle's *Punch and Judy*, Ligeti's *Le Grand Macabre*, Ginastera's *Bomarzo*, or views which the audience is not accustomed to seeing on the operatic stage (as in *Lulu*, *A Quiet Place*, *The Knot Garden*, *Death in Venice*).

Primarily, however, the problem is one that applies not merely to opera but to all contemporary music – the gulf that has since the 1950s grown ever wider between composers and all but a tiny fragment of their audience. It often seems to the listener that the composer displays no interest at all in communicating; or, if the will is there to communicate, it is routinely subordinated to the conflicting demands of dogma.

Abstraction and obscurity are for some reason less palatable now in music than in either theatre or fine art – Jonathan Miller is puzzled as to why music should prove the exception to the rule. 'The odd thing about the visual arts as opposed

OPPOSITE Ligeti's *Le Grand Macabre*, with Anne Howard as Mescalina and Geoffrey Chard as Nekrotzar (ENO, 1982).

to the musical arts is that as visual art becomes more and more abstract, it actually seems to gain a *larger* audience; it's very hard to keep people away from the Museum of Modern Art – it's quite hard to get people *into* the Juilliard when it's playing a very, very modern piece of music. . . . What is it about the senses which enjoys abstraction in the visual mode and is really quite disturbed by abstraction when it's in the acoustic mode?'

One should not discount the efficacy of simple prejudice in keeping audiences away. Thea Musgrave, starting an opera company in a community (Norfolk, Virginia) largely unfamiliar with live opera of any description, found that her own works met with no more resistance than *Madam Butterfly*. 'They didn't know contemporary music was a problem. . . . Neither did they know that there weren't any women composers.' But her music does not fully embody many of the features which initially alienated audiences and helped to entrench prejudice for the future. It is not, for example, wholeheartedly atonal (avoiding any system of key). Whatever the intellectual arguments for atonality, to many it seems unnatural and therefore confusing to the ear. Marvin David Levy, who has in the past used the twelve-tone technique (a systematisation of atonality) quite extensively, owns: 'The physical business of sound is tonal – the harmonic system is based on tonality; it has nothing to do with our ideas or any superimposed law – in nature it is tonal. And you might as well go with nature. Distorting it in many ways is interesting but dangerous, because you clutter up the ear so much with superfluous overtones that, unless you have a very skilled handler of it, you won't know what you're listening to.' Similarly, extreme complexity and irregularity of rhythm can leave the listener floundering. John Eaton: 'The great problem in contemporary music, and perhaps in many of the arts, is not one of unity ("It doesn't hang together") but of continuity ("I can't follow it"). Continuity in music is a matter of arousing and addressing the listener's expectations' – and in the absence of key or regular rhythm, expectation, when it can be formed at all, is more often than not confounded.

For Nicholas Maw, the most serious consequence of the direction taken by much modern music is a loss of expressivity: 'One of the things that makes Mozart one of the greatest composers of opera is the incredible flexibility of his language. He can show any emotion he wants in a character on the stage, he can clothe it all in marvellous music which is all related but is at the same time infinitely flexible. 'Dove sono' and Cherubino's aria, which are as like as chalk and cheese, are still in the same style, in the same opera. It's become more and more difficult for composers to do that in the twentieth century. . . . It's *not* because you get a vocal line which is extremely angular – sometimes that's highly appropriate and works superbly well, as in Berg. It's that the musical language is too inflexible to deal with the complex dramatic situation. . . . Schoenberg was wrestling with this problem in *Moses und Aron* – in my view, that's why he could never get it finished. When he came to write the orgy scene round the Golden Calf, it sounds like a reach-me-down *Rite of Spring*, knock-kneed and double-jointed, because Schoenberg's musical language simply is not flexible enough to deal with it as well as all the other things necessary in the piece.'

But to put it at its simplest, what audiences most often complain of missing in new music is *melody*. Very few twentieth-century operas, even those admired and respected by critics and other composers, have had melody: Placido Domingo has commented on the unlikelihood of any member of the audience emerging from the opera house whistling *Wozzeck*. Paradoxically, prospects are probably better now for melody than in 1925 when Berg wrote *Wozzeck*, as increasing numbers of composers turn back towards tonality and emotionalism, causing musicologists to speak of a 'neo-Romantic' movement. It is a trend that David Blake welcomes: 'What has disappointed me about much of modern music is that it doesn't get me in the guts. So much of it intrigues me and interests me intellectually and aurally, but doesn't actually move me – and this is what we all love music for, the tingles down the spine and the tear glands pricking.' Nicholas Maw would go further than this: 'If we don't learn again how to write melody which is perceivable as such, which somebody can actually go out on the street and whistle – perhaps not the first time, but at least with some sense that this is a melodic phrase – we're going to be in deep trouble. The whole musical art will collapse – and specifically opera. Music is basically related to two primary human needs – one is singing, one dancing. Ezra Pound said, "When music gets too far away from the dance, it rots." I don't quite go along with that, but there's something in it. The same goes for singing – such a basic human activity that it has *got* to be perceivable as being at the centre of the art. . . . There are two strong impulses in opera – the lyrical and the dramatic. It has to be related to both, and it's the lyrical side which has suffered. There are certain modern operas without a lyrical impulse throughout. I think it's going against the nature of the art form – better to be doing something else, and not trying to write operas – writing plays, for instance . . . I can't see the point of it unless you're *really* singing.'

Acknowledgements

This book owes more than most to the expertise and good nature of others, drawing heavily as it does on more than two hundred interviews conducted between January 1984 and April 1985 with people from every corner of the opera world. We have enjoyed our researches inordinately, and should like to thank everyone who gave us their time and encouragement:—

Claudio Abbado, Ande Anderson, Luciana Arrighi, Norman Ayrton, Norman Bailey, John Barker, Josephine Barstow, Chris Bartlett-Judd, Linda Beazer, Anthony Besch, Claire Biddle, Michael Billington, Harrison Birtwistle, David Blake, Rodney Blumer, James Bowman, Mike Bremner, Isobel Buchanan, Paata Burchuladze, Peter Burian, Stuart Burrows, Humphrey Burton, John Bury, José Carreras, Sir Hugh Casson, Nick Chelton, Sir George Christie, Graham Clark, Nicholas Cleobury, Maria Cleva, John Conklin, John Copley, Ileana Cotrubas, Peter Courtier, Gina Cowen, John Cox, F. Mitchell Dana, June Dandridge, Peter Maxwell Davies, Sir Colin Davis, John Dexter, Brian Dickie, Bryan Drake, John Eaton, Mark Elder, Roy Emmerson, Matthew Epstein, Ronald Eyre, Paul Findlay, Gillian Finn, Gerald Fitzgerald, John Fraser, David Freeman, Ronald Freeman, Götz Friedrich, Jonathan Friend, Frank Galea, Erica Gastelli, Bram Gay, Mary Laura Gibbs, Geoffrey Gilbertson, Philip Glass, Jane Glover, Colin Graham, Linda Esther Gray, Terri-Jayne Gray, Romayne Grigorova, Jonathan Groves, Sir Peter Hall, Iain Hamilton, Arthur Hammond, Martin Handley, Lord Harewood, John Harrison, Donald Hassard, Desmond Heeley, Thomas Hemsley, Jocelyn Herbert, Sylvia Holford, Gwynne Howell, Nicholas Hytner, Ted Irwin, Martin Isepp, Sally Jacobs, Stefan Janski, Gwyneth Jones, Wilfred Josephs, Charles Kay, Terry Keen, Peter Knapp, Lady Anne Lancaster, Sir Osbert Lancaster, Michael Langdon, Stefanos Lazaridis, Catherine Lee, Raymond Leppard, Marvin David Levy, Hugh Lloyd, Max Loppert, Barbara Lorber, Felicity Lott, Tom Macarthur, Bill McGee, Donald McIntyre, Sir Charles Mackerras, Brian McMaster, Hugh Maguire, Andrew Marriner, Molly Marriner, Sir Neville Marriner, Nicholas Maw, Colin Maxwell, Clarie Middleton, Ruth Miescucz, Jonathan Miller, Tony Mills, Beni Montresor, Janet Moores, Peter Morrell, Margaret Morton, Richard Morton, Elijah Moshinsky, Thea Musgrave, Stephen Oliver, Dennis O'Neill, Rosalind O'Reagan, Jeffrey Phillips, Clive Pleasants, Andrew Porter, David Pountney, Janice Pullen, Raymond Quinn, Craig Raine, Tom Redman, Tina Reilly, Maria Rich, David Ritch, Phyllida Ritter, Anthony Rolfe Johnson, Harold Rosenthal, John Schlesinger, John Seekings, Peter Sellars, Andrei Serban, Beverly Sills, Ian Sinclair, Erik Smith, Julian Smith, Daniel Snowman, Stephen Sondheim, Mick Spray, Clifford Starr, Larry Stayer, Barbara Stewart, John Streets, Jeremy Sutcliffe, Pauline Tambling, Jeffrey Tate, Hilary Tear, Bob Tear, Dame Kiri te Kanawa, Pippa Thompson, Sir Michael Tippett, Sir John Tooley, Dame Eva Turner, J. Rigbie Turner, Richard Van Allan, Josephine Veasey, Stephanie Ward, Anne Whitley, Anthony Whitworth-Jones, Peter Wood and Julia Wright.

We are particularly grateful to Katharine Wilkinson (Press Officer for the Royal Opera), David Reuben (Press and Public Relations Director at the Metropolitan Opera), Caroline Loeb and Maggie Sedwards at English National Opera, Shelagh Nelson (Press Officer, Welsh National Opera) and Helen O'Neill (Head of Press and Public Relations for Glyndebourne Festival Opera), for arranging many of these interviews for us; to our editor, Jennie Davies, who nursed and championed the book from the beginning; to Penny Mills, who designed it with so much care and thought; to Michèle Young, who tightened and much improved the text; and to Joe Stern, who made the crucial difference in New York. It is perhaps presumptuous, in a book which has been a joint effort, to thank Zoë Dominic and Catherine Ashmore, whose experience was our invaluable guide and whose company was (and is) extremely entertaining.

The authors and publisher would like to thank the following for permission to quote extracts: Bodley Head (*The World of Placido Domingo* by Daniel Snowman); Cambridge University Press (*Otto Klemperer – His Life and Times Vol.1 1885–1933* by Peter Heyworth); Maria Rich and the Central Opera Service ('The Director in the 80s', transcript of the Central Opera Service National Conference 1982); Ernst Eulenberg (*Music of the Angels* by Michael Tippett); Faber & Faber (*Music and Politics – Collected Writings 1953–81* by Hans Werner Henze, transl. Peter Labanyi); Meredith Enterprises (*Bubbles – An Encore* by Beverly Sills); the *Kenyon Review* ('Stories that Break into Song' by John Eaton); the *New Yorker* (Andrew Porter); Ellen Blassingham and OPERA America ('Perspectives – Creating and Producing Contemporary Opera and Musical Theater'); Harold Rosenthal and *Opera* magazine; Sidgwick & Jackson (*My Own Story* by Luciano Pavarotti) and Weidenfeld & Nicolson (*My First Forty Years* by Placido Domingo). The Priestley Report – 'Financial Scrutiny of the Royal Opera House, Covent Garden Ltd: Report to the Earl of Gowrie, Minister for the Arts, by Clive Priestley CB, 1984', *Opera* magazine, and *Opera News* have all been very useful sources of comment and statistics.

Index

Italics refer to illustrations

Abbado, Claudio 25, 52, 99, 101, 105, 106, 115, 120, 125, 126, 135, 140, 151, 152, 156
Albee, Edward 277
Alden, David 3, 33
Allen, Thomas 47, *226, 247*
Anderson, Ande 175, 220, 253
Annenberg, Walter 18
Argento, Dominick 73, 276, 315
Armstrong, Richard 25
Arrighi, Luciana 222, 223, *226,* 228
Auden, W. H. , 274
Ayrton, Norman 72

Bacon, John *263*
Badini, Carlo Maria 25
Baer, Olaf *vi*
Bailey, Norman 59, 62, 84, 88, 95, 240, *263*
Baker, Dame Janet 47, 87
Balk, H. Wesley 241, 271
Baltsa, Agnes 78
Barber, Samuel 311
Barenboim, Daniel 31
Barker, John 117, 119
Barstow, Josephine 47, 92, 95, 144, 223, 240, 246, 261, 268
Bartlett-Judd, Chris 220
Battle, Kathleen 47, 49, *51,* 86
Baylis, Lilian 6
Beckett, Samuel 277
Begley, Kim 237
Bellow, Saul 277
Bennett, Richard Rodney 312
Berganza, Teresa 47, 90
Berghaus, Ruth *109*
Bergman, Ingmar 277
Bergonzi, Carlo 62, 95
Berio, Luciano 317
Bernstein, Leonard 301, 314
Besch, Anthony 6, 166, 236, 244, 245, 251, 309

Bibalo, Antonio 276
Billington, Michael 159, 242, 246
Bing, Sir Rudolph 7, 8, 23, 29, 49, 88, 99, 259
Birtwistle, Harrison 274, 276, 278, 293, 302, 311, 312, 313, 316, 317, 319
Bjørnson, Maria 212
Blake, David 273, 283, 286, 295, 296, 298, 299, 309, 312, 315, 316, 321
Bliss, Anthony 23
Bliss, Sir Arthur 23, 313
Blitzstein, Marc 277
Blumer, Rodney 289
Bogianckino, Massimo 7, 36, 188
Bond, Edward 282, 286
Bonney, Barbara 78, *79*
Bonynge, Richard 82, 84, 120
Boulanger, Nadia 314
Boulez, Pierre 105
Bowman, James 59, 62, 64, *65,* 83, 90, 136, 137, 194, 229, 241, 267
Brain, Denis 127
Brandt, Willi 282
Britten, Benjamin 36, 90, 126, 136, 175, 275, 281, 285, 298, 300, 301, 304, 306, *307,* 311, 313, 316
Brook, Peter 161, 237, 245
Brooks, Mel 57
Bryan, Robert 25
Buchanan, Isobel 74, 84, 89, 141, 261, 264, 266
Bumbry, Grace 49, 62
Burchuladze, Paata 81
Burian, Peter 128, *129,* 130
Burrows, Stuart 54, 59, 85, 147, 262
Bury, John 179, 182, 185, 189, 190, 191, 195, 197, 212, 215, 234
Busch, Fritz 7, 261
Bush, Alan 283

Caballé, Montserrat 47, 81
Cage, John 268
Callas, Maria *1,* 58, 88, 89, 135, *136,* 146
Carreras, José 47, 81, 82, *83,* 88, 89, 93, 106, 115
Casson, Sir Hugh 183, 189, 193
Celletti, Rodolfo 137, 301
Chagall, Marc 178
Chard, Geoffrey *318*
Chelton, Nick 210, 212, 215
Chéreau, Patrice 194
Chirico, Georgio de 178
Christie, Brenda *312*
Christie, Sir George 16, 26, 29, *35,* 45, 49, *312,* 313
Christoff, Boris 74, *75*
Cillario, Carlo Felice *136*
Ciulei, Liviu 161
Clark, Graham 94, 139, 239
Cleobury, Nicholas 113
Cleva, Maria *129,* 139
Coates, Albert 276
Cocteau, Jean *269*
Colette 293
Conklin, John 10, 33, 174, 178, 189, 190
Copley, John 176, 182, 192, 241, 253, 266
Corigliano, John 315
Cotrubas, Ileana 47, 66, 74, 78, 81, 88, *140,* 145, 239, *263*
Cowie, Edward 313
Cox, John 25, 36
Crawford, Bruce 23
Crosse, Gordon 312

Dale, Laurence 237
Dali, Salvador 178, 311
Dallapiccola, Luigi 283, 311
Dam, Jose van *297*
Dana, F. Mitchell 214, 215, 217, 218, 219, 220
Dandridge, June 203
Daniels, Barbara 78
Davies, Arthur *180*
Davies, Dennis Russell 311

Davies, Peter Maxwell 304, *305*, 312, 316, 319
Davis, Sir Colin 7, 25, 42, 99, 102, *104*, 105, 108, 120, 124, 125, 127, *140*, 147, *263*
Della Casa, Lisa 47
Dent, Edward 315
Devine, George 183
Dexter, John 25, 102, 134, 151, 165, 170, 176, 179, *183*, 209, 253, 319
Diaghilev, Serge 25
Dickie, Brian 26, 28, *35*, 36, 41, 45, 47, 49, 50, 313
Dimitrova, Ghena 60
Dohnanyi, Christoph 311
Domingo, Placido 8, *27*, 47, 54, *55*, 60, 62, 64, 74, 77, 82, 88, 89, 95, 106, 108, 135, *141*, 144, *160*, *187*, 228, *249*, 265, 267, 317, 321
Donath, Helen 78, *187*
Downes, Edward *305*
Drake, Bryan 72, 73, 87
Dress, Claus Helmut 25
Druckman, Jacob 315
Dutschke, Rudi 282, 283

Eaton, John 29, 271, 274, 275, 278, 294, 314, 320
Ebert, Carl 7
Egk, Werner 311
Einem, Gottfried von 275, 311
Eisler, Hanns 283, 299
Elder, Mark 10, 25, 36, 42, 52, 80, *110*, *111*, 115, 119, 151, 152
Eliot, T. S. 287, 290
Emmerson, Roy 267
Enzenberger, Hans Magnus 291
Epstein, Matthew 82, 84, 89, 93, 96, 136
Estes, Simon 49
Evans, Sir Geraint 47, *83*, 262
Ewing, Maria 62, *237*
Eyre, Ronald 170, 176, 183, 244, 245

Falk, Mrs Michael 18
Farrell, J. G. 288
Feasey, Norman 70
Felsenstein, Walter 169, 241, 257

Ferro, Gabriele *139*
Field, Helen *280*
Fielding, David 4, 173
Findlay, Paul 6, 16, 29
Fischer-Dieskau, Dietrich 60, 88, 94, 317
Fisher, Sylvia *307*
Fitzgerald, Gerald 30, 195
Flagstad, Kirsten 54
Floyd, Carlisle 287, 315
Forster, E. M. 301
Fortner, Wolfgang 275
Franklin, David 67
Freeman, David 236, 242
Freeman, Ronald 229, 230, *231*
Freni, Mirella 47
Friedrich, Götz 11, 42, 122, 156, 159, *160*, 166, 171, 179, 182, 243, 311
Friend, Jonathan 32, 39, 44, 81

Garrett, Eric *vi*
Gastelli, Erica 69
Gay, Bram 106, 121, 122, 126
Geliot, Michael 25
Getty, Gordon P. 18
Gibson, Sir Alexander 25
Gielen, Michael 23, 311
Gilbertson, Geoffrey 252
Ginastera, Alberto 319
Giulini, Carlo Maria 147, *149*, 150, 156
Glass, Philip 13, 32, 130, 271, *272*, 278, 287, 310, 314
Glover, Jane 113
Gobbi, Tito 89, 146, 246, *265*
Gockley, David 316
Goodall, Sir Reginald 125, 140
Graham, Colin 10, 152, 171, 283, 285, 287, 288, *303*, 306
Gravett, Guy 252
Gray, Linda Esther 66, 72, 113, 115, 137, 259, 261, 265, 266, 317
Greene, Graham 277
Grigorova, Romayne 250
Gruberova, Edita 47
Gui, Vittorio 7, 36
Guthrie, Sir Tyrone 252, 311

Hadley, Jerry 34, 47, 80
Haitink, Sir Bernard 26, *35*, 36

Hall, Sir Peter 26, *35*, 36, 151, 152, *155*, 160, 166, 170, 174, 182, 185, 197, 234, 235, *237*, 245, 257
Hamilton, Iain 271, 275, 281, 283, 291, *292*, 295, 297, 300, 312
Hammond, Arthur 70
Hampe, Michael 23, 156, 193, *247*
Handley, Martin 108, 130, 131, 132, 134
Harewood, Lord 25, 28, 34, 52, 135, 252, 315, 316
Harnoncourt, Nikolaus 31
Harper, Edward 313
Harrington, Mrs Donald D. 18
Harrison, John 25, 196
Havergal, Brian 275
Heeley, Desmond 177, 223
Hellmann, Lilian 277
Hemsley, Thomas 38, 78
Henderson, Alva 276
Hendricks, Barbara 47, 49
Henze, Hans Werner 29, 117, 170, 281, *282*, 283, 286, 290, 291, 311, 313, 319
Hepworth, Barbara 178
Herbert, Jocelyn 182, *183*, 185, 194, 195, 201, 223
Heyworth, Peter 144
Hockney, David 31, 178, 179, 190
Hoddinott, Alun 276, 312
Hofmann, Peter 89, *91*
Holloway, David *237*
Hopper, Edward 178
Horne, Marilyn 62, 67, 78, 89
Hotter, Hans 58, 114
Howard, Ann *318*
Howell, Gwynne 66, 68, 87, 114, 264
Howells, Anne *79*, *303*
Hughes, Owain Arwel 312
Hughes, Spike 261
Hytner, Nicholas 173

Ingpen, Joan 49
Ionesco, Eugène 277
Isepp, Martin 76, 126, 131, 137, *138*, 143, 146, 147

Jacobs, Sally 182, 185, 186, 188, 190, 203, 206, 214, 215, 217, 223, 224, 228, 229, 234, 235, 251

Jacobson, Robert 23
Janski, Stefan 219
Jerusalem, Siegfried 89
Jonas, Peter 25
Jones, Gwyneth *60*, *187*, 229
Josephs, Wilfred 293, 294, 295, 298, 300, 306
Jurinac, Sena 47

Karajan, Herbert von 99, 126, 144, 150
Keen, Terry *232*, 233
Kempe, Rudolf 105, 114
Kenny, Sean 310
Kerman, Joseph 273, 277, 279
King, James 78
Kirchner, Leon 276
Kleiber, Carlos 34, 99, 106, 124, 261
Klemperer, Otto *97*, 144, 150, 176
Knapp, Peter 74
Knussen, Oliver 224, 313
Krainik, Ardis 9, 25
Kraus, Alfredo 95
Křenek, Ernst 274
Kubelik, Rafael 7

La Guardia, Fiorello 6
Lancaster, Sir Osbert 178, 189, 203, *303*
Langdon, Michael 66, 69, 70, *71*, 74, 93, 262, 263, 267
Langridge, Philip 87
Larson, Susan 237
Lazaridis, Stefanos 178, 182, *184*, 185, 186, 191, 198
Leavis, F. R. 170
Lee, Catherine 244
Lefort, Bernard 145
Leggate, Robin *310*
Lehnhoff, Nikolaus 189
Leppard, Raymond 36, 99, 117, 126, *147*, *150*, 152, *155*, 156
Levine, James 8, 23, 40, 99, 101, 105, 148, 156
Levy, Marvin David 274, 290, 315, 320
Liebermann, Rolf 7, 312
Ligeti, György 313, 319
Littlewood, Joan 195
Lloyd, Robert 67, 68, 74
Lloyd-Webber, Andrew 114
Lopez-Cobos, Jesus 119

Lorber, Barbara 18, 19
Lorengar, Pilar 47
Lott, Felicity 89, 94, 264
Luxon, Benjamin 87

Maazel, Lorin 38, 44, 105, 147
Macarthur, Tom 25, 198
McCracken, James 77
McGee, Bill 215
Machin, David 51
McIntyre, Donald 87, 138, 195, *231*, 263
Mackerras, Sir Charles 25, 36, 58, *107*, 114, 118, 119, 122, 127, 132, 135, 144, 264, 266
McLaughlin, Marie *221*
McMaster, Brian 25
MacNeil, Cornell 47
Maguire, Hugh 126, 127
Malfitano, Catherine 86
Marriner, Sir Neville 114, *118*, 127, 146, 152
Marshall, Margaret 89
Martin, Marvis 86
Martinoty, Jean-Louis *153*
Mascagni, Pietro 275
Masterson, Valerie *172*, *180*
Mathias, William 276, 312
Maurier, Daphne du 293
Maw, Nicholas 124, 277, 293, 299, 302, *303*, 309, 312, 313, 320, 321
Mayer, Martin 20
Mayor, William 314
Mazzonis, Cesare 25
Melchior, Lauritz 54
Menotti, Gian Carlo 311
Messel, Oliver 197, 203
Miki, Minuro 276, 314
Milhaud, Darius 274
Miller, Henry 276
Miller, Jonathan 10, 50, 150, 151, 154, 165, 167, 169, 174, 175, 177, 182, 190, 193, 236, 239, 243, 253, 272, 319
Mills, Erie 34
Milnes, Rodney 167, 283, 286
Milnes, Sherill 47, 54, 88
Moholy-Nagy, Laszlo 178
Montressor, Beni 184, 194, 201
Moore, Douglas 311
Moores, Janet 264

Moser, Sir Claus 16
Moshinsky, Elijah 162, 165, 169, 170, 175, 179, 182, 222, 238, 242, 245
Munro, Leigh 5
Murdoch, Iris 276
Murphy, Suzanne 34
Murray, Ann *172*
Musgrave, Thea 275, 296, 299, 300, 306, 312, 317, 320
Muti, Riccardo 25, 99, 106, 121, 140

Nafé, Alicia *139*
Neil, William 315
Nilsson, Birgit *46*, 47, 54, 60, 62, 87, 89, 95
Nobili, Lila de 8
Nolan, Sir Sidney 178, 179
Nono, Luigi 283
Norman, Jessye *vi*, 49, *255*

O'Brien, Timothy 201, 206, 223
Oliver, Stephen 3, 276, 284, 288, 290, 296, 306
Oman, Julia Trevelyan 177
O'Neill, Dennis 62, 64, 76, 84, *85*, 94, 142, 146
Opie, Alan *310*
Orr, Robin 312
Osborne, Nigel 286, 306

Palmer, Tony 174
Pasatieri, Thomas 315
Paulus, Stephen 314
Pavarotti, Luciano *43*, 47, 58, 64, 81, 89, 106, 240, 259, 266
Pearl, Jady *71*
Pears, Sir Peter 136
Penderecki, Krzystof 319
Peyer, Gervase de 317
Pinter, Harold 166, 245, 277, 289
Piper, John 178, 203, 306
Piper, Myfanwy 175, 281
Plowright, Rosalind 34, *209*
Ponnelle, Jean-Pierre 31, 37, 195, 239
Ponselle, Rosa 66
Popp, Lucia 92
Porter, Andrew 21, 116, 117, 150, 156, 161, 194, 300, 301, 317
Pound, Ezra 321

Pountney, David 10, 25, 30, 52, 151, 171, 174, 239, 242
Price, Leontyne 49, *53*, 54
Price, Margaret 47
Pritchard, Sir John 143, 154
Pruslin, Stephen 276, 293
Pullen, Janice 222, 224, 227, 228, 229
Purser, John 312
Putnam, Ashley 47

Quinn, Raymond 244
Quivar, Florence 86

Raimondi, Ruggero 47
Raine, Craig 286, 288, 306, 308
Ramey, Samuel 34, 47
Rankl, Karl 7
Rawnslay, John *180*
Redman, Tom 198
Reimann, Aribert 90, 311, 317
Reinhardt, Max 25
Rennert, Gunther 7, 305
Reuben, David 22
Ricciarelli, Katia *43*
Rich, Maria 32
Rigby, Jean *180*
Rihm, Wolfgang 311
Ritch, David 191, 236
Robertson, Patrick 178, 179
Rockwell, John 278
Rolandi, Gianna 34, 47
Rolfe-Johnson, Anthony 87, 89, 136, 144, 319
Rosenthal, Harold 11, 42, 95, 312
Rudel, Julius 29

Sallinen, Aulis 313
Sargent, Sir Malcolm 183
Sawallisch, Wolfgang 23, 156
Schlesinger, John 122, 159, 186, 236
Schmidgall, Gary 277, 288
Schoenberg, Arnold 282, 301, 304, 311, 320
Schwarzkopf, Elisabeth 87
Sellars, Peter 162, 163, 164, 169, 236, 248, 253, 268, 306, 307, 308, 309
Sendak, Maurice 189, 313

Serban, Andrei *157*, 170, 185, 186, 188, 190, 224, 235, 236, 237, 239, 245, 248, 250, 261, 267
Shaw, Glen Byam 87
Shicoff, Neil 86, 89, 90
Shuard, Amy *168*
Sills, Beverly 5, 10, 12, 19, 24, 25, 31, 32, 47, 54, 57, 59, 66, 80, 95, 246
Sinopoli Giuseppe *141*
Smith, Julian 154
Smyth, Dame Ethel 302
Söderström, Elisabeth 47, 259, 289
Solti, Sir Georg 7, 99, *100*, 105, 106, 113, 115
Sondheim, Stephen 277
Sotin, Hans 47
Stade, Frederica von 47, 90, *92*
Starr, Clifford 39
Stayer, Larry 86
Stein, Erwin 148
Stockhausen, Karlheinz 117, 315, 316
Stoppard, Tom 277
Stratas, Teresa 81
Stravinsky, Igor 164, *269*, 287
Streets, John 61, 67
Susa, Conrad 21, 314
Sutcliffe, James Helme 167
Sutherland, Dame Joan 47, 77, 81, 82, 89, 95, 120, 241, 262
Svoboda, Josef 176, 191, 194, 209, 210

Taplin, Frank 20
Tate, Jeffrey 103, *153*
Tavener, John 312
Tear, Robert 58, 72, 87, 94, *187*, 251, *260*, 261
Te Kanawa, Dame Kiri 47, 61, 62, *63*, 68, 70, 77, 81, 93, 135, 136, *160*, 263, 264
Theodorakis, Mikis 284
Thomson, Virgil 21
Tippett, Sir Michael 90, 198, 273, 276, 277, *279*, 280, 281, 285, 286, 287, 290, 291,

295, 298, 301, 305, 306, 309, 311, 312
Tooley, Sir John 7, 16, 25, 27, 106
Torroba, Moreno 317
Tranchell, Peter 276
Traubel, Helen 54
Treleaven, John *280*
Troyanos, Tatiana 47, 73, 88
Turner, Dame Eva *60*, 61, 66

Valois, Dame Ninette de 250
Van Allan, Richard *4*, 54, 68, 88, 142, 194, *211*
Vaness, Carol 47
Veasey, Josephine 61, 74, 142, 259
Vercoe, Rosemary *178*
Verrett, Shirley 47, *48*, 54
Vick, Graham 25, 185
Vickers, Jon 54, 77, *238*
Visconti, Luchino 156

Wagner, Wieland 162, 169
Wagner, Wolfgang 49, 156, 195
Walton, Sir William 183, 313
Wanamaker, Sam 301, 310
Ward, Anthony 286
White, Willard 50
Whitley, Anne 253
Whitworth-Jones, Anthony 313
Wilkinson, Katharine 257
Williams, Grace 312
Williams, Tennessee 277
Williamson, Malcolm 276
Wilson, Thomas 312
Winkler, Hermann *297*
Wishart, Peter 275
Wixell, Ingvar 47
Wood, Peter 8, 196
Woodhouse, Barbara 57
Workman, William 237

Zancanaro, Giorgio *123*
Zeffirelli, Franco 3, 31, 167, *168*, 177, 196, 236, 252, 261
Ziegler, Delores 47
Zimmermann, Bernd Alois 311

782.1   Harries, Meirion,
HAR   1951-

         Opera today

$19.95

DATE			

871016

© THE BAKER & TAYLOR CO.